LAW & DISORDER

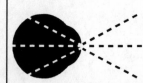

This Large Print Book carries the
Seal of Approval of N.A.V.H.

LAW & DISORDER

JOHN DOUGLAS
AND MARK OLSHAKER

THORNDIKE PRESS

A part of Gale, Cengage Learning

GALE
CENGAGE Learning·

Detroit • New York • San Francisco • New Haven, Conn • Waterville, Maine • London

GALE
CENGAGE Learning®

LIBRARY OF CONGRESS CATALOGING-IN-PUBLICATION DATA

Douglas, John E.
    Law & disorder / by John Douglas and Mark Olshaker. —
Large Print edition.
        pages cm. — (Thorndike Press Large Print Crime Scene)
    ISBN 978-1-4104-6036-3 (hardcover) — ISBN 1-4104-6036-3
(hardcover) 1. Douglas, John E. 2. Police—United
States—Biography. 3. United States. Federal Bureau of
Investigation—Biography. 4. Criminal investigation—United
States. 5. Criminal psychology—United States. 6. Large type
books. I. Olshaker, Mark, 1951– II. Title. III. Title: Law and
disorder.
HV7911.D68A34 2013
363.25092—dc23
[B]   2013013274

Published in 2013 by arrangement with Kensington Books, an imprint
of Kensington Publishing Corp.

Printed in Mexico
2 3 4 5 6 7 17 16 15 14 13

To the women and men who fight for integrity and justice, regardless of the cost or consequences, this book is dedicated with admiration and respect.

Justice is truth in action.
— Benjamin Disraeli
Speech before the House of Commons
February 11, 1851

Injustice anywhere is a threat to justice
everywhere.
— Martin Luther King Jr.
Letter from the Birmingham Jail, 1963

CONTENTS

9

PROLOGUE:
WITCH-HUNTING

Salem Village and Town, Massachusetts Bay Colony — June 1692

She was different, an outsider. And even though she lived in their community, she was not really one of them. The perfect profile of someone to fear.

She always wore black, and often strange outfits, hardly in keeping with the Puritan and proper way of life. So when Sir William Phips — newly appointed governor of the royal colony of Massachusetts Bay — established a Court of Oyer and Terminer (a tradition of British law from the Anglo-French, "to hear and determine"), it was probably not surprising that sixty-year-old Bridget Bishop should be the first one brought before the bar of justice.

It had been more than five months since January 20, when the Reverend Samuel Parris's nine-year-old daughter, Betty, and his eleven-year-old niece, Abigail Williams, had been first afflicted at the parsonage in

Salem Village. They were seized with spontaneous fits that included the sensation of pinches and sharp needle pricks, tongues drawn from their throats, loud sudden outcries, as well as severe pains of the neck and back. Dr. William Griggs examined them thoroughly, but he could find no cause in nature for the girls' terrifying symptoms.

The afflictions quickly spread to Ann Putnam, their twelve-year-old friend, and then to Mary Walcott, Ann's seventeen-year-old friend, and Mercy Lewis, the Putnams' seventeen-year-old servant. Soon ten girls and young women up to the age of twenty were behaving the same way.

The Harvard-educated Reverend Parris and other prominent village elders drew the most logical conclusion: "The Devil hath been raised among us," and witchcraft had invaded their well-ordered community. Cotton Mather, the most learned and influential minister in the colony — son of the Reverend Increase Mather, president of Harvard — had warned of this threat in his landmark treatise, *Memorable Providences,* and had himself examined bewitched children in Boston.

Various scientific methods were employed to confirm the doctor's diagnosis and the minister's conviction. Reverend Parris's neighbor Mary Sibley, whose niece Mary Walcott was one of the afflicted girls, prevailed upon Tituba, Parris's slave, and Tituba's husband, John Indian, to bake a witch cake. This well-established method was first used in England. Instead of milk, urine from the girls was mixed with rye meal. When it came out of the oven and cooled, it was fed to a dog. If the dog displayed similar symptoms to the human victims, it was determined they were, indeed, bewitched. Once a suspected witch was identified, the touch test, based on the Cartesian "Doctrine of Effluvia," could be used. If the suspect touched a victim during a fit and it stopped, that proved it was the suspect who had caused the affliction.

Near the end of February, some of the girls called out the names of three women who were tormenting them. The first was Tituba, who had entertained the girls with her native stories, spells and incantations. The second was Sarah Good, an old homeless beggar who went door-to-door and was known to mutter at those who would not give her alms. The third was Sarah Osborne, a widow who had married an indentured servant, much to the disapproval of town worthies, and who seldom went to church. It was not surprising that these marginal members of the community would consort with the Devil. Warrants were sworn out and the women were arrested on suspicion of witchcraft. Now investigators had solid information and suspects to work with.

On March 1, magistrates John Hathorne and Jonathan Corwin commenced hearings in the Salem Village meetinghouse, converted for the purpose into a makeshift courtroom. The girls all confirmed that Sarah Good's spectral *shape* had attacked them.

Under rigorous questioning, Goodies (for "Goodwives") Good and Osborne denied being witches. Tituba, in an apparent effort to save herself, confessed to having been enticed by the Devil, but she claimed she was no longer working for him. Following a similar tactic, Good claimed it was actually Osborne who was tormenting the children. But the astute investigators realized that if she knew this, it must mean that she was a witch, too.

The following week, the three suspects were sent to jail in Boston, twenty miles away, and the hearings continued. Each person the girls accused was brought in for examination and most were sent to jail. Soon it was no longer just the marginal characters. Before the month was out, regular churchgoers had been called out, such as Rebecca Nurse.

And still the girls were acting up, meaning the Devil had taken firm hold in and around Salem. The situation had reached crisis proportions. It was as if a deadly disease was rapidly spreading and anyone could be a carrier. No one was beyond suspicion.

Martha Corey voiced public skepticism about the girls' credibility. Soon the girls saw her shape sitting on a beam above them in church, suckling a yellow bird from her hand.

One of the girls, Mary Warren, named her mistress, Elizabeth Proctor. Elizabeth's husband, John, was a prominent and upstanding farmer. Like Martha Corey, he did not believe in witchcraft. During Elizabeth's hearing, the girls called out his name; under repeated questioning, Mary asserted he was a wizard.

Outside the meetinghouse, Mary reportedly admitted that John Proctor was not a wizard and suggested that the girls' actions were a "sport." Hearing this, some of the other girls accused her of being a witch. She was arrested and, under repeated formal questioning, declared that the Proctors were, in fact, wizard and witch.

By now, the investigation had grown so large that it had to be moved to the larger meetinghouse in Salem Town, eight miles away.

Meanwhile, Sarah Osborne had died in prison and Sarah Good gave birth to a baby, who died in the jail, confirming suspicions of her evil soul.

On May 31, John Alden answered charges before the magistrates. He was sixty years of age, a well-respected sea captain and Indian fighter and son of the celebrated lovers John and Priscilla Alden. He was among those who didn't believe in witchcraft and had the temerity to suggest that a good beating would cure the girls of their fits. Soon after they named him as the Master Wizard.

The Court of Oyer and Terminer, formed to hear the cases of all those accused, consisted of seven judges, all learned and respectable men. Governor Phips appointed his deputy William Stoughton to preside as chief judge. In consultation, the judges decided on some key rules. Any witch who confessed would not be punished. This would both show mercy and encourage defendants to name the names of others who had practiced the black arts. And Stoughton consulted with the most prominent and expert clergymen throughout Massachusetts Bay before concluding that spectral evidence should be admitted.

Thus was the court prepared for the appearance of its first defendant, Bridget Bishop.

At sixty years of age, Bishop had buried two husbands, the second of whom she had been accused of bewitching before the current panic had broken out. But she had been acquitted on that charge. Now she was married to Edward Bishop, a successful sawmill proprietor.

Five girls had called out her name as one who had dreadfully afflicted them. Samuel Shattuck, who ran a dye house, testified that Goody Bishop brought to him "sundry pieces of lace" that were too small to be used for anything other than a poppet, similar to what we think of as a voodoo doll. And John and William Bly, doing work in her cellar, said they had seen such poppets in the house of this woman who had bewitched their pig to death. Several men testified that Goody Bishop's spectral shape had appeared in their rooms and attacked them in their sleep.

Throughout the court's questioning, Bishop continued to deny she was a witch, that she had afflicted the girls, or made them sign the Devil's book. Her failure to confess pegged her as essentially beyond saving.

By the end of the day, all laws of jurisprudence and procedure having been followed, the jury returned with its verdict, finding Bridget Bishop guilty of all charges of witchcraft.

Eight days later, on June 10, she was taken up to Gallows Hill and hanged.

Five days later, twelve prominent ministers in Massachusetts Bay advised the court by letter that they had had second thoughts about the use of spectral evidence. Cotton Mather was concerned about misinterpretation of the science. Testimony about suspected witches' shapes appearing before various victims was unreliable, he had concluded, because the Devil could simply take the shape of any individual without that person even being aware of it.

That didn't stop the proceedings, though. William Beale told an Essex County grand jury that Philip English's specter came to him and that the next day his son James, who seemed to be recovering from smallpox, died. Fortunately for English, he was able to escape from jail and waited out the panic in New York.

Others weren't so lucky. Five women, including Rebecca Nurse, went on trial on June 29. Goody Nurse, in her seventies, a mother and grandmother from a prominent farming family, was found not guilty by the jury due to lack of evidence. But when the verdict was read, the afflicted girls in the courtroom went into instant fits. To chief judge Stoughton, this was prima facie evidence of her guilt and he insisted that the jury reverse its verdict.

On July 19, all five women were hanged on Gallows Hill.

By the end of September, nineteen defendants — thirteen women and six men — had been convicted of witchcraft and executed by hanging. George Burroughs's case was not helped by his failure to have one of his children baptized, clear evidence of his common cause with Satan. He was hanged on August 19, along with John Proctor and three others. As convicted witches and wizards, they were excommunicated from the Church and refused proper burial.

A twentieth individual, Martha Corey's husband, Giles, was an eighty-year-old farmer who refused to enter a plea, apparently protesting the legitimacy of the entire procedure. The judges ordered that he be taken to a field and have heavy stones piled on his chest until he pled. Every time he was asked, he replied, "More weight!" He died of suffocation without entering a plea.

Meanwhile, the proceedings had created a growing sense of alarm among a progressively more vocal group of critics. Dutch and French Calvinist ministers in New England worried about the validity of the evidence. New York's chief justice expressed concerns over the quality of justice. Thomas Brattle, a noted Boston mathematician and astronomer and a member of London's Royal Society for Improving Natural Knowledge, published a letter critical of the trials that concluded: *I am afraid that ages will not wear off that reproach and those stains which these things will leave behind upon our land.*

Clearly, Governor Phips was getting nervous. He prevailed upon Cotton Mather to publish *Wonders of the Invisible World: Being an Account of the Tryals of Several Witches, Lately Executed in New-England,* which the author hoped would "help very much flatten that fury which we now so much turn upon one another."

In spite of the executions, the resident evil that had taken hold of Salem Village and its neighboring communities continued. And things were beginning to unravel even further. The girls started accusing anyone they could think of, including Mary Phips, wife of the governor. One even accused Cotton Mather.

When Increase Mather visited the Salem Jail in October, he found that several of those who had confessed wanted to recant their testimony. He had been in England for most of the trials. When he returned, he was alarmed by what he learned. He published his own concerns in his tract *Cases of Conscience Concerning Evil Spirits Personating Men, Witchcrafts, Infallible Proofs of Guilt in Such as are Accused with that Crime.*

In that treatise Mather wrote his famous formulation: *It were better that Ten Suspected Witches should escape, than that one Innocent Person should be Condemned.* That sentiment, of course, evolved into the moral underpinning of our modern system of justice.

It is important to note that almost all of the impetus to stop what was going on came from *outside* the Salem community.

Before the month was out, the General Court of the Massachusetts Bay Colony ordered a meeting of ministers to evaluate the current situation. Three days later, Governor Phips dismissed the Court of Oyer and Terminer and all remaining prisoners were released on bond.

Near the end of November, a new Court of Judicature was created to handle the remaining cases, but there were no more convictions or executions. People stopped paying attention to the afflicted girls, they stopped having dramatic fits, and the Salem Witch Trials came to an end. In May of 1693, Governor Phips pardoned all remaining defendants. No one else was executed for witchcraft in the American colonies or the nation that grew out of them.

The cause or causes of the girls' afflictions remains a topic of debate. Some say it was a misunderstood physical disease, possibly a fungal infection from cereal grains now known as ergot poisoning, though this would not explain why the symptoms were confined to girls and young women from ages nine to twenty. It might have begun as two girls just seeking attention, and then later trying to avoid punishment for overstepping their carefully circumscribed social bounds. Or it could have been a case of mass conversion disorder, in which preexisting neurotic conditions were transferred into physical symptoms by several people at once, not as unusual a phenomenon as one might think.

Whatever it started out as, it blossomed into a case of mass hysteria that continued as long as requisite attention was paid.

Reverend Samuel Parris, in whose home the entire affair had begun, was fired from his church and left Salem Village in disgrace.

Deputy Governor William Stoughton, who presided over the trials, firmly believed in witchcraft and bullied the jury into convicting Rebecca Nurse, has both a town in Massachusetts and a building in Harvard Yard named after him.

The great-grandson of investigative magistrate John Hathorne changed the spelling of his last name to dissociate himself from his notorious ancestor. Through his writing, Nathaniel Hawthorne brought fame and honor to the name.

In January 1697, the General Court voted for a fund to make restitution and pay reparations to those accused of witchcraft and the survivors of those who had been executed.

And on August 25, 1706, the now-twenty-six-year-old Ann Putnam who, as a twelve-year-old, had been one of the first accusing girls, petitioned the Salem Village Church for admission, publicly confessing her role in the events of 1692 and begging forgiveness of God and those she had wronged. The congregation voted unanimously to accept her appeal.

Today the village is known as Danvers, and the Salem Witch Museum in Salem Town is a popular tourist attraction that manages to combine solid historical perspective with spooky, Halloween-like thrills and chills. But as we have seen, for those caught in its vortex, the Salem witch furor was deadly serious and a permanent blight on early-American criminal justice. As long as the hysterical girls and their supporters were allowed to dominate public life, no one was safe.

The reason for relating the details of this case from long ago is that, unfortunately, it still has resonance for much that occurs in the criminal justice system today when anyone — prosecutors or defenders, juries, the media, the public at large — places preconceived ideas or beliefs ahead of facts, proof or even common sense. And it doesn't matter whether we're talking about innocent people who have been condemned, or guilty people who have gone free. Injustice works both ways.

In Salem, Satan's presence and influence was an accepted reality, so this preconception, this pre-judgment, was a factor of everyday life. But it could be anything. Assumptions and presumptions, false confessions and recanted testimony, mistrust of outsiders and fear of those who are different, the innate need for certitude, authority and closure . . . these are all part of the Salem story. But they don't end at Salem. We'll see variations on these themes in all of the cases described in the pages to come.

Three hundred years later, many of the lessons of Salem remain unlearned.

■ ■ ■ ■

MY PERSONAL
JOURNEY

■ ■ ■ ■

CHAPTER 1
cATch Me BeFore
I KIll MorE

It was one of the most hideous and brutal murders in the history of Chicago, a city already notorious for the brutality of its crimes.

In the early-morning hours of Monday, January 7, 1946, an adorable, flaxen-haired six-year-old named Suzanne Degnan was snatched from her first-floor bedroom in the family's house at 5943 North Kenmore Avenue, in the Edgewater neighborhood on Chicago's north side. A poorly written ransom note demanded $20,000, warned her parents not to *NoTify FBI oR Police,* and instructed them to *wAITe foR WoRd.* A ladder was found outside Suzanne's bedroom window.

An anonymous caller instructed police to check sewers near Suzanne's home. Before nightfall, police had found her dismembered remains in several sewers near her home, as well as in a bloody basement laundry room, where her body was cut apart in an apartment house on nearby Winthrop Street. The cause of death was apparent strangulation in an unknown location between her home and the laundry room.

This all happened the year after I was born. By the time I got involved with the case, the confessed and convicted defendant had already been in prison thirty-three years.

After tours as a street agent in Detroit and Milwaukee, I'd been assigned in 1977 to the Behavioral Science Unit (BSU) of the FBI Academy in Quantico, Virginia, teaching applied criminal psychology to new agents, seasoned detectives and police brass through the National Academy program. The trouble was, many of these guys (there were very few women students back then) knew more about the cases being taught than I did, and every so often we'd get a chief or senior investigator who'd actually worked the case under review.

In an attempt to keep myself from looking uninformed, stupid or both before the veteran cops in my classroom, I decided to try to meet these violent predators face-to-face, to interview them and find out what was actually going on in their heads when they committed their crimes and what they thought of them afterward. My fellow instructor Robert Ressler and I did regular "road schools" for local police departments and sheriff's offices around the country, which I figured provided us the perfect opportunity to visit these offenders at their various institutions of longterm residence.

Out of those informal and unofficial origins, we began our original serial killer study, which ultimately led to a rigorous study funded by the National Institute of Justice (NIJ). I coauthored two landmark books with Ressler and Dr. Ann Burgess, of the University of Pennsylvania, entitled *Sexual Homicide: Patterns and Motives* and *Crime Classification Manual,* and solidified my career as the Federal Bureau of Investigation's first operational behavioral profiler.

Surprisingly — at least we thought so at the time — virtually every killer on our "wish list" agreed to talk to us. One of the earliest interviews Bob Ressler and I did happened to be with William George Heirens at Statesville Prison in Joliet, Illinois. As a seventeen-year-old, Heirens had confessed and pled guilty to murdering little Suzanne Degnan, as well as two adult women in the preceding months: forty-three-year-old housewife Josephine Ross and thirty-one-year-old Frances Brown, a former Navy WAVE who had served during World War II.

Brown's naked, bloodstained body was discovered in her apartment not far from Ross's home on the morning of December 11, 1945, when housemaid Martha Engels came to clean. She found Brown in the bathtub with a bullet wound to her skull and a butcher knife stabbed into her neck. On the living-room wall, scrawled in Brown's own red lipstick, was the apparent plea or, perhaps, mocking taunt:

For heAVens
Sake cAtch Me
BeFore I Kill More
I cannot control myself

By the next day's editions, Chicago's enterprising newspapers had a name for the unknown subject ("UNSUB" in our terminology) of this disgusting and horrific crime: the "Lipstick Killer."

Before the interview in Joliet, Ressler and I prepared by reviewing the case file and William Heirens's prison record. He had been a model prisoner throughout his incarceration and had become the first inmate in Illinois to complete a college degree. He'd since done graduate work.

Unlike many of the offenders we had or would study, there was nothing arrogant about Heirens, nothing "sinister," egotistical or overbearing. There was nothing intimidating about him; and unlike some we interviewed, he didn't give the impression of wanting to rip off our heads. He was polite and spoke well, but throughout the several-hour interview he insisted he was innocent. He maintained that he'd been intimidated by Chicago police into confessing and was railroaded by his attorneys into taking a plea deal that they had come up with in a bold attempt to keep him out of the Illinois electric chair.

No matter how we approached the case or what we asked him, Heirens had a ready answer. Though he freely admitted to his extended career as a breaking-and-entering man, he swore he had an alibi for the nights of each of the three killings and wasn't even close to any of the scenes. He was so passionate about his innocence, so compelling in his insistence, I was convinced he could have passed a polygraph on the spot. As we left the prison, I was thinking to myself, *Man, maybe this guy really got the shaft!*

One of the ultimate mysteries of the human condition is what really happens between two people in any situation. When that situation is a murder, that mystery can intensify to the extreme. *Is it possible that this given individual is capable of the worst act one person can perpetrate against another? And if not, then who is?*

At its essential level, criminal justice is about assembling evidence, clues and other indicators to come up with, and then telling a logical, consistent and believable story. The investigator has to have one, and so do the defense and the prosecution. The version that the jury buys ultimately determines the outcome of the case. That's what I did and the current profilers still do at Quantico: apply our knowledge, experience and instinct to intuit a story about a known victim and an unknown predator. Like everything else in criminal justice, there are several ways of telling the rest of the William Heirens story.

I was so affected by Heirens's rational-seeming claims of his innocence after so many years in prison that as soon as I got back to Quantico, I dug out my copies of the case materials and reviewed all the critical points.

I took the file over to the second floor of the academy library, where I often went when I needed to concentrate. At my desk, the phone rang constantly and colleagues were always stopping by to ask questions or kibitz. Also, working in a field in which darkness and night are such prevailing metaphors, I liked having sunlight. At the time, Behavioral Science was housed in offices sixty feet underground, in space that had originally been designed as an emergency-command bunker, leading to our frequent quip that we were buried ten times deeper than dead people.

Sure enough, all of the incriminating facts

were plain to see in Heirens's case file. He had the bad background I had come to expect from repeat predators: a risk-taking loner who had almost burned down the house with a chemistry experiment, and later jumped off a garage roof to try out his homemade cardboard wings; parents who had violent arguments and periodic money troubles; a string of burglaries going back at least to the age of thirteen; gun charges; and a record of being in and out of correctional schools. Based on stolen books found in his possession, including Richard von Krafft-Ebing's *Psychopathia Sexualis,* as well as a scrapbook he'd put together on the Nazis, he seemed to have an abiding interest in sexual perversion. He was even found to have his own portable surgical kit. The instruments were too small and delicate to have been used to take apart a body, but the interest it demonstrated in such things didn't exactly look good for someone who'd confessed to the postmortem dismembering of a child.

The confession itself was straightforward enough, except for the parts about a collaborator named "George Murman," who authorities decided was his face-saving alter ego who "drove him to it." George was Heirens's middle name, and Murman, they concluded, was short for "murder man." It appeared to be what our research would soon show us to be a classic case of escalation to murder through two opportunistic situations in which the owners of the premises happened to be home at the time of the break-ins, followed by a further escalation with the savage killing of the little girl. Heirens officially signed off on the confession not once, but twice, both times with attorneys present.

Other elements fit as well. The neighborhoods in which the murders took place were within the areas Heirens had burglarized in the past, what we would call his "comfort zone." He was apprehended in the midst of a burglary and attempted to shoot pursuing police officers before an off-duty cop happened to see what was happening and conked him on the head with a ceramic flowerpot, sending him to Bridewell, the medical lockup associated with Cook County Jail. Despite his checkered academic background, he was sufficiently intelligent to be accepted to the vaunted University of Chicago at age sixteen. In that, he equaled the feat of those other notorious Chicago killers, Nathan Leopold and Richard Loeb, convicted of the thrill murder of Loeb's fourteen-year-old neighbor and distant cousin, Bobby Franks, and only saved from the death chamber by the impassioned defense of Clarence Darrow. The local press saw to it that none of these details was lost on the terrorized and news-hungry public. The *Chicago Tribune* labeled the Suzanne Degnan homicide: *one of the most atro-*

cious American murders since the Loeb-Leopold case.

Once enrolled in the prestigious university, Heirens majored in electrical engineering and continued to burglarize private homes, stores and apartment hotels. The meager cash, jewelry and odd objects he stole speak to someone who was more interested in the kick than in profitable criminal enterprise. If this kid was able to compartmentalize his life to that extent, then maybe the plaintive plea to catch him before he killed more made some sense. You could even explain the immature scrawl as a psychological attempt to separate the highly intelligent "Bill Heirens" from the sinister "George Murman."

Most compelling was the physical evidence: Heirens's fingerprint showed up both on the ransom note and in blood on a doorjamb in Frances Brown's apartment. The ransom note print was eventually questioned as not having the necessary number of points of comparison (this one had nine; the FBI required a minimum of twelve). But the one from the Brown murder scene was unimpeachable.

In this context, the reality of the case became clear. Sitting in prison all those years with endless time to think about it, the intelligent and introspective Heirens had let himself psychologically off the hook and convinced himself that while he was an inveterate serial burglar, he was innocent of the three murders to which he had confessed.

We taught the William Heirens case for years after we included it in our Criminal Personality Research Project, the first organized study that actually correlated each step of a violent crime with what the offender was thinking and doing at the time. That study formed the basis of a discipline that has proven accurate and useful in finding and trying serial murderers, rapists and other violent, predatory criminals over more than forty years, through many thousands of investigations and prosecutions.

In 1987, nearly ten years after my interview with Bill Heirens, a detective from nearby Arlington County, Virginia, named Joe Horgas, came calling at Quantico. Through years of persistent investigative work, which I can only characterize as brilliant and inspired, Horgas thought he had linked bold break-ins, violent rapes and horribly vicious rape-murders that had taken place in Arlington, neighboring Alexandria and down in the Richmond area over a period of years. Others in the various police departments didn't buy the connection. However, Horgas was positive. In his mind, the series of crimes went back to the murder of Carolyn Hamm, a thirty-two-year-old attorney, in Arlington in 1984.

After hearing the detective's presentation and considering everything — from timing and method of entry to physical and behavioral evidence, choice of victims and lab reports — we agreed the cases were almost certainly related. There are very few absolutes in our business, and none in profiling, but this was a pretty damn good matchup.

Then Horgas sprang a major curveball on us. "Hamm is actually a closed case," he explained, "because an individual has been arrested, tried and convicted."

Whoa!

He told us about David Vasquez, a Hispanic male who was thirty-seven years of age when the Arlington Police Department arrested him two weeks after the murder. He'd been living with a friend in Hamm's neighborhood and had been witnessed around her house by two individuals. When detectives searched his room, they found pornography involving bound and gagged women, as well as peeper photos he'd taken surreptitiously of women in various stages of undress. He couldn't be linked to semen samples found on Hamm's body or clothing, though some hair samples were suggestive. But the slam dunk was that he had confessed!

"Do you think there's more than one person involved?" Horgas asked.

This wasn't an idle question. Because Vasquez was demonstrably of very marginal intelligence and the crime was criminally sophisticated, there was some compelling thought that the Hamm murder might have been the work of two offenders, the UNSUB being the dominant one and Vasquez more of a compliant partner. We'd seen a number of examples of this over the years; so while rare, it wasn't beyond the realm of possibility. Normally, there are some pretty strong indicators at the crime scene, with elements representing both organized and disorganized aspects.

But at no point had Vasquez mentioned anyone else, nor was there any reference in his confession, nor was there anything from the Hamm case or any of the others that looked to us like a two-person crime. In fact, from what he told us about Vasquez, it didn't seem that he had the intellectual capability or the experience to have pulled off something this criminally sophisticated.

The fact that the crimes had stopped in Northern Virginia at a certain point, and then similar ones started occurring around Richmond three years later, established a pattern that was highly suggestive: Since this type of offender rarely stops on his own, we speculated that he had been picked up for some crime, like a burglary, which carried a three-year sentence, then was put on some sort of work release in Richmond.

Horgas pursued this idea, following up on

every record of someone who might fit the pattern. He went back to the Arlington neighborhoods where the early crimes took place. Before long, he recalled a troubled African-American teenager named Timothy Wilson Spencer, whom he'd once investigated for a burglary. Several computer checks confirmed a bull's-eye. Spencer was twenty-two when he had been arrested in 1984 for burglary in Alexandria and was released to a halfway house in Richmond in 1987. Once Spencer was targeted as a suspect, everything started falling into place. Most important, his DNA matched three of the murder scenes and several of the rapes.

Though he never confessed, Spencer was convicted of murder in the first degree in three separate trials, and sentenced to death in all three. His convictions represent the first successful use of DNA evidence in the United States. After the failure of all of his appeals, on April 27, 1994, Timothy Wilson Spencer was executed in the electric chair of the Virginia State Penitentiary in Jarratt.

For people like me who have spent our professional lives helping police hunt down the worst of the worst and seeking justice for those who can no longer seek it for themselves, this was a highly gratifying outcome. But one giant loose end persisted. David Vasquez remained in prison for a crime we were convinced was part of a string commit-

41

ted by someone else. The two witnesses against Vasquez would not alter their testimony, and the crime scene samples had degraded to the point of being useless. The best shot at getting him sprung — of demonstrating that the Hamm murder was committed by the same offender as the others — was probably a behavioral science approach. So that was when we took the lead.

The FBI's profiling group is now called the Behavioral Analysis Unit (BAU). When I became the first full-time operational profiler, I was part of the Behavioral Science Unit, which was essentially academic. In an effort to be taken seriously by our police clients, and to "get rid of the BS," I called the new profiling group the Investigative Support Unit (ISU). There were twelve profilers whom I affectionately nicknamed "the Dirty Dozen." Soon we were analyzing more than a thousand cases a year, so we set up a system in which each special agent profiler was assigned a geographic area of the country.

At the time of the Vasquez-Spencer case, the agent overseeing Virginia was Steve Mardigian, who set to work gathering material and analyzing every aspect of each related crime. After months of work, he presented his findings to all of us in a case conference. We all agreed that these were all the work of a resourceful, experienced, angry and manipulative sexual sadist. David Vasquez did not and could not have committed the murder of Carolyn Hamm.

Once we had completed our analysis, we joined with Joe Horgas and the Arlington PD in asking Commonwealth Attorney Helen Fahey, of Arlington County, to ask Governor Gerald Baliles to grant Vasquez a full pardon. A report signed by both Mardigian and me accompanied her petition. Less than three months later, David Vasquez was a free man, having spent four years in prison for a crime he confessed to, but didn't commit.

Had a defense attorney brought this case to us and asked for our assistance, we would have had to decline. There was no federal jurisdiction here, so the only way we could get involved was when local law enforcement asked us in. Also, stretched as thin as we were, we had only offered our services to police, sheriff and other investigating agencies, not those charged with crimes. Even if we had had the resources, I can't imagine the FBI brass letting us work both sides of the street.

In working this case, though, the reality of the confession became equally clear. Scared and isolated during his police interrogation, Vasquez perceived that his only "salvation" was to please and cooperate with his interrogators and give them what they wanted. Either intentionally or not, he had been given way too much information, which he then

43

formed into a "dream" in which he had murdered Carolyn Hamm. Naively, he thought that once he had cooperated with the authorities, they would let him go.

Was the conviction of David Vasquez a horrible miscarriage of justice? Of course, it was. But let me point out one critical factor. Yes, it was law enforcement officials who put Vasquez behind bars. But it was also law enforcement officials who got him out when the mistake was realized, not reporters or lawyers or even crusading civilians. And it is the open-mindedness, impartiality and integrity — or lack of same — of those connected with the criminal justice process that is at the heart of this book.

Stated in its most basic terms, our criminal justice system is an attempt to do the impossible: to make the world as right as possible after someone has done something to upset that rightness. We define this as committing an act that's against the law. And that system knows and understands its own limitations, both in terms of restoring the aggrieved to their previous state and determining the ultimate truth of what happened. Just remember: *No one is ever found innocent.* Not ever. The only distinction the system is capable of making is between "guilty" and "not guilty." Has the evidence reached a level of reasonable human certainty? That's what the system strives to determine in each instance. We know that's the best we can do, so we must try to do it as well as we possibly can.

Long after we'd finished with the Vasquez case, it continued to haunt me, as it should haunt anyone in law enforcement who takes his or her mission seriously. I had always regarded confessions as the gold standard: If you can get a confession, you've made your case! But David Vasquez called everything uncomfortably into question.

Which brings us back to William Heirens.

CHAPTER 2
UPON FURTHER REVIEW

When you start out as a special agent for the FBI and get your first field office assignment, you're pretty naive about certain things, especially if, like me, you had no previous law enforcement experience. The first thing you realize is that not everyone is glad to see you, and I'm not just talking about the bad guys. Some police departments welcome the assistance the Bureau can provide, while others perceive us as the four-hundred-pound gorilla muscling onto their turf.

When you're new, you tend to assume that all PDs and sheriff's offices conduct complete and thorough investigations, just as you've been taught to do at the FBI Academy, and that all the evidence they give you is good and reliable. Well, that one isn't always true, either.

During my years in the Bureau, I was always handling so many active cases and, for much of that time, also heading up the Investigative Support Unit, that I seldom had the luxury to revisit past cases. Only after I retired did I have a chance to consider crimes I'd studied early in my career, cases like the Lipstick Killer of Chicago.

Let's review the case and see if we want to tell the story a different way this time. We'll take a look at some facts and events of which I was unaware at the time of the prison interview, and we'll bring to bear some of the experience, research and knowledge we acquired as my unit's criminal investigative analysis program developed. And we'll begin as if we were profiling an UNSUB for a police consultation.

First, let's make sure we understand the role of profiling in a criminal investigation.

Point Number One: We don't catch criminals. That's what the police do. What we do is assist local law enforcement in focusing their investigation on a particular type of UNSUB. Depending on the type of evidence or clues available, we may be able to give pretty specific details of sex, race, age, area of residence, motive, profession, background, personal relationships and various other aspects of an individual's personality. We will also suggest proactive techniques to draw a criminal into making a move to go in a particular direction. Once the suspect is apprehended, we can aid in interrogation and then prosecution strategy. In the trial, we can provide expert testimony of signature, modus operandi (MO), motive, linkage, crime classification and staging.

This is all based on our research and specialized experience with what is now tens of thousands of cases, many more than any local investigator could ever possibly see. Essentially, we use the same techniques as our fictional forebear, Sherlock Holmes. It is all based on logical, deductive and inductive reasoning and our basic equation is this:

$$\text{WHY?} + \text{HOW?} = \text{WHO}$$

It sounds simple, but there are countless variables that go into the analysis; and to be truly useful, we have to be as specific as possible. We all recognize the cliché of the white male loner in his twenties. But even in instances where that description might be accurate, it doesn't help much unless we can say something about where he lives, what's been happening in his life, what types of changes family, friends and colleagues should be noticing in him, when and where he might strike again, whether and/or how he'll react to the investigation, etc.

One thing I always told new agents in my unit was that it is not enough to profile the UNSUB; you have to profile the victim, too. You have to know whether she or he had a high-risk lifestyle, whether she or he was likely to be passive or aggressive in the face of threats, whether she or he had any enemies or bad relationships in the past, and so on. But I've found that even that is not enough. You also have to profile the *situation*. And by that, I mean taking a look at what is going on in and around the investigation. What is the social environment like? How do people feel about the particular crime? What role do the media play? What is the police culture like? There are any number of important questions you can ask to try to get the lay of the land.

Most people know of Chicago's reputation in the Roaring Twenties, when Prohibition made large-scale criminal enterprise profitable. But in the years since then, it went through a number of rough patches. After a relatively tranquil period during World War II, city officials were concerned that the influx of returning servicemen and a decrease in jobs would boost violent crime rates again. The police were already under intense stress. So when Josephine Ross was murdered in June 1945, just as the war was winding down, and then Frances Brown in December, just four months after VJ Day, the pressure was on.

In my business, you always take into account the role of the media, and Chicago had the most audacious and freewheeling press in the country. Once they had their Lipstick Killer to write about, they began whipping the public into a frenzy. And we can't overlook the fact that throughout the first half of the twentieth century and even later, Chicago had an ongoing problem with public corruption. This, in turn, led to two other results: The public was both cynical and skeptical about the authorities' abilities to solve problems; and the authorities felt a need to produce solutions, whether they had the wherewithal or not.

If I were advising the Chicago PD after studying the Ross and Brown cases, I would tell them to look for a white male in his late twenties to late thirties who already had a history of break-ins and violence against women. This man would be very control-oriented and have a lot of rage as evidenced by the "overkill" of repeated stabbings. Neither woman was aggressive, nor did either victim have a high-risk lifestyle. Their murders were crimes of opportunity in which the victim was unfortunately home when the offender broke in. He would be able to objectify his victims and feel no remorse for the crimes. The murders of victims Ross and Brown — like those by Timothy Spencer in Virginia — show a strong degree of criminal sophistication and a buildup in both learned technique and escalation of acting out rage against women. This is why I would profile an older UNSUB.

I would find the lipstick-scrawled message

at the Brown scene interesting, but I'd also be skeptical. It could be a taunt from a narcissist playing off the press coverage he would be sure to get from such a gruesome crime. But it could also be a complete red herring — something forged by an overly industrious member of the press corps who wanted to up the ante on sensationalism. When Mark Olshaker and I were examining the "Jack the Ripper" Whitechapel murders for our book *The Cases That Haunt Us,* we became convinced that the notorious "Dear Boss" letter, from which the Ripper nickname derives, was a fake, probably written by an enterprising Victorian newsman hoping to gin up interest in the case. Simply put, when subjected to psycholinguistic analysis, it did not conform to the profile we had constructed for the killer based on the totality of evidence, while the subsequent "From Hell" letter — a much more raw and disorganized message — did. I think there may have been a similar instance here with the "Catch Me" message.

Going back to our situational profile for a moment, when Suzanne Degnan was murdered less than three weeks after Frances Brown, everything changed. There is nothing more horrible in the collective consciousness than the murder of a child, and the details of this particular murder were so monstrous that the public and media demanded a swift solution and certain justice. That another little girl might meet Suzanne's fate was unthinkable. The police were now under intense pressure to come up with a suspect. In response, they launched the greatest manhunt in the city's history, involving thousands of leads, nearly a thousand interviews, hundreds of polygraphs and countless handwriting sample comparisons.

It took them only two days to come up with their first good suspect. Hector Verburgh was the sixty-five-year-old janitor of the building where Suzanne's body was butchered in the laundry room. The ransom note had the kinds of dirt smudges consistent with an author whose hands were always grimy. A PD spokesman announced, "This is the man."

This was like their trophy to hold up.

They held Verburgh for forty-eight hours, during which time they beat and abused him so severely that he required ten days of hospitalization. Only the intervention of the janitors' union attorney demanding a writ of habeas corpus finally got him released. Habeas corpus — literally "that you have the body," in Latin — goes back to the era of English common law and gives imprisoned petitioners the right to be brought to court to have their grievances or objections to detention or sentencing reviewed.

Enumerating the horrifying interrogation techniques, Verburgh testified, "Any more and I would have confessed to anything." It also turned out the janitor's writing skills were not even sufficient to have penned the crude ransom note.

The treatment of Mr. Verburgh speaks for itself. So deplorable were the police actions that he sued the Chicago Police Department for $15,000, a considerable sum in those days. The court apparently agreed and awarded him the money and another $5,000 for his wife, whom the police had tried to coerce into testifying against him.

When called into a case by a local law enforcement agency, a profiler's role is to help *refocus* or *redirect* an investigation. The apprehension of Hector Verburgh definitely would have called for a redirection, had I been called in on the case. First of all, he was too far along on the age continuum, particularly with no prior history. People don't suddenly "blossom" into violent sexual killers. From our extensive experience, it just doesn't happen that way. For someone of Verburgh's age to commit this act, there would have had to be other acts of violence, especially against children or other defenseless people, in his past. Other than the happenstance of the location, there was nothing that tied him to the crime.

A number of weak suspects followed. One was a marine combat veteran who lived in the neighborhood who happened to have the same first initial and last name as the laundry mark found on a handkerchief near the crime scene. He had a solid alibi and easily passed a polygraph. Then there was a local kid who'd been in reform school for armed robbery and told another kid he'd killed Suzanne. Again the local papers declared the case solved. After failing to convince a polygraph examiner (in other words, *passing*), he admitted he'd made up the story to get the other kid to try to get the ransom money.

Meanwhile, more than a thousand miles away, police came up with a suspect who definitely would have interested me.

Richard Russell Thomas, a sometimes drifter, forty-four years of age, was in the Maricopa County, Arizona, jail on charges of molesting his thirteen-year-old daughter. Charles B. Arnold, head of the forgery unit of the police department in nearby Phoenix, Thomas's hometown, thought he saw distinct similarities between the ransom note and Thomas's handwriting when he wrote with his nondominant left hand. At the time of the Degnan murder, he had been living in Chicago, working as a nurse at Woodlawn Hospital and was known to hang around an automobile dealership a few blocks from the Degnan home.

When Thomas was questioned, he confessed to the crime. However, police were suspicious, since he didn't seem to know all of the details and appeared to be angling to be extradited out of state so he could beat the molestation rap. Apparently, he felt the devil he didn't know was preferable to the one he knew. Once he had a chance to think about it, though, Thomas recanted his confession pretty quickly.

But aside from the questionable confession, the facts concerning Thomas were compelling:

He was a burglar with a bold and risky MO.

He had a previous conviction for extortion, having sent a ransom note threatening the kidnapping of a little girl.

He had a history of domestic violence and sexual abuse.

He worked as a nurse and several times had tried to pass himself off as a doctor, and he had stolen surgical implements and supplies.

If you also add the fact that he was known to be in and around the Degnans' neighborhood at the time of the murder, and that his left-hand writing was a possible match for the ransom note, this was the kind of guy I would have advised the Chicago PD to put on the front burner. To get to the level of violence and depravity that the Suzanne Degnan murder represented, an offender had to go through a series of evolutionary steps. It often starts with voyeurism and/or petty burglary, but then it keeps escalating. Clearly, Thomas had gone through them.

Then there was the issue of the ransom note, which I would have taken seriously as a piece of evidence, but not as a demand for money. Anyone primarily interested in kidnapping would have "researched" a likely victim — and in the late 1940s, this was still a somewhat active criminal enterprise, much more than it is today — and chosen one whose family clearly had the means to pay. Twenty grand was a large amount of money back then, far more than an average year's salary for a government worker like James Degnan.

If kidnapping was the primary motive for a crime, the criminal would target a victim whose family had the obvious means to lay their hands quickly on the amount of cash demanded. You see, the longer a kidnapping goes on, the more dangerous it becomes for both the victim and the offender. If you put this together with the fact that Suzanne's body parts were discovered before twenty-four hours had passed, or any instructions on delivering the money had been sent, you realize that kidnapping was not the prime motivation for the crime. This was a psychopathic offender for whom the ransom note was a sideline or afterthought.

I can't say for sure from this remove that Richard Thomas was Suzanne's killer. He died in prison in 1974, before I started the FBI prison interviews, so we might never know. But I can say with a fair degree of confidence that Suzanne's killer was *like* Thomas, or shared similar characteristics.

But it was at this point — June 26, 1946 — that seventeen-year-old William Heirens was arrested for burglary of an apartment house and, when trapped by police from two sides, panicked and pulled out his gun and fired. This act, in retrospect, altered the course of his life because it indicated to police that he was capable of violence. And it was at this point that the police apparently lost interest in Richard Thomas. They were confident they had the Lipstick Killer in custody.

Despite the fact that they may have asked federal agents to come into a case, police are often not very happy when you suggest they refocus an investigation away from a particular suspect they feel is good for the crime. Sometimes they're downright pissed off. That's probably what would have happened if I had been working the Degnan case.

Looking at Heirens, I would have considered him too young to pull off a crime of this detail and sophistication, to make the leap from petty burglaries to violent rapes and murders, and much too meek and passive. This would be particularly true after we looked into his personal life and saw that there was no precipitating factor to make him change or escalate his pattern of lawless and antisocial behavior. In other words, nothing had changed in his life at this point to induce the emotional trauma or stimulus that might have propelled him to more aggressive and violent behavior.

He wouldn't go suddenly from causal, if repeated, burglaries to the murder and mutilation of a six-year-old child, brazenly taken from her own bedroom.

It just doesn't happen like that!

Please keep this phrase in mind as we delve further into the minds and methods we'll be exploring as we go along.

I might have pegged this suspect for a voyeur or a fetish burglar, who steals underwear or personal objects; in spite of the way he was caught, and his carrying a gun, he would be essentially nonconfrontational. I wouldn't see this type trying to pull off a kidnapping, or even going through the motions of one, because it would involve too much interaction with a victim and police.

Just as important, whether the ultimate intent in the Degnan case was kidnapping or murder, a guy as young and meek as Heirens would not be able to exert the kind of control over the victim that the evidence clearly indicated. A six-year-old is not going to go willingly or quietly with a stranger who breaks into her room and tries to take her away. This would require more experience and finesse than a seventeen-year-old like Heirens could muster. Even the idea of someone with this personality transporting a live or dead child to another location is almost unthinkable. Also, I would have been surprised by the use of a ladder in the crime, as it had not been previously part of Heirens's breaking-and-entering MO.

And here's the most critical factor of all from a profiling perspective, and this is pretty much an ultimate truth. After the Suzanne Degnan murder and mutilation, *you would have seen a profound change in the offender's actions and personality.* This would be true no matter who the UNSUB was, but it would be even more pronounced the younger the killer. He would become acutely nervous. Those around him would notice negative changes in his appearance. He might lose weight. He might drink heavily. He would seem distant and preoccupied. He would definitely follow the investigation and probably talk about it. He would not have gone unnoticed around his own circle in his home area or in school.

According to multiple accounts he later gave, this is what happened to William Heirens following his arrest:

As we've noted, he was brought to Bridewell Hospital, adjacent to Cook County Jail, to be treated for the injuries sustained when the off-duty police officer knocked him out with the flowerpot. He was questioned for long periods around the clock for six days, during which he was given little to eat or drink and was struck repeatedly. He said he was punched in the testicles and burned with ether. He was refused attorneys and, until near the end of this phase of the confinement, was not able to see his parents.

Two psychiatrists, Dr. Roy Grinker and Dr. William H. Haines, administered Sodium Pentothal — then thought to be a "truth serum" — and questioned him for three hours, during which the "George Murman" alternate personality emerged. Since there are no written or recorded transcripts extant of that session, it is unclear whether Heirens came up with George or whether he was suggested by the doctors or someone else who might have been in the room. What is clear is that several years later, one of the psychiatrists confirmed that Heirens never implicated himself in any of the three murders.

Afterward, in the presence of police captain Michael Ahern, state's attorney for Cook County William Tuohy and a stenographer, Heirens is said to have given additional details about George Murman, who sent him out to rob, and that he was always taking the rap for George. Again, since the transcript no longer exists, I don't know how much is accurate, but had I heard it, I would have been very skeptical. Once this information leaked out, though, the newspapers went crazy with it. Who wouldn't love a *Dr. Jekyll and Mr. Hyde* angle to grisly murders? Add to that the stolen dissecting kit found in his dorm room and the book about deviant sexual practices and you had the perfect portrait of a bright young college student as perverted rapist and killer.

It is not at all unusual for suspects to attribute blame to another imaginary figure. David Berkowitz, known as the "Son of Sam" and the ".44-Caliber Killer," who terrorized New York City in 1976 and 1977, claimed a three-thousand-year-old black dog had ordered him to kill. The shrinks had gone to town with this and labeled him a paranoid schizophrenic. It all sounded too familiar to me, so when I interviewed him years later in Attica State Prison and he started up on this dog, I faced him and said, "Hey, David, knock off the bullshit. The dog had nothing to do with it." He grinned and admitted I was right. The fact was that this was just one angry son of a bitch who came up with the dog to enhance his own image and maybe get himself off the hook mentally.

Convicted killer Sedley Alley at one point claimed that an alternate personality forced him into the absolutely horrific murder of U.S. Marine lance corporal Suzanne Collins. In fact, though I've seen several clearly legitimate cases of multiple personality disorder (MPD) in young children — all of them physically and/or sexually abused — I have yet to see an authentic MPD diagnosis

61

that emerged postarrest for murder.

If I had been presented with this George Murman business, I would have concluded one of two things: Either the suspect was using it to set up an insanity or diminished-capacity plea, or the investigators had suggested it to him as a way to make their case.

Shortly after this, Heirens was subjected to a spinal tap, apparently to rule out any brain damage resulting from being conked on the head by the flowerpot. For reasons unknown, this painful lumbar puncture was performed without anesthesia, and then he was carted over to the detective bureau for a polygraph exam. He was in so much pain that the test was rescheduled for four days later, at which time the results were officially "inconclusive."

I have never been a big fan of the polygraph. Innocent people are often totally spooked by the process and the emotional assault on their honesty, and sociopaths often have no more trouble lying to a box than they do to other humans. It is mainly a tool that investigators will use to segue into an interrogation. In this case, I would consider the test absolutely worthless, regardless of whether it implicated or exculpated the subject.

Various handwriting experts were called in to compare past exemplars of Heirens's handwriting with the lipstick scrawl and ransom note. The best they could come up with was inconclusive. Several found no similarity, nor did they believe the "catch me" slogan and ransom note were written by the same individual. Many years later, in 1996, FBI handwriting expert David Grimes stated that the exemplars of Heirens's handwriting taken from his college notes did not match either the lipstick scrawl or the ransom note, which did not even match each other.

Having discounted the Murman details, the polygraph and the handwriting, I would have fallen back on one of the key principles of profiling: *Past actions suggest future actions.* There was nothing in Bill Heirens's past to suggest that he would even feel comfortable confronting a woman during a break-in, much less killing her so brutally. Even if he had been surprised and panicked at a burglary scene, someone like this might possibly have shot the victim to keep her from pursuing him or testifying against him. He would not have stabbed her multiple times. That is the work of an individual with a long-standing rage against women. When you get to the third crime in the supposed string, as we have shown, it would be incomprehensible for him to deal with a child in the way the Degnan scene and dump site indicated.

As you may have gathered by now, I don't think the Degnan killing was carried out by the same individual who perpetrated the Ross and Brown murders. Those two are more opportunistic, more the work of a thrill-seeking burglar who is sexually motivated and prone to rape if the situation presents itself. This belief is certainly bolstered by the fact that no valuables were taken from either scene. And neither one fits the pattern that Heirens had already established in his own burglaries, nor had anything in his behavior or evidence at any of his scenes given an indication that he had progressed or evolved in his criminal intents.

By the same token, we can't ignore the established past actions of the Chicago police in the Hector Verburgh incident. If they were so hot to get a confession from this poor elderly custodian that they put him in the hospital for ten days and left him with lasting physical problems, how can we suppose that they wouldn't do it again? Whatever confession they got out of Heirens is tainted from the get-go. Even ignoring all other allegations of brutality against the Chicago police of that era, what they did to Verburgh makes Heirens's claims highly plausible and believable.

This was a phenomenon I would see over and over again. Frankly, it has shocked me each time I have come across it: that a suspect who had been grilled for hours and hours in a high-stress environment would not only give interrogators whatever he thought would get them off his back, he would actually start to lose hold of reality and think that maybe he could have done what he was being accused of. And it didn't just happen to individuals of demonstrably low IQ, such as David Vasquez. It has happened to numerous highly intelligent and sophisticated people, too.

As far as the most damning piece of physical evidence — the bloody fingerprint smudge on the doorjamb of the Frances Brown murder scene — we've got to be suspicious of that now, too. It was said to match a print from the ransom note, but that could have been obtained by letting Heirens examine the document. Even more alarming, a number of experts later asserted that the Brown scene print appeared "rolled," as if it had come from the technique used to put prints on a fingerprint card. In other words, it may have been planted. No other physical evidence tied Heirens to any of the three scenes.

There's another factor. Like just about everyone else in Chicago, Heirens's attorneys, brothers Malachy and John Coghlan, along with Alvin Hansen and Roland Towle, were concerned that he was guilty and felt their first responsibility was to keep him out of the electric chair. As it later turned out, while state's attorney Tuohy also felt he was guilty, he wasn't confident about a conviction based on the rather skimpy physical evidence of the one partial print and the possible print on the strange ransom note. So the prosecution and defense lawyers got together to talk about a plea bargain. The general agreement among them was that in exchange for a guilty plea, Heirens would receive a single life sentence for all three murders, saving him from execution and conceivably making him eligible for parole at some time in the distant future.

Four days later, the *Tribune* led with the inside story of Heirens's "second confession," despite the fact that all concerned denied there had been one. So great was the *Tribune*'s prestige with this made-up account that the other Chicago papers quickly followed suit.

As it turned out, though, the *Tribune* version of the murders was helpful to Heirens's lawyers in fashioning the confession they would present for him in court, filling in many of the "details" their client claimed not to know. Heirens agreed to sign, then balked, prompting Tuohy to threaten him with adding yet another unsolved murder. Actually, Heirens was in a reform school in Indiana at the time, though Tuohy might not have been aware of or focused on this fact. Heirens's attorneys pressured him and his parents to confess and take the plea, and as far as I can tell, genuinely thought they were serving their client's best interests.

On July 30, William Tuohy assembled various officials and the press in his office to hear Heirens's official confession. At the last second, though, William Heirens balked. The defense attorneys were shocked and the state's attorney was mortified. As soon as the public spectacle was over, Tuohy changed his offer to three life terms, instead of one, and Heirens's lawyers warned him that the electric chair loomed if he didn't start playing ball.

A week later, on August 7, 1946, Heirens did, reenacting his crimes before an eager mob of media. Then, on September 5, before Chief Justice Harold G. Ward, of the Criminal Court of Cook County, William Heirens presented his confession and pled guilty to the three murders. He later said, "I confessed to save my life." It was an eerie reprise of Hector Verburgh's comment that had he been held and abused any longer, he "would have confessed to anything."

Of all those present, it seemed that the only one who doubted Heirens's guilt was Josephine Ross's daughter, Mary Jane Blanchard. "I cannot believe that young Heirens murdered my mother," she told a reporter from the *Chicago Herald-American.* "He just does not fit into the picture of my mother's death. I have looked at all the things Heirens stole and there was nothing of my mother's things among them."

That evening, he tried to hang himself in his cell in the Cook County Jail, but he was discovered before he suffocated. He said he was in despair over being perceived as guilty and that if he were dead, maybe that perception would be different. To me, what he was saying was that he couldn't tolerate the impossible emotional box in which he'd been placed.

On September 5, after statements from both prosecution and defense, Judge Ward sentenced Heirens to three life terms, effectively eliminating the possibility of future parole. As Heirens was being transferred from Cook County Jail to Statesville Prison, where I would meet him more than thirty years later, Sheriff Michael Mulcahy, one of the few officials who had treated him with kindness and consideration, confided, "You probably didn't realize this, Bill, but I'm a personal friend of Jim Degnan. He wants to know, did his daughter Suzanne suffer?"

"I can't tell you if she suffered, Sheriff Mulcahy," Heirens replied. "I didn't kill her. Tell Mr. Degnan to please look after his other daughter, because whoever killed Suzanne is still out there."

When William Heirens — frail, sickly and wheelchair-bound — passed away on March 5, 2012, at the Dixon Correctional Center, at the age of eighty-three, he was the longest-serving prisoner in the United States. In addition to his previously mentioned educational achievements, his record over the years was essentially spotless, and he had earned the respect of numerous prison officials.

Several efforts to have him pardoned, or at

least paroled and released, were mounted, the most formidable by Dolores Kennedy, a legal assistant with the Northwestern University Center on Wrongful Convictions, and author of the book *William Heirens: His Day in Court/Did an Innocent Teen-ager Confess to Three Grisly Murders?* He was denied parole at least thirty times.

By now, it is probably too late to determine with absolute certainty whether or not William George Heirens actually committed any or all of the three vicious murders to which he confessed. But, after examining all of the available facts and evidence, from my years of experience in profiling and criminal investigative analysis, I no longer believe him to have been a killer, and he spent the vast majority of his life behind bars for nothing. Though he is now beyond our justice, I would be happy to testify to those beliefs under oath in a court of law.

I wish I had known enough when I first encountered Bill Heirens to have come to this conclusion and put forth these views. I have spent considerable energy both in and after my FBI service to make up for my initial naiveté.

I have spent my career helping to put away the bad guys: kidnappers and killers, bombers and sexual predators, the worst of the worst. And I've derived an enormous amount of satisfaction from that pursuit. But for that effort to have any meaning, our first allegiance must always be to justice. And to approach justice, we must first seek truth — whatever it means and wherever it takes us.

The American criminal justice process is an admirable and often copied system. But as we have noted, it is not a perfect one. Innocent people are convicted, and guilty ones evade the law or are let go, and I weep for all the victims. It is therefore incumbent upon all of us to have the humility to realize that we can, and must, improve.

Justice is often uncomfortable, but that doesn't mean we should turn our heads away. And perfect justice is an ultimately unattainable goal for us mere mortals. But that in no way suggests we shouldn't continually strive toward achieving it. The examinations of the cases that follow represent some of my personal steps along the way.

■ ■ ■ ■

MATTERS OF LIFE
AND DEATH

■ ■ ■ ■

Chapter 3
"An Innocent Man Is Going to Be Murdered Tonight"

What is it about murder trials that capture the imagination? For me, they represent the culmination of months, sometimes years, of investigation, analysis, prosecutorial strategy and preparation of witnesses. For "normal" people, though, I think there's something else at work.

A murder trial is the ultimate mystery and morality play — not only a whodunit, but also an examination of what human beings are capable of at their most extreme. It is a contrast between the individual and the society in which he lives, and about emotions that we all experience played out in real life rather than suppressed in conformance to social norms. I think it is interesting to note that three of the great institutional contributions of Western culture — the drama, the Mass and the trial — are all narrative-driven pageants with three acts — a beginning, a middle and an end — that focus on the individual in relation to society, the struggle between right and wrong, and how it may ultimately be resolved.

It is no wonder, then, that murder trials always seem to fascinate. In almost every time and place, the media focus on one particular trial to play out the ongoing conflict between truth and lies, between good and evil, between justice and lawlessness. Nowhere is that more acute than when the defendant's own life hangs in the balance in the determination of whether or not he took the life of another.

In 1976, through a group of five cases clumped together under the heading *Gregg* v. *Georgia,* and called by some scholars the "July 2 Cases" because of the date of the decision, the United States Supreme Court overturned a four-year moratorium on capital punishment and set forth new standards by which the death penalty could be imposed.

Almost immediately, death penalty opponents began a quest for a case that would demonstrate, in the most direct way possible, the folly of allowing the state to execute human beings. This would have to be a case in which it could be proven, beyond all reasonable doubt, that a man or woman had been put to death for a crime he or she did not commit.

They looked for several years without success. Then came the case of Roger Keith

Coleman.

Grundy, Virginia, is in the southwestern corner of the state. It's about thirteen miles to the West Virginia border, fifteen miles to Kentucky, and only about fifty miles from both North Carolina and Tennessee. The seat of Buchanan County, Grundy is in the heart of Appalachia. Like many small towns along that mountain chain, its main livelihood is coal.

On Tuesday, March 10, 1981, at about two-fifteen in the afternoon, twenty-one-year-old Bradley D. McCoy left his small brick and white-siding home near Slate Creek on the outskirts of Grundy for his three o'clock shift at the United Coal Company. Management considered Brad a smart and enthusiastic worker, so he had been assigned to be a parts clerk, rather than being sent down the mine. During a break at about 9:00 P.M., he called his wife, Wanda Faye. Wanda was nineteen, wasn't employed and wasn't all that comfortable being home alone while Brad was at work. So he liked to call around this time and check up on her. They talked about common things, such as what they would do with the tax refund they were expecting.

When Brad returned home around 11:15 P.M., he was surprised that the outside of the house was dark. Wanda usually left the porch light on for him. Also, the storm door was unlocked; Wanda was usually more careful than that. He let himself in the front door with his key and stepped into the living room. The room light and television were on; the coffee table was out of place; he saw what looked like small drops of blood on the floor. He called to Wanda, but he got no response.

Rushing to the bedroom, he found Wanda on the floor on her back. Her arms were over her head. Her hair was pulled across her face, and her legs were spread straight out. Her cable-knit sweater and bra were pushed up around her neck. Her dark blue panties were twisted around her left ankle, and her blue jeans lay on the bed. The only articles of clothing that remained in place were her blue-striped socks. There was significant blood on her chest, her neck and the side of her head.

Horrified as he was, Brad had enough presence of mind not to touch the body. He called his father, Max, a retired coal miner known as "Hezzie," who lived nearby. Hezzie called the Buchanan County Sheriff's Department; then he went to Brad and Wanda's house to await law enforcement.

Sergeant Steven D. Coleman was first on scene, arriving at about 11:25 P.M., accompanied by another officer. He tried to check Wanda's neck for any sign of a pulse, but it was so severely cut that he couldn't even find an intact vessel.

Within minutes, the Grundy chief of police Randall S. Jackson arrived. He felt Wanda's wrist, which he said was still warm, but he couldn't detect any pulse, either. He ordered the entire scene secured and sent for medical examiner (ME) Thomas D. McDonald. Dr. McDonald lived nearby and came quickly. He made the death pronouncement and determined that the "slashing wound to the throat" was the cause. Based on the body temperature and the lack of rigor mortis, he concluded the time of death was within thirty minutes either way of 10:30 P.M. He decided not to move the body until a state police special investigation unit could examine the scene.

Once the crime scene team had finished, the body was transported to Roanoke, where an autopsy performed by Dr. David W. Oxley confirmed Dr. McDonald's findings. The slashing was so brutal and deep that the right carotid artery, jugular vein and larynx were all severed. Two deep stab wounds to the chest had penetrated the heart and lung, but since there was little hemorrhaging, Oxley concluded that they were inflicted postmortem, or at least after the arterial wound cut off blood pressure. He found two foreign hairs in the genital region.

The brutal murder sent predictable shock waves through this small town. Brad told investigators that Wanda was a naturally shy person and skittish about staying home alone, particularly at night. Had I been assisting on this case, this would have been a key piece of the victimology, particularly since the front door was locked when Brad returned home. He said there were only three men in town for whom she comfortably would have opened the door. The police were quickly able to alibi two of them.

The third was Wanda's brother-in-law, Roger Keith Coleman, twenty-two years of age and married to her sixteen-year-old sister, Patricia. Wanda and Patricia were the two youngest of a family of eight boys and eight girls. Like Brad's father, Wanda's dad was a retired coal miner. Roger and Patricia lived in his grandmother's house, about a five-minute walk from the McCoys'.

Coleman was arrested on April 13. He denied any knowledge of the crime, saying he would have no reason or motive to rape and kill his wife's sister. He said he could account for his whereabouts the evening of the murder, with witnesses to alibi him.

On the night in question, he showed up for his shift as a miner at the TJ and M Coal Company, only to learn that the entire shift had been canceled. He detailed for police where he had been since leaving his house, ending up at a bathhouse in town where miners often showered and changed clothes before returning home. He willingly turned over to the state police a plastic bag containing the clothing he was wearing that night. He also agreed to give samples of blood, hair and saliva without the police having to seek a warrant.

Despite his cooperative attitude and profession of innocence, police had a compelling reason to suspect Coleman.

On April 7, 1977, elementary-school teacher Brenda Ratliff's house had been broken into. The intruder pulled a gun on her, made her tie her six-year-old daughter, Megan, to a chair, then forced the woman to an upstairs bedroom, where he tore off her clothing. Despite her pleading, he jumped on top of her and told her, "Don't make me mad!"

As he was assaulting her, he put down his gun, at which point Brenda struggled free, called out to Megan and ran downstairs. She managed to get the still-bound little girl out to the porch before the attacker caught up with them. He tried to drag them both back into the house. But by this point, neighbors had heard Brenda's screams, so the intruder fled.

She identified Roger Coleman as her attacker; and though he claimed it was a case of mistaken identity, she said he stalked her on the street and tried to intimidate her as he was free on bail awaiting trial. He was convicted and served two years in prison for aggravated assault, always claiming he was innocent.

Then, about two months before Wanda McCoy was murdered, county librarian Pat Hatfield said Coleman came into the library shortly before closing time, exposed himself and exhibited what she characterized as hostile behavior. Coleman denied it, but Hatfield insisted her ID was correct.

Things only went downhill for Coleman from there. While he was being held pending trial, a cellmate, Roger Matney, claimed Coleman told him he and another man had raped Wanda McCoy. This became a key piece of the prosecution's case when Coleman went to trial in March 1982, just a little over a year after the murder. A week before the trial began, at the prosecution's urging, Matney was released from serving the remainder of four concurrent four-year prison sentences. At some point later, his mother-in-law claimed he had admitted fabricating the story, but Matney denied this.

In addition to Matney's testimony, Commonwealth Attorneys Michael McGlothlin and Thomas Scott cited the lack of forced entry, as suggesting an offender known to the victim, and several hair and fluid samples. The hairs found on the body were consistent with Coleman's and his semen sample put him in the 10 percent of the population that matched one of the two types found on the body (through blood secretion). The other matched Brad. Some specks found on the defendant's clothing were the same blood type as Wanda McCoy. The prosecutors asserted that wet pant legs on Coleman's jeans came from his having to wade across Slate Creek. Also, given the notoriety of the crime, it's likely most, if not all, of the jurors knew of the previous conviction and might have considered it as evidence of Roger Coleman's emotional and physical capability of committing violent rape.

The defense was headed by Coleman's court-appointed attorney, Terry Jordan, who was just two years out of law school and had tried only one murder case. He expressed hesitation about taking on Coleman's defense. However, when the judge insisted, he proceeded gamely. He countered McGlothlin by showing that a pry mark on the front door was a definite sign of forced entry and that various defensive wounds on the victim showed that she had indeed put up a fight, which would indicate a stranger. Jordan noted that this was a purely circumstantial case, with no established motive and no witnesses, and that while the semen *could* have come from Brad and Roger, it could also have come from a lot of other individuals and certainly was not proof beyond a reasonable doubt. Also, when the evidence team vacuumed the McCoy house, they retrieved numerous hairs that did not match Coleman's. As far as the wet pants legs, Coleman said that easily could have happened when he showered and changed clothes before going home.

There was also the matter of a McCoy neighbor who discovered a bag containing bloody sheets and two Western-style shirts. The prosecution dismissed this potential evidence as irrelevant and the defense made no challenge.

Most tellingly, though, Coleman had several witnesses who could vouch for his whereabouts for almost the entire evening. In other words, there would have been insufficient time for Coleman to park his truck, get down into the creek, cross it in ten-inch-deep water and go up the other side, climb a thousand-foot hill, get to Wanda's house, have her open the door, overpower her, rape her, stab her repeatedly and practically saw off her head, and do it all so carefully and efficiently that he left no obvious traces of himself or his traversing of the creek — not even a muddy smudge or footprint. With the horrifically gory state of the body and the crime scene, the defense reasoned, shouldn't Coleman's clothing have been covered with blood? Despite the defensive wounds on Wanda's body that indicated a struggle, Roger didn't have a scratch on him. And didn't he cooperate with every investigative request of the police and willingly surrender potential evidence? Was that the behavior of a guilty man?

The trial lasted four days, during which the prosecution stressed the supposed jailhouse confession and the suggestive blood and semen evidence, and did its best to poke holes in the defense's timeline covered by witnesses who had seen Coleman at various times during the evening.

The jury took only three hours to deliberate. On March 18, 1982, shortly before 11:00 P.M., they returned a verdict of guilty of rape and first-degree murder. The next morning, Coleman's attorney moved to have the verdict set aside on the grounds of insufficient evidence. The judge denied the motion. The defense had tried for a change of venue before the trial began, arguing that the brutality of the crime had so affected the Grundy community that no one accused could get a fair trial there. A sign put up at the gas station near the somber gray stone courthouse proclaimed: IT'S TIME FOR A NEW HANGING TREE IN GRUNDY. The change of venue request had also been denied.

At the sentencing hearing, the prosecution was allowed to bring in Coleman's prior rape conviction and allowed the victim, Brenda Ratliff, to testify. On April 23, Roger Keith Coleman was sentenced to life imprisonment for the rape and death for the murder.

Coleman didn't give up. He appealed to

the Virginia Supreme Court, but he was denied. The Supreme Court of the United States refused to hear his case. He then filed a writ of habeas corpus with the Buchanan County Circuit Court, raising several constitutional arguments against his sentence. The court held a two-day evidentiary hearing; then it denied all of Coleman's claims, entering its final judgment on September 4, 1986.

He next appealed back to the Virginia Supreme Court, but the court dismissed his motion on a technicality: Coleman's attorneys had not filed the appeal within the statutory thirty days of final judgment. Through a clerical error, they had missed the deadline by three days. He exhausted all of his federal appeals without success.

While sitting on death row, as a result of his continued protestations of "actual innocence" (as opposed to merely a procedural or legal mistake in his arrest or trial), he had attracted a formidable new defense team, far stronger and more experienced than the one that had originally represented him. James McCloskey was an investigator from New Jersey who, convinced of Coleman's innocence, worked for years to prove it. His Centurion Ministries was — and is — an effective innocence project headquartered in Princeton, dedicated to reversing the sentences of those wrongly convicted, particularly in the case of murder. Kathleen "Kitty"

Behan was an attorney with the powerful Washington, DC, law firm Arnold & Porter. Both worked long hours completely pro bono.

In addition to exploring every investigative lead and legal option, Coleman's team did an exemplary job of publicizing his case and making his impending death sentence into a national, then worldwide, cause. This might not seem all that important, since it is the courts and not the public that are the ultimate decision-makers. But in our imperfect and overburdened criminal justice system, effective publicity literally can mean the difference between life and death.

The attorneys pointed out that there were no witnesses for the prosecution and plenty for the defense, no credible motive and that the case against Coleman was purely circumstantial. We must point out here that that, in itself, is not necessarily a negative. Most cases are circumstantial, and circumstantial evidence can often be more reliable than eyewitnesses. Also, except in the instance of felony murder, in which a killing is committed during the performance of another felony, such as a bank robbery, or when one victim escapes after another one has been killed, witnessed murders are rare. By the very nature of the crime, few are alive to tell the tale. Sightings of escaping fugitives are sometimes helpful, but often wrong.

Despite McCloskey's and Behan's best efforts, and despite repeated declarations of innocence, the long legal appeals process moved inexorably toward Roger Coleman's rendezvous with Virginia's electric chair. Protests were coming in from all over the world. Many of these were demanding that the remaining fluid samples be retested, now that DNA science was becoming more sophisticated and specific. The state denied all such requests. By this time, Wanda's sister Patricia had divorced Roger. He now had a girlfriend, Sharon Paul, a college student whom he had met by mail while in prison.

As the date of execution drew near, the public response continued to mount. Pope John Paul II, Mother Teresa and Amnesty International sent pleas to Virginia governor Douglas Wilder to grant clemency. The May 18, 1992, issue of *Time* had a photograph of Coleman on its cover. Sitting against a cinder block wall in a blue shirt, black pants and work boots, hands in his lap, he looked like an ordinary, good-looking everyman. The message of the picture was clear: *If it can happen to him, it can happen to any of us.*

Over the photograph, in type large enough to cover most of the page, was written:

THIS MAN MIGHT BE
INNOCENT
THIS MAN IS DUE TO
DIE

ROGER KEITH COLEMAN WAS
CONVICTED OF KILLING HIS
SISTER-IN-LAW IN 1982. THE COURTS
HAVE REFUSED TO HEAR THE
EVIDENCE THAT COULD SAVE HIM. HIS
EXECUTION IS SET FOR MAY 20.

Mr. Wilder, a former defense attorney and the first African American elected governor of Virginia, was a pro–death penalty Democrat. But he could not have been unaffected by the outpouring of support for Coleman or his own need for some sort of personal validation of justice. So early on the morning of May 20, Coleman was taken from his holding cell in the Virginia death house at the Greensville Correctional Center in Jarratt and driven by prison van seventy miles to a Virginia State Police office in Hanover County, where he was given a polygraph exam. Predictably, he failed.

When you've got a man on the morning of his scheduled execution, who hasn't eaten or slept, knowing that his life literally depends on what some unknown examiner thinks of his responses, how can you possibly consider this test a reliable indicator of anything? Remember, a polygraph works through indirect, nonspecific indicators such as galvanic skin response and respiration, and so in my opinion it shows emotion in general rather than necessarily truthfulness. Under similar conditions, if I stated that the sky was blue, I'd probably come off as untruthful. Also, McCloskey had his own polygraph examiner ready to review the results. However, through some apparent administrative slipup, he was given the wrong address, so he never even got there.

The failed polygraph was enough for Governor Wilder to deny clemency. "I wanted to make certain every avenue was opened and made available so as to remove any vestiges that Virginia was not interested in affording fair and adequate opportunities for persons to receive fair trials," he explained to a group of reporters. Just before noon, the Fourth U.S. Circuit Court of Appeals turned down a request for a stay of execution. The countdown to death was set in motion.

Meanwhile, thousands of letters and phone calls were pouring into the governor's office in Richmond, all but a handful protesting the execution. Of those that favored it, almost all came from the Grundy area, according to one of the governor's aides.

James McCloskey, known as "Jim," and Kitty Behan were with Coleman for several hours and shared his last meal of pepperoni pizza, chocolate marshmallow cookies and 7UP. They noted that he had grown surprisingly calm. "He was in remarkably good humor," McCloskey reported. Behan had not given up and still had a final appeal before the U.S. Supreme Court.

The electrocution was scheduled for 11:00 P.M., but it was held up pending the U.S. Supreme Court's final word. At 10:59 P.M., it announced it was refusing to take any action. The vote was 7–2, with Justices Harry Blackmun and David Souter dissenting.

As he was being strapped into the electric chair, Coleman was given the opportunity to make a final statement: "An innocent man is going to be murdered tonight. When my innocence is proven, I hope Americans will realize the injustice of the death penalty, as all other civilized countries have. My last words are to the woman I love. Love is eternal. My love for you will last forever. I love you, Sharon."

At 11:38 P.M., Roger Keith Coleman was pronounced dead.

By the next day, the first two sentences of his final statement had been spread around the world. Now, whether you're for, undecided or against the death penalty, those words are pretty sobering. Culturally and legally, we tend to give special weight and respect to last words. A "dying declaration" is even generally given a special exception to federal and state rules against hearsay testimony. It has been a long-standing feeling, again going back to the origins of English common law, that individuals who are preparing to meet their Maker, and have nothing more to gain or lose in this earthly life, have no reason to lie and have significant reason to tell the truth.

In fact, when Mark Olshaker and I were investigating the infamous 1932 Lindbergh kidnapping for our book *The Cases That Haunt Us,* the one element that continued to perplex us was that even as he faced the New Jersey electric chair, Bruno Richard Hauptmann refused to confess to the abduction and murder of baby Charlie Lindbergh Jr. or even admit any degree of participation. We had determined beyond any reasonable shadow of a doubt that Hauptmann had to have been involved in the crime; though unlike many of the others who have examined this notorious case over the years, we were convinced he could not have acted alone. Yet, even when he was offered the possibility of a commutation of his sentence from death to life in prison if he would only cooperate and name other names, he continued to maintain his innocence and that he knew nothing about the crime. He went to his execution steadfastly maintaining this stance.

As we carefully constructed Hauptmann's behavioral profile, we concluded that his motivation lay in his personal rigidity and conception of honor. Hauptmann was prepared to die rather than live and leave his family, his wife and young son, with the shame (and, perhaps, attendant financial burden) of a confessed killer.

Roger Coleman had no such incentive or choice to make. He wasn't going to be plea-bargained or have his death sentence commuted for "telling the truth." He had been baptized while in prison and his chaplain said he took his faith seriously, so his final statement was extremely troubling to anyone who cares about justice.

The controversy did not die with Coleman. "I promised Roger Coleman the night he was executed, I would do all within my power to prove that he was innocent," McCloskey announced. "Those were my last words to a dying man."

He was as good as his word. He had investigated claims that another man in Grundy had admitted killing Wanda McCoy and pressed to have the remaining fluid samples retested, now that DNA technology had made significant advances. The office of Virginia attorney general (AG) Jerry Kilgore steadfastly resisted.

"The state keeps telling the citizens that we need the death penalty and that we're doing it right," a spokesman for Centurion Ministries stated. "The public has a right to know if the state is doing it right."

Kilgore countered that the case had been through the courts for more than a decade and that the "doctrine of finality" dictates that at some point the process has to finish. "We have to someday look to finality of judgment. We feel certain in Virginia that Roger Coleman committed the crime and was punished appropriately."

Centurion, joined by four newspapers, including the *Washington Post,* petitioned the Virginia Supreme Court to have the DNA evidence retested. It took more than a year for the court to respond with a denial. They then went to Governor Mark Warner for an executive order. Warner, another pro–death penalty Democrat, also didn't respond right away, but there is strong indication that he had his lawyers look seriously into the matter.

By now, the Coleman case had become a focal point for the ethical and legal struggle over capital punishment, and his ghost haunted the public debate. Abolitionists felt that if they could just get tangible proof that one innocent person had been executed, the entire moral fabric of the argument for execution would be ripped to shreds.

Finally, on January 6, 2006, as Warner was preparing to leave office (Virginia governors are limited to one term), he announced that he had ordered the retesting of the McCoy murder fluid samples. It's unclear whether he had bowed to public pressure or genuinely wanted to know once and for all if Virginia might have carried out a horrible miscarriage of justice. The simplest and most heartfelt explanation is probably the one he gave to Anthony Brooks, of National Public Radio (NPR): "You know, if we have access to the truth, let's figure it out. Let's find out what the truth is, one way or the other."

Though both sides claimed to be confident of the outcome, this was certainly a nervous period all around.

For me, too. Around this time — the mid-2000s — Mark Olshaker and I were both doing a lot of speaking about victims' rights and our feeling that the humanity of individual victims was being overshadowed by emphasis on the rights of convicted offenders, particularly those convicted of murder. This was also a time of heated debate over capital punishment, which I support for certain situations and types of offenders.

I got a request to speak at Vanderbilt University in Nashville, Tennessee. They had been running a series of forums on the death penalty, and they wanted to feature me in one. Scott Turow, the distinguished novelist, attorney and former prosecutor from Chicago, had already appeared. After serving on a blue-ribbon Illinois State commission on the death penalty, and after much analysis, introspection and soul-searching, Turow had concluded that there was no effective way to make the prospect of execution fair, bias free, evenly administered, as well as compellingly foolproof.

Now, I happen to disagree with Turow on some of his conclusions, though there is no denying that he ranks as one of the most thoughtful, rational and articulate voices on the subject. I knew he would have given a stirring and inspiring presentation from his perspective; and though I figured a university atmosphere would not be a particularly welcoming place for mine, I thought they ought to hear the other side.

But the timing couldn't have been worse. *I'm going down there to talk about the death penalty and here's the case that's going to prove that an innocent man was executed!* I thought long and hard about whether I should go through with the talk.

The samples were analyzed in two sets of procedures several weeks apart by the Centre of Forensic Sciences, a distinguished lab in Ontario, Canada, that handles thousands of cases a year. On January 12, 2006, Warner's office announced the results of its findings: Roger Coleman's DNA matched the sample material taken from Wanda McCoy's body with no exclusions. The chance of the attacker being someone other than Coleman — in other words, another intruder whose DNA just happened to match Coleman's — was one in 19 million.

We have sought the truth using DNA technology not available at the time the commonwealth carried out the ultimate criminal sanction, Warner's statement read. *The confirmation that Roger Coleman's DNA was present reaffirms the verdict and the sanction. Again, my prayers are with the family of Wanda McCoy at this time.*

Which was exactly where they should have been.

Reaction was nearly instantaneous. *"How can somebody, with such equanimity, such dignity, such quiet confidence, make those final words even though he was guilty?"* the *Washington Post* quoted a betrayed Jim McCloskey as saying.

Stop the presses — it turns out that rapists and killers are also liars, wrote Michael Paranzino, a Yale– and NYU Law–trained attorney and former Congressional staffer who founded the organization Throw Away the Key.

"Quite frankly, I feel like the weight of the world has been lifted off my shoulders," said lead prosecutor Thomas Scott. "You can imagine, had it turned out differently, we certainly would have been scapegoats."

Later, with great dignity and eloquence, McCloskey told NPR's Anthony Brooks, "This is a very . . . a bitter pill for me to swallow. However, the truth is the truth. We who seek the truth, especially in criminal justice matters, must live or die by the sword of DNA."

■ ■ ■ ■

What are the lessons of the Roger Coleman case? There should be several. Despite the truism that all of us, under certain sets of circumstances, are capable of killing, I would submit that most of us are not capable of murder. That is: Murderers, particularly predatory murderers who force sex and intentionally inflict pain with their acts, are not like us, and it's about time we understand that. We can't imagine ourselves lying about something morally important even if the honesty would go against us. Most of us parents have had the experience of punishing a child more severely for lying than for the initial misbehavior he or she lied about. Truth is that sacred to most of us, at least as a concept.

When I see someone passionately proclaiming his innocence, unrelentingly for years and years, even with all of my experience, my first and most human instinct is to think that he must be telling the truth. We project ourselves and our own sensibilities onto this person. Even if we believe he might have done something wrong or illegal, we like to think that it was some sort of aberration, rather than a deep-seated behavior. It's one of the reasons why good and decent people, like Jim Mc-Closkey, can be taken in by bad and devious people, like Roger Coleman. It's one of the reasons we like to believe that repeat predators can be rehabilitated. And in my opinion, it's one of the reasons for the phenomenon of otherwise intelligent women falling in love with prison inmates.

But what Mr. Paranzino says is actually pretty close to reality. Individuals who are willing to cause extreme harm and suffering to others are, by definition, sociopaths; they have no conscience. Truth is no more important to them than adhering to the law and the decent instincts of ordinary human beings.

So how do we know whether a convicted killer insisting on his innocence is more like William Heirens or more like Bruno Richard Hauptmann and Roger Keith Coleman?

There is no foolproof way. As we say rather too glibly sometimes, criminology is not an exact science. But there are often strong clues, just as there were in each of these three cases.

With William Heirens, there was no previous instance of violence, particularly violence against women, so our experience and research show that it would be essentially unheard of for him to have quickly escalated from petty breaking-and-entering crimes into violent sexual assault, murder and dismemberment of a child. True, he did carry a gun, but the only time he ever attempted to use it was in the heat of the moment as he was being pursued. This doesn't make it right, and might have made him a setup for a felony murder rap, had his burglaries gone unstopped, but there is nothing in his background that suggested intentional and premeditated violence against women. We could say something similar about David Vasquez. Had all of this been factored in during the investigation, police would have come up with a radically different suspect than Heirens.

Bruno Richard Hauptmann, who, like Roger Keith Coleman, went to his highly publicized death asserting his innocence, was a carpenter with a record that fit right in with the type of crime of which he was convicted, including a series of armed robberies and burglaries in his native Germany involving a homemade ladder (the single key piece of evidence in the Lindbergh case). Together with the overwhelming amount of circumstantial evidence and an entire string of provable lies to the police, he was a poor prospect for veracity.

Roger Coleman, of course, had a prior conviction for violent sexual assault and the exposure charge, both of which he claimed were cases of mistaken identity. Without those priors, one might have looked more skeptically at the inconsistencies in the evidence. But without those priors, he probably wouldn't have evolved far enough to kill his sister-in-law so brutally.

As William Shakespeare wrote in *The Tempest*, *"What's past is prologue."*

The other thing we should learn from this case is to give scientific evidence its due — no more, no less.

These days, prosecutors worry about "the *CSI* Effect" on juries: the perception popular television shows have instilled in the public that all murders or other violent crimes can be solved through scientific analysis of blood and other fluids, fingerprints, hair and fiber, etc., all routinely found at the crime scene. The fact is that most scenes do not render up a cornucopia of definitive physical evidence directly linking the UNSUB; and absence of evidence, as we say, is not evidence of absence. So we need to be realistic about our expectations.

The judges in the Salem Witch Trials thought they had good spectral evidence until Cotton Mather and others pointed out that Satan himself could have been the cause of various townspeople's shapes appearing to the afflicted girls.

But in this age of increasingly scientific and technological sophistication, when we do have apparent definitive evidence, it is incumbent on us to use it well. After all these years, for example, I still don't see how the jurors in the trial of O.J. Simpson for the murder of his ex-wife Nicole Brown and Ron Goldman could have interpreted the evidence as they did. They ignored the DNA lab work, which put the defendant unquestionably at, and in, the murder scene, while at the same time setting great store in the idea that a leather glove soaked with the victims' blood did not seem to fit Simpson's hand. One piece of evidence was absolute and incontrovertible. The other was subject to any number of variables, including the well-known fact (at least in climes less temperate than Southern California) that leather can shrink when it gets wet, whether with water or blood! Maybe we haven't come as far from the reasoning and thought processes of Salem as we might have hoped.

At the time of the Coleman trial, blood science could only narrow the evidence to a relatively small percentage of the population. But now, if we do have a sample, and it is untainted from harvesting, with a clear chain of custody, it can tell us a lot about the crime and help determine guilt or innocence. I very much agree with former governor Mark Warner. If we have the evidence, we should not be afraid to employ it, and let the chips fall where they may.

If you're going to consider taking someone's life for a crime, or even putting him away for the rest of it, you'd better be pretty damn sure you've got the right individual. Fortunately, science is helping us with this effort.

Had the evidence gone in Roger Coleman's favor, it might have galvanized the anti–capital punishment ranks and made him a martyr for the cause, instead of what he turned out to be: a lying, violent, sadistic murderer for whom none of us need contribute an ounce of sympathy. On this case, at least, we can have the certainty that is so often elusive, and the victim's family can finally have a measure of peace.

But this is not the end of the argument.

"The results in this case won't end the debate over the death penalty," declared Paul Enzinna, an attorney with the prominent international law firm Baker Botts, when the DNA findings on Coleman were announced.

And indeed, they have not. Nor should they, any more than they should end the continual quest for a better quality of justice.

Chapter 4
The Fire on West Eleventh Street

Roger Keith Coleman, of Grundy, Virginia, didn't turn out to be the poster boy that death penalty opponents have sought for more than three decades. But Cameron Todd Willingham, of Corsicana, Texas, may turn out to be.

The Coleman and Willingham cases share a number of elements. Both men came from working-class backgrounds and grew up in small towns that had seen better days. Both were personable and good-looking, passionate and articulate, despite not having much education. Both married young. Both were quickly arrested for murder and tried in a matter of days. Both had jailhouse snitches testify that they had confessed to the crime in casual conversation. Both were convicted in a matter of hours, and then spent long years on death row. Both went to their executions proclaiming their innocence and attracted a large community of believers. And both cases, to most reasonable observers, were ultimately resolved by science.

Like Coleman, the Willingham case attracted national attention — first through an outstanding and award-winning article, "Trial by Fire," by David Grann, in the September 7, 2009, issue of *The New Yorker,* and the following year in the PBS *Frontline* episode "Death by Fire," by producer-director Jessie Deeter and writer-producers Mike Wiser and Michael Kirk, broadcast on October 19, 2010.

But these similarities are overwhelmed by one glaring difference, as we will see here.

Cameron Todd Willingham, who was known as Todd, had a tough time from the start. He was born in 1968 in Ardmore, in south central Oklahoma, and was abandoned by his divorced mother while he was still a baby. He was raised by his tough, demanding, ex–U.S. Marine father, Gene, who worked in a salvage yard, and his stepmother, Eugenia, whom he adored. He was never much for school, and discovered paint sniffing and drugs when he was eleven. His half brother, Monte, felt he never got much past that age emotionally or intellectually. He dropped out of high school and racked up a record for drunk driving and petty theft.

In 1988, Todd met Stacy Kuykendall, a high-school senior from Corsicana, Texas, a small town about fifty-five miles southeast of Dallas, and moved there with her. Stacy had also come from a tough background. When she was four, her stepfather had strangled her mother as they fought.

According to several accounts, Todd drank, ran around and physically abused Stacy. Police visited the house a number of times on domestic complaints. Still, something kept them together. Within a few years, the couple had three daughters: Amber and twins Karmon and Kameron. Amber and the twins were only a year apart. They rented a small, single-story wood-framed house at 1213 West Eleventh Street in Corsicana. Since Todd was having trouble finding work as a mechanic, Stacy took a job in her brother's bar, while Todd stayed home to take care of the kids. While the evidence of his frequently beating Stacy is solid, even she says he never abused the children. And in the summer of 1991, she and Todd decided to make a real try for the long run. They married on October 1.

The first report of the fire came from eleven-year-old Buffie Barbee. About ten minutes after ten on the morning of December 23, 1991, two days before Christmas, she was playing in her backyard with her sister and a friend when she smelled and saw smoke. She ran inside to tell her mother, Diane, that the house next door was on fire. Diane raced out the front door and realized it was not the neighboring house, but the Willinghams', two doors down.

Diane saw Todd outside the door on the front porch, wearing only a pair of jeans. He was yelling, "My babies are burning up!" and asked her to call the fire department. While Diane ran for a phone, Todd grabbed a stick and jabbed holes in the bedroom window, from which flames shot out. Moments later, all five of the bedroom windows exploded outward and the house was engulfed in flames. Some witnesses said Todd seemed to retreat into a trance at that point. But by the time firefighters arrived a few minutes later, others recalled that he had to be restrained from trying to get back inside.

The firemen immediately laid out their hoses and equipment and attacked the fire. Burvin Terry Smith asked him if there were any other people in the house. Paramedic Ron Franks and firemen Charles Dennison and Steven Vandiver, equipped with oxygen masks and tanks, entered the house through a front window and fought their way through the blaze, trying to "knock it down," in firefighter parlance. Vandiver emerged with Amber's limp body in his arms. She died at the hospital without regaining consciousness. When Assistant Chief Douglas Fogg reached the children's bedroom, he found the one-year-old twins dead. A medical report would find that all three children died of acute carbon monoxide poisoning as a result of smoke inhalation.

Todd told firemen that Stacy had gone out early to shop for Christmas presents for the children and that he was asleep when Amber rushed into his bedroom and woke him up, shouting how the house was on fire. When he opened his eyes, the room was full of smoke and he shouted to Amber to get out of the house.

Almost as soon as the blaze was extinguished, the fire department began investigating. Assistant Chief Fogg went through the house with a video camera, narrating on the tape as he focused on each surface. On December 27, he went back with Manuel Vasquez, a state deputy fire marshal who was one of the most experienced fire investigators in Texas. Both men had impressive backgrounds. Fogg, a local boy, had been a navy medical corpsman in Vietnam, with four Purple Hearts attesting to his dedication and courage. Vasquez was a veteran of army intelligence who had more than twelve hundred fire investigations to his credit.

At the very front of the house, the damage seemed mainly smoke and heat-related, including the master bedroom about halfway back, where Todd had been sleeping and Amber had been found unconscious. The farther down the main hallway they went, the more suspicious they became. There was charring along the base of the walls and the floors, even though fire usually burns upward. The "burn trailer" seemed to go from the children's bedroom in the left front, into this hall and then out the front hall, suggesting the fire started there. Moreover, the intensity of the burn marks on and under the floor of that bedroom suggested that accelerant could have been poured in the middle. The weblike patterns on the broken glass were also evidence of an intensely hot fire in this particular location, further bolstering the accelerant scenario.

As they followed the burn trailer back out to the front, they noted brown staining on the concrete floor of the porch, also consistent with the use of an accelerant. V-shaped soot patterns in the children's bedroom, the hallway and the front porch further documented the three places where the fire had started. If accelerant had been poured at each of those locations and then lit, it would be nearly impossible for anyone inside to escape the burning building alive.

Before they left, Fogg and Vasquez reached an inescapable conclusion: This fire had been intentionally set.

Of all the major crime categories, arson stands alone in one key respect. Except for a rare bombing in which a gas leak might initially be considered a possible cause, arson is the only violent act in which the first stage of the investigation is to determine whether a crime has actually been committed. With a murder or robbery, we know that a crime has taken place and our first priority is to figure out who did it. Even with poisoning, either direct or a product tampering, like the Tylenol case of 1982, experienced investigators can tell very quickly that the sickness or death was intentionally caused.

I have worked many arson cases during my career, usually teamed with an experienced specialist. Dave Icove, a special agent with a Ph.D. in engineering science and mechanics, headed up the Arson and Bombing Investigative Services (ABIS) subunit in our underground lair of offices at the FBI Academy. Icove was an expert I knew I could always count on. His résumé of publications, patents and funded research is many pages long. Later Gus Gary, a special agent for the Bureau of Alcohol, Tobacco and Firearms, came over to Quantico and worked closely with my Investigative Support Unit. As difficult as arson cases can be, Dave, Gus and I had an advantage that most investigators don't have; that is, we already knew it was arson.

By the time we would be called in to profile the UNSUB, there was usually a *pattern* of fires in a given area, meaning that we knew they were intentionally set. For example, when we were presented with a string of fires in synagogues and rabbis' homes in Hartford,

Connecticut, in 1983, we knew these blazes *didn't just all happen accidentally.*

Our job in arson cases was to use locations, types of fires, eyewitness accounts and all of the other tools and tricks in our arsenal to figure out what type of individual was responsible and how to flush him out. In an early form of what is now known as "geographical programming," Dave used a map, ruler and compass; through marking the location and order of each fire and drawing lines between them, he was able to predict with a high degree of specificity where the offender lived.

What we didn't have to figure out, in most instances, was whether these fires were arson or mere accidents. In other words, we didn't have to determine whether or not a crime had even been committed.

Local investigators of individual fires don't have that foreknowledge, so their responsibility is grave and their judgment is critical. Fogg and Vasquez had no doubts about their judgment on West Eleventh Street, though. They compiled and documented a list of twenty separate indicators of arson.

Meanwhile, the behavioral evidence was piling up. Even though it is a town of about twenty thousand, representing more than half the population of Navarro County, Corsicana is a small and close-knit community, where residents pride themselves on knowing most of the other folks in their neighborhood.

Knowing that Todd and Stacy had very little money, Vicki Prater, the proprietor of a local bar and tavern, got together with some of her neighbors to hold a benefit to raise money for the children's funeral and burial.

It was an extremely kind and generous act. However, the way she saw Todd acting at the event left her deeply troubled. He seemed heavily into playing darts, one of his normal pastimes, and generally "too involved in the fun" for someone who had just lost twin babies and a toddler under horrific circumstances.

Fire department lieutenant and paramedic Ron Franks thought it was odd that after the fire was put out, Todd seemed unusually upset about a dartboard and set of darts and asked if he could go back in to look for them.

The Corsicana police had some questions of their own. According to Todd's account, when Amber woke him up, he took just long enough to pull on a pair of jeans. When he was seen outside, that, in fact, was all he was wearing.

So why weren't his feet burned?

As hot as the fire investigators said that hallway floor must have been to leave the burn patterns it did, how could Todd have gotten out of the house without blistering the soles of his bare feet? Other than some minor burns and singeing of his hair, he had escaped virtually unscathed.

When police brought him to the station for questioning on December 31, he replied simply that when he got out, the fire was mostly higher up; and while the floor was hot, it wasn't burning hot at that point. *Then it must have gotten burning hot awfully fast after that,* the officers concluded skeptically. Fogg and Vasquez were both there for the questioning, along with police officer Jimmie Hensley. As far as the cause of the fire, Todd mentioned the three space heaters he and Stacy used to keep the house warm, one of them in the children's bedroom; maybe one of them had shorted out, or the kids had upset it or something. But during his careful examination of the house, Manuel Vasquez had noted the dial on the heater in the children's bedroom was in the "Off" position. Maybe it was something electrical in the house, Todd suggested. He had heard something like a popping or cracking sound.

Todd acknowledged his bad treatment of Stacy. He said that they had split up several times over it, but what kept bringing them back together was the kids. When he was asked why anyone would want to hurt his family, he could not come up with a single thought.

The investigators' impressions of his behavior were similar to Vicki Prater's. Despite his insistence that the children were what kept him with Stacy and led them to marriage, instead of displaying grief or even remorse, he seemed almost cocky. It was as if he were bragging about how he'd rushed back into the house to try to save his children — an action no one had witnessed. The whole thing seemed too rehearsed and calculated. The only time he broke down was when they showed him photographs of his dead children.

This is not an unusual reaction. I have used and suggested this technique and its variations many times when interrogating suspects. I have also coached detectives in its use. On one level, you're trying to get through to something human within the suspect, appealing to his most primal sensibilities. Maybe the comprehension of the moral horror of his act will prompt some feelings of guilt. Maybe there are feelings of guilt because he felt he did not do enough.

On another level, you're evaluating his reaction. Who are the tears for: the victim or himself? Is he sobbing because he is sorry for the victim, or is he sorry for himself that he got caught? I have seen it both ways. But with the predators I hunted throughout my career, the second reason is far more common.

If a case like this had been brought to my unit at Quantico, I think the first thing I would have asked would be "Why are you coming to us? If you know it was a set fire and only one individual was in a position to set it, then you've got a slam dunk here."

Nor would there have been much doubt as to *what type of* arson it was. We break arson down into several general categories: insurance fraud, pyromania and thrill seeking, vandalism, concealing other crimes, revenge, civil disorder and murder. If this one was arson, then it was arson as murder.

When the physical evidence and the behavioral evidence match up, and there aren't any other likely suspects given the time and location of the occurrence, that's a pretty good package to hand to a district attorney (DA).

But if we had been called in, here's where I would have focused: While I would have been skeptical of Todd Willingham's tears at the sight of his kids' photos, I would have also warned about placing too much meaning in his emotional reactions during and immediately after the fire — whether they were "appropriate" or not. Experience and the study of many cases have shown us that reaction to the death of a loved one is a very individual, very personal thing.

When his infant son was kidnapped, Charles Lindbergh was criticized by many and actually suspected by some for seeming so cold and distant. In reality, this was merely his way of coping. It isn't surprising when you consider that this was a man who had been in many harrowing aviation situations and, against all odds, had flown solo across the Atlantic for more than thirty-three sleep-less hours in a rickety plane without even a front window. If he weren't able to control his emotions in moments of crisis, he wouldn't have been the man he was. Everyone reacts differently, and observation during this kind of crisis is one of the least reliable ways of determining personality and motive.

I would have counseled investigators to concentrate on what we generally refer to as postoffense behavior. In the days and weeks following the event, how has the subject's behavior changed? Has he either avoided investigators or inserted himself into the investigation? Has he begun drinking more or abusing drugs? Has his weight changed? What is he doing with himself during the day and at night?

Then I would have asked if the police were sure of the arson investigators' report. Person-ally, I have no expertise in structural or chemical engineering, biochemistry or metal-lurgy, just as I have no expertise in fingerprint analysis or ballistics. So when those disci-plines come into a case investigation, I rely on the best experts I can find. In the Bureau, we are fortunate to have some of the best in-house, and we have called on many others. For example, I had a close working relation-ship with Dr. James Luke, the former ME for Washington, DC. We so completely trusted each other's methods and analysis that I often called him in on cases in which forensic pathology might be a determining factor.

If the locals expressed any doubt about the quality of their own forensic science, I would have asked Dave Icove or Gus Gary to take a look. If either man saw anything that raised red flags in the reports, photos and analysis, he could go down to Texas himself and take a look.

The only other service I would have offered would be prosecution strategy; that is, help figure out how to explain motive to a jury.

Technically, the prosecution doesn't have to establish motive in a criminal trial. If the evidence indicates beyond a reasonable doubt that the defendant did the deed in question, it doesn't matter why he did it. But in the real world of criminal trials, most jury members, consciously or subconsciously, consider motive part of the proof. If they can't figure out why the defendant would have committed such a crime, they have trouble convicting. That's why my unit was often called in by prosecutors, even after the police had already delivered a suspect.

Had this case been brought to us, since the science had already established the fact of arson and there were no suspects other than Todd Willingham, we would have deemphasized his immediate behavior at the fire scene. Instead, we would have pointed to his conduct at the benefit at Vicki Prater's bar as evidence that he was relieved rather than grief-stricken at the loss of his three girls. He was no longer stuck at home, changing three sets of diapers; he could be out doing what men his age normally want to do. Many people saw a similar motive in the behavior of Casey Anthony when she was tried for the alleged murder of her young daughter, Caylee, in Orlando, Florida. While an apparently agonized jury found her not guilty of the charge, it was extremely difficult for many of us to square the image of a young woman partying, drinking and participating in wet T-shirt contests while knowing that Caylee was (depending on which version you believe) either missing or dead.

The prediction of future violence is far from an exact science, but we live by the concept that the *best* predictor of future violence is past violence. And here, Willingham easily qualifies. Any man who regularly beat and mistreated his young wife is certainly capable of other types of violence. That doesn't mean he will do it, but he is certainly capable. And once you've harmed your wife, harming your children is merely an escalation, not a diversion from form.

There is one detail from the reports that I think would have given me pause, and that is the fact that two-year-old Amber was found in her parents' bedroom, while the baby twins were found in the children's bedroom, with more severely burned bodies. This fact would not only tend to confirm Todd's description of how he learned of the fire, but also call into question his methodology if the fire was set. That is, I would have expected to find all three children together if he was trying to kill them. A two-year-old is far more mobile than one-year-olds, but I wouldn't expect her to be able to escape the primary fire site if it had been started by accelerants and therefore burst into flame all of a sudden.

When Amber was found in the master bedroom, she was clad only in underpants and one sock. Had the other sock been found in the debris, it might have indicated her path. But the fact that she was so lightly clad also points to the space heater in the children's bedroom having been on, regardless of what the switch indicated. Malfunction or Amber doing something to it could have been a cause of the fire. Stacy told investigators that several times Amber had played with the space heater and been punished for it. The house was not very well insulated, so it's doubtful Stacy and Todd would have put the kids to bed in so little if a heat source was not nearby.

On the other hand, I would have questioned Todd's just putting on his jeans, but not also picking Amber up and carrying her out under his arm. According to his account, he told her to run right out, and the smoke might

117

have been so thick that he thought she did, but I would certainly want to know more about that moment and press the investigators for the complete evidence.

On January 8, 1992, police arrested Todd Willingham and charged him with three counts of murder in the first degree. In Texas, the multiple counts made him eligible for the death penalty. Since he couldn't afford an attorney, the court appointed two: David Martin and Robert Dunn.

Prosecutor John Jackson thought he had a pretty solid case, and I would have agreed with him. But before the trial, he approached Martin and Dunn with an offer to take execution off the table in exchange for a guilty plea and a life sentence. Jackson was personally against capital punishment, believing it was an ineffective deterrent and a waste of court time and taxpayer money. It also haunted him that there was always a possibility that an innocent man or woman could be executed. If he could get a conviction without a death penalty, that was fine with him.

The defense attorneys, who understandably thought their client was guilty, urged him to take the plea, save his own life and spare the families and the community the anguish of a trial. Willingham steadfastly refused.

"I ain't gonna plead to something I didn't

do," he insisted, "especially killing my own kids."

There are several reasons for maintaining your innocence. The most obvious one is that you're innocent. But as demonstrated in the Hauptmann and Coleman cases, that is not a sure thing, even in the face of a waiting execution. So while one would certainly have given some weight to Willingham's insistence, it could also be chalked up to pride, concern for his reputation or a simple gamble with the criminal justice process, which, in practice, doesn't execute that many convicted murderers — even in Texas, a state that takes its death penalty seriously.

Cameron Todd Willingham's trial began on August 18, 1992, and lasted only three days. Prosecutor John Jackson brought in a witness named Johnny Webb, a convicted felon, who claimed that during a casual jail conversation as he was passing by Willingham's cell, Todd had confessed to setting the fire. He went on to say that Willingham described how he had poured lighter fluid on the floor of the children's bedroom in a pentagram pattern. This was supposed to be evidence of Wicca or some darker satanic cult.

When investigators had first heard that claim from Webb months before, it was seen as the key to Todd Willingham's whole personality. It became a critical element of what became the second phase of the trial.

I don't think much of jailhouse snitches, yet we see them used all the time. The thinking is that if some bad guy is going to shoot his mouth off about what he's done, he's most likely going to do it to one of his own kind. According to David Grann in *The New Yorker*, Jackson didn't believe Webb had any motive for making a statement that wasn't true.

From my experience, jailhouse snitches always have something to gain, or at least perceive that they do. It's the only reason they come out of the woodwork.

"Why did you decide to tell anyone about this conversation?" Jackson asked Webb on the witness stand.

"Because it got to bugging my conscience. I mean, three kids, you know? Someone tells you something like that, it's not something to be taken lightly."

Don't believe any of the pretense of conscience or feeling sorry for the victim or wanting to see justice done when it comes from this type of individual. It's all about them. This doesn't mean they're lying, necessarily. But it does mean that their credibility is always questionable.

I've always said the same thing about prison and parole-mandated psychiatry. Unlike regular therapy, in which the subject has a vested interest in being truthful and candid with the analyst, in a law enforcement situation the subject has a vested interest in telling the analyst whatever will get him out or reduce his sentence.

In this case, the idea that a man who steadfastly maintained his innocence would suddenly spill to another inmate he hardly knew, in full hearing of others, is utterly preposterous, even if the defendant was guilty. If I were a juror, I would have given it no credence. In fact, I might even have held it against the prosecution, figuring they might not be as sure of their case as they seemed if they had to present a loser like this.

The main case against Cameron Todd Willingham, though, was the forensic investigation. On the witness stand, Manuel Vasquez enumerated his twenty indicators of arson, proclaimed his firm belief that it was Todd who had started the fire, and even ventured an opinion as to motive. "The intent was to kill the little girls," he said.

Vasquez seemed to have an almost mystical relationship with fires and arson, claiming that nearly every fire he had investigated had turned out to be intentionally set. Other experts would later raise eyebrows at this claim. "Let me say this," he declared under questioning from coprosecutor Alan Bristol, "the fire is telling me this. The fire tells a story. I am just the interpreter. I am looking at the fire, and I am interpreting the fire. That is what I know. That is what I do best. And the fire does not lie. It tells me the truth."

And the truth, as he interpreted it, was that three fires had been set intentionally in the house that morning in late December. "Based on my experience, and from what I observed at the fire scene, the first fire was in the bedroom, the front bedroom."

"The bedroom where the twins were found?" Bristol clarified.

"Yes, sir. The second fire was in the hallway, and the third fire was on the front door on the porch."

"Deputy Vasquez, during your investigation, did you interview witnesses, including the occupants of this house?"

"Yes, sir. I've talked to the occupant of this house, and I let him talk and he told me a story of pure fabrication."

Todd had wanted to take the stand in his own defense, but his attorneys were concerned he would be his own worst enemy, and prevented him from testifying. They tried to find experts to refute Fogg's and Vasquez's reports, but they couldn't find any. The only witness they ended up putting on was a woman who had babysat for the Willingham children. She said she did not believe Todd capable of harming them. There has been a good deal of criticism of the defense team, which believed their client to be guilty. But from the trial transcripts, even though they presented little evidence of their own, they mounted a vigorous and, to me, effective assault on the prosecution's case and the expert witnesses' assumptions.

The jury went out at 10:25 A.M. on August 20. They returned to the courtroom seventy-seven minutes later with a verdict: guilty of three counts of murder in the first degree.

In the penalty phase, conducted after lunch on the same day, a string of witnesses from law enforcement and the private sector testified to Todd's antisocial acts and "bad reputation." Neighbor John Bailey recalled an argument he'd heard in which Todd taunted Stacy, "Get up, bitch, and I'll hit you again!"

Prosecutors called Stacy to the stand. She proved to be a hostile witness, stating definitively that she believed Todd was innocent and would not have hurt the children. She also minimized his physical abuse of her.

Then they picked up on the satanic theme. The pentagram pattern in which Webb said Willingham poured the accelerant conformed to the pattern of burns Vasquez had noted on the bedroom floor and immediately tied to other aspects of Todd's personality. Jackson pressed Stacy on the significance of Todd's shoulder tattoo of a dragon wrapped around a gaping skull.

"It's just a tattoo," Stacy replied.

Not so, countered Tim Gregory, a prosecution witness with a degree in family counseling. He cited Todd's interest in heavy metal and his posters of Led Zeppelin and Iron Maiden as evidence of his preoccupation with violence and death, cults and satanic activities. "In my opinion," Gregory stated, "there is not much chance of any type of rehabilitation at all." He admitted under cross-examination that he had never interviewed Todd or anyone associated with him. But he had gone goose hunting with the prosecutor John Jackson.

The final witness was Dr. James Grigson, a psychiatrist who had testified so often in capital punishment cases that he had earned the moniker "Dr. Death." He called Willingham a "severe sociopath," beyond the help of psychiatry, despite the fact that, like Gregory, he had never met him.

The next morning, the jury came back to hear final arguments. They retired to deliberate at 10:15 A.M. They returned at five minutes past noon. Taking the scientific proof together with the portrait of a death-obsessed, satanic sociopath beyond reclamation, the jury voted for a sentence of death.

Those who spoke later said they were unimpressed by Johnny Webb's testimony, but they set great store in Manuel Vasquez. They didn't like the fact that Todd Willingham didn't take the stand and explain his own innocence. They also didn't like it that he just stood outside as the fire burned and made no attempt to go back inside to rescue his children.

These issues shouldn't matter in a determination of guilt. But, of course, they do. Regardless of the judge's instructions, once the twelve individuals enter the deliberation room and close the door, it's all up to them.

CHAPTER 5
BURNING QUESTIONS

Cameron Todd Willingham was packed off to death row in E1, the Ellis One Unit at the Texas State Penitentiary, near Huntsville. Like Roger Coleman, he continued to proclaim his innocence.

During that time, an extraordinary event took place at the institution. Ken Light, a well-known and respected documentary photographer, and Suzanne Donovan, a writer who previously had been director of the American Civil Liberties Union (ACLU) of Texas, were granted "unlimited access" to the Texas death row. The two had been teaching colleagues at the journalism school of the University of California, Berkeley. Ken made three trips, spending an aggregate of several weeks there. He made the photograph of Todd Willingham that appears in this book during one of those trips.

From my own experience with penitentiaries throughout the country, I know how difficult it is even for a law officer like me to get all the permissions and clearances to get in to talk to individual inmates. The fact that the toughest capital punishment state in the nation would allow in and give free reign to an ACLU official and writer and a guy with a camera is amazing. So are the results, published in a 1997 book entitled *Texas Death Row.* Their interest was not to make judgments as much as "put a human face on who these men are."

Ken has seen a lot of the world's tragedy and evil during his distinguished career, but the experience in the Texas death house clearly affected him.

"I worked from early in the morning until six or seven, when I was completely exhausted and would go back to my little hotel room and lock the door and just be completely freaked out," the photographer stated.

"Probably for about a year and a half, I had nightmares from the experience, waking up from dreams, sweating, with images of the guys," he added. "Of the guys I photographed, about sixty-five have been executed." For some, Ken's images were the last ever made of them.

The intensity was compounded by what was going on in his own life. "At the same time I was working on this project, my wife was pregnant, so that was an experience of going to the death house, coming back home to my wife, and realizing all these guys started out as babies. You begin to wonder how the hell did they end up here."

As you might expect, he described the atmosphere at Ellis as "dark and gothic." And while most of the inmates would not relate their crimes to him, the chronicler revealed, "Some of them did tell me their stories. And, of course, they're very weird and twisted, with their ethical scale completely stuck. They'll describe, 'Yes, I killed that person, but I didn't rob him, so I shouldn't be here.' "

During his time at Ellis, Ken got friendly with Willingham's bunkmate Danny, and through him got to know Todd. "There is something about that tattoo on his arm that is fairly impressive," Light states, realizing it was that scary, dragon-wrapped skull image that helped convict him nearly as much as the scientific evidence. But Ken found him friendly and cooperative. "A regular guy."

"Some people avoided me because they were afraid their pictures being made would jeopardize their appeals."

Todd had no such qualms, never even talked about his case, and he and Danny allowed Ken in and out of their cell at will. And the image he captured, Ken feels, is representative of the man.

"It was unusual to find an inmate lying in bed in this stark cell in the middle of the afternoon, calmly reading a book. That was part of the interest in taking the picture."

Basically, that was how Todd spent his twelve years on death row.

Like Roger Keith Coleman, Cameron Todd Willingham's long string of appeals went nowhere. Stacy believed him, but she decided to put her life with him behind her and would not come to see him. Eventually, like Coleman's wife, she filed for divorce.

Also, like Coleman, he eventually acquired a female friend on the outside. But instead of a girlfriend, she became his chief advocate. Elizabeth Gilbert was a teacher and writer from Houston, a divorced mother of two, who had acceded to an anti–capital punishment friend's request that she become a pen pal to a prisoner on death row. Willingham turned out to be her assigned prisoner and she was impressed by how articulate he was. Either out of curiosity or just general human compassion, she agreed to his request that she visit him at Huntsville.

Their relationship developed. They continued to correspond and she came to visit him again. All the time, he continued to insist on his innocence. When she had agreed to the pen pal arrangement, it hadn't occurred to Elizabeth that her prisoner might actually be innocent. With this possibility in mind, but also with a writer's skepticism, she set about to investigate the case on her own.

She drove to Corsicana, went to the courthouse and sat down with the court records. She was surprised to note that a number of the eyewitness accounts of Todd's behavior had shifted after the fire investigators' report came out. That is to say, once they knew that the fire had been set intentionally, their interpretations suggested more "inappropriate" behavior than they had originally noticed.

This phenomenon is actually pretty well known to those of us in law enforcement. As David Grann noted in his excellent *New Yorker* article about the case, "Dozens of studies have shown that witnesses' memories of events often change when they are supplied with new contextual information."

I have often said that investigators, including me, can only be as good as the evidence we have to work with. If this issue of witnesses' "evolving impressions" of the subject had been brought to us, I would have tried to make a few points. Most important is that the witnesses were not necessarily wrong in either case. We are always filtering our first-hand experience through a layer of interpretation. Therefore, I would have advised that it is very important to do complete interviews with each of these individuals, to probe their feelings about the crime and their beliefs about Todd Willingham, in order to set these observations in a meaningful context. Otherwise, they aren't going to be very helpful or indicative.

As one telling example, Vicki Prater stated on the *Frontline* program that, given Todd's history of beating up on Stacy, many in the community were unwilling to give him the benefit of the doubt when it came to killing his children. This statement showed a good deal of insight. Essentially, Vicki was profiling Todd and the community. This is just the kind of analysis investigators should use.

Elizabeth Gilbert talked to Todd's parents, Gene and Eugenia, and then Stacy. None of them could conceive of Todd hurting his children. All three described his behavior as normal in the days before the fire — happy anticipation of visiting his parents in Oklahoma.

She also went to see Johnny Webb in prison in Iowa Park, Texas. He described his background of crime and drug abuse and his psychiatric diagnosis of mental impairment. Eventually he would recant his testimony about Willingham admitting to setting the fire. Then he would recant the recantation.

When David Grann interviewed Webb shortly before the publication of his article, he seemed not to remember one way or the other. *After I pressed him,* Grann wrote, *he said, "It's very possible I misunderstood what he said."*

Throughout all of her personal investigation, Elizabeth just couldn't find a motive for Todd killing the three little girls. She found him becoming more emotionally dependent on her. As his situation grew more desperate, and he grew more despondent in prison, she was the only one besides his parents and court-appointed appeals lawyer, Walter Reaves, who came to see him.

The various state court levels continued to refuse Reaves's motions, and after the U.S. Supreme Court refused in December 2003 to hear the case, Willingham's execution by lethal injection was scheduled for February 17, 2004.

It was at this point that the case took two dramatic turns — the most significant since the trial almost twelve years before. Both involved women in Todd Willingham's life.

The first involved Stacy. For the first time in twelve years, she agreed to visit him in prison. The visit did not go well. She had reviewed the court record and fire investigator's report and now believed Todd had set the fire intentionally. For this reason, when he asked her, through the Plexiglas partition that separated them, to have him buried next to the three children, she refused. He was outraged that she denied this final request and that she had come around to believing he was guilty. They argued and shouted, and she stormed away from the prison.

The second turn of events involved Elizabeth Gilbert. Once she concluded that Todd's lack of motive and apparent sincerity about his innocence didn't square with the scientific evidence of arson, she started looking for experts to see if there might be any divergent theories about the fire. If there were other explanations, these might at least be devices to gain a stay from the scheduled execution.

One of the names she came across was Dr. Gerald Hurst in Austin, Texas. Todd's cousin, Patricia Ann Cox, had seen him on television. After a great deal of effort, they reached him.

Hurst is an unusual, intellectually imposing, idiosyncratic fellow. A tall, thin man in his sixties, with large glasses, thinning gray hair and a full gray beard, Hurst was considered brilliant by his colleagues. He had earned a Ph.D. in chemistry from Cambridge. He became an expert on explosives and designed rockets and bombs for a number of American defense contractors. Deciding during the Vietnam war that he no longer felt comfortable in the destruction business, he went on to become an inventor of "civilian" products and various applications to make explosives less likely to detonate accidentally. His knowledge of all subjects relating to fire was so profound that he became a much sought-after expert witness in civil cases of possible insurance fraud. Within the industry, his judgment became the last word and he garnered such fans as John Lentini, an

Atlanta-based, world-renowned fire investigator in his own right who would go on to write the landmark text *Scientific Protocols for Fire Investigation.*

Hurst was not just a prominent expert witness. Since the 1990s, people like him and Lentini had been revolutionizing the science of fire analysis through advanced chemical analysis and complex experiments in which they set fires and then carefully monitored and correlated the results. The results were often surprising and contradicted long-held conventional wisdoms about the differences between set fires and accidental ones. Hurst had been instrumental in having charges dropped or convictions reversed against ten people accused of arson.

He and Lentini both felt that arson investigation had grown up as a set of untested beliefs, passed down from one investigator to the next, without any real scientific correlation. This was understandable, Lentini explained, because most investigators were firefighters, not scientists: "Extinguishing a fire and investigating a fire require two different skill sets and two different mind-sets."

Comfortable from royalties on his various patents and inventions, Dr. Hurst agreed to look at the Willingham case without charge. Only weeks before the execution date, Reaves sent him all relevant materials.

■ ■ ■ ■

The Willingham case reminded Dr. Hurst of the 1990 fire at the home of Gerald Wayne Lewis on Lime Street in Jacksonville, Florida. Six people had perished in that fire, and Lewis, thirty-five years of age with a history, like Willingham, of spousal abuse, was charged with intentionally setting the fire. Lewis had insisted the fire started with his young son playing with matches on the couch. Also like the Willingham case, several witnesses thought Lewis was acting inappropriately around the fire and was slow to seek help. The prosecution called in several arson experts, including Lentini and John DeHaan, an arson expert from the California Department of Justice who would coauthor three arson textbooks with my former FBI colleague Dave Icove. They all noted the telltale V-shaped burn patterns and other evidence of the use of accelerants. In his article, Grann quoted Lentini as saying, *"I was prepared to testify and send this guy to Old Sparky."*

As Grann related, with fire department sanction and the prosecution willing to foot the $20,000 cost, Lentini and DeHaan devised an elaborate experiment at the house next door, nearly identical to Lewis's, which was slated to be torn down. They furnished the house as closely as possible to Lewis's and re-created the fire exactly, even down to the same model sofa. Everything was identical, except for one critical detail: they used no liquid accelerant, merely setting a match to the living-room couch. The idea of the experiment was to be able to show the jury that Lewis was lying, by showing the difference between the two fires. They put in temperature sensors, carbon monitors and video cameras.

The investigators were shocked and stunned by the results. The experimental "accidental" fire reached flashover — the point at which a burning object gets so hot that it sets everything else in the room on fire — just as quickly as an accelerant-fueled blaze would have. The critical point for fire scientists and investigators is that once that happens, it is no longer fuel that controls and determines the direction of the fire; it is air supply, or sources of ventilation. It turned out that flashover left burn patterns that looked just like pour patterns from gasoline or other accelerants.

The Lime Street experiment proved that a flashover in one room could cause a flashover in an adjacent room, and the resulting burn patterns are indistinguishable from pour or puddle patterns.

In an admirable display of courage and responsibility, prosecutor Frank Ashton moved to have the charges against Gerald Lewis dismissed. His eloquent argument acknowledged that it was "horrible to take somebody who is totally innocent and to try them for a crime because there is some circumstantial evidence that they might be guilty, and convict them of it and send them to death row."

He went on to observe that by the time a case gets to a jury, the defendant "has two strikes against him" because the police have arrested him and the prosecutor has charged him. "So you run a great risk of having an innocent man convicted."

All in all, the course of the two fires was identical. Lentini suddenly realized that much of what had been accepted for decades as fire science was assumption. "Witchcraft, really."

"This was my epiphany. I almost sent a man to die based on theories that were a load of crap."

Gerald Hurst had similar feelings about much of what passed for arson investigation in the early years of the twenty-first century. He concluded that the fire path at the Willingham home, rather than being caused by accelerants, had been caused by ventilation from the front door when Todd escaped and left it open. Then, when the fire reached flashover in the front bedroom and the windows blew out, there was an entirely new source of air. The supposedly pentagram-shaped pattern the original inspectors thought they had seen actually represented the burn patterns created by the air supply from the five windows in the room!

Todd's account of running down the hall in his bare feet was totally consistent with the evidence, Hurst concluded. Since he had opened up the ventilation path with the front door, the hallway would not have been on fire yet, and the floor would have been the last element to burn since heat travels upward. Even the smoke fumes and carbon dioxide would not have traveled fast enough to do him serious harm, a revelation that came out of the Lime Street fire investigation and its follow-up.

Even the chemical detection of accelerant on the concrete slab of the front porch had an innocent explanation, Hurst realized. Photographic evidence of the house before the fire showed a charcoal grill and a can of lighter fluid were on the front porch. Finding no evidence of "accelerant," therefore, would have been more surprising than not. By the time he had finished his analysis, Hurst had refuted every one of the original investigators' twenty points supporting an intentionally lit fire. His two most likely causes were one of the three space heaters or electrical wiring.

"Todd Willingham's case falls into that

category where there is not one iota of evidence that the fire was arson," he declared on the *Frontline* program. "Not one iota."

By the time Walter Reaves received Hurst's report, it was less than a week until the execution. He immediately sent it to Governor James Richard "Rick" Perry and the Texas Board of Pardons and Paroles, and filed a series of emergency motions claiming legal and factual innocence. With only four days remaining, Reaves got word that the fifteen-member commission had voted unanimously to deny Willingham's petition for relief. Reaves and Hurst were shocked. Since hearing proceedings were closed, there wasn't any way to tell whether they had rejected the report or hadn't even bothered to read it. Stacy's brother Ronnie filed an affidavit in Navarro County Court stating that during her prison visit, Todd had confessed to her. Todd adamantly denied it, but the damage was done. Once again, the state and U.S. Supreme Court refused to act. Governor Perry turned down his plea for a stay, choosing to ignore the Hurst report.

Todd, who had started to have some hope, prepared to face his own death.

I'm no fire scientist, so it would be foolish for me to come to an independent conclusion without scientific evidence. But while the evidence presented at trial may have seemed compelling, when a new analysis, based on state-of-the-art science and presented by a leading world expert surfaces, there is no good reason for not paying attention to it. What possible criminal justice value could be served by not taking the amount of time necessary to evaluate the report properly? Cameron Todd Willingham had been on death row for twelve years. Another month or two or three would make very little difference to authorities, but it might mean all the difference in the world for one individual and his family.

The courts, the pardons board and the governor didn't see it that way.

On February 17, 2004, Todd met with his parents for the last time. He did have one confession to make — one that had been bothering him for all the years since the fire. Contrary to what he had reported, he did not actually make his way into the children's room to try to rescue them. The fire there was just too intense, so he rushed outside to try to get to them from the outside. He had maintained the fiction for so long because he didn't want people to think he was a coward. Hurst and Lentini both later acknowledged that anyone who has never been inside a fire has no concept of what it is like to face flames and try to go through them. That is why you don't hear more about people rushing triumphantly out of burning buildings carrying loved ones.

At 4:00 P.M., Todd had his last meal of barbecued pork ribs, onion rings, fried okra, beef enchiladas and lemon cream pie. Not resisting, but refusing to be an accomplice in his own execution, he lay down, forcing prison guards to carry him to the execution chamber. He was strapped onto the cross-shaped table and a needle was inserted into his arm. As he looked out through the glass window to the viewing area, he saw Stacy.

When the warden asked him if he had any last words, he replied, "The only statement I want to make is that I am an innocent man convicted of a crime I did not commit. I have been persecuted for twelve years for something I did not do. From God's dust I came and to dust I will return, so the earth shall become my throne."

Then he went off on Stacy in extremely vitriolic and explicit language, stating that he hoped she "rots in hell," presumably for refusing his burial request and claiming he had confessed to her. The lethal injection began at 6:13 P.M. Seven minutes later, he was pronounced dead.

After the execution, Todd's parents were finally allowed to touch him at the funeral home. His body was still warm. According to his instructions, it was cremated and his ashes were secretly spread over his children's graves.

Some have suggested that Todd's final rant

against Stacy demonstrated the way his mind actually worked and the violence of which he was capable. But no statement makes sense outside its full context. Facing immediate death and feeling *I have been publicly betrayed by a person I have counted on,* I think I, too, might have said something similar if I had been in his shoes.

As with Roger Coleman, the controversy did not cease with the defendant's death. Reporters for the *Chicago Tribune* asked Lentini and other fire experts to review the evidence in the Willingham case. All four agreed with Hurst.

In 2005, the state legislature created the nine-member Texas Forensic Science Commission under the leadership of chairman Sam Bassett, an attorney from Austin. Its charge was to review possible errors in the gathering and analysis of scientific evidence for trial. It remained virtually unknown until 2008, when it responded to a request from the Innocence Project, led by Professor Barry Scheck, of Benjamin Cardozo School of Law in New York, and took on the Willingham case. After reviewing the evidence, the commission solicited an independent report from Dr. Craig Beyler, of Baltimore, a Harvard- and Cornell-educated engineer considered one of the top fire experts in the world. Beyler agreed with Hurst and Lentini that there was absolutely no factual basis for concluding the fire was set. He tore into the evidence and procedures presented at trial, stating that the original investigators had no understanding of flashover and ignored scientific methodology, even that which was already established at the time.

As this was happening, two members of Governor Rick Perry's staff asked Bassett to a meeting during which they delivered a message in no uncertain terms: The review was a waste of state time and money and should be halted. Bassett refused.

Just as the commission's report was to be issued, Governor Perry appointed three new members and fired Sam Bassett. According to England's *Guardian* newspaper, *[The Innocence Project] likened the action to Richard Nixon's dismissal of the Watergate prosecutor in the so-called "Saturday night massacre."*

During the 2010 Republican gubernatorial primary, Senator Kay Bailey Hutchison, who was challenging Perry for the nomination, accused him of "trying to ramrod a covering-up."

Perry countered through a spokesman that critics "should just say so" if they disagreed with the death penalty for a man who had killed his three children, beaten his wife, had been convicted and had his conviction upheld in various courts. And I'm sure many Texans would think such a man ought to be executed.

I know that as a law-and-order professional I certainly would.

But the real point was made by John Lentini in the *Frontline* film:

"The State of Texas executed a man for a crime that they couldn't prove was really a crime. And the evidence says, this is an accidental fire. And if it was an accidental fire, it doesn't matter how many posters of Iron Maiden Cameron Todd Willingham had on his wall, or Led Zeppelin, or whether he liked to play darts or drink beer, or whether he smacked his wife around. It only matters that a fire was not really a set fire."

In Bassett's place, Perry appointed his political ally John Bradley, the district attorney for Williamson County. The *Texas Tribune* characterized Bradley as "an outspoken conservative with a tough law-and-order reputation." When challenged, according to the *Tribune,* "Perry said he simply replaced commissioners whose terms had expired, and he rejected the work of those who had questioned the arson findings as that of 'latter-day supposed experts.' "

"*Supposed* experts?" Excuse me, Governor. How about taking a leaf from Virginia governor Mark Warner's playbook with the Roger Coleman case? I find this statement from the chief executive of the state with the most executions breathtaking in its insensitivity and obtuseness. Three giants of the field independently found no basis for a claim of arson. If that were true, it not only meant Todd Willingham was innocent, it meant *no crime had been committed*. Justice is not a political game; it is a search for truth. This was not a commitment to toughness on law and order; this was a close-minded attempt to avoid confronting a miscarriage of justice in its most blatant and egregious form. It is not surprising that this same governor, while campaigning for the Republican nomination for president in 2011, characterized evolution as a theory that's "got some gaps in it," and believes "intelligent design" "should be presented in schools alongside the theories of evolution."

If this is the standard that is to be used to review scientific evidence in criminal cases in the state of Texas, we can expect a lot more tragic fiascos like Willingham's.

While on the commission, Bradley called Willingham "a guilty monster"; the DA was replaced when the Texas Senate refused to reappoint him. Bradley was replaced by Dr. Nizam Peerwani, a medical doctor and medical examiner of Tarrant County who seemed to have a respect for science.

The commission has already acknowledged flaws and mistakes in the Willingham investigation. Whether they will deal with his actual innocence is an open question.

The Willingham case, unfortunately, is far

from an isolated incident. All over the country, John Lentini and his associates are testifying in cases of fires that were deemed arson, against modern scientific standards.

For people in my line of work, there are a lot of reasons why a particular case might haunt you. It might be that an UNSUB was never caught and a killer was not brought to justice. It might be the especially hideous nature of the crime itself — the sadism and brutality evidenced by the crime scene. It might be that the victim was a child and you can't bear to imagine what you would do if it was your child. It might even be that the killer got off on a legal technicality, sloppy police work or a botched investigation. But in terms of the criminal justice process itself, a case like Cameron Todd Willingham's is about the most difficult to deal with.

Throughout my career, I've often been taken to task — face-to-face, around the Bureau and in the media — for my so-called cockiness and overconfidence in dealing with local law enforcement agencies. It's been said that I'm a loose cannon and a risk taker, though I would argue that those risks have all been extremely calculated ones. I have been called a publicity hound who "went Hollywood." I've heard jokes like, "The most dangerous action you can take at Quantico is trying to get between John Douglas and a camera." None of this went over big in the old Hoover-dominated "just the facts, ma'am" FBI.

I neither deny those charges nor regret the actions that prompted them. Starting the operational profiling program when I did, I had to "go Hollywood" and appeal to the media, promote the program to get us on the map. I've always said one of the smartest things I did was cooperate with Thomas Harris when he wanted to come to my unit to research *Red Dragon* and *Silence of the Lambs,* because it led to the Jonathan Demme Academy Award–winning feature film. That helped put us on the map to as great an extent as any success we had with a real case, such as the Atlanta Child Murders or the "Trailside Killer" in San Francisco.

But the reason a case like Willingham's troubles me so much is that, had it been brought to us, I fear we might have blown it. When my unit provided a written profile, we always included a paragraph similar to this:

This analysis is based upon information available at the time this report was prepared and assumes that the information provided was obtained through a comprehensive, thorough, and well-planned investigation. Should any additional information or case materials become available at a later date those materials would be reviewed in order to determine whether they are germane to issues discussed herein. Subsequent to such a review, certain aspects of this analysis may be subject to modification or change.

In any criminal case, these written analyses would be discoverable by the defense, so there is nothing secret about this; it is not something we hide. It is simply a statement of fact: We can only work with what we're given.

Had the local police assured me they were solid with the arson findings, I'm afraid we might have been led, like most everyone else was, to interpret Todd's background and behavior after the fire as evidence of guilt. In many of the cases my unit and I worked over the years, our profiles and criminal investigative analysis did not lead to a prosecution or identification of an UNSUB, and I'm okay with that. You don't bat a thousand in this business; and in almost all of those instances, I would still say that the profile was correct, even though it didn't lead to an arrest. And in the many cases in which a suspect was already in custody and we were asked to either confirm or redirect an investigation, I think our track record is pretty damn good.

This one, though, I might not have been proud of. We had too many cases and too much pressure to question what looked like strong and reliable evidence. I would not have questioned the arson report, which, as an investigator, would have oriented me in a specific direction. The only mitigating thing I will say is that had we worked this case and then been informed of the eleventh hour turnaround in the forensic evidence, I would have moved heaven and earth, camped out on the FBI director's doorstep, if necessary, and tried to throw the entire resources of the Bureau behind getting a stay of execution. Even that, though, probably wouldn't have been enough.

Like the Coleman case, this one was ultimately resolved by state-of-the-art science. The *CSI* Effect notwithstanding, this is possible in only a small minority of cases. Most have no definitive physical evidence; rather, there are individual elements that have to be put into a larger context from which conclusions may be drawn. As these two cases together demonstrate, achieving justice can be a complicated business and a morally perilous journey for which we have no easy answers to offer. The only completely reliable guidance is always to be aware of those perils so that we may hope to avoid them.

I'm not sure whether it is ironic or understandable that of these two cases — Coleman's and Willingham's — the man for whom justice was done spoke as his final words, "Love is eternal. My love for you will last forever. I love you, Sharon." The one for whom it was miscarried chose to end his life with profanities and expletives.

Because of what he did, Cameron Todd Willingham may be labeled a school failure, a wife abuser, a runaround and a general ne'er-do-well. Because of what was done to him, he became a martyr for justice and truth. And that is the legacy that will survive him.

BALANCING THE SCALES

CHAPTER 6
SUZANNE'S STORY

When it comes to murder, there are no effective legal remedies. There is no way to right the wrong and no possibility of restoring the victim to his or her family, friends and lifestyle. Given this impossible situation, many victims' families and advocates, law enforcement personnel and ordinary members of the public, feel that in cases of intentional and particularly brutal or sadistic murder, the closest the state can come to balancing the scales judicially is to take the life of the individual who took the life of his or her innocent victim.

As a result of my experience in decades of work in law enforcement, I place myself in that camp.

While I fully accept and respect the views of those who oppose capital punishment on moral or practical grounds, there is one argument I will not accept. In fact, I resist it vigorously. That is, that capital punishment is legalized murder — that if the state takes a life, it is just as morally culpable as the defendant who committed murder. This, frankly, is nonsense. Not only is it nonsense, it is morally offensive. It is morally offensive because it trivializes the distinction between the victim and the perpetrator, between the innocent and the guilty. And if we ever lose that distinction, we are done for as an ethical and just society.

Every other aspect of the argument is up for grabs.

People often ask me and other investigators who share my views, with all we know about the varying degrees of competence and sophistication of police work, investigating agencies and criminal justice procedures, how we can be in favor of capital punishment? How can we support this irreversible act, especially in light of a case like Todd Willingham's or Dr. Gerald Hurst's suspicion that there are probably many more like it? And that's only in the realm of arson.

The answer is, we support it for certain types of crimes and certain circumstances. But rather than beginning with a theoretical, academic discussion of the death penalty, let's bring it down to the personal level. Because life doesn't get any less theoretical and more personal than murder. Let's focus on individuals rather than abstractions, on experience rather than supposition, on facts rather than opinions.

I want to relate a case that I first described in *Journey Into Darkness.* But since that book was published, there is a critical, agonizing and ultimately enlightening new chapter to be written. This is a story that will illuminate many key issues: the strengths and weaknesses of the death penalty; the parameters and limits of a fair trial, as well as a reasonable appeals process; the uses of scientific evidence, especially after the trial is over and the verdict rendered; and the human toll all of this takes on each of the participants.

This is the story of Suzanne Marie Collins and Sedley Alley.

I use the two names in the same sentence, but it is not because there is any similarity or moral equivalence between them. It is because Sedley Alley did something that created a connection and a relationship, a horrible association that resulted in death. As we discuss the criminal justice system and the pros and cons of capital punishment, don't let that forced connection stray from your thoughts.

Of all the cases I worked, and that Mark Olshaker and I have written about, none has elicited as much passionate reader response as the Suzanne Collins murder. Corn-silk blond when she was little, tawny-maned as she grew older, athletically buff and strikingly beautiful, Suzanne was, in many ways, the epitome of the all-American girl. She was the daughter of John A. Collins, an American Foreign Service officer and attorney universally known as "Jack," and his wife, Gertrude, known as "Trudy." Suzanne and her older brother, Stephen, were both adopted, and Jack and Trudy devoted their lives to them.

With her looks and charm, she might easily have been a heartbreaker at Robert E. Lee High School in Springfield, Virginia, where the family settled after stints in Greece and a special State Department assignment in Madison, Wisconsin. But she was so popular and friendly, so interested in everyone else's life, that everyone loved her and she became the school's social organizer. By this time Steve was both an academic and wrestling star, and it became well known how protective he was. Any guy wanting to approach Suzanne on more than a casual level had to pass Steve's muster.

Her charm and popularity also led to some problems in high school. Although she was a good language and science student, between socializing and sports, studying was not her top priority. Despite warnings and encouragement, inspiration and threats from her parents, Suzanne ended her high-school career as something less than optimum college material.

She didn't want to go to community college and live at home, and she didn't want what she characterized as some "rinky-dink job," so she decided to enlist in the United States Marine Corps.

Her decision was a surprise to everyone — her family, her friends and her teachers. When her navy veteran father asked her how she had arrived at this decision, she replied simply that she wanted to challenge herself and the marines were "the best."

"What could I say to that?" Jack recalled. "So I answered, 'Well, you're the best, Suzanne, so that's fine.'"

Suzanne graduated from high school in June 1984 and began basic training the same month at the Marine Corps Recruit Depot, Parris Island, South Carolina. She threw herself into the grueling boot camp regime, pushing her mind and body as she never had before. When her parents came down for graduation, Jack was amazed by her physical prowess and self-confidence. Trudy was amazed that this girl whose room was always a cyclone-like wreck could now make a bed tight enough to bounce a quarter.

Jack and Trudy both cherished the official portrait photo they received of their smiling, bright-eyed daughter. Her once-long blond hair was cut fashionably and sensibly to chin length. She was proudly wearing her green marine cap, with its black eagle, globe and anchor, and the American flag waved behind her.

Suzanne had also done a lot of thinking

during basic training and for the first time in her life had articulated and solidified her goals. She wanted to go to the Naval Academy, hoping a strong military record would offset her lackluster high-school performance. And she wanted to become part of the first class of female marine fighters, banking on the hope that the restriction against women in aerial combat positions eventually would be lifted. As a first step in proving herself, she applied to and was accepted in avionics training — electronics applied to aviation.

Private First Class Suzanne Marie Collins reported to Marine Aviation Training Support Squadron 902, Memphis Naval Air Station, Millington, Tennessee, on October 20, 1984. On and around the base, she was hard to miss — a tall, gorgeous blonde who kept herself in tip-top shape through constant exercise. She had developed an easy, graceful manner that seemed to appeal to everyone, except, perhaps, some of her fellow recruits and military wives who noticed their husbands' heads snap every time Suzanne passed by.

She found her best friend shortly after Susan Hand arrived in March 1985. Susan, from Lisle, Illinois, was another beautiful blonde, a year older than Suzanne, and at Millington for air traffic control school. She was bunked downstairs from Suzanne in the same barracks building. Both women were five-seven and 118 pounds; they swapped clothes and shared secrets. They were always together during off-duty hours and soon everyone on the base knew them. Both acquired boyfriends from the air traffic control department, and they were the only two women deemed good enough to be invited to play soccer with the guys' teams. They were also great dancers and often went to clubs on Beale Street in Memphis. Despite her popularity and athleticism, there was an aura of sweetness and innocence about Suzanne that men and women found genuine and endearing.

Her busy off-duty life notwithstanding, Suzanne was turning into a first-rate marine. Around the time Susan Hand arrived, Suzanne had been promoted to lance corporal and appointed to the honor deck, a ceremonial troop made up of "only the most motivated students." Her parents were thrilled and surprised, because to be recommended for honor deck, a student had to maintain a top academic average, a feat Suzanne had never before been motivated to attempt.

This also represented another accomplishment. Prior to Suzanne's appointment, all members of the Memphis Naval Air Station Honor Deck had been male. For weeks, she was harassed by many of the men and derided by many of the women, who thought she had achieved this honor because of her looks. But she stuck it out and took all the abuse and hazing thrown her way. Within a few weeks, Suzanne had convinced everyone that she was the real deal. Cracking this barrier gave her confidence that she would one day achieve her goal of getting into Annapolis and making it as a U.S. Marine flier.

There was only one thing that bothered Suzanne and Susan as graduation day approached. Suzanne had been assigned to Cherry Point, North Carolina, Marine Corps Air Station (MCAS), while Susan had been assigned to El Toro MCAS in California. Their plan was to take up their assignments, then figure out a way to get Suzanne assigned to El Toro, too. They envisioned their lives together, including fleet appointments to Annapolis and eventually settling down near each other and raising their kids together. Suzanne's boyfriend, Greg, was all in favor of this because he was also going to California. He had already set his sights on marrying Suzanne, though Susan says that her friend was still having too much fun to think about settling down quite yet.

Susan's mother and four-year-old sister came down from Illinois for the graduation. On July 11, 1985, the night before the ceremony, Mrs. Hand invited Suzanne to join them all for dinner at a friend's house in a Memphis suburb. Shortly before they were to leave, the barracks staff sergeant assigned Suzanne as Duty NCO for the day. It basically meant sitting behind a desk outside the barracks building, checking people in and out, and then once an hour making a circuit around the building and recording her findings in a logbook. Suzanne told them to go without her, saying they would meet at the base park the next morning before the graduation. But Susan was seething, feeling the sergeant was jealous of Suzanne and had it in for her. She had one last chance to punish her for all her attributes and she was going to take advantage of it. Susan didn't think someone who was graduating the next day should have to be on duty when anyone could have been assigned, particularly someone who didn't already have plans.

The watch was uneventful. By the time Suzanne finished her duty assignment, she was restless and wanted some exercise. She went to her room and changed from her uniform to a red Marine Corps T-shirt, shorts, white socks and her Nike sneakers. She wrapped a white bandanna around her forehead and a blue sweat belt around her waist. When she came out, she told her friend Janet Cooper, who had watch duty, that she was going for a run and that she'd probably be out for a half hour or so. They talked while Suzanne stretched, and Janet said she seemed in a good and happy mood.

It was understandable. She was nineteen

161

years old, beautiful and in the best physical condition of her life. The regrets of high school seemed far behind her. She had a boyfriend, a best friend, a brother and two parents who worshipped her. She was well on her way to all of her lofty goals. Tomorrow she would graduate from avionics school and begin the next adventure, one she was primed for and anxious to get started on.

That tomorrow never arrived for Lance Corporal Suzanne Marie Collins.

CHAPTER 7
THE BODY IN THE PARK

Susan Hand learned the horrible news early Friday afternoon, July 12, after Suzanne didn't show up in the park as they'd arranged the night before. She was called into Captain Nowag's office, where the captain told her she'd better sit down. He came over and put a hand on her shoulder. Then he pulled up a chair and sat with his arm around her.

Steve Collins found out at home in Springfield, where he was recovering from a foot injury. He saw a military car pull up and figured his wily sister must have connived an official ride home. Instead, it was a marine officer and a chaplain.

Trudy was out at a senior citizens' luncheon with her parents. When they returned home, Steve intercepted her and made her get out of the car on her own.

Jack was in New York, helping his brother-in-law with a patent application issue, when a secretary pulled him out of a meeting for an urgent phone call. Being a devout Catholic who believed fervently in the power of prayer, he asked the mixed group of Christians and Jews he was with to pray for his daughter.

At those moments, Suzanne Marie Collins — dear friend, sister and daughter, lance corporal in the United States Marine Corps — was lying on an autopsy table in the office of the Shelby County, Tennessee, medical examiner. Dr. James Spencer Bell had just finished his examination and report. He later said it was the worst case he had ever seen.

Around the time of the Roger Coleman DNA testing early in 2006, I got a request to speak at a series of lectures at Vanderbilt University in Nashville, Tennessee, on the death penalty. Concerned that I could be bushwhacked if the tests were negative and the indication was that Virginia had executed an innocent man, I planned my appearance carefully. I said I wanted to be able to talk about individual cases — one in particular — and that I wanted to be able to use actual crime scene photos as part of my PowerPoint presentation.

The organizers objected to this last condition. When I pressed them on it, they said it would be exploitive to the victim and revictimize his or her family.

"Don't you think I'm sensitive to that after all the cases I've handled?" I countered. Yes, seeing a lot of gore over a long period of time does make you less vulnerable to its effects and the gross-out factor eventually goes away. But the feeling about the victims and their families never dulls. If anything, it gets stronger.

"The family *wants* this information to get out," I explained. "They want people to know what their child suffered. They want people to understand what murder is really all about."

People often ask me if putting myself "inside the minds" of killers and violent predators has taken an emotional toll. The answer is always, "No." That's what I do, and through a combination of natural talent, exhaustive research and plain hard work, I'm good at it. Any investigator who can't handle the psychic burden is in the wrong business. And all the serial killer novels that tell you otherwise — *He had a rare gift . . . or was it a curse?* — are just so much fiction.

The real emotional toll comes from putting myself inside the mind of the victim at the moment she is being violently raped or beaten, or when his life is coming to an end with no support or help or love or caring anywhere around. It's when I envision the victims staring unmitigated evil right in the face. Then it's watching the faces of their survivors — the family and friends and colleagues — when I try to explain "how this could have happened" and "how someone could do this." That's my baggage. But you know something? It's baggage I'll proudly carry for the rest of my life.

I told the lecture organizers they were wrong about the revictimization. The real revictimization comes when the loved ones realize that the justice that had been promised to them is an elusive mirage always looming just over the horizon; and that the system meant to give them a measure of peace is often just one more implement for brutalizing them.

When I went down to Nashville and did the lecture, I was surprised by the size of the crowd. The auditorium held five hundred and was packed. People were standing in the aisles.

I said, "You people here in Tennessee have the death penalty on your books, but you almost never use it. Since the Supreme Court reinstated capital punishment, you've executed exactly one person, five years ago. Yet your juries — your representatives of the people — keep imposing it. So something's out of whack with the system. And as citizens of this state, it is up to you to decide whether you want it or not. And if not, you should get rid of it."

Then I told them about Suzanne Collins. I told them about how she'd gone out to run on base the night before avionics school graduation and never returned to her barracks. Shelby County sheriff's deputies discovered her naked and mutilated body around six in the morning of Friday, July 12, 1985, in Edmund Orgill Park in Millington, just east of the Naval Air Station. Around five in the morning, her bunkmate and close friend, Patti Coon, awoke and saw that Suzanne's bed had not been slept in and worriedly called security. Soon an all-points bulletin (APB) was issued for the base, Millington PD and the county sheriff's department.

The deputies found Suzanne's body facedown about 150 feet from the road, with her shirt and athletic shorts, socks, underwear and exercise belt scattered nearby.

This is what Dr. Bell wrote in his autopsy report: *Death was due to multiple injuries inflicted by blunt trauma to the head, pressing on the neck and pushing 20 1/2 inches of a 31 inch long, 1 1/2 inch diameter sharply beveled tree limb up the perineum through the abdomen into the right chest tearing abdominal and chest organs and producing internal hemorrhaging.*

That was the summary. The entire report was twenty-one pages long. It detailed a bloody head, a left eye swollen shut and bite marks on the left breast. Bruises covered both shoulder blades, and scratches ran from the shoulders to the waist. What it did not mention was that her face was so badly beaten that the photographs the Navy Security personnel had furnished to the police and sheriff's deputies couldn't help much in the identification.

"Okay," I challenged my audience after reading this description out loud and showing some of the least graphic crime scene photos, "do you understand what this means? It means she was overpowered in a surprise attack while she was jogging. That someone hit her repeatedly on the head with a hard object. It could have been anything — a hammer, a baseball bat, the effect would have been the same. It means this beautiful blond girl, this young woman who had proven herself as a U.S. Marine, had been so brutalized that she didn't look like herself anymore."

My hands were shaking and my fingers were gripped into claws as I talked, because I can't describe a victim's ordeal without emotion, as many times as I've been over it, as many times as I've presented it to law enforcement groups.

When I present this case, as I've done frequently, I use descriptions like this:

It's dark. He gets her in his car and he drives her off base. Whenever she comes to enough to try to resist, he hits her again. When they get to this park, he drags her out of the car, rips all her clothes off. Then he breaks a limb off a tree. The report says it's an inch and a half in diameter and almost a yard long. And in some kind of inhuman sexual rage, he takes this sharp, jagged tree limb and he shoves it. He forces it between her legs and pushes it up as far as he can, as hard as he can. The medical examiner measured how far that it was — it was almost two feet. What I'm saying is that he raped her with this thick sharp stick and shoved it up so hard and so far that he tore through every organ in its path, up to and including her right lung.

Witnesses later testified that they heard a hideous "death scream" coming from somewhere in the park.

I looked out over my audience. I wanted them to understand, to feel at least a little of the revulsion, at least a little of the horror. Some of them were crying. Some of them had an almost blank expression on their faces. Most likely, they were all feeling, *How could anyone do something like this to another human being?*

The attempt to answer that question, or at least the explanation for it, is the reason I got involved in the case. The prosecution asked me to help them explain that very question to an uncomprehending jury in light of the defense that was being offered. But let's not get ahead of the story.

It didn't take police long to come up with a

suspect. In fact, Navy Security officials identified him even before they knew Suzanne had been murdered.

Around eleven on the night of July 11, two marines, Private First Class Michael Howard and Private First Class Mark Shotwell, were jogging when they saw a female jogger matching Suzanne's description. Soon after, they noticed a car — a dark-colored, mid-1970s Ford wagon, they thought — with its high beams on, heading in the same direction as the jogger.

They heard screams and immediately took off in that direction, but they were suddenly blinded by the glare of oncoming headlights. In the few moments before they regained their night vision, they lost the car they were pursuing, so they ran to the nearest base gate and told the guard on duty, David Davenport. Davenport called base security, adding that he had seen a car of the same description leaving the base. The driver was male and had his arm around a woman. He recalled that the plates on the car were from Kentucky. Richard Rogers, chief of the watch for that part of the base, issued a "be on the lookout" (BOLO) to the entire base, Millington PD and Shelby County Sherriff's Department. Then he sent a security unit over to the gate and got in his own car to help look for the Kentucky car himself.

About ten minutes after midnight on July

12, Rogers spotted a car matching Davenport's description and stopped it. He brought the driver back to the security office for questioning.

His name was Sedley Alley. He was a white male, twenty-nine years of age. He was six feet four inches tall and weighed 220 pounds. His wife, Lynne, was an enlisted woman in the navy, working at the air base. He was a laborer who had had a string of jobs, most recently working for a company that did air-conditioning installations and repairs.

Rogers called Lynne Alley and asked her to come in. She seemed to match the description of the woman in the car. Sedley said the scream the two joggers heard was actually just part of a domestic dispute that had now been settled. Rogers had no choice but to let them go. Shotwell and Howard were in the security office at the time, giving their statements. As they drove off, both said they were certain from the loud muffler sound that this was the car they had seen and heard.

As soon as Rogers had been notified about the discovery of Suzanne's body, he directed two of his patrolmen to arrest Sedley Alley and bring him back in. Since the abduction had occurred on a federal reservation, he also called the FBI Resident Agency in Memphis, which sent two agents to the scene. When agents of the Naval Investigative Service seized Alley's car, they found several bloodstains, both inside and out.

At first, Alley denied any knowledge or involvement in the crime and asked for an attorney. But as that was being arranged, he said he changed his mind and wanted to tell what had happened.

He had been out drinking. Then, back in his car, he had spotted the pretty blond marine jogging. He pulled over to talk to her, but accidentally rammed her with his car. She fell down, unconscious or semiconscious, so he picked her up and put her in his car to take her to the emergency room. As they were en route, she woke up and started resisting, fighting with him, trying to get out. It got so intense, so quickly, that before he could explain to her what had happened and where he was taking her, he leaned over in a panic and hit her on the head to keep her quiet, not realizing he was holding a screwdriver in his hand. The screwdriver was at hand because it was a beat-up old car that wouldn't start with a key, and so he would use the screwdriver to start it.

She was suddenly quiet and stopped moving, so he was afraid he'd hit her harder than he intended and accidentally killed her. Panicking even more, he stopped at Edmund Orgill Park. He checked her vitals and he was pretty sure she was dead. That's when he got the idea to divert suspicion from what really happened by staging a sexual assault. He carried her into the park and removed her clothing. Then he broke off the tree limb and inserted it into her dead body in a sexualized manner.

There are three true statements in this account. He had been out drinking; he did spot the pretty blond marine jogging; he did use a screwdriver to start his car. It was found less than half a mile away from the park in the direction of the base. Everything else is a blatant and self-serving fabrication.

With the numerous wounds all over Suzanne's body, none matched up with either being struck by an automobile or jabbed in the head with a screwdriver. The medical examiner was quite clear that the horrific attack with the tree limb occurred while she was still alive and the "death scream" heard by three earwitnesses in the park corresponded to the time Suzanne would have died. Moreover, the damage to the internal organs strongly indicated that the offender had pulled the jagged tree limb out and shoved it in again, three or four times. This is not staging. This is intentional behavior of the most hideous form imaginable.

Alley was nine inches taller and nearly twice Suzanne's weight. Given the fact that he took her by surprise, even in marine fighting trim, it would have been virtually impossible for her to fend him off.

Lynne told investigators that she had been

out at a Tupperware party with girlfriends, and Sedley wasn't home when she returned. She didn't see him until she was called in for questioning by Navy Security during the night. The next morning, she noticed grass stains inside the car, but she figured they had been caused by their two dogs, which frequently rode in the car.

Other details about Sedley Alley quickly emerged. He had been married before, in Ashland, Kentucky. On February 28, 1980, three days after his twenty-year-old first wife, Debra, filed for divorce, she was found dead in the bathtub. Alley had told investigators she was out drinking that night with other men, had come home drunk, took a bath and must have drowned. It was several hours before Sedley called for an ambulance. The ME noted numerous bruises and strangulation marks on her neck. She had a French fry stuck in her throat and it was ruled that she had asphyxiated, choking on her own vomit.

The death was ruled questionable and Sedley Alley was never prosecuted. Shelby County assistant district attorney (ADA) Henry "Hank" Williams told us that if he had been the prosecutor in Kentucky, he definitely would have pursued the case and gone for a murder indictment. Had that been done, Suzanne Collins would almost assuredly still be alive today.

Murder cases tend to emphasize the extremes of human behavior, motive and principles, both bad and good. And Hank Williams is one of the genuine heroes of this one, as well as an exemplar of what a righteous prosecutor and a complete human being should be. A former FBI special agent, he knew as soon as he was handed the case and went over the file that he was going all the way. If ever a crime called for the death penalty, Williams thought, this was it. The ADA made it clear he was not interested in even talking about a plea bargain.

Aside from fervently prosecuting the case, he also became a supportive friend to the Collins family, spending countless hours listening to their anguish and fears and concerns, counseling them, trying to give them the psychological support he felt they needed.

And he had good support. Assistant U.S. Attorney Lawrence Laurenzi, who had been brought up to speed by both the Naval Investigative Service and the FBI, assured Williams's office that if, for any reason, he couldn't secure a capital indictment in state court, he was prepared to seek one in the federal system, since kidnapping is a federal crime. It turned out not to be an issue. Sedley Alley was charged with murder in the first degree of Suzanne Marie Collins.

CHAPTER 8
AN EMPTY SEAT, A FLAG AT HALF-STAFF

The graduation ceremony for Marine Aviation Support Squadron 902 was a solemn affair. The flag flew at half-staff and an empty seat was prominent among the graduates, who had expected to feel so happy.

The following Wednesday, July 17, Memphis Naval Air Station held a memorial service for Suzanne at the base chapel, officiated by her commanding officer, Colonel Robert Clapp. At the end, when the band played the "Marines' Hymn," and then a lone bugler played "Taps," there were hardly any dry eyes in the audience of the toughest of America's fighting forces.

Though the viciousness of the attack had left Suzanne so disfigured that her parents had already decided on a closed-casket funeral, when her body arrived back in Virginia, Jack and Trudy and Stephen had to look upon her one final time.

"We had to know, as best we could, everything that had happened to her," Jack explained.

When the casket was opened and they saw her, in blue dress uniform and white gloves, they could not believe anyone could possibly do anything so savage, so horrible, to another human being.

"My heart cried. My soul cried. I was screaming inside," Jack recalled.

The following month, they would travel down to Millington and visit the spot where Suzanne was found. They would insist on reading the autopsy report, on seeing the photographs of her body, the close-ups of every wound. When they arrived at the Shelby County Sheriff's Office, Sergeant Gordon Neighbours introduced himself and spontaneously hugged Trudy.

In any civilized society, I don't think there is any category of death worse than the death of a child while his or her parents still live. It is an experience that turns the natural order upside down, that demands more in the way of strength and emotional resources than any rational person has to give. It can bring family members together or tear them apart; it can test faith or destroy it. But it leaves none as they were; it is utterly transformative. And within this unfortunate category, there can be no death more horrible than the death of a child by murder. You would be hard-pressed to come up with a more devastating occurrence in the entire world.

Though it had to rank as the most dreadful experience of their lives, this act of Jack and Trudy's — this final bearing of witness — is not an uncommon one among the parents of murdered children.

Our book *Obsession* told the story of Katie Sousa, whose beautiful little eight-year-old daughter, Destiny, known as "Dee," was horrifically beaten to death by Katie's sister's boyfriend, Robert Miller. Katie had generously let her sister and Miller live in her house while they got back on their feet. After the murder, Katie insisted that she wanted to see everything: the murder file, the medical examiner's report, the autopsy photos. Then, when she went to the funeral home to make arrangements for Dee's burial, Katie insisted that they bring out Dee's body for her to examine.

The funeral director and the friend who accompanied her both pled with her not to go through with this. The body had just arrived and they hadn't had time to prepare it yet for viewing.

That was exactly the condition in which Katie wanted to see her. "Bring her out!" she ordered.

They had Katie go to a viewing room and brought Dee's body, cold from refrigeration, covered by a sheet. She was not content just to see her daughter's bruised face and the dotted puncture wound on her scalp, where her plastic barrette literally had been driven into her skull when Miller smashed her head with a heavy wooden jewelry box, ostensibly to punish her for "mouthing off" to him.

She described for us how she told them to remove the sheet. She wanted to examine Dee's naked body, inch by inch, from the top of her skull to the soles of her feet. She spent about forty-five minutes doing this. She wanted to understand — to experience — everything that had been done to this innocent child. She needed to take the suffering and pain onto herself and make it hers. With her little girl dead, that was the only way she felt she could go on living.

Carroll Ellis, who was then director of the Victim Services Section of the Fairfax County, Virginia, Police Department, likened it to the image of the *Pietà*. "I still see in my mind this Madonna with child in this private moment, seeing her child's wounds with her own eyes."

This is what Jack and Trudy and Stephen Collins experienced as they stared at Suzanne's unrecognizable face. Though the morticians had done their best, it looked nothing like the beautiful girl they had loved.

This quiet insistence on confronting the murder in all its brutality speaks to the love and courage and passion of so many of the parents of murdered children we have known. When I think of the individuals who have carried out this final viewing of their beloved children, I know I speak for all law enforcement officers when I quote Carroll's simple rhetorical question: "In the name of God, how dare they?"

Lance Corporal Suzanne Marie Collins, who had died on active duty in a uniformed service of the United States, was laid to rest with full military honors in Arlington National Cemetery on July 18, 1985. It was a warm and sunny afternoon. There were too many mourners for the funeral service at the old Fort Myer Chapel. Many had to listen from outside.

In the weeks following the funeral, Jack and Trudy were overwhelmed by the number of letters, phone calls, gifts and other tributes they received — many from people they had never met, all of whom attested to the effect Suzanne had had on their lives. Apparently, others had known the same wonderful girl, with the same magical personality, as they had. But each had a personal and individual story to tell about what Suzanne had meant to them.

That was the kind of girl . . . that was the kind of woman Suzanne was.

CHAPTER 9
DEFENDING THE INDEFENSIBLE

Sedley Alley, meanwhile, had several stories of his own to tell. But not, of course, about Suzanne Collins. Someone like Alley would only be concerned about himself and how the whole situation had affected *his* life.

After first admitting that he had killed Suzanne (though accidentally, in his rendition) and walking police through the various crime sites, he said he didn't remember any of it. This was the story he told his two court-appointed attorneys, Robert Jones and Ed Thompson, both prominent and highly respected members of the Memphis defense bar. After they brought in a psychologist, who examined and hypnotized their client, Alley came down (or up, depending on your interpretation) with multiple personality disorder (MPD). It seemed there were three warring personalities in that hulking body: regular Sedley, a female persona named Billie and Death. He later told state psychologist Dr. Samuel Craddock that it was Death who killed Suzanne, though Craddock testified at trial that the so-called normal Sedley personality showed no remorse for the victim. None of this had turned up in Alley's initial statement to the police, which was recorded in full, further refuting the MPD claim.

Dr. Craddock saw no evidence of MPD, but he came up with a very reasonable diagnosis of borderline personality disorder (BPD). So named because it was thought to exist on the borderline between neurosis and psychosis, this disorder is characterized by severe emotional instability, anger, rigid thinking, narcissism, paranoia and a general lack of empathy, among other characteristics. Various other members of the examining team came up with a similar diagnosis.

The defense said it needed more time to evaluate Alley's condition and got a six-month postponement in the trial that Hank Williams had been pushing hard to get started.

From my experience in all the investigations and trials I've worked and studied, MPD is one of the great classic nonsense defenses. If you've pretty much tied yourself to the crime, and the physical evidence has done the rest, it's one of the few strategies available that can at least deny or mitigate your culpability. A traditional insanity plea is pretty much an uphill climb: "You mean, at the time, you couldn't tell it was wrong to abduct a young woman, beat her senseless and then shove a tree branch between her legs and up through her body?" Not likely to go over with any sane and rational jury.

But MPD? Well, that might have some potential. For one thing, no one's really going to understand it; it's kind of mysterious and spooky. And it maintains the logic that the "real" you is an okay guy; it's just these demons messing with your mind that are doing the bad stuff.

I don't mean to suggest that multiple personality disorder doesn't exist, because it definitely does. The problem with it as a defense against a charge of violent crime is that it is very rare, and at that, much more prevalent in women than in men, and nearly always first manifests itself in early to middle childhood. All the MPD cases we've seen are a reaction to severe sexual and physical abuse, a coping mechanism allowing the child victim to split off into safer or stronger personalities to separate from his or her grim reality. Sometimes one of these personalities is an avenger who can get back at the abuser, but it is a fantasy existence. MPD cases are not always easy to diagnose, but any competent individual in the health or education field will be able to tell that something is wrong, and should seek help for the child.

None of the experts we've consulted knows of a case in which MPD makes a nonviolent person become violent. I am particularly skeptical when an MPD diagnosis arises not in childhood, but in postarrest adulthood.

Alley's psychiatrists concluded that his MPD had come from a combination of emotional abuse at the hands of his father and a childhood urinary tract infection that had prompted him to create a female persona.

After four postponements, each of which the Collinses found excruciating, Sedley Alley's trial commenced in March 1987. Fearing that the jury might not be able to comprehend a motive for so horrific and senseless a crime other than insanity, Hank Williams contacted the FBI's Memphis Field Office, which relayed the request that I come down to help with prosecutorial strategy. There was also hope that Alley might take the stand; if he did, I could help the prosecutors draw him out and show the jury the kind of person he really was. This approach had worked quite well in the Wayne Williams Atlanta Child Murders trial, when my coaching had helped the prosecutor to get Williams to explode. I sat behind the prosecutor's table, made observations and offered my perspective.

As it turned out, though, Alley did not choose to testify in his own defense. It certainly wouldn't have helped him.

During that trial, I got to know Jack and Trudy Collins quite well. We were staying at the same hotel and became close friends. I could see that they were devastated — shell-shocked, even — but their courage and fortitude were consistent and amazing. Despite Jack's law degree and their sophisticated background in the American Foreign Service, they still couldn't fathom how one human being could do this to another. It was as if they were coming to me for answers.

I tried to give them the same analysis of Alley's behavior that I had given Hank Williams: that even though the crime was as depraved as any I had seen, it was still the work of someone who knew what he was doing. There were some mixed elements to the evidence, but we were definitely dealing with an organized type of killer, rather than a disorganized one. When you see a genuinely, severely mentally ill individual commit a murder — which is rare — the presentation is overwhelmingly disorganized.

Seeing a young woman jogging on base at night, the offender had to assume she was a service member in excellent physical condition, with knowledge of close-order combat and an aggressive disposition if attacked. In spite of this, using his overwhelming height and weight advantage, he was able to blitz attack her by surprise, get her into his car and drive her to a familiar location, where he knew he could be alone with her. He was able to accomplish this even with two marines running after him as fast as they could. These are all indications of an organized offender.

The targeting of Suzanne was clearly a matter of opportunity, but it didn't "just happen." There would have been a precipitating event or series of them. He would already have been in a murderous rage, to begin with; his inhibitions would have been further lowered by alcohol. Likewise, the handiness of the tree limb was a matter of opportunity, but thrusting a sharp, phallic-like object between the victim's legs is the fulfillment of a developed fantasy. In a storage room in Alley's house, police found a twenty-inch-long stick wrapped with tape and bearing an unidentified stain.

This is all completely characteristic of a "lust murderer," a term Special Agent Roy Hazelwood and I coined more than thirty years ago for an analytical article we did for the *FBI Law Enforcement Bulletin.* The lust murderer is a particularly repulsive form of sociopath who kills — and kills the way he does — quite simply because it makes him feel good, because it fulfills an urge in him, a lust, that is satisfied in no other way than by literally destroying his victim.

This type of individual is continually wrestling with deep-seated feelings of inadequacy, which is why the perverse sexuality of the crime is often manifested in forms other than traditional rape. There is no evidence that Alley penetrated Suzanne with his penis, though that in no way negates the sexualized nature of the crime. The fact that blood was found on Alley's shorts suggests that he rubbed himself up against her after killing her. Not terribly surprising, investigators found a mail order penis-enlarging device in Alley's toolbox. He probably kept it there to avoid the humiliation of Lynne finding it somewhere in the house.

The necrophilia aspect of the crime points us in two complementary directions. It underscores the inadequacy of the individual, who knows he could never make it with a girl of Suzanne's caliber under "normal" circumstances. It also demonstrates the perpetrator's need to control, in ways he cannot do in real life. We'll never know whether he tried to come on to Suzanne and she quickly rejected him, or if he didn't even bother and just decided to take her forcefully. In the end, it doesn't really matter.

And this gets us back to the precipitating factors. Despite the unspeakable cruelty and brutality of the crime, the offender was not a sexual sadist like others we have seen. He did not hurt her for the sexual pleasure he would derive from seeing her suffer and hearing her scream. The savage beating around the head, something we often see in the murder of spouses or former girlfriends, is not to punish or cause pain so much as to dominate and then obliterate. In other words, what he wanted to do was destroy this woman and her beauty and all they represented to him.

Though it might seem a subtle distinction in the midst of this inhuman barbarity, I would want the jury to understand that all of the behavioral indicators told us that this rage was displaced anger against someone else, as well as a general hostility toward women. As we will soon see, this proved to be prophetically true.

Let's get back to the insanity defense that was employed at the trial, and review insanity in its legal sense. Actually, its legal sense is the only official sense it has, because "insanity" is not a term used by modern psychiatrists and mental-health workers.

The insanity defense has undergone many attempts at definition and interpretation since it was first used in England in the trial of Daniel M'Naghten who wanted to assassinate Prime Minster Robert Peel in 1843. Instead, he actually murdered Peel's private secretary Edward Drummond whom he shot at point-blank range emerging from Peel's house. Despite the years since then, this type of defense relies on the same basic and commonsense principles: Did the defendant know right from wrong? Did the defendant know that his actions were wrong? Was the defendant able to conform his behavior to the rules and norms of society?

The last two questions are stated in a neat hypothetical construct known popularly as the "policeman at the elbow" doctrine. It posits: If the perpetrator saw a uniformed police officer nearby, would he have still committed the act or would he have restrained himself? If he would have gone ahead and done it, he was probably suffering from an "irresistible impulse" and is therefore not guilty for his actions by reason of insanity. But if he could restrain himself, that suggests that he could conform his behavior and also knew his intentions to be wrong, something the officer would not tolerate.

Defense attorney Robert Jones tried to get the jury to buy the idea that the crime was so horrible, it had to be the work of some deranged mind because no one in his right mind could have done such a thing. I was there to counteract the concept of being able to use the monstrousness of the crime itself as a mitigating defense.

Am I implying that Sedley Alley did not have severe emotional problems or was not mentally ill? Not at all. I assume he did have severe emotional problems, and I have no real way of knowing whether he was mentally ill or not. However, I think it's fair to say that on a certain level, most, if not all, individuals who commit violent and intentional murder probably have some significant degree of mental illness — significantly further along the mental-health continuum than "normal" people. This distinction, however, falls more into the realm of psychiatry than law enforcement. And though the two fields often work hand in hand, they each have their own agendas.

When laypeople consider the insanity issue, it is sometimes difficult for good and decent folks to understand that a suspect can be mentally ill and still be sane and rational. The question is not whether Suzanne Collins's killer was mentally ill, emotionally disturbed or suffering from a character disorder. The question is whether he knew right from wrong, understood that what he did was wrong and could control himself to the point of not doing it *if* he thought he would be seen and caught.

In my mind, there was no question from the physical evidence and the behavioral presentation that Suzanne's killer was sane and capable of comprehending and controlling his actions.

Nothing came out during the trial that in any way supported the claim of multiple personality disorder or any other crippling mental disease. The closest was Alley's mother, Jane, who testified, "There's always been something wrong with him."

Yeah, he's a sociopath. But that doesn't make him legally insane.

In his closing arguments, prosecution co-counsel Bobby Carter said to the jury, "You've observed him for two weeks now, and he's been able to control his behavior."

On March 18, 1987, the jury of ten women and two men received the case. They deliberated for about six hours before returning a verdict of guilty of murder in the first degree, aggravated kidnapping and aggravated rape. They took another two hours to ponder the punishment, during which time they determined that the murder was "especially heinous, atrocious or cruel," and that it was committed during a kidnapping or rape. They recommended execution, a recommendation Judge W. Fred Axley accepted, along with the imposition of consecutive forty-year prison sentences for the two lesser charges. Judge Axley set the date for death by electrocution as September 11, though everyone knew that was merely a formality. The appeals process was the beginning of the next stage of the family's ordeal.

CHAPTER 10
ONE INDIVIDUAL STORY

"So here he sits on death row," I said as I concluded my presentation at Vanderbilt, "and he's been on death row longer than Suzanne Collins was alive. How about that?" I turned off the PowerPoint and looked out into the silent audience.

Then I told them about the Collins family, about how they had pledged themselves to "going the distance" with Suzanne, until justice was finally carried out, and that they could not rest until that happened. I told them that when Jack and Trudy, who had moved out of the area, came back up to Washington, DC, they would stay with Mark and his wife, Carolyn, and how we would all go out to Arlington Cemetery together to visit Suzanne's grave.

Jack would talk to her; his strong religious faith had convinced him that there was an existence beyond death. "Sue, it's Mom and Dad. Carolyn and Mark and John are here with us. They're fighting our battle for justice for you. You're not alone, Sue. You'll never be alone, and your friends will always be there for you, active in the fight."

It was difficult to maintain our composure.

Shortly after Suzanne's burial, Jack had taken up the Jewish custom of having each visitor find a small stone and place it on top of her gravestone. There are several interpretations of what this custom signifies. To Jack, as to others, it was a way of commemorating the visit and showing that those who loved and cared about Suzanne were with her spiritually twenty-four hours a day.

His ritual also included asking visitors with any kind of religious orientation to recite the appropriate memorial prayer from their own faith, after which he would recite the last verse of the English-Irish folk ballad "Danny Boy":

And if you come, when all the flowers are
    dying
And I am dead, as dead I well may be
You'll come and find the place where I am
    lying
And kneel and say an "Ave" there for me.
And I shall hear, though soft you tread
    above me
And all my grave will warmer, sweeter be
For you will bend and tell me that you love
    me

And I shall sleep in peace until you come
   to me.

As his final act, he would kneel and kiss the headstone.

But this was only the beginning of his and Trudy's devotion. They became part of the Fairfax, Virginia, homicide support group (officially known as the Peer Survivors Group) run by Carroll Ellis, and began attending their regular meetings. They reached out to other survivors of loved ones' deaths, and eventually appeared on television and radio shows, presenting the victims' points of view.

Their message was simple and powerful, and still is. They discussed the ineffable grief that they and Steve had all been through — grief that challenged even Jack's strong Catholic faith — that threatened to tear them apart or leave them unable to even function. They described how the death of a child, particularly a violent death, can rend a marriage and how they struggled to keep each other afloat when either of them was dangerously down. They explained how they would never be the same again, that the pain would never leave them, but that they found they were able to go on to a rich and full life — a life even more suffused with meaning than their previous ones had been.

And they pointed out that theirs was only

one individual story.

There is an old principle in journalism that showing an entire battlefield of bodies is not nearly as effective as focusing on a single one. Similarly, statistics are not nearly as compelling to emotional response as a single story. But the Collinses' message was akin to the one we have tried to deliver in presenting narratives of individual cases: Their single loss was devastating to so many people who knew and loved their daughter. Yet it was only one. Murders take place all the time, all over the nation and the world (though more, proportionately, in the United States than virtually any other Westernized nation). So take the grief and anguish from our case, Jack and Trudy were saying, and multiply it by all the cases every year and you get a sense of the enormity of the evil.

Crime victims and their survivors tend to be leery of the term "vengeance" because of its implications of vindictiveness and retaliation. Personally, I see nothing wrong with those sentiments, but I get their point. The term many of them prefer is "retribution," meaning something justly deserved, a punishment or repayment based on action or performance. Either way, the point is that the justice system, in the limited way in which it is able, attempts to balance the scales between the victim and the offender.

As we've noted, even at its best, this is a

very imperfect resolution, particularly in the case of murder. We can't bring back the dead. But even *trying* to establish some moral equilibrium in society is, I think, absolutely critical. Without the sense that individuals are responsible for their own actions, and that there are appropriate consequences to violating society's most basic values, the concepts of morality and right and wrong become meaningless.

And then you have no society.

CHAPTER 11
GOING THE DISTANCE

"You citizens of Tennessee voted for politicians who supported the death penalty," I said to my audience at Vanderbilt. "So you carry it on the books, you let your juries who represent you impose it, but you don't carry it out."

I told them how the organizers of the conference didn't want me to show crime scene photos because their use would revictimize the family. "But that's not what revictimizes the family. What revictimizes the family is announcing what the sentence is supposed to be, then not imposing it in twenty years. How can the family rest easy when they haven't been able to see that sentence carried out?"

"What about life without parole?" someone asked.

"That's fine, if that's what your law says, and you really mean it," I replied. "Some states have that. And if that was the sentence the jury and judge handed down, and you could be sure of it, okay. But if you support the death penalty in this state, then what possible crime could be more deserving of death than this one? If you don't use it here, then it's meaningless, and then what you have is a travesty of justice."

Here's how it went with Sedley Alley's case, and it's pretty routine for death penalty states.

After a death sentence is imposed, there is an automatic appeal to the Tennessee Supreme Court, bypassing the court of criminal appeals under the reasonable logic that it would end up in the supreme court, anyway. By the time a trial transcript was prepared, new appeals attorneys had come on board and oral arguments had been made, it was two and a half years after the trial, and four since Suzanne's murder. The state supreme court reviewed the full record and unanimously affirmed Alley's conviction and sentence.

Defendant's guilt in this case was established at the level of absolute certainty, the written decision declared. Yet this was only the beginning.

Art Quinn and Tim Holton, Alley's new attorneys, appealed to the U.S. Supreme Court, which denied the request for certiorari, suggesting they saw nothing noteworthy or reversible in the case. The attorneys then hit the habeas corpus circuit.

We're not going to review the entire legal

and political history of the habeas writ here. Let us only say that it is a noble and fundamental principle of our justice system that was designed as a procedural bulwark against unreasonable and illegal searches and seizures, unlawful imprisonment and other abuses of the system. What it was not meant to be was a second, third or fourth trial that could open up and overturn the findings and verdict of the original one. Yet, since the 1953 Supreme Court case of *Brown v. Allen,* that is just what it has evolved to become.

I certainly don't fault Quinn and Holton for taking advantage of every procedural nuance available to them — that was their job for their client — but the invocation of habeas corpus and its state court equivalent, "petition for postconviction relief," effectively allowed them to throw everything at the wall in the hope that something would stick. And that is what they did.

Alley filed a petition claiming his original trial lawyers were incompetent — a common ploy — even though Jones and Thompson were considered among the top capital murder defenders in the state. He claimed all sorts of procedural irregularities that kept him from getting a fair trial because the judge was biased. He even claimed he should get a new trial because Jack Collins had been allowed to get a cup of coffee from a pot in the judge's antechamber. Not only does this type of claim clog up the courts, each one represents a significant delay in carrying out the sentence, adding cumulatively to the victims' anguish.

By the time the very fair and responsible Judge Axley had decided there was no merit to Alley's petition, another year and a half had been eaten up.

Jack Collins was so disturbed by the inherent abuses he saw in the habeas system that he returned to the law library for the first time since law school and began reading up. He offered to testify for congressional hearings, noting that no victim or survivor had ever been in that role. He came to the attention of the national victims' rights organization, Citizens for Law and Order. He and Trudy became their Eastern Regional directors. They spoke to citizens' groups and law enforcement organizations, and I met up with them again when they came to Quantico to speak to FBI Academy classes.

At Attorney General Richard Thornburgh's Crime Summit in Washington, DC, in March 1991, the meeting where Supreme Court justice Sandra Day O'Connor voiced the opinion that current habeas procedures represented a potentially endless round of appeals *after* normal safeguards had been observed and normal appeals exhausted, Jack spoke for all crime victims, stating, "Until we know that the punishment of those who savaged us — or our loved ones — is final, we cannot begin to put our lives back together."

Though no one identified it at the time, this was one of the opening salvos in what became known as the victims' rights movement. It posited an extremely simple and basic premise that had hitherto been largely absent from criminal justice discussions: By virtue of the unwanted relationship the offender established when he committed the crime, victims and their families have a right to standing and a say in the disposition of his case.

For example, if at sentencing, the defendant is allowed to introduce any mitigating fact or evidence he can think of, why shouldn't the victim or her survivors be able to show what the crime has done to them? Out of this type of advocacy, the victim impact statement was born.

The Collinses didn't stop there. Jack testified before the U.S. Congress, giving them the victim's perspective. They appeared on national television shows. As they had encouraged me to do at Vanderbilt, they described the hideous details of their daughter's murder so that audiences would come to understand the kind of individual who would do such a thing. They pulled no punches. In their retirement years, they became militants.

In recognition of their advocacy, Jack was asked by AG William Barr, who succeeded

Thornburgh, to join the justice department as special assistant to the director of the Office for Victims of Crime. He accepted, and for two years he liaised with victims and victims' organizations, advised on legislative initiatives, figured out ways to make the office more efficient and responsive, and tried to demonstrate that the government did care about victims and their families. Until he reached his goals, Jack considered his business unfinished.

Meanwhile, Sedley Alley and his defense team were doing everything they could to keep that business unfinished. Having lost his petition for postconviction relief — that is, his claim that there were reversible irregularities in the trial — he appealed that turndown to the Tennessee Court of Criminal Appeals.

That appeal and decision ate up another year and a half. In April 1994, the appeals court handed down a decision that Judge Axley should have recused himself because of an offhand comment he had made before a Rotary Club group that one way to reduce overcrowding in jails was to "just execute some of these people that are already in line for it." So they ordered a new lower-court hearing with a new judge, and *only after that* would they rule on the merits of the claim itself. Another fourteen months went by.

In that hearing, the issue of ineffective counsel was again raised, with the charge that the original lawyers should have brought in more medical evidence and testimony about Alley's mental state. Since I was there, I can tell you there was plenty of testimony on that subject, as well as several pretrial delays for medical evaluations. Not only that, but in all the time since the trial, Alley had manifested no signs of multiple personality or again spoken of Billie or Death or any of the identities that supposedly cohabited inside his head.

The stress level on Jack and Trudy had grown severe. They didn't want to give up their advocacy, but they knew that if they didn't remove themselves from the fray, at least to some extent, they would collapse. In 1994, they moved away from the Washington, DC, area and settled into a comfortable house in a smaller community near the Atlantic coast.

The following year, the Tennessee Court of Criminal Appeals in Jackson ruled there was no basis for a claim of ineffective counsel or any other material defect. These findings of proper jurisprudence and jury verdict, and no indication of any exculpatory evidence, were repeated over and over again throughout the protracted appeals process. By this point, the court record ran to fifty volumes, taking up ten linear feet of shelf space.

That same year, largely through the work of the Collinses and people and groups like them, Congress passed and President Bill Clinton signed Public Law 104-132, the Anti-Terrorism and Effective Death Penalty Act, part of which was aimed at preventing the endless recycling of habeas corpus petitions. The act set up a process of judicial review before a petition could be heard by a federal district court. It wasn't a full solution to the problem, but it certainly was a start.

Suzanne had now been dead for almost eleven years. At no time had Alley denied the killing, expressed any remorse, or reached out to the Collins family in any way. In 2002, Alley went back to the Federal District Court for the Western District of Tennessee for federal habeas corpus relief. He was turned down and appealed to the Sixth Circuit Court of Appeals in Cincinnati, which covers Kentucky, Michigan, Ohio and Tennessee. Another complete review of the case, and another turndown. Every finding of fact and law had been consistent.

You might have thought this would have ended it and let the state get on with its business. The district attorney filed a motion with the state supreme court requesting a new execution date; it was at least the third by my count. On January 16, 2004, the court granted the motion and set the execution date for June 3.

At that point, Alley's tactics changed. He no longer claimed he was not guilty by reason of insanity. Now he was just plain *not guilty.* He recanted his confession and all of the details he had provided investigators and said he hadn't done it; he hadn't killed Suzanne Collins. He offered no substantiation, alibi or corroborating detail. He just said he wasn't there; and if the physical evidence was tested, his DNA would not be found and he would be vindicated.

On May 4, less than a month before his latest date with lethal injection, he petitioned the Shelby County Criminal Court, which heard the case and produced a twenty-three-page order denying his motion. The order stated: *[The] petitioner has failed to demonstrate that a reasonable probability exists that . . . he would not have been prosecuted or convicted if exculpatory results had been obtained through DNA analysis of the requested samples, and [The] petitioner has failed to demonstrate that a reasonable probability exists that analysis of said evidence will produce DNA results which would have rendered the petitioner's verdict or sentence more favorable if the results had been available at the proceeding leading to the judgment of conviction.*

In other words, the court was saying, had testing turned up Sedley Alley's DNA, it would have confirmed the verdict, but an absence of his DNA would not have negated or altered the verdict, since there was no testimony or evidence that Alley had penetrated Suzanne Collins with his penis or masturbated on or near her, or that she had been able to inflict any wounds that would have caused him to bleed. His conviction was based on a large amount of evidence, but none of it was related to DNA findings. This was definitely a sexual crime, but not one involving the exchange of bodily fluids.

He appealed once again to the Tennessee Court of Criminal Appeals. In another lengthy ruling, the three-judge panel reviewed every point of the trial and claim in the case. In a masterfully written unanimous denial of the appeal, Judge David G. Hayes responded, one by one, to Alley's arguments on why various sites of possible DNA evidence were irrelevant to the verdict or findings of actual innocence. For example, the court reasoned, a medium brown body hair found in the waistband of Suzanne's shorts did not convict him and would not have exonerated him, had it been shown to belong to someone other than Alley. They pointed out that Suzanne lived in a public barracks, where there were numerous opportunities for hair and fibers to be picked up in her commonly laundered clothing.

Moreover, the opinion stated, since her bloody hair and blood type were found on and in Alley's vehicle, *[it was] not reasonable to conclude that, even if the DNA of the samples revealed semen from another individual present on the victim* (and there is no evidence that it would), *the State would not have sought prosecution or the jury would not have convicted.*

Finally the court expressed serious questions as to whether Alley had requested this hearing to establish actual innocence rather than merely to delay execution, which is specifically prohibited in the statute (though I suspect, as Hamlet would say, "more honored in the breach than the observance").

But then the execution order was stayed once again when the federal district court filed a procedural motion. While waiting for its disposition, on March 28, 2005, the U.S. Supreme Court refused to hear Alley's case without comment.

This was where matters stood in January 2006, when I made my presentation at Vanderbilt. One of the reasons I was so forceful in my disgust with the system was that although Tennessee had about a hundred individuals on death row, they had carried out only one execution since 1960 — that of a child rapist and killer in 2000. Was capital punishment just on the books for some sort of symbolic value?

Word got back to the Collinses about the lecture and I got a call from Jack. "Do you know who was in the audience at your talk?" Jack asked.

"No, who?" I responded.

"Andrea Conte, Governor Bredesen's wife." Now, that was interesting, because not only was Ms. Conte the first lady of Tennessee, she was also a registered nurse, who also had an M.B.A., and was a hero of the victims' movement.

In December 1988, she was walking across a parking lot in Nashville when she was abducted by a man in a car. She fought him courageously and fiercely, and though she was hurt, she managed to jump out of his car as he drove. He was caught and identified the next year after murdering a woman in a Nashville park. In reaction to her experience, she founded the nonprofit organization You Have the Power to advocate for victims' rights and help them through the criminal justice system. In 2004, she walked more than six hundred miles across Tennessee to publicize and raise money for child advocacy facilities. She spoke frequently about victim issues, not only in her state, but also across the nation.

This was someone who would be able to break away from abstract statistics and procedure and understand the feelings and experiences of real people.

"It would be great if you could write her a letter," Jack said.

I didn't know how much influence she exerted with her husband or whether it would accomplish anything, but it sounded like a good idea. In a letter addressed to her at the state capital, dated February 1, 2006, I wrote:

Dear Mrs. Bredesen:

I heard that you were in the audience last Thursday evening at Vanderbilt University when I gave a presentation on the death penalty. I'm so sorry I didn't have the chance to meet you and chat with you. I heard some great things about you and your deep concern for crime victims. I understand you were a victim of criminal abduction several years ago and but for your own initiative and courage might well have become a murder statistic. Thank God that was not the case!

As you may remember from my presentation, one of the most horrific cases I have ever been personally involved in was the 1985 rape/torture/murder of Suzanne Collins, a 19-year-old Marine stationed at the Naval Air Base in Millington, just north of Memphis. Even though her killer, Sedley Alley, was convicted of first-degree murder/abduction/rape and sentenced to death in 1987, his appeals are still ongoing with no end in sight. In my opinion, this flagrant abuse of the appellate process is truly an obscenity.

The impact of Suzanne's murder on her parents and brother these past twenty years beggars description. As painful as her loss is to them, however, the failure of the judicial system to deliver final justice has had a dreadful multiplier effect on their sorrow. As a crime victim yourself, you have a unique basis for understanding how they must feel.

I don't know what, if anything, you can do about this situation. However, as a caring and concerned victim advocate and as a Tennessean, you should know the strength of my own feelings on this case, both professional and personally. It is one of the worst of the very worst that I have ever dealt with.

Thank you for your courtesy in hearing me out.

Sincerely,
John E. Douglas

Two months later, on March 29, 2006 — another year and a day after the U.S. Supreme Court turndown and now more than twenty years since the murder — the district court rejected Alley's procedural motion and the Tennessee Supreme Court set a new execution date of May 17.

In all the years since the trial, Sedley Alley had not been able to convince a single juror or jurist that he was not guilty or that there might have been the remotest reason to believe he was. But that didn't stop him. On April 11, thirty-six days before the once-again rescheduled execution, Alley went back to the federal district court with a new complaint.

Tennessee's lethal injection protocol, it seemed, might cause pain and distress and therefore violated his Eighth Amendment rights. The court stayed the execution until they could consider this.

Now, I am against cruel and unusual punishment, but lethal injection is the result of an ongoing search for ever-more "humane" methods of execution. Observation of the process suggests only a quick and peaceful end. But since the subject is no longer around to report on the experience after the fact, we don't know for sure how much pain and suffering it actually causes. I do know one thing: It causes infinitely less pain and suffering than being beaten viciously over your entire body, having your face and head pummeled until they are unrecognizable, and then having a thirty-one-inch tree branch shoved forcibly into and past your vagina four times.

The Sixth Circuit Court of Appeals must have had some sympathy for this point of view when they vacated the stay on May 12. The execution was on again for May 17. After all those years, it looked like the day of reckoning would finally come.

But then Alley's lawyers went before the Tennessee Board of Probation and Parole, asking for another stay so they could *go back to the trial court* and ask to have *other* items tested that were not included in his 2004 request! These included skin cells from the underpants found near Suzanne's body that were presumed to belong to her attacker, any cells or tissue found on the end of the tree branch and any material from underneath Suzanne's fingernails.

This time around the team was bolstered by a legal big shot. Barry Scheck achieved national prominence in 1995 as one of the lawyers on the team that successfully defended O.J. Simpson from the charge of first-degree murder in the deaths of his ex-wife Nicole Brown and her friend Ron Goldman. After that verdict, I had worked with attorney Daniel Petrocelli in the Goldman family's successful wrongful death civil suit against Simpson. So here was one more case in which Scheck and I had radically different views.

But I did respect him. Three years before the Brown-Goldman murders, as a longtime professor at the Benjamin Cardozo School of Law in New York, Scheck had cofounded the Innocence Project with Peter Neufeld, organized to use DNA and other scientific evidence to exonerate people who had been wrongly convicted of violent crimes. He had worked hard to get the new scientific analyses introduced before Cameron Todd Willingham's execution in Texas. Though that effort had failed, the project has managed to get

212

more than two hundred wrongful convictions overturned and a number of death row residents freed.

But I had to question why he was coming into the Alley appeal at this late stage. Like the Simpson case, I knew this one inside and out; and unlike Willingham or others Scheck and his team had worked on, sophisticated science or DNA analysis wasn't going to lead to a different conclusion or suggest a different killer.

The Innocence Project has done a lot of heroic work and championed people who were in jail erroneously. But Sedley Alley wasn't one of them, and that should have been clear to any experienced professional who took a close look at the original trial and evidence, or read the appeals decisions that had come out since then. I knew about false confessions, and this clearly wasn't one of them. The details were all correct, there was no police leading of the witness, and Alley's original story had been complete and made total sense in context.

I wondered how much of this maneuvering was about establishing actual innocence and how much was about trying to thwart the death penalty. If he was serious about showing that Sedley Alley was innocent and that someone else had brutally murdered Suzanne Collins, did he want to see that theoretical guilty person brought to the Tennessee death chamber, or would he then have tried to have that execution stopped as well? I felt bad for the Collins family, to have this new stumbling block put in front of them. I felt bad for the prosecutors and state attorney general Paul Summers's office, whose staff had put so much work into this case for more than two decades. And in a strange way, I even felt bad for the Innocence Project, because they were squandering their credibility on someone who was clearly not innocent, and had never shown an ounce of remorse for one of the most horrible crimes I had ever investigated.

When Jack and Trudy found out about the hearing, they traveled to Nashville at their own expense. This time, Stephen came with them. Jack and Trudy had tried to shelter him as much as possible, but his sister's loss had been at least as hard on him as it had been on his parents, and his normally serious disposition had grown darker and even more intense. He had been married and divorced, and some of his friends thought his marriage had broken up because he was unsuccessfully trying to find a woman who could live up to all Suzanne had meant to him. That had begun to change when he met Kassandra, whom he married in 2002. She was a strong, resolute and beautiful woman who had faced challenges of her own, and who understood the valleys Stephen had walked through. Now he was a successful telecommunications executive living outside of Denver. Before long, he and Kassandra would adopt a little girl, whom they would name Sienna. Her middle name would be Suzanne.

Through a member of the AG's team, Barry Scheck asked to meet Jack and shake hands with him. Jack refused, saying he wouldn't shake hands with someone who was trying to thwart the sentence a jury had imposed on his daughter's killer more than twenty years earlier. To him and Trudy and Stephen, anything or anyone who got in the way of the sentence being carried out was standing in the way of justice for Suzanne.

The defense team presented its case, which was essentially a rehash of the arguments they had made unsuccessfully before the trial and appeals courts. Then the Collinses read statements they had written. The chairman seemed particularly impressed with Stephen, and asked him to summarize the family's perspective.

The panel then left the room; when they returned, the chairman announced a split vote in favor of granting Sedley Alley a fifteen-day reprieve to try to make his case in court one more time for DNA testing.

The Collinses had been accompanied to the hearing by Lisa Helton, the empathic and highly respected and effective victim liaison in the attorney general's office. When Jack said he wanted to make certain that the governor had all of the facts, Lisa suggested they go over to the governor's office and see if he was in.

When they got to the state capitol building and went to Governor Philip Bredesen's office, the receptionist not surprisingly said he wasn't available. But shortly after that, he came out of his private office on his way to an appointment. Governor Bredesen cordially invited them in for a brief meeting. By this point, Jack said, he was completely exhausted and afraid he no longer had the energy to make the case forcefully.

Stephen took over, reviewed what had happened for the governor, and said that once the fifteen-day reprieve had passed, they expected him to let justice take its course. Stephen was strong and persuasive; and while Bredesen made no promises or offers, it was clear he had taken Stephen's passion to heart.

On May 31, the trial court denied the new petition for DNA testing, basically reaffirming every previous court ruling. By this time, Governor Bredesen's fifteen-day reprieve had run out. The state supreme court granted a motion to set a new execution date: June 28, 2006.

On June 7, Alley appealed, and the appeals court expedited the motion. Going through all of the twenty-plus-year history — factual and procedural — yet again, and taking the requests for DNA testing item by item, Judge

David Hayes wrote a thirty-one-page decision affirming the trial court's denial.

On June 26 came a final appeal to the state supreme court. Once again, Alley's lawyers made their arguments. The district attorney's office countered, "The petitioner has raised no additional arguments that would justify a different judicial ruling than the one previously rendered by the trial court and affirmed by the Tennessee Court of Criminal Appeals in 2004."

The court apparently agreed, turning down the appeal. The mechanics of the execution process began.

For a long time, Jack and Trudy Collins had resolved that if Sedley Alley ever was executed, and it happened in their lifetime, that they would attend. They had not been able to be with Suzanne when she died, so they felt that while watching her killer pay the price for his barbarism would not make up for that, it would represent the final steps in walking the entire journey with her.

But as the appeals dragged on, year after year, their thinking and feelings evolved. They had never hated Alley — it was unproductive. All they wanted was to see the scales of justice finally balanced, as much as the system was able to do, to show that Suzanne's life mattered at least as much as that of her killer. As a human being, Alley was now simply beneath their contempt. They decided not to dignify him by attending the execution.

"It was time for us to go home and for the state to do its work," Jack explained.

As they hoped, Governor Bredesen refused to intervene in the execution. Lydia Lenker, the governor's spokesperson, said that he "believes that this matter has been thoroughly and appropriately reviewed by the courts and therefore has denied clemency."

A final plea to the U.S. Supreme Court also was denied. In the afternoon on June 27, Alley was moved to a holding cell at Riverbend Maximum Security Institution in Nashville. Execution was scheduled for 1:00 A.M. on June 28, 2006.

In the flurry of activity that always seems to accompany the lead-up to executions in the United States, Alley's attorneys *once again* (a phrase which became all too common in describing this case) hit the Sixth Circuit Court of Appeals, this time through a hearing held at 10:00 P.M. at the Nashville home of Judge Gilbert S. Merritt Jr. Around 11:00 P.M., in a stunning move, Judge Merritt granted a habeas corpus motion based on a claim of actual innocence and DNA testing. The order, partly printed and partly handwritten, called for a hearing on July 7 to determine jurisdiction in the case and promised to render: *an opinion within the next three days further detailing the reasons for the entry of this order.*

Everyone on the prosecution side and among Suzanne's family and friends knew what this meant. Any question of jurisdiction would become a legal morass and begin a whole new cycle of procedures. God knew what the defense team would bring up once they had the chance. Maybe this time Alley would claim he had been abducted by aliens and they were the ones who had committed the murder. With execution supposed to take place within two hours, the prospect of more years of this ordeal still loomed.

Instantly AG Summers's office sprang into action and filed a motion to vacate the stay. It was signed by Summers himself, Solicitor General Michael Moore and Associate Deputy AG Jennifer Smith. It called the invoked procedure: *highly irregular and in brazen violation of every rule that applied to this situation, and because Judge Merritt's stay order is unlawful, the Court should immediately vacate the stay of execution.* They then went on to elaborate why Judge Merritt, who wasn't one of the judges who had heard the original case, should not even have been involved and had no standing to issue the order.

At 1:18 A.M., a fax went out from Leonard Green, Clerk of the Court. It was a two-page order from circuit court chief judge Danny J. Boggs and judge James L. Ryan assertively vacating the stay.

At 1:46 A.M., Sedley Alley was brought into the Riverbend death chamber. Through the viewing glass, he said good-bye to his grown son and daughter, and the lethal injection was administered. He exhaled twice, and otherwise seemed peaceful. He was pronounced dead at 2:12 A.M., central daylight time. He was fifty years of age. It had been twenty years, eleven months and fourteen days since Suzanne's murder. She had been nineteen years, one month and four days old when she died.

Verna Wyatt, head of You Have the Power, the organization Governor Bredesen's wife, Andrea, founded, read a statement from the Collins family. The statement began: *Rest in peace, Suzanne. The jury's sentence has been carried out.*

CHAPTER 12
"I CAN'T STOP THINKING ABOUT THEM"

The more-than-two-decade story we've just related is an achingly sad one. Yet by the grim calculus of murder, it has a "happy" ending. At least it does by our standards, and from the perspective of the victim's family and friends and the many who loved her. If there is a more perfect justice beyond our human experience, Sedley Alley was now consigned to it. And in our own human realm, the scales were balanced to the degree the system could do so.

After the case was finally resolved, we heard from two women, seemingly very different. Yet, both had been victimized, and both clearly were affected, each in her own way.

I had been surprised and somewhat disappointed not to hear from Governor Bredesen's wife after I had written to her. But it was what it was. Then, about two weeks after Alley's execution, I received a letter, dated July 11, 2006, and written on the stationery of the State of Tennessee, Office of the First Lady.

She acknowledged my letter and said she wanted me to know that my voice, as well as the Collinses' and other crime victim advocates', had been heard.

Of the entire gracious note, the sentences that stood out most poignantly for me were: *My heart goes out to the Collins family for an ordeal no one should have to bear. There are no words to repair the hurt and cruelty they have endured these past 21 years.*

Now I understood why I had not heard back from Andrea Conte; not because she was ignoring my comments or putting me off, but because she took me and my message seriously. If she had just wanted to put me off, it would have been easy to send a bland note thanking me for my interest and saying she had looked into it.

I doubt we will ever know what went into Governor Bredesen's ultimate decision to let the execution go forward in a state that continues to collect convicted killers on death row but seldom goes through with the punishment assigned to them. I'm sure he studied the case record and read the Tennessee Board of Probation and Parole report. But I would be surprised if the righteous, experience-based passion of both his wife and Steve Collins didn't also have their effect.

■ ■ ■ ■

Early in May 2010, I got a call from our lawyer, Steven Mark, that someone named Lynne wanted to get in touch with me. I have Steve's name as the contact on our website for book and media inquiries. She hadn't noted any publishing or media affiliation and her last name didn't ring a bell, so I asked Steve if he would call her back and find out what she wanted to talk to me about.

"I was married to Sedley Alley," she explained.

Wow, I thought. I had only seen her once briefly at the courthouse and I'd never had the opportunity to talk to her; so whatever she had to say, I wanted to hear it.

I sent her a confirming e-mail, then called Mark Olshaker. We decided it would be best if we talked to her together, so we'd make sure not to miss anything. We arranged a time with her; then a few days later, I went over to Mark's place. We got on extensions in different rooms and called the number she had given me. She suggested we refer to her here as "Lynne S."

She was living in Southern Indiana, the mother of four children. She was up-front and candid that she was a recovering alcoholic and drug addict, who had been struggling for years to get her life in order. This was a regrettable and damaging, but perfectly understandable, coping mechanism given the overwhelming circumstances she had had to face.

This interview, or debriefing, as it turned out, was highly informative and valuable for us. It confirmed the behavioral profile of an angry, abusive, inadequate and manipulative predator that I had constructed of Suzanne's killer. It filled in details that wouldn't have been in the voluminous court record. The conversation connected a lot of dots I had been speculating about for twenty years. It told the story from another character's point of view. And it provided some firsthand insight on what it is like to live with this type of personality.

The first thing I always want to know in any situation is: *Why?* Why did she suddenly contact me, almost four years after Sedley's execution? What did she want?

I asked why she had approached me at this point. She explained about a year before, she had Googled "Sedley Alley" and learned about our book *Journey Into Darkness*. She hadn't known about it before, but she read it and said she had learned things she had never known.

Much as I'd like to take this as a compliment, this is not an unusual phenomenon. In many ways, a violent crime is like a battle. As with the fog of war, every participant has a different perspective, and few, if any, have a complete overview. Witnesses see only a limited angle for a limited time. Physical evidence, hair and fiber, even fingerprints, only refer to one aspect of a scene. Not only are the prosecution and defense teams trying to offer divergently different narratives and slants on what happened, in most cases even the lead detective and district attorney will see things differently. The jury seldom gets all the facts or the full story, such as a defendant's previous record. If you compound all of this with the fact that Lynne, as a potential witness, was kept out of most of the trial proceedings, she would have a narrow window on this determinative event in her own life.

What she wanted to know was how the Collinses were doing. Better, we said, since her former husband had been executed. "I can't stop thinking about them," she revealed.

I knew she hadn't been at the execution and asked how she'd found out about it. "In the Louisville paper," she replied, and it became clear where her sympathies lay.

"At first, for an instant, I felt sad. I called my brother and I said, 'I feel bad about it.' And they said he was a model prisoner, and I thought, 'At least he got to live. The victim didn't.' "

Lynne had made her own journey in the last twenty years.

I was interested in her recollections of July 11, 1985, and the following day.

Had I been profiling the case without a known suspect, the behavioral evidence would have led me in one of two directions right off the bat. With the degree of rage, cruelty and overkill demonstrated by the evidence at the crime scene, the UNSUB would have been someone who either: (1) knew the victim well or (2) was displacing his rage from another young white woman who, for one reason or another, he didn't feel he could kill.

The next investigative step would have been to turn to victimology to determine which of the two types we were dealing with. Since a thorough examination had revealed no bad or even suggestive male relationships with Suzanne, this had to be an individual who matched the second description. For a stranger murder to be this brutal, it almost had to represent an instance of emotional displacement.

I had seen this phenomenon a lot. When I had conducted an extensive prison interview with Edmund Kemper, the so-called "Coed Killer" in California, he had ultimately admitted to me that the young women who attended the University of California, Santa Cruz, whom he'd picked up and killed were all in some way a substitution for his hated mother. When he finally got up the nerve to batter her to death in her bed with a claw hammer, he gave himself up to police. He had accomplished what he set out to do.

The same was true with Gary Heidnik, another case I worked on. This was a guy — a very bright guy, I might add, who made himself a fortune in the stock market — who kept women in a pit in the basement of his house in Philadelphia, raping them at will and punishing them as necessary. Finally he killed some of them. When I interviewed him in prison after his conviction, he was completely rational and matter-of-fact about his actions, until I mentioned his mother. Then he went nuts on me. In his case, his rage against women had been precipitated by his strange mother having committed suicide without ever having become the loving and nurturing presence Gary dreamed of experiencing.

In Alley's case, though, I didn't think the murder had anything to do with the offender's mother. Everything about the crime pointed to a lover or partner as the object of his wrath, possibly a series of lovers or partners. This was clearly someone who wanted to punish women, not for the sexual satisfaction of seeing them suffer as a sadist would, but to vent his built-up anger and frustration.

The other factor I was pretty sure of was

that there would have been a precipitating stressor or series of events that would make the subject want to strike back at someone. In many cases, the stressor is the loss of a job, but because of the sexualized nature of the crime, despite the lack of body-to-body penetration, I figured it had to be the loss of a relationship or some perceived slight or misbehavior on the part of his wife or girlfriend.

Lynne confirmed that she had been out at a Tupperware party that night. "When I got home he was gone, and the car was gone, and the phone rang and it was the base police and they said, 'Where's your husband?'

"And I said, 'You must know or you wouldn't be calling.' And they said he was down here and there's been a possible abduction. 'Can you come down here?'

"And I said, 'As you know, I have no car.'

"Well, they came and got me and took me down there and I knew something had happened just by looking at him. He was breathing fast and hard, and I remember his socks were inside out or something was inside out, and grass clippings were on him.

"I knew something had happened."

The base police, on the other hand, did not. Sedley had managed to convince them that what the witnesses had observed was a lovers' quarrel, that it was Lynne next to him in the car, and that it had all been an easily resolved misunderstanding. She got in the car with him and they returned home to their apartment on base. Lynne was twenty — a year older than Suzanne Collins.

"I remember he had some kind of compressor in the backseat, and I said, 'What is that?'

"And he said, 'I stole it from a captain's house.'

"I went off. I said, 'Are you crazy?' Then I said, 'We'll talk about this tomorrow.' I didn't want any part of whatever it was."

Lynne had signed up for base housing for herself and Sedley; though she acknowledged that even at the time, she was ambivalent about whether she wanted Sedley to join her there. When the apartment came through and they were together again, he got a job at a convenience store in Millington. But her husband was fired after substantial losses of inventory became apparent to the owner. A few days before, he'd gotten part-time work with an air-conditioning installation and service company, and now he was risking everything in using that position to steal.

"I went to bed. I woke up earlier than usual. He had never come to bed, and he was pacing the floor and drinking coffee."

The story she told of meeting and getting together with Sedley Alley was typical of many predator relationships.

They met in her home state of Michigan

when she was a fifteen-year-old high-school girl. She came from what she characterized as a "dysfunctional family." She was about five feet three inches tall, and was living with a female former staff member of the group home where she'd resided for a while. Recently her boyfriend had gone off the deep end and had committed "suicide by cop," shot down from a rooftop in Detroit.

Alley was nearly ten years older, more than a foot taller and weighed at least twice as much. He had come up from Kentucky to Ypsilanti, Michigan, following the tragic and pathetic death of his first wife, Debra. The late twenty-year-old had a drinking problem, he told Lynne, and one night she choked in the bathtub on her own vomit. The medical examiner's report classified it as an accidental drowning and choking on the French fry that was found lodged in her throat.

"He could be funny and superficially charming," Lynne reported. "But the bizarre thing is that I would go somewhere and I'd run into him. He was always there. I was in a Laundromat washing clothes and there he was. I didn't realize until afterward that he was stalking me."

All of this fits into the predator pattern. And leaving town right after the death of someone whom the police can associate you with is also a very predictable form of postoffense behavior.

The overwhelming number of predators I have dealt with and studied have two emotional pictures of themselves that are constantly at war with each other. The first is a sense of power and grandiosity, that they are special and not bound by the rules of conventional society. The second is a sense of powerlessness and inadequacy that often has its roots even further back than they can remember. The only way they can overcome this second sensation is by exercising the first. In my FBI unit, I used to teach that the three techniques they commonly use are *manipulation, domination* and *control.*

Remember, predators are profilers, too. So it is understandable that guys like this — and as we've noted, they are almost all guys — gravitate to women upon whom they can most easily practice these techniques. Women who are small, poor, lost, have low self-esteem, or are emotionally vulnerable because of some recent tragedy or uprooting in their lives, are all candidates. Lynne had just the profile that an inadequate, angry predator like Alley would look for. She fit the bill on many counts.

"I started hanging out with him and stopped going to school."

Once he had his hooks in her, he took her back to Ashland, Kentucky, in his own comfort zone, but not in hers. This is a typical move of predators — they try to isolate their wives or girlfriends, remove them from whatever support systems they have, make them emotionally and physically dependent. *Manipulation. Domination. Control.*

He used various techniques to break down her defenses, to desensitize her to his aberrations. "I remember one time him telling me that when he lived in Michigan, he entered a male-on-male oral sex contest in a bar, and he won. Even at the young age I was, that was pretty repulsive."

Frequently, she said, he would have sex with her after she had passed out from drinking. He would do things to her that she would never have agreed to of her own free will. This perfectly demonstrates the predator's need to dominate and humiliate, but at the same time his inadequacy, knowing that truly to have his own way his partner/victim somehow had to be disabled.

"I didn't like having sex with him on a good day," she commented. "I came to hate it. He was repulsive and nauseating, and I had to drink before I could face it. But even that didn't work."

The more resistant Lynne became, the more resentful Sedley grew.

"I got a little tougher, and I pushed him and he pushed me back. We got to where we didn't have sex at all." Which must have represented a huge threat and insult to Alley's sense of his own power and potency.

When predators can't effectively control their victims, their entire sense of self-esteem is challenged.

Sometimes Lynne would need to get away from him, but she had few options for refuge. She went to stay with his brother several times. Once or twice, she went to her mother and the elderly man she was caring for.

We were convinced that a crime as horrific as the one perpetrated on Suzanne Collins did not come out of nowhere. There had to have been significant violence in his past.

"Lynne, were you ever afraid for your own safety?" Mark asked.

"Oh, yeah," she replied. "One night we went to the drive-in, and it was he and I and a friend.

"We're all drinking and I was sitting in the middle and had a blanket over me. His friend was kind of feeling my leg, feeling me up, and then I black out.

"The next thing I know, I come to. I'm in my bed and he's straddling me with all his weight, and he's pressing down on my throat, and I'm trying to push him off me and I realize I can't. I'm saying to myself, 'God, forgive me for my sins. Here I come.' "

"Did you think he was trying to kill you?" I asked. "Did you actually think you were dying?"

"I *knew* I was dying. I knew I was going to die. I let go. And then he stopped. He finally stopped.

"The next day, I had to cover every mirror in the house because I'd get hysterical when I looked in the mirror. My face was swollen like a basketball. One eye was swollen shut. The other was a slit. My face was purple. The whites in my eyes were busted, and I couldn't even eat anything."

The eye injury she referred to is called petechial hemorrhaging, and it is something we look for in cases of suspected strangulation murders. With the force he was capable of exerting, she was lucky he didn't kill her. But the aftermath was also typical of abusers.

"The next day, there was all this remorse — 'I'm sorry' and 'I'll leave.' And I said, 'You're not going anywhere. You're going to look at my face!'"

She did call a spousal-abuse center. "But they said I couldn't bring my dog, and the dog was my baby." Again, this is not an unusual situation. Abused women or children will cling to anyone or anything they have for love or comfort.

When prosecutor Hank Williams received the Suzanne Collins murder case and looked into Sedley Alley's background, he was convinced, he told us, that this was not the defendant's first murder. He was upset that the death of Alley's first wife, Debra, in Kentucky had been ruled accidental. Williams felt that if it had been properly investigated and pros-ecuted, the Collins murder never would have happened. So we were extremely interested in whether Sedley Alley had ever talked to Lynne about Debra, beyond his initial play for sympathy as a grieving widower when they first met in Michigan.

"As time went on, he actually confessed to me that he killed her. He told me how he did it."

I had figured that if he had killed Debra he might have told Lynne, and not because he trusted her or felt a need to get it off his chest. Telling her would serve the dual purpose of letting him relive and reaffirm his own power and sense of not having to live within normal rules, and also as a veiled warning of what could happen to her if she didn't toe the line. After all, he'd already choked her nearly to death.

"The way he told the story, he kind of had you convinced, almost, that she had it com-ing. At least, I was so sick that that's the way I interpreted it, coming from him." To live with someone like this, you pretty much have to buy in emotionally to his perverted view of reality.

"He said he peeled her clothes off the same way you would as if you were peeling your (own) clothes off, where your underwear is kind of inside your pants inside out. And he said what he did was he choked her and then held her underwater. And he got her in the bathtub and made the water hotter than he normally would, so it would screw up the time of death. He used to tell me that her mom thought he did it."

Despite the series of hard knocks her life had been, Lynne was always looking for ways to improve herself. She got her GED, but could only get a job in a doughnut shop. Not satisfied, she took a navy entrance exam and scored well. She was sent through basic training in Orlando, specialist schooling in San Diego and was then assigned to the Memphis Naval Air Station in Millington. As soon as she got there, she went to the housing office to try to secure a place she and Sedley could live in together.

"I had fun in the navy," she reported.

With all that she had been through with Alley, I wondered what made her go to the effort to make it possible for Sedley to live with her on base.

"He had my dog," she explained. "I wanted my dog."

But she soon began to question her own efforts to bring him to Millington, just as she had wondered about it before he came. "As soon as he got there, I had intuition speaking to me: 'Ooh, what have I done?' But I didn't listen.

"He knew our marriage was over pretty much as soon as he got there. I'd come home from work and he'd be drunk. I didn't want to hurt his feelings, so I used to pray to God to please let him meet somebody and leave. Maybe that's where some of my guilt comes from."

Several of Lynne's friends and associates had uneasy feelings about Sedley. Her close friend Tammy came over to the apartment one day after Sedley had arrived. "She told me something about him scared her. Something about him just creeped her out."

We always say that if an individual makes you viscerally uncomfortable, there is probably a legitimate reason and you should pay attention to that feeling.

While Sedley was working part-time at the convenience store in Millington, she coped by doing more and more things without him. "I worked a second job in the theater on base. He pressured me to quit."

As Sedley warred within himself with his conflicting senses of entitlement and inadequacy, Lynne, like most similar victims, had her own conflicts between wanting to assert herself and have the relationship end and also blaming herself for their shared situation. When the base police brought her and Sedley in for questioning following the discovery of Suzanne Collins's body, she was at first defiant.

"They had me in one room and him in the other, and I didn't know anything. So I said,

'I want a lawyer.'

"And then they pulled out the picture of her with the branch sticking out. And that's when I broke down. I told them everything I knew, which wasn't much."

They had been to Edmund Orgill Park together, she and Sedley. Now to see photographs of this battered and mutilated dead body lying on the same grass where they'd let their Great Dane puppy run free was too much for her.

Even after Sedley was charged and put in jail awaiting trial, Lynne continued to be emotionally confused. "He had manipulated me so much, I even had letters where I would apologize to him and say, 'I'm so sorry this happened,' as though I drove him to do it. And he would say, 'It's not all your fault.'"

What an extraordinary — but sadly predictable — reaction! Imagine the absolute, unmitigated gall of magnanimously condescending to *share the responsibility* for this unspeakable crime with his innocent and repeatedly victimized wife. Just from this statement, it should be obvious why, in more than twenty years, he never accepted guilt or responsibility for the murder. Rather, he kept making excuses that it was an accident, then shifting blame to other personalities, then finally denying he was involved altogether. He couldn't deny it to his wife, who knew he had done it, but he was willing to let her take the emotional rap. *Anyone but himself.* In my mind, he met the purest definition of a coward.

As the trial got under way, she saw the manipulation continue. "The lawyers told Sedley to wear light blue," she recalls, "because it was an 'innocent' color."

Several times in court, she wanted to go over to Jack and Trudy Collins to tell them how sorry she felt. "I wanted to hug them." But she didn't feel it was her place to intrude on their grief.

She visited Sedley in prison a number of times, before, during and after the trial. At first, she would give him small amounts of money for prison commissary. Even here, she continued to show kindness, even though none had been shown to her. After a while, she would only go see him with his sister coming along, because she was afraid of being locked in the visiting room alone with him. The two women had a plan in case he "tried anything."

Lynne's life spiraled downward. "No one would talk to me, because they didn't know what to say." She couldn't deal with the fact that she had been living with a monster.

"I started doing drugs real heavy. Before I would go see him, I'd do cocaine or go get drunk. I remember when he was in the mental hospital for the criminally insane in Nashville (for pretrial evaluation), I was so wasted. I was AWOL. I just decompensated."

The navy career she had enjoyed so much was now unbearable. "I wanted out of the navy and they wouldn't let me out. I kept going AWOL. I became a drug user and had a bad car wreck. I hit a car stopped at a light, when I was high. I had the chance to run, but I said, 'No, I want this to be over with,' so I just waited for the police to show up."

Ultimately she was court-martialed, but Lynne doesn't blame the navy. "They really tried. I can look back and say they really tried. They were very kind."

She went to Louisville and stayed with Sedley's sister. She got a job doing data entry. Then she enrolled in college, kept at it for over a year and maintained a 4.0 average.

She saw Sedley for the last time about a year after the trial. "The last time I went, I remember just looking at his hands and thinking, 'Those hands did that to her.'"

It was only when she was sufficiently removed from his toxic presence that she could begin to think clearly enough to separate her life from his emotionally.

At some time around 2004, when Alley changed his defense strategy from not guilty by reason of insanity to denying he had committed the murder altogether, Lynne recalled she was visited by two female public defenders who asked her to help them with the appeals case. "They were really nice, so I invited

240

them in and they stayed a couple of hours."

But she said she couldn't help them because she knew that he did it; he had been the one who murdered Suzanne Collins.

They implied they could accept that, but she could be helpful, anyway, if she'd be willing to testify or sign an affidavit to the effect that during the original questioning, she had requested an attorney and had been denied. They explained that short of proving actual innocence, they might be able to get his death sentence lifted or postponed by showing irregularities in the criminal procedure.

Politely but firmly, she told them there was nothing she could do for them or her former husband.

Life hadn't been easy for Lynne. She married twice more after Sedley Alley. She had two sets of children with two husbands. But all through her experiences with drugs and alcohol, she never gave up hope or stopped thinking about trying to better herself. She enrolled in college again, with the goal of going into nursing or some field of medical technology. Though in a twelve-step recovery program, she said she continues to struggle with addiction. You can't help but admire the courage and fortitude of someone who has been through so much and still perseveres. She told us that she is more than willing to try to help other victims in any way she can.

Throughout all of the years since that horrible night in Millington in July 1985, one thought continued to haunt her.

"When he did that to her, I personally think he was thinking of me — that he remembered after he choked me that time, I told him, 'If you ever do it again, you'd better kill me, because if you don't, I'm going to kill you!'

"And that night he killed her, he knew he couldn't kill me because he'd definitely be caught." She added wistfully and sadly, "I looked at pictures of her. She was beautiful."

I asked Lynne if there was anything she'd like us to tell the Collinses when we next spoke to them.

"Let them know that I was a victim, too," she said with mounting emotion, "but that I'm okay now and living each day the way God wants me to. And that I can't stop thinking about their daughter."

People tend to forget that every homicide leaves many victims on many different levels. Sedley Alley's monstrosity took Suzanne Collins's life and ruined Lynne's.

Lynne S. firmly believed that Suzanne died in her place. I agree. Though, as we've noted, she was a victim, too, being saved by someone else's death is a heavy burden to have to carry. But it is one that Lynne hopes and prays has given Suzanne a special place in heaven.

CHAPTER 13
WHO SHOULD BE EXECUTED?

In previous chapters, we've described the capital punishment process from the defendant's perspective and specifically Cameron Todd Willingham's futile quest to achieve justice. So how, justifiably, can we support a protracted appeals process in one case and condemn it in another?

The fact is that we can't and don't.

It is legitimate and necessary to go through all reasonable appeals — to examine all of the facts and procedures and effectively deal with all of the issues of proper jurisprudence and the possibility of actual innocence. If any evidence comes up during that time, as it did in the Willingham case, it should be addressed and acted upon. That should be a no-brainer, even though it doesn't always happen that way. But an endless retrying of every element, and then appeal of each of those hearings, is absurd, denies justice and makes a mockery of the system.

The flaw in the Sedley Alley case was that

it dragged on too darn long for any rational reason. The flaw in the Cameron Todd Willingham case was that when evidence of actual innocence surfaced, it was ignored.

Ah, but if Willingham had been executed earlier, say three or four years after his conviction, Dr. Gerald Hurst's report never would have been written. That's true. And what about all these other cases where DNA had exonerated prisoners sitting on death row awaiting execution? That's a good point, too. Some will argue that had those prisoners *not* been condemned to death, no one would have bothered to review their cases and get them set free. But that's a pretty lame argument for keeping the death penalty.

Both the Willingham and Alley cases do get to the heart of my personal take on the proper uses of the death penalty. In other words, who should be executed and who should not?

The arguments for and against the death penalty are complex and diverse. There is a charge that it is imposed disproportionately upon minorities and the poor, who have little standing in society and can't afford the best attorneys. And there is merit in this argument.

There is the observation that the United States is one of the few civilized nations that still maintains capital punishment. This is also true, but irrelevant, I think. We are also one of the few civilized nations that still permit nearly limitless access to handguns. We can argue the meaning and relative merits of the Second Amendment; but as a career law officer and gun owner, I'm here to tell you that if you allow handguns, you are going to have more murders and more accidental deaths — a lot more. During the time we were writing this book, there were mass shootings in Arizona, Colorado and Wisconsin, to name but a few.

Easy access to guns is not the only reason we have so many more murders than other advanced countries. The reasons we do are as complex and disputed as the death penalty itself, and involve our relative freedom over many other societies, the size and diversity of our population, and the legacy of our often ugly history of race relations. But I think an argument can be made that a nation that suffers more violent crime, proportionately, than other seemingly similar nations has its own particular needs regarding criminal justice.

So having acknowledged these two factors, what are, and should be, the real dynamics of the situation?

First, while I certainly don't condone the fact that the death penalty does seem to be arbitrarily applied, we consider that an impetus for reform in the mode of fairer application rather than a reason for eliminating it altogether.

Second, even if one individual is sentenced to death and a second person is not for the same or a similar crime, that fact does not imply that the first individual did not deserve the sentence.

Now, let's look at who — and the type of crime — is actually deserving of that kind of sentence.

If you believe, through unshakeable religious or ethical belief, that the state never has a right to take a human life under any circumstances, including war or any instances short of immediate self-defense, then I am not going to convince you otherwise. I think there are some practical problems with this point of view, but I respect you for it if you are completely consistent, like ethical vegetarians who also don't wear leather belts and leather shoes. Surveys and polls repeatedly show that this is not, however, a majority opinion; most people do support capital punishment in certain circumstances. So what we want to do here is sort out a few of the important considerations in application of the death penalty and try to figure out if it does, in fact, serve any useful moral or societal purpose.

We have examined cases in the two states with the greatest number of executions since the 1976 U.S. Supreme Court decision: Texas and Virginia. The next two in the lineup are

246

Oklahoma and Florida.

Before his three distinguished terms as a United States senator, Democrat Bob Graham served two terms as the governor of Florida, from 1979 to 1987. A Harvard Law School graduate and highly popular politician, considered a moderate to liberal and widely respected by members of both parties in his home state and on Capitol Hill, Graham has supported capital punishment since he first had to put his vote on the line as a member of the Florida Legislature. But his *specific* views on the death penalty are instructive.

More than any other elected official, a governor in one of the thirty-four states with capital punishment on its books has to think about this on a personal level. In most of those states, the governor has the final word on whether a condemned prisoner lives or dies. Most of them face this responsibility with utmost seriousness, and Bob Graham, a deeply moral individual, is a prime example.

During his two terms in the Tallahassee governor's mansion, Graham was presented with scores of death warrants, of which he signed all but one. We asked him how many of those he considered not signing.

"Every one," he replied matter-of-factly, explaining that he took each case individually and seriously. "In order for me to not sign a death warrant, there would have had to be some flaw in the long process of reviews. By the time a person gets to the gubernatorial level, they have been through a very elaborate process. Had a set of facts come before me of actual innocence, I would have acted."

This did not mean an execution was carried out for each of those orders, however. By way of example, Graham explained, "I signed Ted Bundy's original death warrant. But he was not executed on my watch. In fact, I can't think of a single instance in which a first death warrant had been carried out. It would usually go on for years."

Graham has no moral qualms about the death penalty in the proper circumstances, but he believes the extended time leading to most executions "becomes a quagmire of process."

He notes that "the system is designed to protect the innocent. That builds in a lot of checks to protect the guilty, so sometimes you have the issue of executing a fundamentally different person than you started with."

This issue that former Governor Graham points out has come up several times in my career. In early 1998, the state of Texas prepared to execute Karla Faye Tucker for the 1983 murders of an acquaintance, Jerry Lynn Dean, and another woman named Deborah Thornton. There was a wave of international protest as the process went forward. The situation was unusual in several respects.

First, it was unusual for a woman to be facing capital punishment, and this was to be the first execution of a woman in Texas since 1863. Second, more than the traditional anti–death penalty crowd was lobbying for a commutation of her sentence. Not only were the pope and several Nobel Peace Prize laureates speaking out, but also such hard-line conservatives as Speaker of the House Newt Gingrich and televangelist Pat Robertson pled for her life on the grounds that she had found God and converted to Christianity during her long stay on death row.

A fair number of reporters and other media representatives approached me for my reaction; and to each, I said some version of the following: "I would hope in all those years in prison with nothing else to do that at least she found God and some sense of morality, and I'm happy that she did. But that doesn't change the law or the legal and moral obligation to carry out the jury's verdict."

I went on to explain that I feel it is always better to go to your death having made peace with your God or, for nonbelievers, with your own moral code. But the fact that the process dragged on for so long did not erase the crime, which in Ms. Tucker's case involved hacking two innocent people to death with a pickax when an attempted robbery went bad. If she had accepted God and truly felt sorry for her actions — and I am not questioning that she had — she should have been willing to pay for them on earth with her own life and face perfect justice and ultimate redemption in whatever existence may follow. Her final words suggest that she had embraced this idea, and I therefore have no problem praying for her immortal soul.

During the time he spent photographing the Texas death row, Ken Light recorded the final hours of Richard Beavers, before his execution. "Beavers had been a heroin addict," Ken related. "He had robbed his next-door neighbors in Houston and had taken them to the ATM and had them withdraw money and then shot them point-blank in the head. One of them died. The other survived and testified against him. He had been convinced by the fundamentalist preachers who came onto the row that if he gave up his appeal that he would go to heaven. The other inmates said, 'Oh, he was just tired of being here so long.' They were really pissed off because they felt that in giving up his appeal, that they were all being jeopardized — that you have to fight. You just can't give up."

This mirrors the case of Gary Mark Gilmore in Utah, the first individual executed in the United States after the Supreme Court upheld new death penalty statutes in 1976. This was a case made famous by Norman Mailer's Pulitzer Prize–winning epic *The*

Executioner's Song. Like Beavers almost twenty years later, Gilmore accepted his sentence and successfully prevented would-be supporters from keeping him from the execution chamber.

In both cases, it was as if the admitted killer had committed some further outrage by not fighting his sentence. To me, this is indicative of some screwed-up attitudes and values regarding the death penalty.

But it leads to an even more fundamental question. Is Karla Faye Tucker, despite the brutality of her crime, the kind of killer who *should* be executed?

Bob Graham would say, *not necessarily.*

"I'm less of a punishment person than I am a deterrent person," he explains. "The types of events that lead to the death penalty should be those that have the capacity to deter. For example, the death penalty doesn't work well in domestic cases because they're so highly emotional that the killer isn't likely to be deterred by the threat of punishment if he's caught."

One could argue the same thing for an offender like Tucker, who was hanging with a tough biker crowd and doing heavy drugs when she and her boyfriend went to Dean's apartment. While I don't consider her sentence inappropriate for what she did, I don't know that anyone was deterred from committing another crime by her well-publicized execution. And in my opinion, had she received a life sentence and spent her time in jail spiritually ministering to other inmates, that alternative punishment would have been okay, too.

But what if, after the trial and verdict, she or Richard Beavers had continued professing innocence, as Cameron Todd Willingham and Roger Keith Coleman did? It wouldn't be quite the same — they would have had to claim a mistaken ID and a strong alibi for the time and place, but let's say there was some doubt about their guilt, which there wasn't.

Then I would not have favored executing them. I wouldn't have taken the small chance on being wrong.

For sincere supporters and opponents of the death penalty alike, the one searing commonality should be absolute revulsion at the prospect of executing an innocent human being. As we were writing this book, the case of Troy Anthony Davis in Georgia was playing out its final act.

On the night of August 19, 1989, police officer Mark MacPhail was moonlighting as a security guard for a Burger King restaurant in Savannah. Spotting a mugging under way in the parking lot, MacPhail did what any dedicated cop would do, whether he was on duty or not. He rushed outside to aid the victim and apprehend the attacker. In the ensuing melee, MacPhail was fatally shot, and seven eyewitnesses identified Davis as the man they saw standing over the fallen officer and shooting him before fleeing the scene. There was little physical evidence and the murder weapon was not recovered. Davis admitted being at the scene, but he denied that he was the gunman. Two other witnesses contradicted this, stating Davis had admitting the killing to them. He was convicted and sentenced to death in 1991.

Though Davis was an African American, it's doubtful race played a significant role in the verdict or sentence. The jury was mixed: seven black and five white members.

For two decades, in a manner similar to what we have already noted, the case wended its way through the appeals process, including three encounters with the United States Supreme Court, the final one as a last-ditch effort to avoid execution. During that time, a number of witnesses recanted either all or part of their testimony, claiming in some instances that they had been mistaken, and in others that police had coerced or pressured their responses. During an August 2009 review, the U.S. Supreme Court granted a stay of execution on the basis of a "substantial risk of putting an innocent man to death" and directed the U.S. District Court in Savannah to review the case in an evidentiary hearing. Unlike his original trial, this time Davis opted not to take the stand in his own defense. Nor did his attorneys call two of the recanting witnesses or the man the defense claimed was the actual shooter.

In a 172-page ruling released in August 2010, Chief Judge William T. Moore upheld the trial court verdict and found no compelling evidence of actual innocence: *Ultimately, while Mr. Davis' new evidence casts some additional, minimal doubt on his conviction, it is largely smoke and mirrors. The vast majority of the evidence at trial remains largely intact, and the new evidence is largely not credible or lacking in probative value,* Moore wrote.

That was not enough for some observers. Like many defendants facing the ultimate sanction, Davis garnered a number of high-power sympathizers, including former president Jimmy Carter, my former boss ex–FBI director and federal district court judge William Sessions and former Georgia Republican congressman and U.S. Attorney Robert L. Barr Jr. I don't think anyone would accuse either Judge Sessions or Congressman Barr of being soft on crime.

In a letter to the Georgia State Board of Pardons and Paroles partially reprinted in the *Washington Post,* Barr wrote that while he supported capital punishment, that support was based on "assurances of fundamental fairness" and "accuracy." He didn't think those assurances had been present for Troy Davis.

Davis, by then forty-two years of age, was executed by lethal injection on September 21, 2011. His last words were a profession of his innocence.

It is not my intention here to second-guess the trial jury or Judge Moore's obviously detailed and careful review of the case. But this and other capital cases of this nature trouble me deeply. While the evidence in the case looks pretty good, no one seems *absolutely* convinced of his guilt. I know "absolute" is often a just-about impossible standard; but if we're going to take someone's life for having taken someone else's life, *we'd better be pretty damn sure.*

So other than the defendant's ongoing claim of innocence, what is it about *this kind of case* that makes me squeamish about the death penalty?

First, it's a one-off, not part of a pattern or spree, which makes it difficult to draw connections to previous behavior in support of motive or tendency to violence.

Second, it's a felony murder — that is, a killing perpetrated during the commission of another crime. Most felony murders are spontaneous reactions to immediate situations rather than planned events. While I have no beef with the principle that someone who takes a life while perpetrating another crime is just as culpable as someone who plans out a cold-blooded murder in advance, in actual practice these are often difficult situations to sort out. In my investigative experience, I've run up against such questions as: What really happened? Did the gun go off accidentally during a fight or melee? Who was the actual triggerman?

Felony murders tend to happen very fast, so even if there are eyewitnesses, they can't always tell exactly what they saw. The most compelling felony murders are often the ones where a firearm found in the suspect's possession matches up to the ballistics on the bullet or bullets taken from the victim's body. But that was not the case with Davis.

In December 2011, Michael Morton was exonerated of the 1986 beating death of his wife, Christine, in Austin, Texas, after almost twenty-five years in prison. DNA testing ultimately proved that Mark Norwood, a convicted felon with a long criminal history, was the actual killer. Though it was the DNA that proved exculpatory, it was the defense's discovery of long-suppressed investigative evidence that drove the reversal. Barry Scheck's Innocence Project petitioned for a court of inquiry to determine whether the prosecution had unlawfully suppressed the evidence at the original trial.

What is deeply troubling about the Morton

case is not only the quarter century during which this man was vilified and robbed of his freedom, but also the fact that this was the forty-fifth case in Texas in which a prisoner or death row inmate had been exonerated by DNA evidence. When you add to this number all of the murder cases in which DNA would not be dispositive, you've got a margin for error that simply can't support capital punishment for felony murder or single, patternless murders without an overwhelming amount of evidence in each individual case.

At the very least, there has to be some independent system of review.

When he was Florida governor, Bob Graham instituted yet one more level of protection for those facing capital punishment. It didn't draw out the process needlessly, and it made the possibility of a wrongful execution remote. Private attorneys were appointed as special counsels outside the normal bureaucracy, law enforcement and political system for six-month periods, during which it was their responsibility to review and investigate all processes with an item that might warrant commutation. The special counsel could then report directly to the governor.

Had this system been in place in Texas during the Cameron Todd Willingham appeals process, and had the governor had the same open attitude as Graham, it is highly doubtful that execution would have taken place.

But as many of us have acknowledged, time and again, there are certain crimes for which anything less than execution just seems morally deficient for a decent and humane society.

On the same night that Troy Davis was put to death in Georgia, Lawrence Russell Brewer was executed in Texas for the murder of James Byrd Jr.

On June 7, 1998, Byrd, a forty-nine-year-old African-American male, accepted a ride home from three men in a pickup truck who recognized him from around town in Jasper, Texas, northeast of Houston. The driver was Shawn Berry, age twenty-four. Lawrence Brewer, age thirty-one, and John King, age twenty-three, were riding with him. Instead of driving Byrd home, the three men took him to a remote location out of town; there, they beat him, urinated on him and then chained his ankles to the pickup. They drove him three miles along a bumpy asphalt road until his head and arm came off. Then they dumped the severely mutilated body in front of an African-American church and went off to a barbecue. Despite the fact that police found eighty-one separate pieces of Byrd's body, medical examination of his head and brain indicated he was alive for most of the dragging ordeal.

We pay a lot of attention to the specter of

domestic terrorism these days. But lynching was an accepted and tolerated method of terrorism against blacks throughout the South for a hundred years, and so represents perhaps the ugliest and most repugnant aspect of our national history since slavery itself. And this crime was among the most reprehensible since the horrendous murder of fourteen-year-old Emmett Till in Money, Mississippi, in 1955, a case that shocked and outraged the nation and galvanized the Civil Rights movement.

The difference here was that unlike the shameful complicity of the Money community, the Texas State Police, the prosecutors and the good citizens of Jasper demanded justice. The three men's involvement was quickly determined from evidence along the crime scene. Since Brewer and King were well known to be white supremacists, the police and DA labeled this a hate crime and called in the FBI.

All three men were convicted of murder in the first degree. Brewer and King received death sentences. Berry was sentenced to life since he was not known to have expressed anti-black sentiments, meaning his action could not specifically be classified as a hate crime. I consider this a somewhat esoteric distinction, given that all three were in on the murder together, but that's the way it went.

The day before Brewer's execution, he gave

an interview to a Houston television station in which he commented, "As far as any regrets, no, I have no regrets. No, I'd do it all over again, to tell you the truth."

It doesn't get much more depraved than this. There was no question of Lawrence Brewer's guilt, no question of the sickening evil of the crime, and no question of his attitude toward it. In my opinion, this is the kind of crime the death penalty was made for.

People often ask me, given my stance on capital punishment, if I would be willing personally to throw the switch, push the button or what have you that would end another human being's life. In a case like Lawrence Brewer and John King, or Sedley Alley, or any of those whose evil is tangible in their deeds, I would be happy to do so. I can think of few more righteous acts a just society can realize than sending a monster like this straight to hell.

In the months before Brewer's execution, much of the nation was horrified by reports from the first trial resulting from the murders of three members of the Petit family in Cheshire, Connecticut, in July 2007.

Early on the morning of July 23, Steven Hayes, forty-four, and Joshua Komisarjevsky, less than a month shy of twenty-seven, approached the home on Sorghum Mill Drive where William and Jennifer Petit lived with their two daughters, Michaela and Hayley. William was a well-known endocrinologist and Jennifer was a nurse and codirector of the health center at Cheshire Academy, a boarding school in town. Seventeen-year-old Hayley had just graduated from the prestigious Miss Porter's School and had been accepted at Dartmouth, where she wanted to major in biology so she could follow her father into the medical profession. Eleven-year-old Michaela was a student at Chase Collegiate School. Hayes and Komisarjevsky had staked out the house for a robbery, which they planned to perpetrate long after the family had gone to sleep.

When they arrived, though, they found Dr. Petit asleep on a couch on the porch. Grabbing a baseball bat he spied in the yard, Komisarjevsky bludgeoned William and then forced him at gunpoint into the basement, where he and Hayes bound him. They then went upstairs, grabbed Jennifer and the two girls, tied them up and left them locked in their own bedrooms. We can imagine the family's terror at this point.

The two intruders searched the house for money and valuables and were disappointed in their take. But they did find a bankbook. Hayes found two gasoline cans in the garage, which he took to a nearby station. Records showed he purchased ten dollars' worth of gasoline, which he took back to the house. He then forced Jennifer to drive with him to the bank to withdraw $15,000 on a line of credit. Jennifer managed to whisper to the teller what was going on. The teller called 911 while Jennifer left the bank and was picked up by Hayes, terrified of what would happen to her family if she didn't cooperate.

When they returned to the Petit home, the true horror began. Komisarjevsky raped Michaela, capturing the act on his cell phone camera. He then goaded the older Hayes into raping Jennifer.

At this point, Komisarjevsky realized that William, despite his severe injuries and being bound, had escaped. He told Hayes, who then strangled Jennifer and poured the gasoline he had purchased that morning over her, Michaela and Hayley and their rooms. The two intruders lit the accelerant and fled the scene and got into the Petits' Chrysler Pacifica.

While this was all happening, Dr. Petit had managed to wriggle free and get out. He said he felt a "jolt of adrenaline" when he heard one of the intruders say to his wife or daughter, "Don't worry. It's all going to be over in a couple of minutes." He got himself to the home of his neighbor, who didn't even recognize him at first because he was so badly beaten up.

When the 911 call had come in, police had

set up a perimeter around the house, trying to evaluate the situation before taking action to avoid innocent bloodshed. They had no idea what was actually happening inside. But when Hayes and Komisarjevsky drove away, they were apprehended only a block away from the house when they ran into a police car.

The medical examiner confirmed that Jennifer Petit had died from manual strangulation. Hayley and Michaela succumbed to smoke inhalation.

Now let's look for a moment at the particular dynamics of this crime. It began as what we categorize as a "criminal enterprise," that is, a crime for profit. Certain methodologies are needed to accomplish the crime. We collectively call these the modus operandi. We've all heard detectives on police dramas refer to the MO. The MO for this particular crime would include a way to get safely into and out of the house, time to look for valuables and a way to escape without being identified.

"Smart" robbers try to accomplish these goals as cleanly and with as little interaction with the victims as possible. It doesn't take a criminal mastermind to realize that this is best done when no one is home. But clearly, that was not Komisarjevsky and Hayes's plan. Part of their MO was to neutralize the inhabitants. Also, despite Hayes's later pathetic claims that "things just got out of control," the fact that they bought gasoline suggests that their plan for avoiding identification by their victims was to burn the house down and the family members with it.

Then, of course, there are the vicious assaults on the Petit family members. You could stretch the definition of MO enough to include the beating of Dr. Petit when the intruders were surprised by his presence on the porch. But the attacks on Jennifer and the two girls can only be chalked up to sexual cruelty and the desire to dominate and control. We refer to those aspects of the crime as "signature" to distinguish them from MO. They are not needed to accomplish the primary crime — in this case, the criminal enterprise — but are actions the offender takes because they make him feel better or fulfill some emotional desire. In other words, torturing the family had nothing to do with the initial criminal enterprise. The intruders did this because they *wanted to,* and that tells us a lot about them as individuals.

Among the great individual tragedies of this horrible crime is that the police, who had been alerted by the bank teller, did not intervene in time to save the lives of the three Petit women. I am sure they were doing what they thought was best not to risk the safety of the hostages; clearly, though, they did not know what was going on inside the house until it was too late. I am equally sure that this response will be reviewed and second-guessed for a long time to come. But regardless of what may have been the shortcomings of the police plan, nothing takes away from the enormity of the two offenders' evil.

The two suspects were tried separately. Each suspect's defense blamed the other as the leader and instigator. Two separate juries found them guilty of murder, capital felony and sexual assault, among other charges. Hayes was sentenced to death plus 106 years. The testimony and exhibits in the trial were so harrowing that for the first time in state history, its judicial branch offered post-traumatic stress counseling to jurors.

Komisarjevsky went on trial on September 19, 2011. His defense team blamed the older Hayes for the crime "getting out of hand" and suggested Hayes was the criminal mastermind; their client was only an unwitting accomplice. Of course, that's what an unwitting accomplice would do: rape a naked eleven-year-old and take photos of the act with his cell phone. There are no words in my vocabulary that can adequately express my contempt for this type of individual.

He was convicted on seventeen counts. Following six weeks of testimony in the penalty phase, in December the jury reconvened to deliberate on his sentence for the most serious of those counts. After five days, they decided he should be put to death. On January 27, 2012, Connecticut Superior Court judge Jon Blue formally sentenced him to death on six counts. I say, "God bless Judge Blue and all the jurors!"

Following the murders and anguishing trial, Dr. William Petit did not return to his medical practice. Instead, he established and runs the Petit Family Foundation and scholarship funds in memory of each of his daughters. It is one of the ironies of victimization that individuals who are good, caring and productive to begin with, often become even more so after their encounters with human horror.

In the Petit case, what happened and who did it are not in dispute. The crimes speak for themselves. The only issue is what should be done about them. As in the Brewer and King case, there is zero chance that police apprehended the wrong men or the juries reached inaccurate verdicts. Whether you are for or against the death penalty, I would challenge any decent human being to state that these men didn't *deserve to die* for what they did.

To the defendants themselves, I would like to say: "Given what you've done, the cruelty you intentionally inflicted, what right can you claim to live after you willfully denied that right to others?"

And to those, just as appalled as I am, who would say that the civilized state must rise above the actions of perverse and conscienceless killers, I would respond: "They refuse to behave on our level, so we must behave on theirs. It is a simple matter of self-defense for our society."

Those of us in law enforcement for any length of time all have our perfect examples of perfect candidates for capital punishment.

"Ted Bundy was a classic case for when the death penalty was appropriate," stated former governor Graham.

I can't disagree with that one.

Between 1974 and 1978, Theodore Robert Bundy, better known as "Ted," killed at least thirty women in seven states. There were probably a lot more, though we'll never know. His victims of preference were pretty, college-age women, with long, straight hair. If it was parted in the middle, that was even better. He was sufficiently good-looking, glib, charming and sophisticated that he could often find these particular victims, either by feigning a broken arm with a removable cast and asking for help, picking up hitchhikers or simply coming on to them. Once they were inside his VW Beetle, they would realize that the passenger-door handle had been removed and there was no escape.

Despite his college education, acceptance at the University of Utah College of Law and previous participation in both a Seattle suicide hotline crisis center and the Young

Republicans, Bundy's main motivation in life was to capture beautiful young women, hurt them, violate them and then butcher them. Crime scene evidence shows that he continued to enjoy relations with a number of them even after they were dead.

After escaping from jail while awaiting trial for murder in Colorado, he made his way to Florida by a combination of busses and stolen cars, and rented a room near Florida State University in Tallahassee, to be as close as possible to his victims of choice. On the night of Saturday, January 14, 1978 or the early hours of the 15th, he broke into the Chi Omega sorority house, because he had heard it had the most beautiful girls on campus. When he left only fifteen minutes later, two young women were dead in their beds — beaten, bitten and molested. A few blocks away, he broke into another apartment, where he attacked the attractive resident, leaving her covered with her own blood and her skull fractured in five places. Miraculously, she lived, but her permanent injuries destroyed her dreams of becoming a professional dancer.

His final victim, less than a month later, was a beautiful, dark-haired twelve-year-old named Kimberly Leach. She was last seen in the courtyard of Lake City Junior High School talking to a stranger, who was motioning her toward a white van. Her body was found two months later in an abandoned hog shed; her neck was sliced through and there was massive trauma to her pelvic area. The position of the body suggested that the choice of the hog shed had not been accidental. He had slaughtered her like a pig.

The Pensacola PD finally caught up with him on February 12, 1978, when an officer ran the plates on his stolen VW (he even stole his car of preference). Even then, Ted tried to escape, but he was overpowered.

At his trial, Bundy arrogantly opted to serve as his own attorney and may even have been surprised when he was convicted. It wasn't until the day of his execution — January 24, 1989, in the electric chair of the Florida State Penitentiary at Starke — that he finally realized he wasn't going to manipulate or bargain his way out of his sentence. I only hope that in the hours leading up to his confrontation with his own fate, he suffered one tiny percentage of what he put his victims through. And having both studied and consulted on this case, I can tell you that though he'd been in prison for more than a decade, hearing about his execution was the first time I rested easy that this monster would not kill again.

We can talk about Bundy's bad background and the social upheaval of his youth. We can speculate that had someone noticed his early cruelty, lack of empathy and antisocial behavior, perhaps there could have been some intervention that would have set him up on the right path, or at least made authorities aware of him. And if he had been incarcerated for his early burglaries and car thefts, maybe he wouldn't have had the opportunity to kill those women.

But a lot of people have bad backgrounds — a lot worse than Ted Bundy's — and they don't end up as serial killers. Bundy did what he did because he wanted to, because it gave him greater pleasure and satisfaction than any other life experience or endeavor. I defy anyone to tell me that an individual such as this could be rehabilitated.

Even one of his own defense attorneys, Polly Nelson, stated that, "Ted was the very definition of heartless evil."

With violent, serial sexual predators like Ted Bundy, the normal rules don't apply. They have no conscience and cannot be given one through any known means of therapy, correction or behavioral modification. By their very definition, they have killed repeatedly and in a definable pattern, so we are virtually never worried that we have caught or convicted the wrong man. Because their motive has to do with the emotional satisfactions of manipulation, domination and control, and therefore tend to be particularly cruel and sadistic, involving a maximum amount of suffering on the part of the victim, their crimes generally qualify as "special circumstances." And we now know enough about their pathology to know that the vast majority of them, if ever freed or able to escape from prison, will kill again.

What is the point of keeping individuals like this in prison for the rest of their lives — people who we know are guilty and know would kill again, if given the chance — other than the moral abstraction that the state should not take a life? If we are not going to let them out, if we know we cannot change their attitudes, why would we warehouse them for thirty or forty years?

Of course, this is not a universally held opinion. In November 2011, Oregon Democratic governor John Kitzhaber issued a temporary reprieve from execution for Gary Haugen, a twice-convicted murderer. Kitzhaber, a physician, health care policy expert and well known as a deeply moral man, stated, "It is time for Oregon to consider a different approach. I refuse to be a part of this compromised and inequitable system any longer, and I will not allow further executions while I am governor."

He went on to say that the two executions carried out during his first term "were the most agonizing and difficult decisions I have made as governor, and I have revisited and questioned them over and over again during the past fourteen years. I do not believe that those executions made us safe, and certainly they did not make us nobler as a society. And I simply cannot participate once again in something I believe to be morally wrong."

This mirrors Illinois Republican governor George Ryan's actions in 2000, when he instituted a moratorium on execution in the state, declaring, "We have now freed more people than we have put to death under our system. There is a flaw in the system, without question, and it needs to be studied." Before he left office in January 2003, he commuted to life the death sentences of the 167 residents on the state's death row. "I still believe the death penalty is a proper response to heinous crimes," he explained. "But I believe it has to be where we don't put innocent people to death."

Unfortunately for himself and the citizens of Illinois, Ryan was subsequently convicted of public corruption, not a unique charge among Illinois governors. But I have no doubt regarding the sincerity of his feelings on capital punishment. And there is no doubt that as an institution, it has to be reformed.

I agree with Governor Ryan that it is still dangerously possible that an innocent person can be executed. And I agree with Governor Kitzhaber that as sporadically and inconsistently as they are carried out, executions don't make us any safer on a certain level.

But on another level, they do. As we say in law enforcement: Capital punishment may or may not be a *general deterrent* to violent crime, but it sure is a *specific deterrent*. According to our statistics, no one who has been executed has ever killed again. No other means of punishment or correction has such a consistent and predictable record.

But as to the second point, while I appreciate his intention and message, I respectfully disagree with Governor Kitzhaber. I believe we have to maintain some standards and say there are certain crimes that are just so heinous that the noblest thing we can do is remove their perpetrators from our midst.

In 1960, the Mossad, Israel's Secret Service, captured Adolf Eichmann, one of the key administrative architects of the Nazi "Final Solution" against the Jews. He was apprehended in Argentina and was brought back to Israel for trial. Before the trial began, Israel instituted a civilian death penalty, which the nation had not felt it needed before then. But for a monster that had done what Eichmann had, no other punishment seemed adequate. Few rational, compassionate people around the world disagreed with this action.

Moral equivalence often leads down a slippery philosophical slope. But we need to ask: Is an individual any less morally culpable if he willfully tortures to death *only* one or two or five innocent people than if he oversees the destruction of as much of an entire ethnic group as he can? I say no. Certainly, a genocidal crime like Eichmann's has a larger impact on society and the human race, and so is greater from a macro, sociopolitical point of view. But the Talmud, the centuries-old collection of Jewish law and commentary, states that saving a single life is like saving the world, and taking a single life is like destroying the entire world.

In her landmark philosophical tract, *Eichmann in Jerusalem: A Report on the Banality of Evil,* Hannah Arendt was highly critical of the trial and the way it was conducted by "the victors," just as she had been of the Nuremberg trials fifteen years earlier. But she was not critical of the sentence. It was natural and understandable, she felt, that the people with whom Eichmann did not want to share the earth would not want to share the earth with him.

Anyone who has committed hideous, intentional murder against another person, it seems to me, is equally liable to Professor Arendt's logic.

You probably will have noted that most of the defendants we are dealing with in this book — the ones we say are innocent, as well as the ones we say are not — are white. This is not to suggest that an unfair and inappropriate percentage of capital sentences are not handed out to African Americans, Hispanics and other minorities. We are only pointing out that the kinds of offenders we feel the death penalty is most appropriate for tend to be white males. While a disproportionate number of felony murderers may be black, it is predominantly whites that commit the sexually violent, predatory-type crimes. This is not a discriminatory statement, merely a statistical observation. But the numbers are not an abstraction to me. I have seen the absolute horror of what these vicious predators are capable of doing. Because of these types of individuals, I believe the death penalty needs to be maintained.

There is power to the argument that as long as we can't have godlike certainty, we shouldn't take on the godlike power of life and death. But as long as the types of people I've just described continue to exist in our midst, we need an effective way to purge ourselves of them, and a way to make an ultimate moral judgment and demonstration.

Bottom line: The system is not perfect and never will be, despite advances in science and our best efforts. But there are certain crimes — certain willful acts by human beings that are so vile and hideous and remorseless — that no other response from society can appropriately address them.

If and when we can ever come up with a

system that can tell for sure whether "routine" one or two-time murder defendants are guilty, and can evaluate to a psychiatric certainty that they acted out of a free will not completely neutralized by a horrible childhood, I will embrace the death penalty for a good many premeditated murders. Until then, I will be satisfied to settle for applying it to those predators whose guilt is unquestionable, whose intentions are unmistakable, whose cruelty is despicable, and whose values fly in the face of everything it means to live in a civilized society.

Sedley Alley, Lawrence Russell Brewer, John King, Steven Hayes, Joshua Komisarjevsky — if you want to reserve the death penalty for the worst of the worst, I think we've just defined it. And I, for one, don't want to share the earth with any of them.

....

PROSECUTION V. PERSECUTION OR GETTING TO THE TRUTH ABOUT RAMSEY

....

CHAPTER 14
A CHRISTMAS NIGHTMARE

PREJUDICE: an adverse judgment or opinion formed beforehand or without knowledge or examination of the facts.
— *American Heritage Dictionary of the English Language*

Throughout my career, I've gotten used to taking a lot of criticism as the price for furthering what I believed in and wanted to do. But I was totally unprepared for the barrage of condemnation that came my way when, after I'd already left the Bureau, I became involved in the JonBenét Ramsey murder case. I was taken to task for selling out, for thwarting justice, for grabbing publicity at the expense of a murdered child. Some of my former FBI colleagues said I had "gone over to the dark side."

The Ramsey case and the reaction to it — by many in the public, the media and law enforcement — represented just about everything we've been criticizing here: overreliance on statistics to the disadvantage of specifics, impressions and theory over evidence, and the relentless pursuit of a *good* story over a *true* story.

Daniel Kahneman, the Princeton psychologist who won the 2002 Nobel Memorial Prize in Economic Sciences for his work on prospect theory, put it succinctly in his brilliant book *Thinking, Fast and Slow: When people believe a conclusion to be true, they are also very likely to believe arguments that appear to support it, even when these arguments are unsound.*

As the cases in my and Mark's book demonstrate, determining *who didn't commit the crime* can be equally as critical as who did. That's where the Ramsey case comes in.

For whatever reason, certain murder cases, as we've seen, acquire a "life of their own." What was it that so captured the public's imagination and the media's attention in this case: The angelic little victim? The indelible contest images of her two-stepping in rhinestone-cowgirl duds and strutting her prepubescent stuff as a mini Vegas showgirl? The wealthy and prominent parents who lawyered up as soon as the going got rough? The intimations of a father's sexual abuse and a mother's barely suppressed jealousy and violent streak? The fact that it happened on Christmas Day?

All of the above, and more. Perhaps the

most elemental factor is that JonBenét, with her blond tresses, luminous blue eyes and sparkling personality, became everyone's child, an idealized "little girl next door." The death of this charming, magical little miss brought home to all of us the vulnerability of childhood and the fragility of happiness.

The case has been written about extensively, so there is no need to repeat all of the details. What is important here is to show the points at which critical errors of judgment or interpretation sent the investigation completely off track and nearly doomed two innocent and grieving victims.

To give you my perspective, we'll start where I came in.

On Monday, January 6, 1997, I was in Provo, Utah, with the chief of police there, Greg Cooper. Greg had been one of the best profilers in my unit at Quantico, and I was working with him to prepare a training seminar for police officers. I'd been retired from the Bureau for about a year and a half.

Some former special agents from my unit, like Greg, remained in formal law enforcement. A number of others had joined organizations like the Academy Group, a forensic consulting and training firm built around veterans from the FBI Academy. In addition to writing books with Mark, I decided to go it alone, figuring I would have more freedom and flexibility to investigate, do research and speak as I wished. Like all special agents, I had spent my FBI career in a group setting, with a lot of time devoted to training and supervising others. Now I relished the idea of working on my own, choosing projects that meant something to me, like this seminar with Greg.

When I checked my voice mail, there was a message from a man who identified himself as a private investigator from Denver named H. Ellis Armistead. He said he had been hired by John and Patricia "Patsy" Ramsey regarding the homicide of their daughter and asked if I was available to provide assistance in the investigation. I replied that I had several more days here in Provo, but that if they still wanted me later in the week, I thought I was available. Like everyone else, I had heard about the murder of this little girl, but with the holidays, travel and preparing for the seminar, I didn't know many of the details.

I learned later that another former member of my unit had also been approached, but he had declined based on his assumption that the Ramseys were guilty. He did not want to work on behalf of murderers. Based on the sketchy details I had heard, I thought there was a pretty good chance one or both of the parents were responsible for the murder, but I didn't presume to know enough to make that judgment on a factual basis. Statistically, most murders of children occurring inside the house are committed by parents or other close relatives; but in our business, statistics are only a starting point. Each case is unique and has to be figured out on its own specific terms. Also, I didn't want to get the reputation of someone who makes up his mind before examining the evidence. So as long as my terms were agreed to, I said I would take the case.

Lee Foreman, a member attorney with Haddon, Morgan, and Foreman, the firm John Ramsey hired, called and said I would be dealing with and reporting to them. On the January 8 flight from Salt Lake City to Denver, I made some general notes to organize the case in my own mind. I was interested in knowing:

1. The basic facts of the case: who was in the house, when did the murder happen, what was the cause of death, how was the body found and by whom, was there much blood or any evidence of sexual assault?
2. Where was the ransom note found, and what did it say?
3. What were the profiles of the family members, and did they have any known enemies?
4. Who had access to the house?
5. How many people knew about the

child's talent show appearances?

When I arrived in Denver, I met with Lee Foreman and Bryan Morgan in their offices. As a private consultant, I knew my working rules had to be different than they'd been in the Bureau. There, I had only been working for one "side": the law enforcement agency. I explained that, as with my FBI clients, I would conduct an independent examination of the facts and evidence made available to me. Whatever I came up with, they could use or ignore as they saw fit, but I would not alter my findings to suit anyone else's purposes or theory of the case.

I told Foreman and Morgan they could buy my time and expertise, and I would give them a report, verbal at first. If they chose to use it — fine. I would write it up with the mutual understanding that since I am not an attorney, it may be subject to subpoena. If they didn't want to use it, I would not speak publicly or reveal what I had learned, but I reserved the right to speak on publicly available information. In either case, I would not shade or alter any opinion to suit a client.

Much of that first meeting was devoted to disabusing me of some of my preconceived notions about the case, about which I still knew very little.

For example, I was under the impression

that JonBenét had been a professional model rather than just a participant in child beauty pageants. Second, I thought there had been some considerable delay in contacting the police. In fact, it had happened as soon as Patsy had noticed the ransom note on the bottom of a circular staircase, despite the note's warnings not to contact law enforcement authorities. Third, it was my impression that John and Patsy had been uncooperative and had been stonewalling the police in their investigation. Morgan informed me that they had been completely cooperative, that they had welcomed a complete search of their house, had answered all questions and offered blood and handwriting samples.

They had only "lawyered up," the attorneys told me, when John and Patsy had perceived that the Boulder Police Department and the Boulder County District Attorney's Office considered them leading suspects in the murder.

When I asked how the body was found, the attorneys told me that with the knowledge and consent of the officer on the scene, John Ramsey and his close friend Fleet White had searched the house, and that ultimately John himself had discovered the bound and gagged body of his daughter on the floor of a remote basement storage room, which they called "the wine cellar."

This fact intrigued me more than any other.

In my unit's long and extensive experience with child abduction and murder, if a family member has committed the crime, then it has to be staged to look like something else, such as a kidnapping or a burglary gone bad, or even a rape. You can't just report to the police that your child has been mysteriously murdered, because the suspicion naturally falls directly on you, unless there is evidence of someone else having done it. As a result, the killer almost always "arranges" to have someone else find the body. In this case, it would have been quite easy for John Ramsey to suggest to Fleet White that he go look around the area of the wine cellar, but instead he did it himself.

When the body was discovered, a blanket was wrapped around the torso, but the arms and legs were sticking out. This also didn't seem like a parental murder to me. Normally, when a parent kills a child, there is some care given to covering the body and making it dignified and protected. We sometimes call this a "softening" of the appearance in which the body will be found. No matter what kind of parent you are, it's hard to kill your child without some sense of guilt or remorse.

There was hardly any blood in the area that constituted the extended murder scene — from JonBenét's second-floor bedroom, down the circular staircase to the kitchen, then down another set of stairs to the basement landing, through the boiler room and into the wine cellar. There was a small amount of blood in the crotch of her panties, and another stain that the lawyers said appeared to be semen. If it was semen and matched John Ramsey's DNA, then that would be the case right there.

But I was doubtful it would prove to be semen — John's or anyone else's — and I wrote that in the notes I took at the time. JonBenét suffered massive blunt-force trauma to the head, and it was not our collective experience that offenders with this much obvious rage and aggression would engage in penile rape. Some other form of abuse — inserting fingers or an object — might be expected if he wanted to show his contempt or sense of control, which is what I believed the blood on the panties represented. This was about anger and retaliation, probably against John and merely taken out on his innocent and defenseless daughter. But this was not the presentation of someone who was primarily obsessed with having sex with a little girl.

We would later learn that the semen report was erroneous.

The evening of my arrival, Bryan Morgan and Ellis Armistead took me to the Ramsey house in Boulder. The neighborhood was definitely upscale, the kind you'd target if you were a sophisticated burglar. I was also told that the home recently had been part of a charity open-house tour, which is among the easiest ways for would-be intruders to case potential targets. I didn't like the fact that anyone could have learned the layout of the place this way. And I didn't like it when I found out that though the house had a functioning alarm system, the Ramseys had stopped using it because JonBenét and her nine-year-old brother, Burke, kept setting it off by accident.

The house had been added onto by the Ramseys and had a somewhat choppy layout, suggesting that whoever the killer was, he or she probably had some familiarity with the interior to maneuver around, enter Jon-Benét's bedroom and ultimately find the wine cellar.

I tried several experiments to find out what could be heard in the parents' third-floor bedroom from elsewhere in the house. Not much. On the other hand, given the complicated layout of the house and the location of the body, this was a high-risk crime on the part of the perpetrator. Had he been confronted in the wine cellar, there would have been no other route out. He would have been trapped.

There were also about six entry doors on the first floor and a balcony off JonBenét's room, which wouldn't have been difficult to reach with a stepladder or by climbing on a garbage can. So as far as the house layout was concerned, this crime could have been committed by either an insider or an intruder.

The next day, I met with the Ramseys at the Haddon, Morgan, and Foreman offices. First, I asked to meet alone with John Ramsey. He seemed appropriately sad and depressed. Five years earlier, John's oldest daughter from his first marriage, Elizabeth ("Beth"), had been killed in an automobile accident in Chicago with her friend Matt Darrington. Beth was twenty-two, and John had gone into the depths of an extended mourning. This might have accounted for the books I had noticed in his house on grieving and loss. And about two years after the accident, Patsy had been diagnosed with stage III ovarian cancer, soon downgraded to stage IV. She had undergone months of rigorous and debilitating treatment at the National Cancer Institute in Bethesda, Maryland. She was currently in remission from this deadly specter. (Sadly, the cancer ultimately returned and she passed away in 2006.)

John had run a computer distribution company in Atlanta called Microsouth. A divorced man, with older children, he had met Patricia Paugh and they had married. Patsy's father, Donald, a former Union Carbide executive, worked for John's company. It had merged with two other companies to form Access Graphics. John moved with Patsy, son Burke, daughter JonBenét and father-in-law Donald to Colorado, to become chief executive. The company topped a billion dollars in annual sales and was sold to Lockheed Martin. John stayed on as chief. At this point, he and Patsy had been married for sixteen years.

John took me through the entire day of Christmas: the children waking up early to open their presents while he and Patsy took photographs; their 4:00 P.M. dinner at Fleet and Priscilla White's house, six blocks away; two brief stops to exchange gifts with other friends; then they went back home, where he carried a sleeping JonBenét up to her bedroom, played a game with Burke and set the alarm for 5:30 A.M. They would pick up his two older children and his prospective son-in-law at the airport, who were coming in to join them for the family's flight to Michigan. After that, they were heading to Florida with Burke and JonBenét for a cruise on Disney's *Big Red Boat.* John described the horror and panic of finding the ransom note, the arrival of Officer Rick French, then other police personnel responding, as well as the Whites and other friends, John and Barbara Fernie, coming to the house. And he recalled finding JonBenét's body, ripping off the black duct tape that covered her mouth and carrying her upstairs to the living room.

That detail interested me just as much as

John being the one to discover the body. If he, or he and Patsy, had killed their daughter, then staged it to look like some other kind of crime, why would he *unstage* it before authorities got to see it? Not only did he rip off the duct tape, he tried hard to loosen the cord that bound her wrists.

The more I learned about this case and the prime suspects, the less the police theory held together.

After about two hours of our conversation, John Ramsey excused himself to use the restroom. I turned to Bryan Morgan and said, "I believe him."

"Oh, God, what a relief!" Morgan responded.

A personal interview doesn't tell you everything you want to know about an individual, but when you've talked to as many suspects and convicts as I have over the years — in the depth that I've dealt with them — you get a pretty good feel for whether they are telling the truth and telling *the whole truth.* Some of it is speech and hesitation; some is body language; some is just the look in their eyes. In fact, when asked about our parenting skills, most of my FBI and detective colleagues admit that while we're probably no better than other mothers and fathers at bringing up our children, we're head and shoulders better at interrogation. We can usually get to the truth pretty quickly with our kids and their friends.

"Look me in the eye and say that" is usually enough to send a preteen into a cowering confession, and our teenaged daughters often complain that their dates don't stand a chance against us.

With John Ramsey, there was just no indication he was lying or holding anything back, or that his professed grief was other than genuine. Particularly in light of his reaction to Beth's death, it seemed inconceivable that he could have taken part in the murder of JonBenét by either strangulation or blunt-force trauma, or even a cover-up of such a crime by his wife without giving it away in an extensive conversation with me.

Also, keep in mind that this was not an individual used to lying, like a habitual offender would be. If he were now trying to lie about something as monstrous as his daughter's murder, there would likely be a number of "tells" that would be obvious to any experienced investigator. And there were not.

I know what I have just stated is not proof of anything, but the interview was the tipping point for me. Once a good and responsible investigator has an informed opinion on a case, he or she will subject it to as much opposing evidence and logic as possible. That is: I went into this figuring the parents were probably guilty, so I would be looking for anything I could find to tell me otherwise. Now that I thought they were probably innocent, I would start looking for evidence to see if I could convince myself that I was wrong.

Bryan Morgan asked if I would participate in a meeting scheduled for the afternoon with Boulder police chief Tom Koby and others directly concerned with the case. I agreed.

The meeting was cordial enough, but the police seemed to have little interest in what I had to say. Several times, Chief Koby left, leaving in charge Commander John Eller, head of the detective division. Eller appeared not to want to be bothered by outside influence of any kind. This idea was confirmed for me when he seemed indifferent to my suggestion that Boulder PD contact Special Agent Ron Walker in the FBI's Denver Field Office. I had no particular ax to grind, and even though I was working with the Ramseys' attorneys, the only thing I really cared about was that this case be solved and this little girl's killer brought to justice. I thought using Ron Walker might give them just the boost they needed.

Ron was a longtime colleague of mine and, in fact, had saved my life. In December 1983, during a period of tremendous professional and personal stress, I had been out in Seattle working on the Green River Murders case.

After addressing the police and the regional task force on a Wednesday, I hadn't been feeling well and asked the two young agents working with me, Ron Walker and Blaine McIlwain, to cover for me with the police on Thursday. I went to my room at the Hilton, hung out the DO NOT DISTURB sign, and went to bed to try to sleep it off.

When I didn't show up at breakfast Friday and didn't answer their calls, they demanded my room key from the manager. They opened the lock, but the security chain was on. Without hesitation, they broke open the door. They found me on the floor, comatose and near death, with what turned out to be viral encephalitis. Several times in Swedish Hospital that week, I almost died. I didn't return to work until the following May and still have lasting effects of the illness.

I had not contacted or talked to Ron about the Ramsey case, but I thought his input could be tremendously valuable. We use the analogy of rare or unusual diseases in medicine. Your normal primary-care physician is a highly competent and effective generalist who knows your situation and history well and will give you good medical care. But if he or she is presented with something that only comes up once every couple of years, or perhaps never before, the standard of care is to bring in a specialist in that particular discipline. If you need complicated heart surgery, you want to bring in a highly experienced cardiothoracic surgeon.

In the same manner, most small to medium-size law enforcement agencies don't deal with many homicides, particularly ones that appear to involve kidnapping and sexually oriented violence. But we in the Behavioral Science Unit, and those we've trained, are specialists. We see those cases every day; we know how to investigate them; we know how to keep those investigations from getting bogged down, off-track or seriously compromised.

Had the body not been found and the case therefore continued to be classified as an abduction, the Federal Kidnapping Statute of 1932 would have gone into effect and the FBI would have had primary jurisdiction. That statute, unofficially known as the "Lindbergh Law," was enacted after the kidnapping of Charles and Anne Morrow Lindbergh's baby son from their home in Hopewell, New Jersey. It holds that after twenty-four hours have passed, there is a legal presumption that the kidnapper has crossed state lines. Therefore, it becomes a federal rather than state crime. But once the body was discovered, it became a murder, and murder is a state matter. The only way the FBI or other federal agency could enter the case was on request.

Boulder was averaging only about one homicide a year and therefore didn't even have a dedicated homicide detective staff. While the police department did ultimately get some input from Ron Walker and the FBI, as well as offers from Denver PD and the Colorado Bureau of Investigation, they essentially decided to go it alone. Normally, when a small department does this, it's because they are pretty confident that they already have the suspect in focus.

As far as I was concerned, this was their first critical mistake.

At nine o'clock on Friday morning, Bryan Morgan and I met with Detectives Steve Thomas and Thomas Trujillo in an interview room at police headquarters. Thomas and Morgan agreed that the meeting was not to be adversarial, nor would we exchange information. We were meeting to see if I could offer anything useful to the detectives as they carried out their investigation.

I told them that after touring the house, I was convinced the UNSUB had been in it before and knew his way around. Otherwise, the crime would have been too high-risk for him to be confident of pulling it off. I told them I felt this was primarily a personal-cause homicide directed against John Ramsey, and I thought that was supported by the degree of overkill.

This was most likely one offender, I said, because two or more would have been able to control the child and the plan would not have gone to hell as it did.

Once the child was dead, he covered her up quickly and left her where she was with a blanket halfway covering her. I didn't think this looked like evidence of a parental killing, either. There was no care taken with the body, which, as I've said, we almost always see when a parent murders a child.

The most fruitful direction for the investigation, I thought, was first to examine anyone who could have had access to the house — including cleaning people, all the way up to employees of John's company. The crime showed a lot of anger. Who had that kind of anger for John or the family?

I gave them some interrogation suggestions, which I won't divulge here because they are useful in a variety of cases. I also said I thought it would be helpful to have the police chief describe the kind of postoffense behavior we would expect and ask anyone who notices it in a friend, family member or acquaintance to get in touch with the investigators. Undoubtedly, the UNSUB would be following the media coverage closely; the more tension and anxiety you could create in him, the better.

Chapter 15
What We Know, and How We Know It

With that background, let's analyze the case as I did, element by element. These are the factors that made a difference in the way the case developed. If any loose ends stick out along the way, we'll try to deal with them as they come up.

The 911 Call and the Ransom Note

At 5:52 A.M., on December 26, 1996, the following call was received by the police dispatcher in Boulder, Colorado, from Patricia Ann Ramsey:

Patsy Ramsey: (inaudible) police.

Dispatcher: (inaudible)

Patsy Ramsey: 755 Fifteenth Street.

Dispatcher: What's going on there, ma'am?

Patsy Ramsey: We have a kidnapping.

298

Hurry, please.

Dispatcher: Explain to me what's going on, okay?

Patsy Ramsey: There we have a . . . There's a note left, and our daughter's gone.

Dispatcher: A note was left, and your daughter is gone?

Patsy Ramsey: Yes.

Dispatcher: How old is your daughter?

Patsy Ramsey: She's six years old. She's blond . . . six years old.

Dispatcher: How long ago was this?

Patsy Ramsey: I don't know. I just found the note and my daughter's (inaudible).

Dispatcher: Does it say who took her?

Patsy Ramsey: No. I don't know. . . . It's there . . . there's a ransom note here.

Dispatcher: It's a ransom note?

Patsy Ramsey: It says "S.B.T.C. Victory." Please —

Dispatcher: Okay, what's your name? Are you . . . ?

Patsy Ramsey: Patsy Ramsey. I'm the mother. Oh, my God, please . . .

Dispatcher: I'm . . . Okay, I'm sending an officer over, okay?

Patsy Ramsey: Please.

Dispatcher: Do you know how long she's been gone?

Patsy Ramsey: No, I don't. Please, we just got up and she's not here. Oh, my God, please.

Dispatcher: Okay.

Patsy Ramsey: Please send somebody.

Dispatcher: I am, honey.

Patsy Ramsey: Please.

Dispatcher: Take a deep breath (inaudible).

Patsy Ramsey: Hurry, hurry, hurry (inaudible).

Dispatcher: Patsy? Patsy? Patsy? Patsy? Patsy?

What can we glean from this call?

Well, first, understandably, the caller is very upset and agitated. But this, in itself, tells us nothing about her possible involvement or whether the crime was staged. For that, we have to go a level deeper, to what we in profiling refer to as "psycholinguistic analysis" — the actual choice and use of words.

The first thing we notice is that she gives the dispatcher disjointed, random pieces of information that make little sense out of context, such as, "It says 'S.B.T.C. Victory,' " as if she is just scanning it for the first or second time and discovering new elements in it. She announces that there has been a kidnapping, but she doesn't immediately follow it up with helpful facts. She has to be prodded for information that comes out in a disorganized way: "She's six years old. She's blond . . . six years old." She is trying to get everything out as quickly as possible rather than in a methodical, coherent narrative.

Had Patsy authored the note herself, as many investigators and much of the public came to believe, she would have been more specific on the phone. The information would have been more coherent; she would have given a better and more organized description of her daughter. Here, she doesn't even offer her daughter's name, a basic piece of information.

Surprisingly, extreme emotional distress is a very difficult sensation to fake. Try it with a friend if you don't believe me and see if you sound phony or rehearsed to them.

Officer Rick French arrived a few minutes later at the redbrick Tudor-style house in the fashionable University Hill neighborhood, where he was met by Patsy Ramsey. She was three days shy of her fortieth birthday. She was clearly agitated and distraught. Her husband, John Bennett Ramsey, fifty-three, came into the hallway. He appeared tense but under control.

Patsy said that she had come down from her third-floor bedroom, at about 5:45 A.M., to awaken six-year-old JonBenét and nine-year-old Burke to get them ready for a private plane flight to their vacation home in Charlevoix, Michigan. When she entered Jon-Benét's room, it was empty. She took the spiral back staircase down to the first floor to look for her. On one of the lower steps, she found three sheets of lined white paper, side by side. On them was written the now-famous ransom note.

It was written with a black felt-tip marker

and appeared to be penned by someone either extremely nervous or trying to disguise his or her handwriting.

In rambling, semicoherent prose, the note, addressed to Mr. Ramsey, purported to be from S.B.T.C.: *a group of individuals that represent a small foreign faction.* They claimed to have his daughter "safe" and "un harmed" [*sic*] and asked for $118,000 in hundreds and twenties. It had all of the normal threats about not involving the police or FBI and warned: *[We] are familiar with Law enforcement countermeasures and tactics. You stand a 99% chance of killing your daughter if you try to out smart [sic] us. Follow our instructions and you stand a 100% chance of getting her back.*

Now, by ransom note standards, this one is very peculiar. I had initially suggested to the Ramseys' attorneys and the police that I thought the UNSUB was a white male in his midthirties to midforties. But when I had the opportunity to study the note closely, I revised my age estimate downward. It is what we would call a mixed presentation — containing both organized and disorganized elements — that generally suggests a younger and less sophisticated offender.

So does the amount of money demanded: $118,000. Normally, we would expect to see a much larger amount asked for from someone with the real or perceived wealth of the

Ramseys, so the police rightly fixed on the amount as a clue in itself.

There are several possible explanations for the sum. One is that it represents around 1 million Mexican pesos at the prevailing exchange rate, suggesting that the intruder or intruders planned to escape to Mexico. A more prevalent theory is that it referred to the amount of money John Ramsey was given as a performance bonus. If this is true, it suggests an offender with some sort of inside knowledge. The Boulder Police Department fixed on Patsy as the only one who would have had such knowledge.

As soon as it was explained to me, I disagreed. I was told that the amount had appeared on several documents, including a tax return that was in the house, and that a number of individuals at his company could have had knowledge. Even more to the point, learning that the Ramseys were not meticulous housekeepers and let all manner of things lie around, it is more than possible that anyone in the house could have seen a pay stub and concluded that he had at least this much in ready cash. The note didn't just say to "bring us this much money." It directed Mr. Ramsey to "withdraw $118,000 *from your account*" (italics added for emphasis by author). Again, this underscores the possibility that the writer was someone with inside knowledge, either through the business or from simple observation.

It is also possible, based on my experience, that the figure is a complete red herring, a coincidental number snatched out of the air — though I didn't think so at the time and still do not. But the one thing it tells us for sure is that if this was either a criminal enterprise — in other words, a crime mainly for profit — or one staged to *look like a kidnapping,* then it was the work of a younger or criminally unsophisticated individual.

The note itself confirms this for us. Remember what we said about modus operandi versus signature. To attempt to complete a successful criminal enterprise, all the kidnapper has to do is say how much he wants, what form he wants it in and how it is to be delivered. Then they add all of the window dressing about not contacting the police or FBI, and not having the drop site surveilled, which almost no one follows. Even the kidnappers don't expect you to comply with this part.

The same ambiguity attaches to the signature: S.B.T.C. Some suggested it was an inside reference to John Ramsey's naval service in the Philippines and stood for "Subic Bay Training Center," even though there is no entity with that specific name. Others, citing Patsy's religiosity, thought it stood for "Saved By the Cross," and referred to her cancer remission. "Victory" meant victory over Satan. This would be difficult to square with the supposed staging of another crime, unless it was some sort of ritual sacrifice on Patsy's part. To believe this, though, you would have to suppose that she was out-and-out crazy, a hypothesis for which there is absolutely no evidence.

Who knows what S.B.T.C. means? It would certainly be nice to know, but ultimately, it may not matter. In any complex case, there are always anomalies that don't add up. People have spent endless hours debating this point, and we may never know.

But there is a lot more to this note. Putting things into the plural is standard form; you want to make your victims feel you are larger and more powerful than you are. Declaring yourselves a "foreign faction" makes you even scarier and more mysterious.

As we have said, the note gave all of the standard warnings, but did so in a taunting, repetitive style apparently intended to raise John Ramsey's level of anguish as high as possible. Also, note the unintentional switch from plural to singular in these remarks:

> Any deviation of my instruction will result in the immediate execution of your daughter. You will also be denied her remains for proper burial. The two gentlemen watching over your daughter do not particularly like you so I advise you not

to provoke them. Speaking to anyone about your situation, such as Police, F.B.I., etc., will result in your daughter being beheaded. If we catch you talking to a stray dog, she dies. If you alert bank authorities, she dies. If the money is in any way marked or tampered with, she dies. You will be scanned for electronic devices and if any are found, she dies.

The writer goes on to say: *Don't try to grow a brain John. You are not the only fat cat around so don't think that killing will be difficult. Do not underestimate us John. Use that good southern common sense of yours.*

This reference to John's Southern origins also points to someone who either knew him well or knew a good deal about him.

There are a number of contemporary movie references, such as *"Don't try to grow a brain John."* This seems to have been taken from *Speed,* the Sandra Bullock–Keanu Reeves thriller then out on video, in which extortionist Dennis Hopper says, "You know that I'm on top of you. Do not attempt to grow a brain."

"Speaking to anyone about your situation, such as Police, F.B.I., etc., will result in your daughter being beheaded," could have come from the Mel Gibson–Renee Russo film *Ransom,* then in theaters. Kidnapper and rogue

cop Gary Sinise warns, "Do not involve the police or the FBI. If you do, I will kill him."

And then there is the opening of the note: *"Listen carefully!"* That easily could have come from Clint Eastwood's immortal *Dirty Harry.*

Maybe they're all coincidences, but three phrases like that start to look like a pattern to me. I didn't think John or Patsy would necessarily know these references; and if they were sitting down under extreme stress trying to come up with what they thought a ransom note should look like, they were not the things I would expect them to call to mind. So this also made me think about a younger offender.

There is one thing about which I felt absolutely sure as soon as I saw the note and learned of its circumstances. The note was written *before the murder,* not, as some have suggested, afterward as a hasty and desperate attempt to stage the crime. No one would have that kind of patience, boldness and presence of mind to sit down and write it in the house afterward. The language seems more fitting to a male than a female offender.

I've seen a lot of ransom notes in my time, and this one clearly falls into one of two possible categories. The first possibility is that it was an actual ransom note with the intention of extorting money out of John Ramsey. The second is that it was part of an elaborate staging to mislead investigators from the actual intended crime, which was murder of the child for whatever reason.

If we assume the first intention, then we must conclude that the murder was unintended, at least initially. And then we can go on to conclude either that it turned out to be harder to control a six-year-old than anticipated and she was accidentally killed in trying to deal with her, or that some sexual perversity or paraphilia led the UNSUB into some signature-type behavior — autoerotic asphyxiation, for example — that ended in the death of the victim.

If we assume the second scenario, what are the possible reasons for a staging? The only logical ones have to do with trying to make the death of this child look like it happened for reasons other than the actual ones. Who would have a motive to do that?

We can come up with numerous far-fetched scenarios in which an intruder might stage a crime to look like one thing, when it is actually another. Mystery writers and crime shows love this kind of exercise. But this is not what happens in real life. Practically speaking, if this were staged to appear to be a kidnapping attempt, when it was actually something else, this would almost have to involve the parents or someone inside the house. No one else would have a reasonable motive to deflect the investigation into this other direction.

But the psycholinguistics point away from the mother. A mother under this kind of stress wouldn't think of her daughter's death as an "execution." If she had been trying to send a message to John — in other words, to "stick it to him" for some real or imagined domestic offense — it is conceivable she might have threatened him with the death of his beloved child. It is nearly inconceivable that she could talk about denying her remains a proper burial. It would be just too painful for her to think about.

I feel the same way about words such as "beheaded." No matter their motives, it seems highly unlikely that the parents could conceive of cutting their child's head off, or even using such a relatively archaic term. When Mark and I discussed the note with some of the Ramsey-hired investigators, he suggested it sounded like what a teen would take away from watching *Hercules* or *Xena, Warrior Princess* or playing Dungeons & Dragons, again pointing to a younger offender.

If Patsy were actually trying to get back at John in this note and in the crime itself, we would have expected her behavior to be consistent in various ways postoffense. But there is absolutely no evidence that she did this, either in word or dead. Yes, we could speculate that the actual murder had shocked her out of this mode of thinking and made her fear for her own safety, but now we're jumping through those logical hoops again.

I also find it significant that as vicious and specific as the note is, with frequent references to all of the horrible things the writer wants to do to this little girl, *nowhere* is she mentioned by name. Perhaps the writer didn't know her name, or didn't know the unusual spelling, based on her father's names.

If either of the parents had killed the child, either purposefully or by accident, it would make sense for them to stage the scene to deflect attention away from themselves. We see this frequently in domestic homicides. But the question remains: *Why?*

It soon became clear where the material for the ransom note had come from. On the afternoon of the murder, Detective Thomas Trujillo came over with a consent-to-search form. John signed it without question. The police asked the Ramseys to submit blood, hair and biological samples. They complied willingly. They were also asked for exemplars of their handwriting to match up against the ransom note. John gave them two white lined pads. One was from the kitchen countertop and contained Patsy's notes, shopping lists and some doodles. The other was on a hallway table near the spiral staircase and had pages written by John. Sergeant Robert Whitson marked them "John" and "Patsy" and submitted them to Detective Jeff Kithcart, the department's forgery and fraud expert.

As he was examining the pads, Kithcart noticed some writing toward the middle of Patsy's tablet. At the top of the page, in the same black felt-tip marker someone had written "Mr. and Mrs." And then a downstroke line could have been the beginning of a capital *R,* had it been completed. He concluded that this was a first draft of the ransom note and that the writer had then decided to address it to Mr. Ramsey only.

This was a critically important discovery. It meant either that the intruder or intruders had been in the house for some considerable period of time, or that JonBenét had been killed by someone known to be in the house — her mother, her father or her nine-year-old brother, Burke.

The inevitable question arises: If it wasn't someone who lived in the house, why would an intruder wait to write the convoluted note in the house and on paper he found there? I don't think we have a perfect answer. It makes no more sense than the ransom note itself. We could speculate that the intruder was young and unsophisticated and so did not think to bring a note with him. He may have had one, but in his time alone in the house decided to write a better one with materials readily at hand. It may be he wanted to implicate the parents by using their own pad. Or he may have wanted to show how bold he was. Or it may have been none of these. But does that make it any more likely that either John or Patsy wrote the note?

Boulder PD brought in four experts to examine the note and match it against handwriting exemplars from both John and Patsy. All four eliminated John as the author. Three out of the four eliminated Patsy; the fourth said he did not think she was, but he could not tell for sure. This was the origin of the story that Patsy's handwriting had matched up to the note.

The note told me that whether it started out as a kidnapping for ransom, or the communication was merely to deflect attention from the actual purpose, the UNSUB planned to remove the victim from the house. There would be no point to this elaborate note if it was intended that anyone in the house should find the body in the basement.

Again, we come back to the question: *Why would Patsy do it?*

Another popular movie out at the time was *Jerry Maguire*. Most of us remember the classic line in which Cuba Gooding Jr. tells Tom Cruise, "Show me the money!"

We operate on a similar mantra: *Show me the motive!* Keep all of the other facts and pieces of evidence in mind as we search for the fulfillment of that demand.

The People in the House

As soon as word got out that JonBenét was missing, friends and supporters started arriving at the house, along with a growing law enforcement contingent. In addition to Officer Rick French and the Ramseys' friends Fleet and Priscilla White and John and Barbara Fernie, Sergeant Paul Reichenbach showed up. He got the telephone company to set up a trap and trace on the Ramseys' line and put out an order to cease all police radio traffic on the crime, in case the kidnapper was listening to a police scanner. These were both good moves.

Fleet White wanted to help out, so he started out on his own search throughout the house. In the basement, he discovered a small broken window. If John Ramsey wanted to divert attention away from him and Patsy, this would have been a perfect opportunity. Instead, he explained that he had arrived home several months ago without his key and had broken the window himself to gain entry.

Sometime before 8:00 A.M., Burke woke up. John and Patsy told him his sister was missing, got him dressed, and then had him taken over to the Whites' house to remove him from the tense scene. Right after this, Sergeant Whitson contacted John Eller, the head of the police department's detective division. Eller was on vacation in Florida with his family, but Detectives Linda Arndt and

Fred Patterson soon arrived on the scene, having been brought up to speed on the details of the case thus far.

Arndt tried to be as reassuring as she could to Patsy and everyone at the scene. Accounts say that she treated both parents with great compassion. She rehearsed with John what he should do if and when a call came in from the kidnapper. Most important was to keep the kidnapper on the phone as long as possible so that the call could be traced.

By this point, without anyone intending to do anything wrong, the investigation already had been compromised to a critical degree. As far as the police could tell, this was a kidnapping, and so the entire house was a crime scene. And yet, here they had all these people in the house, wandering all over, searching on their own, trampling any evidence that might have proven useful in identifying the intruder or intruders. The police had not focused on John and Patsy yet. Once the crime scene has been disturbed, the fine and subtle evidence is gone for good.

While I'm sure the police had the same interests as the Ramseys in not subjecting Burke to any more stress and anguish than necessary, letting Burke leave the house for an unprotected location, when no UNSUBs had been identified, was bad practice. One can figure that if the kidnapper did not get him to begin with, perhaps he was not a target and therefore safe, but that is not a decision I would have wanted to make as a police officer.

By noon, no call had come from the kidnapper. The various police personnel and victim advocates departed, leaving Linda Arndt as the only police official on scene, along with the Ramseys, the Fernies, the Whites, who had returned after bringing Burke to their house to be watched, and the Ramseys' Episcopal pastor, Reverend Rol Hoverstock.

Around one o'clock, possibly to give John something to do as they waited in vain for the phone call, Arndt suggested that he take another look through the house to see if he could find anything that had been overlooked that might be helpful. He agreed and took Fleet White with him. That was when he found JonBenét's rigid body in the basement wine cellar.

Now comes one of the strangest incidents in the case, at least from one perspective. No one disputes Arndt's kindness and sensitive treatment of both Ramseys. In the following days, in fact, several other detectives were annoyed that Arndt was the only detective Patsy would talk to, because she felt a strong sense of trust. Yet, three years after the murder, and after she had left Boulder PD, Arndt appeared on a national television program and described the moment when she and John were kneeling over the body. She had searched in vain for a pulse in JonBenét and had to tell John that his daughter was dead. John groaned in anguish.

"And as we looked at each other," she recalled, "and I wore a shoulder holster, tucking my gun right next to me and consciously counting, 'I've got eighteen bullets,' because I didn't know if we'd all be alive when people showed up."

She further clarified, "Everything made sense in that instance. And I knew what happened."

What did she mean by that? Clearly, she thought that John Ramsey was capable of murder, and either had killed his daughter by himself or with the help of his wife. But why? What about the look in his eyes told her that? And what's this about eighteen bullets? Was he going to try to kill her right then and there? With what — his bare hands? Was he that dangerous that it was going to take an entire clip of bullets to neutralize him? Or did she think everyone else in the room was in on it with him and would have to be shot as well? It just doesn't make any sense and, I'm afraid, points up the confusion and lack of proper control that the Boulder PD exhibited during this case. Was she just stressed out as a result of having the body found in the house by civilians after the police had failed to find it? Was she disturbed that her kidnapping scene had turned into a murder?

Her comments are particularly strange, given that all reports at the time peg Detective Arndt's behavior as exemplary toward the Ramseys.

The incident points up a fundamental rift — a divergence in focus and perspective — that would soon emerge within the Boulder PD. The police department and, to a certain extent, the district attorney's office believed that the parents were culpable in JonBenét's death.

But they couldn't decide which one!

Linda Arndt evidently considered John the dangerous one, while Detective Steve Thomas, who ultimately took over the case, believed it was Patsy. The tensions that this must have produced within the investigation would have made this an extremely difficult case to prosecute. And as far as I could see, there was no hard evidence supporting any of the assumptions about either parent. The closest to actual evidence connecting the Ramseys was the fact that the ransom note was written on Patsy's pad. But handwriting experts eliminated John as the author and only found the most tangential possibility that Patsy could have written it.

I kept waiting for more compelling evidence to surface, but I never saw any.

The Pageant Videos

If there is a single factor that made this case

go global and turn public opinion against the parents, it was the images of pageant videos that flooded the media and the just emerging Internet. In addition to the Vegas showgirl, there was also the red-white-and-blue outfit for her singing of "God Bless America," the rhinestone-cowgirl attire of "Cowboy Sweetheart," the sequined snow princess, the mini Upper East Side sophisticate, with her fancy feathered hat, and so many more.

The contests had names like All Star Pageant and National Sunburst Pageant and Royal Miss, and they disturbed a lot of people. There was a jarring disconnect between the adorable, innocent child and the adult outfits she was wearing and the adult poses she was striking, with the imitation adult hairstyles and adult makeup, all overlaid with an implied sexuality that seemed inappropriate at best and downright exploitative at worst. Some of the investigators and many in the public concluded that JonBenét's reported habitual bedwetting was a result of the pressures and conflicts imposed on her by the demands of pageant participation. I admit that my wife, Pam, and I, parents of two daughters, were uncomfortable watching the videos.

But what do the pageant videos actually tell us about John and Patsy Ramsey? The couple would have said that these beauty pageants were no different from any other organized children's activity, be it Little League baseball or youth league soccer, Cub Scouts or Brownies, music, dance or skating lessons, or anything else. It is a common interest throughout the Southeast, enjoyed by generations of little girls and their families. Patsy had participated as a young girl and it had prepared her for the grown-up pageants and her role as Miss West Virginia in the Miss America pageant. She would also have said that participation in these events develops poise, talent, self-discipline and confidence — all great assets to little girls as they grow up.

As it turned out, almost all of the images were from a few pageants in which JonBenét participated during a very limited interval of time. The videos themselves were not fancy productions; they were made to be sold to parents and grandparents. Most important, JonBenét was a natural performer and pushed her mother to let her participate. At home, she would act out strutting down the runway and make Patsy the emcee, who would introduce her and announce her as the winner.

Regardless of whether we approve of these pageants or would want our daughters to participate, there is no indication they contributed to any personal or family pathology, and certainly provided no motive for a murder. At the time, there was some speculation that JonBenét had abruptly decided she didn't want to participate any longer, and her mother, living through her and distraught over her decision, had struck out in a moment of insane despair and rage. This idea is patently ridiculous and there is no psychological or physical evidence to support it.

Still, once the pageant videos went viral, a large sector of law enforcement, the media and the public decided that John and Patricia Ramsey had to be guilty of *something.*

Lawyering Up

This was another element that severely damaged public perception of the Ramseys.

Around two in the afternoon, the police decided the house should be cleared; and after John's son and daughter, John Andrew and Melinda, and Melinda's fiancé, Stewart Long, arrived (they were originally to meet the family for the flight to Charlevoix, Michigan), the Ramseys decided they would go to the Fernies' house, where the police would provide an around-the-clock guard. They didn't know that the officers had been instructed to listen to everything John or Patsy said.

The next day, Detectives Linda Arndt and Larry Mason came over to the Fernies' house to talk to the Ramseys. At one point, Arndt asked them to go to the police station for a formal interview. John was quietly trying to hold it together; Patsy was almost suicidally distraught; understandably, they were hesitant.

This was all observed by Michael Bynum, an attorney friend of the Ramseys who had come to the Fernies' to pay a condolence call. Though he was now in private practice, he had once been a prosecutor in the Boulder County District Attorney's Office and knew his way around the criminal justice system. Seeing how the police seemed to be focusing on the Ramseys rather than looking for any other leads, Bynum took John aside and asked if he could take it upon himself to make some legal decisions for them. John was grateful for any burden that could be taken off his shoulders, particularly by a trusted friend who was also a lawyer.

Bynum announced to the detectives that the Ramseys were not in shape to be interviewed and would not be going down to the station. He then called two prominent attorneys he knew, Hal Haddon and Patrick Burke. He asked Haddon to represent John and Burke to represent Patsy.

This move immediately triggered suspicion on the part of the police. But if you've read this far already, you know from previous cases we've discussed that this was a very reasonable and intelligent move by Michael Bynum and John Ramsey. The police investigators have certain legal obligations regarding suspects, but they are not out there primarily to protect your rights. They are there to try to figure out who committed a crime and line up the proof to convince a judge and jury. With all my experience, if I were ever a suspect, you can bet I would have legal representation, the best I could find.

It is up to an attorney to call the shots to protect his client, whether the client is innocent or guilty. Though it had no legal or procedural impact on the case, it is a matter of record that the Ramseys' attorneys did believe they were innocent. And it is also a matter of record that they were following their attorneys' advice, not calling the shots themselves. During our meeting with the detectives, Bryan Morgan stated, "It is I who have said you [John Ramsey] may not talk to police. And take that or leave it, but I want to put that on the record now. It was I who stopped the process."

Another hot point that was exacerbated by the entrance into the fray of heavy legal talent was the simmering conflict between the police and the DA's office.

Keep in mind the context. John Ramsey was a corporate executive whose company had been merged, then sold, and constantly had to answer to stockholders, regulators and others. He was accustomed to having things done through lawyers. This was just the way things were done in his world.

Ironically, John and Patsy had no problem

cooperating with the police. "We were perfectly willing to talk and didn't understand exactly why our lawyers didn't want us to," John told us recently. "Looking back on it, from what I learned, I would tell anyone wrongly accused of murder to make sure he has the best lawyer he can get."

But the police saw this move the way much of the public did: anyone who needs to lawyer up must be guilty. The lawyers are there not to get to the truth but to keep the police away from the truth about their clients. This perception fed into the spiral of mistrust, which was already forming.

As soon as possible, the Ramseys wanted to take JonBenét back to Atlanta for burial in the family plot next to Beth. Detective Commander John Eller wasn't happy about the phalanx of attorneys that stood between the department and those he considered his two prime suspects. What's more, he didn't like the Haddon, Morgan, and Foreman firm's apparently close ties to members of DA Alex Hunter's office. In what seemed to be a ploy to gain leverage and force the Ramseys' cooperation, Eller told Assistant District Attorney Pete Hofstrom, head of the felony division, that the coroner would hold the body for some indeterminate time for further tests.

This announcement ignited a firestorm, recalling as it did the threats in the ransom note to deny the family the victim's remains for proper burial. ADA Hofstrom was outraged, and so were the Ramseys' attorneys. The police were forced to back down and release the body for the funeral and burial in Atlanta.

If the case was getting off on the wrong track, this was nearly a point of no return. How could the police have any semblance of objectivity after this? How could they separate genuine behavioral evidence from resentment that their alleged suspects were getting away with murder?

We asked John how he and Patsy reacted, in the midst of their deep grief, to everyone thinking they had done it. "Frankly," he said, "it was mostly background noise. We were concerned with burying our daughter and protecting our son. I don't think we really understood why it was all happening, but it was never our primary consideration."

Looking for a Motive

One of the guiding principles of criminal investigative analysis is that past behavior suggests future behavior. Another way of saying this is that *people do not act out of character.* If they seem to be doing so, it is only because you don't properly know or understand their true character.

Let's start with what we know, or can learn, about John and Patricia Ramsey. This is the beginning of the profiling process.

There is nothing in the background of either parent to suggest they were capable of murdering their child in cold blood. There are no indications of any kind of sexual aberration or paraphilia, particularly involving children. Not only is there no indication that either one was sexually abusive, there is no indication that they were physically or emotionally abusive. Even John's first wife and older children had nothing bad or suspicious to say about him.

JonBenét's pediatrician was contacted and asked point-blank if during any of his examinations he had observed the remotest evidence of any abuse. None whatsoever, he responded. Quite the contrary, John and Patsy were the most loving and caring of parents.

The police hunted for any clue or evidence, and what's more, so did the tabloid press, which was even more motivated and had far less in the way of scruples when digging for information.

No one found anything.

If you don't even spank or slap your child, you aren't likely to bash her brains out, even in a moment of extreme rage (and there is absolutely no indication there ever was such a moment).

You don't just suddenly blossom into a killer out of nowhere. Even for people who kill with no previous criminal history, there is always a specific reason. The most common instance we tend to see in the media: A single mom is just barely getting by, financially and emotionally, and she meets some guy who somehow gives her the message that he would like her in his life, but there is no room for her kids. Maybe he wants them to have kids together, or maybe he doesn't want to be saddled with children at all. In either case, if she wants to change her life, she has to get rid of her children.

Another variation on this is the same woman, without a new man in her life, still wants to start over and seek something better, but feels she can't do it if she is tied down. Certainly, this was the theme of the 2011 trial of Casey Anthony in Orlando, Florida, for the murder of her nearly three-year-old daughter, Caylee. Though she was acquitted by an agonized jury, the impression remained locked in the public conscience.

Lest you think it is always a desperate woman who goes in this appalling direction, the counterpart phenomenon is a man who kills his wife or girlfriend in her eighth month of pregnancy. Up until then, it seems, the life-changing reality of birth is an abstraction. But once this man realizes his baby is imminently due, panic starts to set in. If he doesn't do something soon, he will be trapped. This appears to be the motivation in the 2002 murder of Laci Peterson and her unborn son by her husband Scott.

But neither of these scenarios had anything to do with the Ramseys' domestic situation. So if we want to pursue the case against either John or Patsy, we still need a believable motive.

Point A to Point Z

To make plausible the idea that either of the parents could have or would have murdered their daughter, we have to show how they *could come to do this.* In other words, unless they had been planning to kill their daughter for some time, something would have to have happened between the time they got up in the morning until the time JonBenét died to transform them from ordinary parents into murderers.

We start from Point A by observing that Christmas was a happy time for the Ramseys. They looked forward to it every year as the traditional time of joy and family togetherness. John's older son, daughter and her fiancé were coming to town and they were all flying up to the beloved weekend/summer home in Michigan to spend time together. Then John and Patsy were going to Florida to take the younger children on the Disney-themed cruise, which they were anticipating with great excitement. They had begun the day opening presents and had gone to visit good friends for dinner. They stopped at other friends' houses to exchange greetings and gifts. JonBenét fell asleep in the car on the way home. John carried her upstairs, and Patsy put her to bed as John played a game with Burke before he, too, fell asleep. John's business was doing well. Patsy's cancer was in remission. Life was good, and so was the day.

Point Z is JonBenét's bound, strangled and beaten body lying in the wine cellar, the remotest room in the basement. As I told the detectives during our January 10 meeting, "You don't just act one way at a party, and then, all of a sudden, another way and commit this type of crime."

So how do we get from Point A to Point Z with either or both of the Ramsey parents as the killer?

Before we do that, let's divert for a moment to consider one other possibility, which, believe it or not, became a popular theory of the crime. This one has nine-year-old Burke as the killer.

We can dispense with this one pretty quickly. First, there is no motive, though children don't have the same motives or understanding of lasting consequences that adults do. It is conceivable that brother and sister got into some sort of squabble, he decked her, and then the parents had to deal with it. But would they have gone to elaborate steps to stage a kidnapping, write a ransom note and then set up a weird strangulation scenario in the basement? It makes no sense because a nine-year-old would not be subject to the same legal sanctions as an adult.

There is no way Burke would have the strength either to deliver the fatal head blow, twist the garrote or move his sister's weight. And then the parents never would have sent him to the Whites' house, knowing that kids tend to talk about whatever enters their minds. So let's just move on.

The Police Theory

After some shifting around, Boulder Police Department detective Steve Thomas took over as the primary investigator on the case. As we have noted, Boulder fortunately did not have many homicides; so in the rare instance that one occurred, a detective from another area or squad was put on the case. Thomas had little experience with homicide investigation, but he had spent considerable time on narcotics.

After conducting his own investigation, Thomas came to believe that the happy anticipation of the Christmas Day we've just described was actually a veneer over the tension Patsy was feeling about the holidays in general and several run-ins she'd already had with JonBenét. According to Detective Thomas, Patsy had not wanted to make the

330

hectic trip up to Michigan, and she was upset over her daughter's stubborn refusal to put on the dress Patsy had selected for their dinner at the Whites'.

This was all brought to a head during the night when JonBenét woke up with a wet bed. He speculates that a red turtleneck found balled up in the bathroom must have been what she had worn to bed, and that Patsy had angrily stripped it off her when the little girl had had another accident.

He goes on to speculate that while Patsy had her undressed, cleaning her up before putting her in the clothing in which she was found, she used some sort of cloth to roughly or violently wipe the little girl between the legs. In other words, by this account, the abrasions in her vaginal area were not the result of the digital penetration of some perverse sex play by an intruder, but were a form of intended or unintended punishment for JonBenét's frequent urinary accidents. This could also account for the small amount of blood in her panties.

I find this theory bizarre, but the next part of the scenario is even more far-fetched. Thomas imagines "some sort of explosive encounter in the child's bathroom." In a moment of uncontrolled rage, Patsy either struck JonBenét on the head or threw her across the room. Either way, the child landed against a hard surface, causing the large skull fracture described by the medical examiner. It's hard to believe, even for Thomas, that Patsy meant to hit her or slam her this hard. So when she saw what she had done, she panicked. What to do next?

The rational thing is to call 911 and say it was an accident, but Thomas believed that her first instinct, and presumably that of her husband, was to stage the injury to look like something else. This presupposes that Patsy knew her daughter was dead from the first blow, or was so frightened of getting caught that she was willing to let her daughter die rather than seek help. Then she and John went through the elaborate setup with a garrote and duct tape and all the rest to throw police off. They came up with a three-page-long ransom note on the spur of the moment, and Patsy managed to sound suitably surprised and hysterical when she finally did call 911 to report her daughter missing. And . . . and . . . and these people, who had never pulled off a crime before, manage to make it all so realistic that they take in the police, who at first believe it really is a kidnapping. How logical or believable does that all sound?

Now let's take it from John's point of view. Even if everything Steve Thomas suggests did take place between JonBenét and Patsy, does John just go along with it? Does he buy into her insane plan? What would make John go along with this? Would it be that he had already lost his eldest daughter and now his youngest, and so he didn't want to lose his wife, too? I have yet to see a parent who would favor a spouse over a murdered child. None of this scenario is believable.

But before we leave this point, we have to go back to the supposed inciting incident itself. Patsy lost it when she found out that JonBenét had wet herself and smacked her across the bathroom. Why? First of all, we don't even know that the child had an accident that night. The urine stains in her underwear and long johns could also have been a result of bladder tension release at time of death. But let's say she did wet her pants that night. JonBenét was a habitual bed wetter. It was such a commonplace occurrence that Patsy commonly stripped her bedsheets in the morning before her housekeeper arrived and put them in the stacked washer-dryer unit near JonBenét's bedroom.

So what happened?

On this particular night, because of all the pent-up stress involving Christmas and travel arrangements and having John's older children coming and whatever else, JonBenét wet the bed one too many times and Patsy snapped? She snapped so completely that she hauled off and knocked her child across the room? Is this believable — that a mother who had calmly dealt with hundreds of bed-wetting incidents suddenly acted so violently that she cracked her daughter's skull? Is it any more believable than as she's being put to bed, JonBenét tells her mother that she doesn't want to do any more pageants, so Patsy goes berserk and hits her daughter hard enough to open a seven inch gash on the right side of her head?

In this scenario, overwhelmed by remorse at having done such a horrible thing, Patsy and/or John would have dragged the little girl down to the farthest room in the basement, covered her mouth with duct tape and bound her neck and wrists with cord. Then either one or both parents grabbed a paintbrush from Patsy's painting-supply box, broke off the handle and inserted it into the neck binding to make a garrote they could twist so tightly it compressed the neck. Or maybe this part was intentional — some kind of bizarre ritual sacrifice.

Then one of them would go back up to the kitchen to compose the weird ransom note. "Let's see, John, what movies have we seen recently that we can use in the writing?"

Not finished yet, they'd have to get rid of the rolls of duct tape and cord so that these items were nowhere in the house. But no doubt, in the general panic and confusion of the whole process, they would forget to get rid of the remains of the paintbrush and the pad that the ransom note was written on, leaving them for the police to find. (In fact, to make themselves look even more innocent, they would hand over the pad as an example of Patsy's handwriting and then feign surprise when it had a first attempt at the note on one of the lower pages.) They would also have to head back upstairs to clean up all the blood in the bathroom.

Or let's say that Patsy did all this herself, without John's knowledge. We know for a fact that she was good at cleaning up urine. Maybe that experience helped her clean up all the blood that would have gushed out of so large a head wound (more on that a little later). In this variation, she would have been truly clever, because in the ransom note she would have been sending John a veiled message with the $118,000 reference and *Saved By The Cross,* but she must have figured no one else would pick that up and she could disguise her handwriting on her very own legal pad. It's amazing to think that a wife and mother with no prior experience could summon forth such a high degree of criminal sophistication at the very moment she needed it. If she'd thought to open a door to the outside or smash a window, she could have made the scene even better.

You can make that all work in the movies. It's a lot harder in real life.

What I saw the Boulder PD and others in law enforcement doing was taking a statistical fact — that most young children murdered in their homes are killed by someone related who lives in the house — and trying to make the specific evidence fit the statistic.

Some of this meant going down strange pathways with little relevance. For example, there was a bowl of cut pineapple on the kitchen counter, and the autopsy found some undigested pineapple in JonBenét's stomach. Yet both Patsy and John denied that they had given her any pineapple during the day, and she was asleep by the time they got home in the evening. Detective Thomas made a big deal out of this; yet what could it ultimately prove? Maybe one of the parents did give her pineapple and forgot. Maybe she got up on her own during the night, went downstairs and ate some on her own. Maybe an intruder gave it to her. So what?

More to the point, if it was a material point in the case that gave the detectives some insight into the parents' connection to the crime, John and Patsy would know or sense this, and try to give some plausible explanation — very easy to do — instead of leaving the question hanging. But they didn't try, because it didn't seem to mean anything.

This assumption is typical of mistakes inexperienced investigators make when approaching a complicated case. I used to tell agents who had just come to work for me: "Don't start out looking at the case from too close-up. Step back and look at it in its entirety before you focus on details." Here, the police selectively emphasized certain aspects that they thought bolstered their theory.

On the other hand, they were quick to dismiss unidentified DNA under JonBenét's fingernails, in her panties and in her long johns — *DNA that matched no one in the house.* The police speculated that some of it might have come from the manufacturing and packaging process of the clothing itself; therefore, it was a red herring.

Okay, maybe it was. Maybe JonBenét was playing in the dirt and got some organic material under her fingernails. Maybe she and another little girl had worn each other's clothing at some point and the genetic material was her friend's. It's unlikely, though certainly possible. But doesn't it seem to be a strange unbalancing and prioritizing of evidence? You make a big deal out of the pineapple and don't consider that the foreign DNA *might* point to an intruder?

Then there was the pubic hair found on her blanket. Again, it may mean nothing; hair and fiber transfer is routine. But since it didn't match anyone known to be in the house, shouldn't it at least be regarded as a *possible* indication of an outsider?

And then when you factor in that Detective Linda Arndt felt that John was the one capable of violence, you have a very confused and not very compelling police theory of the case. But there is one piece of evidence that to my mind cinches it.

The Medical Examiner's Report

Dr. John E. Meyer, coroner of Boulder County, board certified in anatomic, clinical and forensic pathology, pronounced JonBenét dead after he'd been called to the house by the police. Once the body had been transported back to the coroner's lab in the basement of Boulder Community Hospital, he conducted a full autopsy.

A ligature garrote around her neck had been tightened to such a degree with a broken-off paintbrush handle that it created a furrow all the way around her neck. Dr. Meyer had to cut it off with a pair of angled bandage scissors. A gold cross and chain were tangled in the ligature. There was an abrasion on her right cheek near the ear, and another on the lower left side of her neck. The petechial hemorrhages on the insides of the eyelids and other places about the head were consistent with strangulation.

At the time of her death, JonBenét was wearing long underwear over floral print panties whose crotch, as we have noted, bore a small bloodstain, in addition to the urine stain that also appeared on her long johns. There was dried blood as well around the entrance to the vagina and hyperemia — engorged blood vessels — that might have indicated trauma just inside the vagina opening. There were further abrasions along the vaginal wall, and the hymen was not intact. Petechial hemorrhaging was noted scattered along the surface of both lungs and the anterior surface of the heart.

When Meyer pulled back the scalp from the large head wound on the right side, he noted a seven-by-four-inch hemorrhage. Underneath the hemorrhage area was an even larger fracture of the skull, measuring eight and a half inches from one end to the other. There was further hemorrhaging under the arachnoid membrane, which covers the brain. Underneath that, the gray matter of the brain itself showed substantial bruising.

Dr. Meyer listed the official cause of death as asphyxia by strangulation associated with craniocerebral trauma.

These findings by a highly distinguished ME, in conjunction with the findings at the scene, became for me the most compelling evidence in the entire case. They represent what Dr. Lester Adelson, longtime Cleveland, Ohio, chief deputy coroner and author of *The Pathology of Homicide,* famously referred to as the "dialogue with the dead." Frankly, I didn't — and don't — see how the police, the district attorney's office, my old FBI unit in Quantico and so many others could fail to interpret this information properly with regard to the victim's parents. It is unfortunately representative of the kind of theory-before-evidence reasoning we've seen throughout the cases in this book.

The blunt-force trauma to the head was severe enough to kill anyone. The details are also much more consistent with a blow from a hard and heavy object than the accidental collision with a fixed hard surface. Investigators identified several items found in the house that could have caused this wound. Most prominent among them were a large metal flashlight and a golf club. So we start from the premise that Detective Thomas's theory of incidental contact with a bathtub or other object is less forensically plausible than an *intentional* blow to the head with a makeshift weapon.

Should we believe that a mother or father with no prior history of violence, domestic or otherwise, would purposely pick up an object and strike a six-year-old with sufficient force to crack her skull and bruise her brain? And should we believe that this parent would *bring the object into her bedroom,* planning to hit her with it? If not, should we believe that this mother or father picked up the child and carried her down to the basement with the intention of assaulting her there? It doesn't work for me.

But here's the kicker! The entire area inside

the house and the yard around it has to be considered a crime scene. Once the initial morning of confusion was past, investigators combed it meticulously. Within that boundary, the primary scene is the area from Jon-Benét's bedroom into the hallway and bathroom, down the circular stairs all the way to the basement, then back to the wine cellar — in other words, the setting in which she was last seen alive to the setting where her body was discovered.

So where along that trail was all the blood?

This is perhaps the most important single question of the entire investigation. The scalp is highly vascular and head wounds tend to bleed profusely, even when they're not serious. This one was deadly serious. A trauma that lacerates the scalp, cracks the skull and causes subdural and subarachnoid bleeding will certainly bleed on the outside, too.

So where was all the blood?

Did Patsy clean it up? And if she did, what did she do with the numerous towels and other cleaning supplies she would have needed? Did she take the car out in the middle of the night and dump them somewhere? It would be virtually impossible to clean up as much blood as would gush from a head wound of this nature and not leave traces that crime scene specialists and/or luminol would pick up. In all of my years of investigative experience, I have never witnessed a crime scene in which the blood from a violent act could be covered up or eliminated completely.

Given all of this, there is only one reasonable explanation: There was no blood because at the time of the blunt-force trauma, Jon-Benét was either dead or near death. For her not to have bled profusely at the scene, her heart was not pumping, or was hardly pumping, and her blood pressure was extremely weak or nonexistent. This means that the blow to the head had to have come *after* the ligature strangulation.

Now, then, what does that suggest to us?

Even if we could imagine a loving mother striking out in a moment of rage, can we imagine a mother binding her young daughter, covering her mouth with duct tape, fitting a cord around her neck and gradually twisting the makeshift handle until she died from asphyxiation? Under what circumstances could this possibly have happened? Was this a severe punishment for her years of bed-wetting? Was it Patsy's way of getting back at a husband who had been sexually abusing his daughter, or favoring her over his own wife? Were John and/or Patsy secret Satanists, and was this a Christmas ritual they felt compelled to perform? And how does this all fit into the context of the planned trips to Michigan and the vacation cruise?

No matter how you break it out, it just

doesn't make sense. The medical and crime scene evidence is clear that strangulation was the cause of death. I have never come across a case in which parents have done anything like this to a child. Could the Ramseys be the first? And could they be so slick and criminally sophisticated that none of their post-offense behavior would give them away? Unless, that is, you consider Linda Arndt's sensation that eighteen bullets might not be enough to deal with the "grieving" father staring across his daughter's rigid body from her.

In Summary

What we've tried to do here is approach the murder of JonBenét Ramsey from a number of different angles, just as we would do in a case consultation when I was leading the Investigative Support Unit. No matter which angle we approach it from, we come to the same conclusion: John and Patricia Ramsey did not murder their daughter, either together or separately. And that means it had to be an intruder.

Despite all of this, my old unit in Quantico continued to be convinced that the parents were the prime suspects. Is it *possible* that one or both of the parents could have killed their young child by progressively tightening a garrote around her neck while her hands were bound? Yes, it's possible; but so unlikely that given the context, it is the absolutely last possibility you would think of. The only way it would work was if everything else in the case tied directly to the parents. But in this case — other than the statistic we've noted that most domestic homicides of children are committed by individuals who belong in the house — nothing tied John and Patsy Ramsey to the murder of their child.

But that didn't seem to matter.

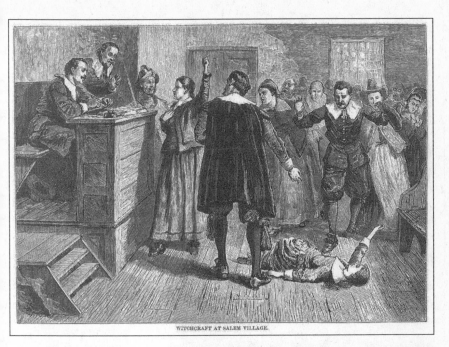

WITCHCRAFT AT SALEM VILLAGE.

The first defendant to be convicted and executed in the Salem witch trials of 1692 and 1693 was Bridget Bishop. Like Damien Echols in West Memphis, Arkansas, three centuries later, she wore black and was considered "different."

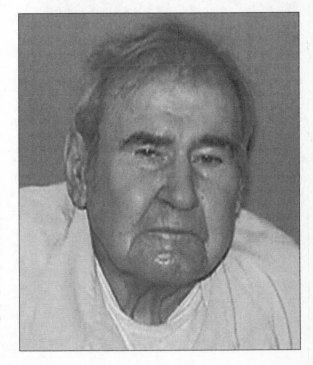

When I interviewed William Heirens in prison, I believed he had committed the murders to which he pled guilty. Now, I think I may have been wrong. He died on March 5, 2012 at age 83. *(Courtesy of the Illinois Department of Corrections)*

When I was in the FBI, we had to do much of our analysis from case files. But whenever possible, I like to visit the actual scene, as Mark and I are doing here. *(© Philip Bermingham)*

At Cameron Todd Willingham's trial, a so-called expert witness claimed his tattoos and heavy metal posters showed his violent personality. He proclaimed his innocence up to the moment of his execution. Later, scientific evidence showed him to be innocent.
(© Ken Light)

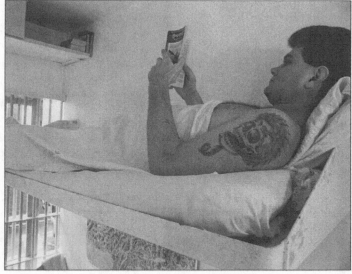

Suzanne Collins with her father, Jack, in West Redding, Connecticut. The photograph is dated July 1983, two years before she was murdered in Millington, Tennessee.
(Courtesy of Jack and Trudy Collins)

Suzanne Collins with her Marine Corps recruiter, brother Steve, and mother Trudy in Springfield, Virginia, just before she left for boot camp, June 1984.
(Courtesy of Jack and Trudy Collins)

A proud Suzanne Collins in her official Marine Corps photograph, taken just after
completing boot camp at Parris Island, South Carolina, August 1984.

(Courtesy of Jack and Trudy Collins)

Sedley Alley brutally murdered Suzanne Collins on July 12, 1985. By the time he was executed on June 28, 2006, he had managed to postpone his sentence longer than Suzanne was alive. *(Courtesy of the Tennessee Department of Corrections)*

Former United States senator and Florida governor Bob Graham served two terms in the Tallahassee state house, during which he signed a number of death warrants. When asked if he had questioned the justice of any of them before signing, he replied, "All of them." Below, he explains his position on capital punishment to Mark Olshaker.

(Courtesy of Mark and Carolyn Olshaker)

In matching sweaters, Patsy, JonBenet, and Burke Ramsey pose in front of their Boulder home during the 1994 Christmas season. The following Christmas, the beautiful JonBenet was murdered inside her home at age six. *(Courtesy of John Ramsey)*

The Ramsey family gathers for Thanksgiving in Atlanta, 1995. From left: John, JonBenet, Burke, Patsy, John Andrew, and Melinda. *(Courtesy of John Ramsey)*

This kindergarten photo shows the real JonBenet Ramsey, a far cry from the pageant images that prejudiced so much of the media, public, and law enforcement establishment against her grieving parents. (Courtesy of John Ramsey)

Employing the inspired and meticulous detective work that had been the hallmark of his celebrated career, Lou Smit came to the same conclusion I had: that an intruder had killed JonBenet. (Courtesy of Mark A. Smit)

Michael Moore   Chris Byers   Steve Branch

The three eight-year-old murder victims in the West Memphis Three case. This composite was widely circulated after the boys went missing May 5, 1993, and came to represent the depraved murder of innocence. *(Courtesy of* Memphis Commercial Appeal)

Booking photos of Jessie Misskelley and Charles Jason Baldwin, two of the West Memphis Three. After analyzing the case, I concluded they were innocent.
(Courtesy of West Memphis Police Department)

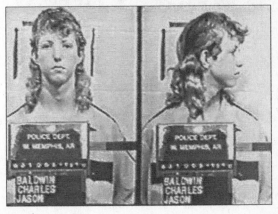

Booking photo of Damien Echols.
(Courtesy of West Memphis Police Department)

Damien Echols, convicted as the ringleader in the 1993 West Memphis Three killings, liked to wear black as a teenager. *(Photo by Bill Templeton, courtesy of* The Jonesboro Sun*)*

Damien Echols still likes to
wear black today.
(© Mark Olshaker)

On November 17, 1993, Arkansas State Police divers recovered a large survivalist-type knife from a lake near Jason Baldwin's home. Prosecutors claimed it was the weapon used to kill the three boys. Scientific experts ultimately concluded the wounds on the victims' bodies were caused by postmortem animal predation. *(Photo by Lisa Waddell, courtesy of Memphis Commercial Appeal)*

At the 1994 trial of Damien Echols and Jason Baldwin, Judge David Burnett allowed self-proclaimed cult expert Dale Griffis to testify how Echols's notebook showed involvement with Satanism, which lead to murder. *(Photo by Robert Cohen, courtesy of Memphis Commercial Appeal)*

John Mark Byers, stepfather of Christopher Byers and himself once a suspect, believed vehemently in the guilt of the West Memphis Three for years. After I convinced him of their innocence, he fought for their release and exoneration. *(Photo by Matthew Craig, courtesy of Memphis Commercial Appeal)*

Washington attorney Stephen Braga took over as lead attorney in Damien Echols's appeal and came up with the Alford plea strategy that ultimately got the West Memphis Three out of prison. *(© Mark Olshaker)*

More than anything, what kept Damien Echols alive, sane, and hopeful throughout his years on death row was Lorri Davis, the woman who gave up her career and lifestyle to fight for his freedom. They married on December 3, 1999. *(© Mark Olshaker)*

After the West Memphis Three's release from prison in August, 2011, Damien and Lorri went to New Zealand to visit Fran Walsh and Peter Jackson, who had become their key supporters, benefactors, strategists, and friends. *(Courtesy of Fran Walsh)*

I did not want to meet Damien Echols in prison, because I wanted to keep my objectivity. Once he was free and had had some time to gain perspective, we met for an extended time to review the case. Below, Damien shares a lighter moment with Lorri and me at Fran and Peter's U.S. apartment. *(© Mark Olshaker)*

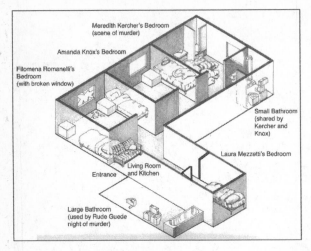

The floor plan of the upper floor of the house on Via della Pergola, on a hill near Perugia's center. Meredith, Amanda, and two Italian women shared this floor. The lower floor, accessible by a separate entrance, was occupied by four male Italian students. *(© Benjamin Cheshire)*

Meredith Kercher's Bedroom (scene of murder)

Amanda Knox's Bedroom

Filomena Romanelli's Bedroom (with broken window)

Small Bathroom (shared by Kercher and Knox)

Laura Mezzetti's Bedroom

Living Room and Kitchen

Entrance

Large Bathroom (used by Rude Guede night of murder)

The real Amanda Knox was neither "Foxy Knoxy" nor the beguiling temptress she was made out to be. She was a bright, industrious, fun-loving, and normal young woman looking to broaden her horizons with foreign study and travel. *(© Madison Paxton)*

Journalist Krista Errickson was assigned to interview me for the Italian daily *Il Messagero*. When editors received her story, which stated my confidence in Amanda Knox's innocence, they demanded changes. Krista refused and the story never ran. *(Courtesy of Guy Webster)*

CHAPTER 16
ENTER LOU SMIT

Once I got involved with the Ramsey case, my public and professional image seemed to change overnight. No longer was I perceived as Agent Jack Crawford, the straight-shooting, justice-seeking character in the trim black suit Scott Glenn had portrayed in *The Silence of the Lambs,* which was reputedly based on me. Now I was seen as the hired gun that would say anything for a price. Ironically, once I determined that the Ramseys were not offenders but surviving victims, I stopped accepting their money altogether.

Mark and I were stunned by the reactions. Nearly everyone we talked to about the case, either personally or through media interviews, seemed to discount our observations out of hand and implied that we were naive in our belief in the Ramseys' innocence. Mark talked to several agents at Quantico and came away surprised and confused about why they weren't looking at the totality of the evidence.

No one, it appeared, agreed with us or even allowed for the possibility that my assessment might be correct.

No one, that is, until Lou Smit entered the picture.

If there was anyone whom I considered a genuine hero in this case, anyone in whom I had complete faith and confidence, it was Detective Andrew Louis "Lou" Smit. By the time he entered the investigation, he was already a law enforcement legend in Colorado, having cleared over 90 percent of the more than two hundred homicide cases he'd investigated. He felt such a personal connection to the victims of the murders he'd handled that he kept small photographs of some of them in his wallet.

In March 1997, three months after the murder with the case at a standstill, with John and Patricia Ramsey still under the glare of prime suspicion, with the police department and district attorney's office in a Cold War–type relationship, DA Alex Hunter hired Lou Smit to consult on the case. At the time, Smit was retired from the El Paso County Sheriff's Office, an area due south of Denver that encompasses Colorado Springs and the United States Air Force Academy. Hunter's reasoning was solid. This case had shone an international spotlight on Boulder; it needed to be moved forward; and no one could assail the integrity, objectivity, talent and experience of a man like Smit.

Smit meticulously went through all of the now-voluminous evidence and concluded that JonBenét had been killed by an intruder. It reminded him of a case he had worked six years before — the 1991 murder of thirteen-year-old Heather Dawn Church, killed in her house near Colorado Springs. For four years, the community and police were convinced that someone in the house was responsible, and the case went nowhere. Smit, with a nearly superhuman attention to detail, discovered an overlooked fingerprint that he was able to match to a suspect arrested in Florida. Robert Charles Browne at first pled not guilty. But realizing he was facing the death penalty if Smit's work held up in court, he took a life plea. Altogether, he may have killed more than forty more. God only knows how many others would have lost their lives but for Lou Smit.

Smit's working theory was that the UN-SUB intruder had gotten in the basement through a loose grate in a window well and gained access to the entire house. While I believed the intruder to be someone who had a grudge against John Ramsey, Smit thought he was probably a pedophile who had seen JonBenét either casually around town, in school or in one or more of her pageants. He used the pad he found in the kitchen to write the strange ransom note and then hid out until the family returned home and went to bed.

Some people may tend to discount this theory because slipping into the house and hiding there for so long is such a bold and gutsy move. But it's important to remember that while "normal" people may find this unimaginable, it's what burglars and robbers do for a living. I don't know how many cases I've had over the years in which a woman wakes up to find an intruder standing over her bed, watching her. And I've dealt with a large number of break-and-enter guys — many of them essentially nonviolent — who have no problem spending long periods in a target house, sometimes entering when the household is still awake. For some of them, that's the main thrill of the crime.

After coming up with his particular slant on the intruder theory, Smit contributed another crucial element through his meticulous observation. Studying photographs of JonBenét's body, inch by inch, he noticed two strange lesions — one on the right side of her neck near her jawline and the other on the lower-left portion of her back. The two lesions appeared virtually identical, each consisting of twin, parallel red welts, about three and a half centimeters apart.

Smit consulted with several of his colleagues before turning to Dr. Michael Dobersen, an M.D., Ph.D., certified forensic pathologist and the coroner of Arapahoe County, Colorado. Though he wouldn't fully commit without being able to examine the body himself, Dobersen agreed with Smit that the lesions were consistent with the results of having been shot with a stun gun. Further consultation with experts helped Smit narrow down the particular spacing of the two marks in each wound to what would have been produced by an Air Taser Model 34000. Smit also examined the last photographs taken of JonBenét when she was still alive. Though her lower back was covered up, he noted distinctly that there were no corresponding marks on the right side of her face and neck.

I didn't know much about stun guns or Tasers, but I was greatly interested in the theory. If a stun gun, in fact, was used on this six-year-old, there were only two possible reasons: to immobilize and therefore control her, or to torture her for the sexual pleasure and satisfaction of the UNSUB. Either of these scenarios would logically rule out either of the parents. First of all, they didn't previously own a stun gun, so it would have had to be specially purchased and brought into the house, for which there was no evidence. Also, they wouldn't need a way of controlling her, the way a stranger would. For two people with absolutely no history of any sort of sexual perversion or pedophilia to inflict this on their own daughter was unthinkable.

It was leaked to the media that John Ramsey had a book about stun guns in his house. This is typical of the lies and half-truths that were legitimatized and regularly published. In fact, he had a book about industrial security, which had a mention of stun guns in the context of a variety of security measures. This was similar to the rumor that our book *Mindhunter* was on the bedroom shelf at the time of the murder. This was completely untrue. John Ramsey did not know who I was and had never heard of the book. It was only after we met and I concluded he was not a legitimate suspect that he obtained and read the book, thus unwittingly starting the rumor.

If a stun gun was part of the crime scenario — and it would seem to me pretty coincidental to have two sets of marks that just happen to correspond to a particular Air Taser model — then that further delineates the evidence. The notepad on which the ransom note was written, the paintbrush handle that was used as a makeshift garrote and the two most likely blunt-force weapons (the golf club and the flashlight) were all found in plain sight in the house. But items intended *to control* the victim — the roll from which duct tape on her mouth came, the spool for the cord used to bind her, and now the possibility of a stun gun to briefly but completely immobilize her — were not found in the house and therefore had to have come from outside. These were all elements that most of the investigators either overlooked or inexplicably dismissed out of hand.

Smit believed the intruder used the stun gun to render JonBenét defenseless, taped her mouth and carried her to the basement room, where he would be able to take her out of the house. He fashioned the garrote with the cord he'd brought and the paintbrush handle he broke off. While he tightened the neck cord as part of his erotic fantasy, he put his hand into her pants and penetrated her with his fingers. Smit ascribed the unidentified evidence found at the scene to this UNSUB: the pubic hair, the DNA deposits, a Hi-Tec brand boot print on the floor, a scuff mark on the basement wall near the window.

The fact that there was DNA under JonBenét's fingernails led Smit to believe that she came to at some point in the ordeal and struggled to fight him off. He also noted a number of half-moon–shaped abrasions on her neck around the ligature. He interpreted these as JonBenét's own desperate attempt to remove or loosen the garrote, again showing that this six-year-old fought to save her own life. Can you imagine a mother struggling with her young daughter as she tightens a noose around her neck? From my work, I can imagine a lot of sick things, but that one is beyond me.

Smit thought that with JonBenét struggling and not fully subdued, the UNSUB panicked and struck her with what was handy, probably the flashlight. Believing he had killed her, he escaped from the house with the items and implements he'd brought with him, leaving everything else behind.

Smit and I differed on several interpretations. He believed the motive was obsession with the child, while I thought it more likely the obsession was with her father. Mark thought the crime was most likely an actual criminal-enterprise kidnapping that had gone bad, staged by one or more young and unsophisticated offenders. The ransom note's demand of $118,000 probably supports Mark's or my interpretation more than Lou's in terms of inside information. But any of these is a likely scenario, far more likely than the exasperation at bed-wetting portrait painted by Detective Steve Thomas. In any of our theories, you'd conduct the investigation the same way and look for the same kind of postoffense behavior. While the investigators interviewed hundreds of witnesses and persons of interest, and came up with some potentially interesting leads, as far as I could see they did not concentrate on these behaviors, or shift their focus away from the parents.

The investigation continued to be beset by

problems, internal divisions and ongoing conflict between the police department and Alex Hunter's DA's office. The police very much wanted a grand jury to be impaneled, since it could compel testimony that detectives could not.

On September 15, 1998, closing in on two years after the murder, a grand jury of four women and eight men began work. Hunter appointed attorney Michael Kane to head its investigation. By that time, Detective Steve Thomas had submitted his resignation, citing disagreements with the police over how the investigation was being handled and with the district attorney's office for having failed thus far to indict the Ramseys.

A week after the grand jury began, Lou Smit submitted his own resignation, but for opposite reasons. In a letter to Alex Hunter, he wrote, *I cannot in good conscience be a part of the persecution of innocent people. It would be highly improper and unethical for me to stay when I so strongly believe this.*

The following March, with the grand jury still impaneled and conducting its own investigation, Linda Arndt also resigned. There were now few left who had been with the case since the beginning.

Lou Smit and I both testified before the grand jury, and we were among the last witnesses. He went before the panel on March 11, 1999. My own testimony was heard on

April 26 and 27. Smit had requested he be allowed to testify, but his participation was rebuffed by prosecutor Michael Kane, who also ordered him to turn over all of the material he had gathered. With the help of other prosecutors he knew around the state, who respected him and agreed that the grand jury was not listening to all relevant evidence, Smit got both rulings reversed. It was my impression that it was not the prosecuting attorneys but the grand jurors themselves who wanted to hear from both of us.

Since grand jury proceedings are held in secret, I don't know what Smit testified to or whether it conformed to what I said. But a number of media sources wrote of a general consensus that what we both told the grand jurors focused them to their final result.

Bryan Morgan had called to tell me the grand jury wanted me to testify and to bring any notes I had. "I told them you didn't have any notes," he said.

"I do have notes," I said.

"You do?"

I did bring them with me; and when I got in the grand jury room, they let me read my notes pretty much verbatim into the record, including my candid observations on many of the key players.

Two of the grand jurors had backgrounds in science, so I knew it would be important to explain to them what I did and how we had developed the discipline. I recall one member asking me something like, "What if we told you there was evidence that two people were involved in this crime?"

"I've investigated and testified in cases in which I thought there were two people involved," I replied, "but I don't see it here." Then I added, "But if you actually have the evidence you mention, then why am I here? Why are you talking to me? Go with your evidence."

He backed off.

On October 13, 1999, the grand jury and Alex Hunter announced they had found insufficient evidence to indict anyone in the murder of JonBenét Ramsey. Since Colorado law specified that a true bill of indictment must be signed by both the jury foreman and the district attorney, it remained ambiguous which party had led the way in not indicting the Ramseys or anyone else.

Lou Smit and I didn't formally meet until after the grand jury testimony. But once we did, we quickly became friends, based on mutual admiration and respect. After I completed my grand jury appearance, the Ramsey lawyers said that Smit wanted to meet me. We drove out to his home in Colorado Springs.

When he opened the front door, he greeted me with, "John, it took me ten months to conclude that the Ramseys were innocent and it only took you four days." The situations weren't exactly comparable; I was doing a quick criminal investigative analysis and he had undertaken a full-scale police-type investigation. But I have to say, a statement like that from an individual of the stature of Lou Smit was one of the greatest compliments I've ever received.

He admitted that like me, he went into the investigation assuming the Ramseys were probably the killers. He took me inside and showed me a PowerPoint presentation he had put together. Seeing the way Smit had gone about his own research and analysis reinforced my belief in the Ramseys' innocence.

As he went over his case materials and presentation with me, I told him how impressed I was by his work. Then he told me some things that didn't come as much of a surprise. One was about a visit he, Steve Thomas and Alex Hunter had made to Quantico, to consult with the successor of my old group, renamed the Child Abduction and Serial Killer Unit (CASKU).

As they were piecing together evidence and making a case for the Ramseys as the killers, Smit declared that the evidence just didn't fit. At that point, he related, the unit chief made a show of throwing his credentials down on the conference table and saying something to the effect, "If the Ramseys didn't do it, I'll turn in my creds!"

This squared with another report I received from Kenneth Lanning, a member of the Behavioral Science Unit and the Bureau's leading expert on crimes against children. Ken's research, writing and teaching have been groundbreaking, and his influence on the field is profound. At one point, Ken was asked to sit in on a conference on the case. After hearing the presentation, he told the other agents that they weren't allowing for the possibility of an intruder, and what they had presented didn't fit with the Ramseys as suspects.

"Ken, you're not saying the Ramseys didn't do it, are you?" one of the special agents asked.

Lanning was never invited back on the case.

The investigation ground on, coming to no conclusion. In 2000, both Steve Thomas and the Ramseys published books. Thomas's chronicle, *JonBenét: Inside the Ramsey Murder Investigation,* fingered Patsy as the killer and John as her accomplice in the cover-up. In *The Death of Innocence,* the Ramseys gave their own side of the story.

In that book, the Ramseys mentioned a local journalist named Robert Christian "Chris" Wolf as a possible suspect and said he "represented too many unanswered questions." Wolf had written about Access Graphics, John Ramsey's company; and according to a former girlfriend, he had acted strangely the day of the murder when he stormed out of his own house, returned muddy the next day and followed the case obsessively. The police had interviewed Wolf and cleared him. He denied any involvement, said he had not even heard of JonBenét before the murder and sued the Ramseys for $50 million for defamation in the U.S. District Court in Atlanta.

Wolf's complaint stated that the Ramseys knew he was not a legitimate suspect, because Patsy had killed her daughter "either accidentally or intentionally" and then undertook "an elaborate and transparent attempt to cover up her crime." His scenario was essentially the same as that in Thomas's book.

On March 31, 2003, Judge Julie E. Carnes, a former federal prosecutor, dismissed the case on a motion for summary judgment on the ground that if Wolf could not prove by clear and convincing evidence (the standard in a civil case) that his theory that the Ramseys killed JonBenét was true; *then he cannot demonstrate that their Statement concerning his status as a suspect was made with the requisite malice* (a critical element in defamation).

In her ninety-three-page dismissal order, Carnes stated that if anything, the Ramseys' book "understated" the police department's interest in Wolf. She took it upon herself to evaluate all the evidence and strongly criticized Boulder PD and the FBI for trying to use the media to create a guilty image of the Ramseys in the collective mind of the public. She had particular criticism for Steve Thomas, comparing his work unfavorably to that of Lou Smit:

> Whereas Detective Smit's summary testimony concerning the investigation is based on evidence, Detective Thomas' theories appear to lack substantial evidentiary support. Indeed, while Detective Smit is an experienced and respected homicide detective, Detective Thomas had no investigative experience concerning homicide cases prior to this case. In short, the plaintiff's evidence that the [Ramseys] killed their daughter and covered up their crime is based on little more than the fact that the defendants were present in the house during the murder.

There was, she wrote, *abundant evidence . . . that an intruder entered their [the Ramseys'] home at some point during the night of Dec. 25, 1996, and killed their daughter.*
On all major points, Judge Carnes used solid legal and investigative reasoning in a statement more far-reaching in its assertion

of the Ramseys' innocence than any official document or opinion before. She dismissed the idea that Patsy would have staged the body to make it look as if her accidental killing of her daughter had been some other kind of crime, as well as the theory that she committed the crime out of depression over a supposedly failing marriage.

Although plaintiff presents such evidence in support of his theory, Carnes wrote, *if accepted as true, [it] cuts against plaintiff's theory that Mr. Ramsey assisted his wife in the "cover-up" of JonBenét's murder. In other words, if the marriage was shaky, it arguably seems less likely that the innocent spouse would help the guilty spouse cover up her murder of their child.*

She also put to rest the notion that the Ramseys, in spite of lawyering up, had not cooperated with the police: *Despite widespread criticism that defendants failed to cooperate in the murder investigation, defendants note that they agreed, on at least three occasions, to be interviewed separately by representatives of the police and of the Boulder County district attorney's office.*

Furthermore, she wrote: *During the course of the investigation, defendants signed over one hundred releases for information requested by the police, and provided all evidence and information requested by the police.*

I found this ruling highly gratifying because

Judge Carnes summed up what I had been trying to get across for years: To use any of the physical or behavioral evidence against the Ramseys, you have to jump through so many logical hoops that the whole theory falls apart.

While this case was unfolding, I got a call from Bryan Morgan, who said that the new Boulder County district attorney Mary Keenan wanted to talk to me. I flew out and met with her and her staff. This was the first time in my career I'd been asked to provide an analysis to the defense and prosecution in the same case.

The same month that Judge Carnes's ruling came down, Keenan issued the following statement:

DISTRICT ATTORNEY'S OFFICE —
  TWENTIETH JUDICIAL
  DISTRICT
MARY I. KEENAN, DISTRICT
  ATTORNEY
April 7, 2003

I have carefully reviewed the Order of United States District Court Judge Julie Carnes in the civil case of *Wolf* v. *John Ramsey and Patricia Ramsey.* I agree with the Court's conclusion that "the weight of the evidence is more consistent with a theory that an intruder murdered Jon-

Benét than it is with a theory that Mrs. Ramsey did so."

Although issued in the context of a civil case, the Court's ruling is a thoughtful and well reasoned decision based on the evidence that was presented by the parties in that case. It should be read in its entirety.

John and Patricia Ramsey have been the focus of an exhaustive investigation with regard to the murder of their daughter, JonBenét, for more than six years. People charged with a crime are presumed to be innocent until proven guilty in court. Since Mr. and Mrs. Ramsey have not even been charged, much less convicted, they must be presumed innocent and must be treated accordingly.

For several months, my office has been investigating new and other unpursued leads, most of which involve the possibility that an intruder committed this crime. We are proceeding with the full co-operation of the Ramseys, Detective Lou Smit, and the Boulder Police Department. We are all focused on the apprehension and successful prosecution of the killer of JonBenét.

Sadly, neither Patsy Ramsey nor Lou Smit lived to see that happen. Three years after her cancer recurred, Patsy passed away on

June 24, 2006, at forty-nine years of age. She died in her father's house with John by her side. She is buried in Georgia, next to Jon-Benét.

After experiencing abdominal pain that turned out to be the result of metastasized colon cancer, Lou Smit died at seventy-five years of age on August 11, 2010, at Pikes Peak Hospice in Colorado Springs, Colorado. Shortly before Lou's passing, John Ramsey had come to the hospice, where he was staying, to spend several hours with him and pray at his bedside. John told us he felt honored to speak at Lou's funeral.

Mark and I have written that probably the worst thing that can happen to a person or couple is to have their child die by violence. Because of the Ramsey case, we realize that there is something even worse: to be falsely accused of that crime.

There is one strange coda to this case that shows how anyone can be taken in by assumptions, even us.

On August 16, 2006, authorities in Bangkok, Thailand, arrested a forty-one-year-old expatriate primary-school teacher named John Mark Karr. He was a divorced father of three from Petaluma, California, with a previous charge of possession of child pornography. He had come to the attention of the Boulder DA's Office when Michael Tracey, a journalism professor at the University of Colorado, very responsibly turned over copies of e-mails he had exchanged with Karr for four years. The Thai authorities were working from a sealed arrest warrant signed by Boulder County District Court judge Roxanne Bailin.

Clearly, there was something strange about Karr. When he was questioned by the police in Bangkok, he said he was with JonBenét when she died. He told a subsequent press conference, "I love JonBenét," and that she died accidentally. When he was asked if he was innocent, he replied, "No." Lieutenant General Suwat Tumrongsiskul, of the Thai Immigration Police, reported that Karr admitted attempting to kidnap JonBenét and strangled her after his plan went bad.

Karr was brought back to Los Angeles, where he waived extradition to Colorado.

As soon as we heard about Karr, Mark and I figured the case had finally been solved and the long quest for justice for JonBenét was nearing its conclusion. Karr seemed weird enough and amoral enough to have pulled this off. He had been married twice, first to a thirteen-year-old and then to a sixteen-year-old, and had become a substitute teacher so he could hang around children.

But it wasn't the evidence that most convinced us. Frankly, we didn't even look at it very closely. We reasoned that with all of the sorry mistakes and embarrassments of this globally publicized case, the Boulder authorities must be absolutely certain they had this guy dead to rights before they brought him halfway around the world to face the music.

So we were as shocked as anyone when Boulder County District Attorney Mary Lacy announced that DNA samples given up by the suspect did not match the evidence found on JonBenét's body and so "the case of the *People* versus *John Mark Karr* has been vacated."

We couldn't believe it! They had been mistaken yet again, and we had fallen for it for the same reason we had criticized others — for going in with a preconceived idea rather than letting facts and evidence direct our thinking. Despite all of our experience, we had fallen for a false confession and were just relieved that neither of us had accepted any media invitations when the Karr story first broke.

To be fair, I think Mary Lacy would have preferred to gather all of the evidence first and then act, but the publicity that leaked out forced her hand. But we can't deny that we jumped to an improper conclusion without full information. The lesson was well learned.

As of this writing, Karr is living under the name "Alexis Valoran Reich" and is preparing to transition into a woman.

■ ■ ■

Who did kill JonBenét Ramsey during the night of Christmas, 1996? I don't know. As a profiler, with the information and resources I had to work with, I can suggest the *type of person* who did it and the strategies that might help identify him and bring him to justice. Equally important, I can suggest who *did not do it,* and my views on that have not altered at all since the day I first met John and Patricia Ramsey. As I've explained, the role of the profiler is to redirect or refocus an investigation and to help police narrow and analyze their suspect list.

Will the case ultimately be solved? Who knows? At this point, it is doubtful, since the heat is long off. The best chance would probably be if the subject is arrested for something else and certain critical dots get connected. When last we spoke to John Ramsey, he felt as I did that it was probably someone who had a deep grudge against him and was getting revenge through his child. He confided a few possibilities to us.

Could the case have been solved if it was handled properly from the beginning? I told the police detectives at the time that I thought it definitely was solvable. Had Lou Smit or someone of his experience, stature and wisdom led from the beginning, I think it would have been solved.

Each murder leaves a terrible legacy in its wake, rippling out in ever-expanding circles from the victim. This one left an even larger and deeper wake than most with its compounding of injustice. Not only were two kind and upstanding people robbed of their beloved child, but because of a vicious and malicious rush to judgment — fueled by a media that couldn't get enough of it — they were tormented and isolated for years by accusations that they were killers, while the real killer remains free. How can you properly grieve under such a burden?

We know that the aftermath of a child's death — whether by disease, accident or crime — can either tear a couple apart or bring them closer together.

"It was really Patsy and me against the world," John recalled. "We were pretty close to begin with, but this probably made us even closer. And if there is any lesson in all of this, it isn't that an innocent child was murdered — because, unfortunately, that happens all too often — but that the police persecuted innocent people."

No matter your faith, no matter your inner strength, when something like this happens, there are wounds that never heal. "Your primary responsibility as a father is to protect your children, and I couldn't do that," John reflected.

How has his life changed since the tragedy? "Before all this happened, I used to worry all the time. Even when things were going great, I'd worry about what would happen if I lost my job — how would I support my family? I could always find something to worry about. Now I just don't pay any attention to that sort of thing. I'm beyond it."

We asked him if having lost two daughters and a wife — having already undergone the cruelest that life could throw at him — made him "emotionally untouchable."

"No, I'm not emotionally untouchable. After JonBenét died, I didn't care what happened. I wouldn't have taken my own life, but if something had happened to me, it would have been fine. Then gradually I came to accept that I still had other children to take care of, and other things to live for. I realized that I had to do what I could to clear the family name — if not for my own sake, then for my children's. And so no matter what, I think each of us has to work toward the idea that our best days are still ahead of us."

With John Ramsey's faith and strength of character, and concern for others, he just might achieve that goal. He remarried in 2011, to a fashion designer named Jan Rousseaux, and we wish them the best of everything.

Any highly publicized murder case becomes

representative and symbolic — of our own fears, our fascination with and repulsion from evil, and of our involvement and inter-relationship with our fellow human beings. They work as real-life embodiments of classic tragedies.

Knowing John Ramsey as I do, having known his late wife, Patsy, I can only think of them as individual human beings rather than symbols or pop culture celebrities. Like so many others, they were fine, loving, generous people; and in spite of everything, John still is.

I hope, with all that this tragedy represents, that we will not lose sight of the most basic and obvious element of all: A beautiful and unique child has been prevented from growing up, from living her life and fulfilling her own special destiny. The family that raised her has had to endure the unendurable, and beyond. That is something that every decent human being must mourn.

■ ■ ■ ■

SATANIC PANIC

■ ■ ■ ■

CHAPTER 17
ROBIN HOOD HILLS

"Hello, this is John Douglas. I understand you want to talk to me."

It was March of 2006. My website directed inquiries to my attorney in New York, Steven Mark, who had given me the name and number of someone who wanted me to consult on a case. This was an Arkansas phone number.

"Yes, thank you for calling. My name is Lorri Davis." She had a nice voice. My instantaneous profile was early thirties, educated and sophisticated, maybe a professional of some sort. "Are you familiar with the West Memphis Three case?" she asked.

"No," I said.

"Three young men were convicted of killing three 8-year-old boys in West Memphis, Arkansas, in 1993. But every one of them is innocent."

Of course they are. No murder defendant is ever really guilty.

"Powerful people in Hollywood are fans of

yours and believe in the work you do," she went on. "Would you look at the case?"

"What is your relationship to it?" I inquired.

"I'm married to Damien Echols, one of the defendants," she explained. "He was already in prison when we married."

Okay, profile's wrong! She may be educated and sophisticated, but this is another nut job.

I say "another" because this was a phenomenon well known to many of us involved with the criminal justice field. For various reasons, certain women tend to fall in love with incarcerated killers. It often starts out as a pen pal relationship, either out of altruism or simple curiosity. It can then blossom into love, and then even marriage with the full knowledge that her spouse will likely forever remain behind bars. And that is a good thing, because this individual is a violent offender; and if he ever got out, she would likely end up one of his victims.

The various reasons for these women's behavior include loneliness and a real or perceived inability to make it with "normal" men; a vicarious fascination with excitement, violence or the taboo; a desire to nurture or "mother" those who have never had sufficient attention or "understanding." This is often combined with the seemingly contradictory feelings of low self-esteem and an illogical, self-righteous confidence in their ability to "reform" the killer and make him a peaceful and productive member of society. Then, of course, some of them marry because it is "safe"; they can feel married without actually having to go through the accommodations of living with a husband.

There can be other motivations as well, but these are the ones we see over and over again. As much as it annoys me, since I think their sympathy is misdirected, I often feel sorry for these women. They can be pretty pathetic.

And who were these "powerful people in Hollywood" who were such big fans? The whole thing sounded strange.

But the more she talked, the more I sensed there was something different about Lorri Davis that just refused to fit this mold. She explained she was a landscape architect in New York who had seen an HBO documentary film entitled *Paradise Lost: The Child Murders at Robin Hood Hills* and had become convinced the three convicted defendants were innocent. She had begun corresponding with Damien Echols, the so-called ringleader who was on death row in Arkansas. Eventually they had fallen in love and decided to get married, even though their lives would essentially be lived apart and their relationship potentially short.

"I don't know anything about the case," I repeated, "so I don't know what conclusions I can draw. We'll have to get an attorney involved to write up an agreement." The contract was important, because if I did get involved and my conclusions were not to the client's liking, it had to be clear that my findings would not be altered.

I gave the standard rap about buying my time, but not my opinion; that they would be free to use or not use my conclusions as they wished; that I would not reveal any negative information obtained through nonpublic sources, but to remember that anything they asked me to put in writing would be discoverable by the prosecution in any future legal proceeding. I ended by saying that when I worked on a case like this, I was always ultimately working for the victims, no matter who brought me in.

Lorri said she thought all that was fine.

"Would the agreement be with you?" I asked.

No, she said, it would be with the lead appellate attorney, Dennis Riordan, of Riordan and Horgan in San Francisco.

"And who are these powerful Hollywood people, and how are they involved?"

"I can't tell you that until after you've signed the agreement," she stated. Very strange.

From there, things progressed quickly. She talked to Steve Mark, who wrote up an agreement. The "they" turned out to be a number of prominent show business people who, like Lorri, had seen the *Paradise Lost* film and concluded that the West Memphis Three were wrongly charged and convicted.

I began speaking regularly with Lorri. Normally, as I've suggested, I find women who fall in love with convicted murderers to be creepy and cripplingly dependent. But as I listened to Lorri, I could tell something else was going on here. Despite the seeming illogic of involving yourself with someone who is going to spend the rest of his (probably short) life in prison, she seemed to have her logic system and critical ego in perfect working order. She seemed neither dependent nor needy. Rather, she was extremely mission-oriented, but without losing her sense of humor or concern for the normal considerations of everyday life.

I received a voluminous amount of case material — forensic reports, interrogation accounts, photographs, newspaper clippings, maps, disks, timelines and the entire trial record. I set to work, immersing myself in the case.

Lorri suggested I interview Damien in prison, but I told her that wouldn't be helpful to me. At this stage, I didn't want to get emotionally involved or be influenced by personal relationships. I wanted to base my opinion strictly on the facts of the case.

West Memphis, a city of some 27,000 residents, lies just to the west, or the Arkansas side, of the Mississippi River. It connects to its larger and distinctly more cosmopolitan namesake — Memphis, Tennessee — by bridges for Interstates 40 and 55, which split off from each other near the northeastern edge of town. These two highways join the country from coast to coast and from Lake Michigan to the Gulf of Mexico. The fact that the east-west I-40 and north-south I-55 come together for several miles here makes West Memphis an attractive place of business for anyone servicing the trucking industry.

The Blue Beacon Truck Wash, part of a hundred-plus location chain throughout the United States and Canada, was one such establishment. This particular location closed in 2012, but in 1993 it was a thriving business just off the interstates' South Service Road. South of the highway there is a long channel running roughly east to west that came off Ten Mile Bayou, one of the many such waterways in the area. It is called, appropriately enough, the Ten Mile Bayou Diversion Ditch. Its function is to take up the rainwater that normally would flow into the Mississippi from the bayou, but is blocked because of the levee system that keeps the river from flooding. The channel carries water south to a point beyond the levee.

Back then, squeezed in between the highway and Ten Mile Bayou Diversion Ditch, was a heavily wooded patch of land known locally as Robin Hood Hills, or just plain Robin Hood. There was a creeklike drainage channel coming off the diversion ditch, which ran into the heart of the woods, and a large sewage drainpipe supported by metal beams across the channel, which allowed brave souls, or those wanting to seem brave, access to Robin Hood from the neighborhood of modest houses to the south.

Parents tried to keep their kids out of Robin Hood Hills. It was reputed to be a haven for drug use and disreputable transients from the interstates. But the creek, hiking and bike-riding trails, rope swing and dense foliage, where any fantasy adventure was possible, were too much of a temptation for all but the most obedient or timid of children.

On May 5, 1993, Christopher "Chris" Byers, Michael Moore and Steven "Stevie" Branch, all eight-year-olds from the adjoining neighborhood, went missing. They were best friends and often hung out together. All three were second graders at nearby Weaver Elementary School.

John Mark Byers, Christopher's stepfather, was the first to report his concerns to the West Memphis Police Department (WMPD), at about 8:00 P.M. He said neither he nor his wife, Melissa, Chris's mother, had seen him since 5:30 P.M., nor was it like him to be late.

Officer Regina Meek responded to Byers'

call at 8:08. While she was taking his information, Dana Moore, who lived across Barton Street from the Byers, came over and reported that her son Michael was also missing. She had last seen him around 6:00 P.M., riding bikes with Stevie. Chris was on the back of Stevie's bike. She'd lost sight of them and sent her nine-year-old daughter, Dawn, to find them. Dawn went after them, but she couldn't keep up. Dana Moore described the brown-haired, blue-eyed boy in his habitual outfit: his blue Cub Scouts uniform.

Stevie Branch's mom, Pamela "Pam" Hobbs, was equally distressed. They lived a few blocks away from the Byers and Moores, and she had not seen him since right after he came home from school. Her husband, Terry — Stevie's stepfather — got up and left the house early each morning for his job distributing ice cream to retail stores. He said he hadn't seen Stevie all day. The boy had brown hair and blue eyes. Chris's hair and eyes were light brown. All three were proud Cub Scouts, though Chris and Stevie didn't wear their uniforms everywhere like Michael did.

As the alarm spread, neighborhood parents and friends joined the police and began searching — anywhere they thought the boys might be. Some even ventured into Robin Hood Hills, which took on a distinctly sinister and forbidding aura once the sun went down. It was difficult to see anything at night in the dense woods, but the search was resumed at sunup. Nobody found anything, not even a clue as to which direction the boys might have gone. By now, the parents were beside themselves with worry.

Meanwhile, Gary Gitchell, chief inspector of the West Memphis PD detective division, had requested a search-and-rescue team from the Crittenden County Sheriff's Office. The Memphis, Tennessee, PD sent its own helicopter to join the search, but the foliage in the Robin Hood area was too dense for any kind of ground visualization.

By 1:30 P.M. the next day, most of the searchers had abandoned Robin Hood Hills. But that was when Steve Jones, a county juvenile officer, glanced down the steep sides of the creek near the Blue Beacon Truck Wash and saw a black tennis shoe. He radioed for backup before he tried to retrieve it. Police Sergeant Mike Allen was on the other side of the woods, in the neighborhood. He made his way across the sewage drainpipe over the overflow ditch and rushed to meet Jones, where he was waiting.

As soon as Jones pointed to what he had seen, Allen clambered down into the water to retrieve the sneaker. He lost his balance and fell in. As he later described it, "I raised my right foot up and a body floated to the surface."

It was a child. He was naked and his back

381

was severely arched. Soon police were all over the site. Gary Gitchell established a crime scene perimeter and his men began looking to see if there were two more bodies nearby.

Detective Bryn Ridge took on the unpleasant task of climbing down into the stream and searching, foot by foot, on his hands and knees. He was hoping against hope that he would not find anything, but he knew that at any step he might. Instead, he ran into a stick stuck upright in the mud. When he pulled it up, there was a child's white shirt attached, twisted around the end of the stick as if someone had been trying to hide it by pushing it down into the streambed.

The police had not wanted to disturb the crime scene, but personnel felt they couldn't just leave the body in the water. While this was an understandable human and humane response, it was the wrong one. The victim was dead, beyond help. The scene should have been left alone until the medical examiner and crime scene technicians arrived.

Instead, Ridge waded back and carefully lifted the corpse onto the creek bank. From photos the officers had been given, they identified it as Michael Moore. The unnatural arch of his back was because he had been hog-tied — left wrist to left ankle and right wrist to right ankle — but not with rope or cord. Rather, he had been restrained with shoelaces, presumably his own. Wounds to the head made it look like he had been struck hard, more than once.

Men and women in the operational end of law enforcement get hardened to seeing horrible things, but almost no one can harden him or herself to something like this.

Ridge got back in the water. Tracing the bottom with his hands, he found more clothing, including Michael's Cub Scout cap and shirt and two more pairs of sneakers — both with their laces missing. Soon they had an almost complete collection of what the three boys had been wearing, most of it secured with sticks beneath the bottom of the creek. *What was that all about?* I wondered. Significantly, much of the clothing was turned inside out, suggesting it had been hurriedly pulled off, either by the boys themselves or their attacker.

Now there was no hope among the officers, only the waiting horror of where the next body would turn up. Ridge discovered it downstream, adhering to the soft mud. He pulled it loose with a firm tug and guided it to the surface. It was Stevie Branch, naked and hog-tied with shoelaces like Michael.

Christopher Byers was found a few minutes later, facedown in the muddy water. He was naked and similarly tied, but it was even worse: it seemed he had been castrated. Only skin remained where his genital organs should have been. Puncture marks, such as would be made with a large knife, surrounded the area.

Detectives found two bicycles in the water, one red and one green, not far from where the large drainpipe allowed access to Robin Hood over the diversion ditch. By that time, county coroner Ken Hale had been called. He examined all three bodies, where the officers had left them on the creek bank, and pronounced death at around four in the afternoon. At that point, no determination was made as to when the boys had actually died.

Gitchell directed that the entire scene be photographed and videotaped and also ordered sandbagging of the stream above where the bodies and clothing had been found so they could search for more evidence, as well as Chris Byers's missing body parts.

I noted in my reading that investigators had not retrieved and catalogued the sticks used to submerge the clothing in the mud.

After giving his orders, Gitchell came back out of the woods, where an anxious crowd had gathered behind the yellow police tape. The first person he talked to was Terry Hobbs, Stevie Branch's stepfather, who crumpled to the ground and began weeping. As soon as she heard, Pam — his wife and Stevie's mother — fainted. Gitchell spoke briefly to some reporters; then he went over to Christopher's stepfather, John Mark Byers.

Byers said he had been out searching the area most of the night and thought he must have come within ten or fifteen feet of where Gitchell said the bodies were found.

The community went into mourning. Grief counselors were brought into the boys' elementary school. A sizable reward was established for information leading to the arrest and prosecution of the killer or killers. Neighbors and church groups took up collections to help pay for the funerals and burials. Gary Gitchell said his detectives were looking into a wide range of possibilities, including that the murders might have resulted from "gang or cult activity" — though he didn't say if there was any evidence to support this hypothesis.

News of the horrendous crime spread quickly. Governor James "Jim" Guy Tucker contacted Gitchell and offered the services of the Arkansas State Police to help in the investigation. But as would happen three years later with the JonBenét Ramsey case in Colorado, Gitchell turned down the state police. It is possible, like the Boulder PD, he was confident his department could close the case itself. But there might have been another reason. At the time, WMPD was under investigation by the state police for corruption, resulting from allegations that one or more of the officers had taken confiscated drugs from the evidence room and had sold them for his own illegal purposes. If that was what was going through Gitchell's mind, working with the state police could have been extremely awkward.

When I read the initial reports, my first thought was a mixed sexual homicide: that is, a crime committed for sexual gratification with elements of both organization and pre-planning and disorganization, or reacting to the scene. It was unclear whether murder was the initial intention, but it seemed likely that the crime got out of hand, since there were three victims, resulting in the killing of all of them. When we see a homicide in which the genitals, buttocks, anus and/or female breasts are primarily involved, we further classify it as a lust murder. Since there appeared to be a castration and all three boys were stripped and suggestively bound, that designation seemed likely here. But I wanted to withhold judgment until I had immersed myself completely in the case.

The autopsies were performed by Dr. Frank J. Peretti, a pathologist with the Arkansas State Crime Lab. Chris Byers, he reported, had died of multiple injuries, while Stevie Branch and Michael Moore had drowned in about two feet of water after receiving less intensive wounds. Unlike Chris, neither one of them appeared to have any defensive wounds, suggesting they had not struggled.

As details of the murders spread throughout the community, residents began to speak of the undertones of evil and darkness attending the case. Lieutenant James Sudbury, of the West Memphis PD, contacted Steve Jones, the juvenile probation officer who had made the first horrible discovery in Robin Hood Hills. Both men thought this looked like a cult-type crime, and Sudbury wanted to know if any of Jones's young charges was capable of this kind of atrocity.

Jones's boss, Jerry Driver, was the senior juvenile probation officer. He was a former airline pilot who had retired and opened a housecleaning service, but it didn't last long. Afterward, he went into probation work. The bearded, bearlike Driver had become deeply concerned about satanic cult activity and saw signs everywhere that it was coming to east-central Arkansas. When the three boys were murdered, he realized his worst fears had come true. He made up a list of the eight young men he considered most capable of committing a crime like this. On the top of that list were Damien Wayne Echols and another boy known to be his close friend, Charles Jason Baldwin. I wondered why he had put them on this list. He shared his list with the local police agencies.

Damien Echols, eighteen years of age, was what was commonly identified as a troubled kid. He had been born Michael Wayne Hutchison, and as long as his parents Eddie Joe and Pamela Hutchison were married, he was constantly being moved around due to Joe's work. *By the age of twelve or thirteen,* he wrote in his memoir *Almost Home, I had already decided life was hopeless.* Because of all this, he developed into a loner, turning inward to reading, music and an apparently long-term quest for spiritual meaning, which involved moving from his Pentecostal background into Buddhism, Hinduism, Islam and eventually Catholicism. Along the way he looked into Wicca.

At one point homeless, the family moved in with Pamela's mother, Francis, and her new husband, Ivan, in West Memphis, while Joe looked for a permanent place for them. But the strain between Joe and Pamela had been building for years, and the marriage fell apart. Michael had grown very attached to Ivan and was devastated when the man died a few years later.

Sometime after her divorce from Joe, Pamela married Jack Echols and moved into his house in West Memphis. In 1990, Jack adopted Michael, who reluctantly took his stepfather's last name. Since he was changing his surname, he decided to change his first name to Damien, having been inspired by reading the story of Father Damien de Veuster, the Belgian Catholic priest who dedicated his life to the lepers of Molokai, Hawaii. Ironically, once Damien was associated with the Robin Hood Hills murders, the story spread that the new name came from *The Omen* movie series about the earthly appearance of the Antichrist.

The life Damien describes with Jack, his mother and his sister, Michelle, was bleak. Jack joined a succession of small Pentecostal churches and moved the family into smaller shacks, each sending them further down the poverty ladder. When his grandmother had a heart attack and needed care, they moved into her trailer park house.

I've heard many jokes about poor people living in trailer parks, Damien wrote, *but I no longer considered myself poor. I was now in the lap of luxury — I could take a shower whenever I wanted, there was central heat for the winter, and a window unit air conditioner for the summer. The toilet flushed, there were no crop dusters, and we had neighbors. It was heaven.*

In junior high school, Damien developed the persona that ultimately brought him to the attention of the authorities. He later conceded he was suffering from depression, which was certainly understandable, given his circumstances. His grades slipped and he became disruptive in class. He developed a passion for heavy metal, especially the bands Metallica, Iron Maiden, Megadeth, Slayer and Anthrax. He also liked the popular Irish rock band U2. He dressed all in black, wearing a secondhand black trench coat even in the humid Arkansas summer. He shaved one side of his head and let the hair on the other side grow long. In his ongoing spiritual quest, he embraced paganism, mysticism and the occult. He became a Wiccan, following a path that he equated with nature and the creative force of life.

And he found his new best friend.

CHAPTER 18
DAMIEN AND JASON

On the surface, Charles Jason Baldwin, known by his middle name, was nothing like Damien. Two years younger, with a slight build and curly blond hair he wore long, Jason was a diligent student with a recognized talent in art. Some of his teachers had encouraged him to pursue it as a career. But the two boys hit it off, talking big ideas, swapping information about the latest counterculture bands, sensing a kinship they felt was absent from the rest of the narrow-minded rural community. Jason, whom most people described as quiet and polite, liked to hunt and fish and kept pet snakes. His mother, Angela Gail Grinnell, had a history of mental illness and drug abuse. At one point, she had been involuntarily committed to the East Arkansas Regional Mental Health Center.

Jason came from a similar background to Damien's and so many others in this poor, semi-rural community, including two of the slain boys. His parents had divorced and remarried several times, so it became a challenge to keep all the last names straight. Jason's father, Larry, lived in central Arkansas. He and Gail were second cousins.

By his middle teen years, Damien was getting into minor scrapes with the law. He and a girlfriend ran away together one night and went into an abandoned house to sleep. Police arrested him and turned him over to juvenile authorities for evaluation. He was sent to Charter Hospital, near Little Rock, where he was diagnosed as manic-depressive and put on the antidepressant drug Trofanil. When he was released and sent back to West Memphis, he was placed under the supervision of juvenile probation officer Jerry Driver.

This was not his first encounter with Jerry Driver. "Jerry Driver harassed and tormented me for years. He's the one who had me put in those mental institutions," Damien said, adding that Driver cruised near his trailer home frequently, looking for kids in some kind of trouble. For whatever reason or combination of reasons, Driver was a figure of fear and loathing in the poorer neighborhoods he patrolled.

"What brought me to his attention in the very first place," Damien recalled, "I have a teenaged girlfriend, her parents find out we're having sex, and say, 'You're not allowed to see each other anymore.'

"So we come up with the ingenious plan —

'Well, let's just run away, then.' So we run away. Her parents call the cops to come and find us. They find us, they take us in. That's when we encounter Jerry Driver. We're juveniles, so they bring Jerry Driver in. It's the first time he sees me. That's when he targets me, zeroes in on me.

"Immediately, the first night, he starts asking me all these satanic questions: 'Well, have you heard anything? Do you know anything about a satanic cult in the area? What have you heard? Have you seen anything strange going on? You know, we really need some help with this.' This was years before the murders. I was, like, sixteen, seventeen, something like that."

The instability that had characterized Damien's life continued. His mother, Pamela, finally divorced Jack Echols and remarried Joe Hutchison, moving with him to Portland, Oregon, and securing the parole office's permission to bring Damien with her. Damien's mental condition worsened; he took to drinking heavily, and his parents were afraid several times he was going to commit suicide.

Damien decided to go back to West Memphis. Staying with a friend, he applied for readmission to high school, but he was told he would need a letter from his parents. As soon as he left the school campus, Jerry Driver arrested him on the grounds that he had violated his parole by leaving his parents' custody in Oregon.

"I went to the high school to register and they said, 'You can't register without a parent or guardian because you're under eighteen.'

"So I go back to my friend's house. Next thing you know, I hear a knock on the door. It's Jerry Driver. He says, 'I'm gonna have to arrest you.'

"I say, 'For what?'

"He says, 'Because you're not living with your parents. Therefore, you're violating the law.' He arrests me and has me put in the mental institution for a month."

Damien was sent back to Charter Hospital; but in the weeks he was there, he seemed to feel better, possibly because of a doctor's insistence that he focus outside of himself and interact with other patients. When he returned to West Memphis, he took his high-school GED exam and passed. He moved in with his girlfriend, Domini Teer, a cute, slender, freckle-faced redhead. She soon became pregnant. When his parents moved back to West Memphis, he lived part-time with them.

Around noon on Friday, May 7, 1993, Lieutenant James Sudbury and Steve Jones came over to the Hutchisons' house in the Broadway Trailer Park and secured their permission to talk to Damien. Sudbury snapped a Polaroid photo of Damien showing a pentagram tattoo on his chest and another arm tattoo they couldn't identify. They asked him if he was involved in cult activities. He said he wasn't.

"They start asking me and telling me things," Damien recounted. "They take me into a bedroom at my house and they say, 'What if the bodies were found in the water? Why do you think they would be in the water?'

"I say, 'I guess to hide them.'

" 'Well, what do you think if maybe somebody urinated in the mouths and they pushed the bodies into the water to wash the urine out of them? Do you think maybe that's a possibility?' "

Damien recollected that he was surprised by the conversation: " 'Okay,' I'm thinking, 'that's some freaky stuff that you would even think to ask me that, but 'Okay.'

"The next thing I know, we get to trial and they're saying, 'He told us they were pushed in the water to wash the urine out of them.' "

The following day, Inspector Gitchell interviewed John Mark Byers, which would be standard practice in any murder case involving children. You always investigate those closest and with the most ready access to the young victim first. Interestingly, although they were interviewed for routine information, there was no organized investigation of his wife, Melissa, or of the other parents, Pam and Terry Hobbs, or Dana and Todd Moore.

The day after the Byers interview, the officers requested an official interview with Damien. They also talked to Jason Baldwin, knowing he was a close friend. Despite an absence of any kind of direct or inferential evidence, they were convinced the boys had something to do with the child murders and put them under even closer surveillance.

Police followed up on various tips, though some were mishandled from the beginning. One such was the unidentified person of interest who came to be referred to as "Mr. Bojangles." According to police reports, around eight-forty on the night of the murders, Marty King, manager of a Bojangles' restaurant about a mile from the crime scene across Ten Mile Bayou, called West Memphis PD to report that someone had seen a black male "dazed and covered with blood and mud" inside the ladies' room. It was unclear whether all of the blood was his or not, but he left some on the restroom wall when his arm brushed against it. He had also defecated on the floor.

About forty-five minutes later, Officer Regina Meek arrived at the scene and drove her scout car into the drive-through lane to inquire. By this time, the man was long gone, so she just took the report and left without going inside.

When news of the murders came out the next day, Marty King very responsibly thought there could be a connection and called the police twice. Crime scene investigators came over after finishing at the Robin Hood Hills site and gathered evidence from the Bojangles' ladies' room. They had not changed their clothing or shoes, which means there was now no way to determine if the two scenes had been cross-contaminated. Also, not knowing his ladies' room might be an accessory site to a murder investigation, King had routinely ordered the restroom cleaned. Dried blood was still visible on the wall and floor tiles and scrapings were taken. By the time anyone was brought to trial, no one knew what had happened to them, though.

A Negroid hair was found on the sheet in which Chris Byers's body had been wrapped when it was transported to the pathology lab. This made the connection to the strange man in the ladies' room all the more tantalizing.

At such an early stage of the investigation before any dots had been connected, it would be impossible to know if Mr. Bojangles was a possible killer, a panicked drifter, who might have stumbled upon the scene at the wrong time, or a totally unrelated red herring. But without physical evidence and not even a contemporaneous visual inspection by the responding officer, an important person of interest was lost.

The police didn't seem that worked up about it, though. Mainly, they were fixated on Damien Echols and his pal Jason Baldwin. As Jerry Driver had noted almost immediately after the discovery of the crime, Damien seemed to fit their image of what a killer of three young boys would be. With nothing but this hunch, they began closely following Damien, parking in front of his house, harassing him, watching his every move. Damien thought they would eventually tire of this and move on. But they didn't. Because they were pretty sure they had their motive:

Satanic-ritual murder.

CHAPTER 19
LOOKING FOR LUCIFER

I didn't know everything about the case yet, but from the facts and the evidence I'd reviewed, already I knew one thing for certain: The police and the investigators were wrong. *This crime had nothing to do with Satanism or any other kind of dark ritual.* There were simply no indicators and frankly, the idea was far-fetched to begin with.

But the police were not alone in their idea about perverse, ritualized murder. They had seen pentagrams and other perceived symbols of Devil worship painted on walls and concrete bridge abutments on the outskirts of town. In fact, around this time, stories of cult-oriented activity had been surfacing all over the country.

TV talk shows featured so-called cult experts, as well as young people who had been "saved" from damnation and renounced their evil ways. Over and over, the public was given the figure of fifty thousand child abductions per year. While this figure was about right, it gave a completely inaccurate impression, since it mainly referred to abductions by noncustodial parents. The real figure for abductions by strangers was closer to one hundred.

That didn't stop local law enforcement agencies in various parts of the country from holding courses on how to deal with this perceived phenomenon, bringing in the experts to tell them how to recognize the beginnings of Satanism and confront it before it got out of hand. Some said it had always been around, but only now were police and academic institutions paying serious attention. Others said it had grown out of the rebellious 1960s, the "anything goes" era during which lawlessness and disrespect for the rules of God and man were accepted as the norm. Now we were paying the social price as the children raised by that disorderly generation had reached their teens.

What many people didn't realize or refused to accept was that the preoccupation with Satanism was just like any other social vogue whose currency suddenly reaches critical mass in the public imagination. Within a few years, the next vogue would be recovered memory, in which adolescents or adults (often but not exclusively women) would either spontaneously, or under the guidance of a therapist, "recall" an event or pattern of abuse that had happened to them long ago and accounted for current emotional distress. I am sure that many of these memories were genuine, but a great number — quite possibly a majority or even a vast majority — were not. They were merely influenced by the publicity and scrutiny given to the subject. We are always looking for ways to understand and change ourselves, and if the cause of our unhappiness or discomfort can be shown to have come from outside ourselves, it may be easier to deal with.

There is also another phenomenon well known to those of us in law enforcement, medicine, and numerous other fields: The more you focus on something, the more of it you will find, if that's what you're looking for and *want to find.* It is like the first-year medical students who spontaneously develop symptoms of whatever disease they happen to be studying that week.

In the case of organized cult or satanic involvement, we in the FBI looked long and hard for reliable data to back up all the assertions, but we came up pretty empty.

When Ann and Allen Burgess, Robert Ressler and I were putting together the *Crime Classification Manual* in the early 1990s, along with a large committee of specific subject experts, we delved deeply into the idea of satanic murder and related violence. *But we didn't find any.* When we published the second edition in 2006, there was no change, nor will there be any in the third edition we are currently preparing.

The closest we could get was a subcategory of *Extremist Homicide* (itself a subcategory of *Personal Cause Homicide*) that we classified "Religious Extremist Homicide," and a subcategory of *Group Cause Homicide* that we classified "Cult Murder." Religious homicide, though, is seen when religious extremists kill with the perception that they are defending their religion against attacks from outsiders or nonbelievers. Cult murders were seen in small fringe groups organized around a charismatic leader with weird ideas and virtually never had anything to do with religious ritual or symbology. The illustration we cited in *CCM* was the killing of some former members who had strayed away from the cult. Another widely known example would be the 1969 Tate-LaBianca murders in Los Angeles carried out by the Charles Manson "family."

In fact, under the *Group Cause Homicide* section, we felt obliged to insert an explanation:

The National Center for the Analysis of Violent Crime's definition of true occult/satanic murder is murder committed by two or more individuals who rationally plan the crime and whose primary motivation is to fulfill a prescribed satanic ritual calling for the murder. Committee members raised the question of whether occult/satanic murder, as defined above, truly exists aside from the media hype surrounding this subject.

The popularity of occultism/Satanism with the mass media has only served to cloud the issue and sometimes interfere with the objective investigation of a crime. The religious beliefs of a law enforcement officer may further complicate the process of objectively investigating an alleged satanic murder.

We went on to conclude:

In regard to the occurrence of satanic murder, the NCAVC has attempted to solicit cases from several sources who have made such claims. The analysis of crime scene photos from the few cases the NCAVC did receive failed to support the definition of occult/satanic murder or the defining characteristics of crime scene indicators and forensics derived from satanic crime conference material.

Many of the cases we looked at, such as Richard Ramirez, "The Night Stalker," and David Berkowitz, "Son of Sam," exhibited possible indicators of Satanism. However, we found the primary motive in each case was driven by sex, money or interpersonal conflicts that did not satisfy any logical definition of occultism or Satanism. A pentagram left at a crime scene no more made it a satanic crime than a Bible left at the scene made it Christian. In either case, that was more an indicator of a disorganized offender with an unstable personality.

It was determined in every case analyzed that the actual involvement of Satanism was secondary, insignificant or nonexistent. It was also revealed during legal proceedings that it was the *defense* that attempted to introduce Satanism in an effort to escape criminal responsibility or minimize punishment for their client, rather than the prosecution. It reminded me of the late brilliant comedian Flip Wilson's character Geraldine who, when confronted, would say, "The Devil made me do it."

The *Crime Classification Manual* was published and widely available in 1992. But it didn't stop people from believing that the criminal dangers of Satanism were all around them and that everyone was vulnerable, particularly children.

My Quantico colleague Ken Lanning, mentioned earlier in reference to the Ramsey case, was a *CCM* contributor and the FBI's foremost expert on crimes against children. Around the same time the *Manual* was published, Ken wrote a groundbreaking treatise entitled *Investigator's Guide to Allegations of Ritual Child Abuse,* in which he stated that while there had always been belief in a connection between Satanism and crime, it had no basis in fact: *In none of the cases of which I am aware has any evidence of a well-organized satanic cult been found.* He likened the phenomenon to the consistency of alien abduction stories over the years.

The West Memphis police were getting enough similar stories that Gary Gitchell and his detectives were confident they were on the right track. A number of strange or unusual witnesses had come forward with information about Damien and his alleged coparticipant.

The day after the murders, Detective Donald Bray, of the Marion Police Department, a community next to West Memphis, was in the process of administering a polygraph examination to Vicki Hutcheson, a thirty-two-year-old waitress, regarding charges that she had stolen money from her employer. (Don't be confused by the similarity to Damien's birth surname, Hutchison.) With her, she had her eight-year-old son, Aaron, who knew the three slain boys. Aaron told Bray he knew where the boys had been killed; and when he correctly identified the area, Bray took notice and called West Memphis PD.

From then on, though, Aaron's story started to fall apart. First he said he had seen men dressed up in costumes and speaking Spanish; then later he said he had seen John Mark Byers kill his stepson and the two others. He didn't pick out either Damien Echols or Jason Baldwin from photo arrays. But once his story leaked out to the press, the satanic angle picked up steam nonetheless.

Aaron's failure to supply a consistent and convincing story apparently disappointed his mom, Vicki, who was interested in cashing in on some of the reward money, as well as having police forget about the charges against her. She told them that shortly after the murders, she had had a hunch about who the killers might be, and she had wanted to play detective. She said she would allow police to wire her for an intended conversation with Damien, her primary "suspect." The only problem was that she really didn't know Damien, so she asked Aaron's frequent babysitter, seventeen-year-old Jessie Misskelley Jr., to introduce her. She used the pretext that she wanted to go out with him and was interested in the occult.

Jessie was a dropout doing roofing and other odd jobs. He was a slow but obliging kid, with a quick smile but a quicker temper; he had an IQ reported to be seventy-two. He was short, which was one of the things that gave him the nickname "Little Jessie." The other was that his father, a tough and burly auto mechanic, was "Big Jessie." His mother had abandoned the home when he was young. Jessie had been raised by Big Jessie and a series of stepmothers, older siblings and Big Jessie's girlfriends. He said he had always had to stand up for himself, and that had also made him tough. Despite the fact that Big Jessie could be rough, he and Little Jessie adored each other. Jessie depended on him for advice and guidance. The other key adult in his life was Shelby Misskelley, Big Jessie's former wife and the woman who had raised him since he was four.

Jessie told Vicki he hardly knew Damien himself, but he would try to get him to come to her home.

Jessie lived near her in a trailer park in Marion. Based on her statement to the police, Jessie would do odd jobs for her and they became friendly. Vicki claimed he told her how strange Damien seemed, so she thought she had a real chance to entrap Damien through Jessie.

He later explained, "She asked me, was he into witchcraft? I told her, 'I didn't really know. I just knowed [sic] he was a weird person.' "

When Vicki asked him about Jason, Jessie told her he had known him since the sixth grade, that he was a nice person and that they'd always gotten along.

The next time he saw Jason and Damien in the neighborhood, he explained that Vicki wanted to meet them and took them over to her trailer home. Damien later said he didn't know Jessie well; but since he had asked him to meet Vicki, he saw no reason not to oblige.

Damien later told us, "I knew who he was. I'd seen him. It was one of those situations where I was like, 'I don't even really know this kid. I have no idea who this woman is. What the hell's going on?' "

Once he had made the introductions, Jessie left, and he reported that within fifteen minutes Damien's mother, Pamela, came and picked up the two boys. He said he knew nothing about any further relationship.

Vicki was wired for this encounter, but whether the recording of their conversation was audible or not is in dispute. Police claimed they couldn't hear anything, while Vicki said she heard the entire playback at WMPD headquarters. Apparently, though, nothing of use came out of it.

On June 2, she told police that after this first meeting, she had developed an intense but nonsexual relationship with Damien for the sole purpose of getting information from him. She claimed that about two weeks after the murders, she had gone with him and Jessie to a Wiccan *"esbat"* in Turrell, Arkansas. She explained that the *esbat* was a pagan ceremony in observance of the full moon. Recall that Jessie said he knew nothing about any contact between Vicki and Damien after the initial meeting, which he certainly would have noticed had he been with them at the *esbat*. So already we have a conflict of stories.

Damien quickly came to regret agreeing to meet Vicki, but by then it was too late. "When you see crazy coming down the street, cross to the other side," he commented. "And see, my problem my whole life is I'd see crazy coming down the street and I'd say, 'Hey, what's over there?' And it was the same with this situation. The Vicki Hutcheson situation comes up, and I see crazy coming, and I say, 'Hey, what's going on?'"

Though Vicki couldn't identify anyone else at this *esbat* or specify exactly where it had taken place, she stated assuredly to investigators that Damien had driven the three of them in his red Ford Fiesta. This should have sent up some red flags, since a cursory investigation would have revealed that Damien did not own or have access to a red Ford Fiesta, or any other car. It was also well known in the neighborhood that he couldn't drive and didn't even have a license. Instead, Vicki was never charged with theft from her boss, and her tale fit in quite comfortably with the satanic theory of the case.

As did a statement by a teenager named William Jones. He told his mother that while drunk, Damien had confessed to the murders, describing how he had raped all three boys and then killed them with a knife. His mother called the police. Detectives videotaped his statement. The pieces were falling into place.

On June 3, the day after Vicki made her report about the *esbat,* West Memphis police made the move upon which, in retrospect, the entire case would turn. Jessie was brought to police headquarters and given a polygraph exam by Detective Bill Durham. He was asked whether he knew who had killed the three boys. He answered no. He was asked if he would tell the truth. He answered yes. Then he was told — erroneously — that he had failed.

This got Jessie confused. Dan Stidham, who would become one of Jessie's defense attorneys, later said the police told him that "they knew he was lying because his brain was telling them so." Jessie didn't understand how he would know something was true, but a machine that could read his brain would tell the examiner something different.

As it later became clear, the only question on which he was perceived to dissemble was whether or not he had ever smoked dope. This was only the beginning of what I — and I am far from alone on this — consider to be egregious police behavior.

Jessie had been approached and agreed to go to the police station with Detective Sergeant Mike Allen with the understanding that he might know something that could lead to his receiving some of the reward money. In his simple reasoning, Jessie didn't know what he might know that could be valuable; but if the police thought there was something, then maybe he did and he could use the money to help Big Jessie buy a new truck. The police did not ask Big Jessie's permission, as they should have done in the case of a minor, nor had they secured from Big Jessie a waiver of Miranda rights for his son.

The police kept Jessie at the blocklike, two-story gray brick department building for about twelve hours, increasingly turning up the pressure to get him to confess to the murders and implicate Damien and Jason. According to Jessie, Gary Gitchell and Bryn Ridge kept hammering on him, saying he must have something to do with the murders because people had told them he did. It was clear — or should have been — that Jessie had no real understanding of what was going on. As the hours dragged on, he only had two goals: to get some of the reward money if he could, and to get the hell out of there and back to the security of his home with Big Jessie.

Ultimately Jessie told police the story they wanted to hear. It had to do with him getting a call from Jason early on the morning of May 5, asking him to go with Jason and Damien to Robin Hood Hills. The three of them were in the creek when the three boys rode up on their bicycles. Damien and Jason had called them over; and when they came, they overpowered and beat all three, then forced at least two of them into performing oral sex on them, then anally raped all three. During this time, Michael Moore tried to run away, but Jessie, up to this point only an observer, grabbed him and brought him back.

Jason pulled out a knife and cut his victims' faces; then he used it on Chris Byers's genital area. Damien hit one of the other two with a "big ole stick" he had found and strangled the other one. Then they stripped off the boys' clothing and tied them up. That was when Jessie said he left.

Later, when he got home, he got a call from Jason, who exclaimed, "We done it!" but then worried out loud what they would do if someone had seen them.

The detectives asked if this was part of a cult. Jessie said he, Jason and Damien had formed a cult about three months before, and that they met in the woods, held orgies and participated in ceremonies involving killing and eating dogs.

Of the twelve hours police questioned Jessie, they only recorded two sessions totaling about forty-five minutes. This in itself is extremely suspect. What we hear is more than troubling. For starters, here's what Jessie got

412

"wrong" in his supposed confession:

1. He said that the crime took place in the morning, when the three boys and Jason would have been in school.
2. He said the boys were bound with brown rope. In fact, they were bound with their own shoelaces.
3. He described Michael Moore trying to run away, when that would have been physically impossible, given that he and the other boys were bound hand to foot.
4. The medical examiner's report showed no evidence of anal penetration, contrary to Jessie's description.
5. There was no evidence of strangulation, as Jessie had described.
6. Jessie contradicted himself on whether Jason had called him that morning or the night before.

On "important" points, like the time and the means of binding, the interrogators tried to "correct" Jessie and steer him back to a narrative that conformed better to the evidence. Not only did Jessie tell the police nothing they did not know, which is unusual in a genuine confession, they clearly told him things *he* did not know, and added them to his story as they were supplied.

"I figured something was wrong," he said

later, " 'cause if I'da killed 'em, I'da known how I done it."

He knew he had been at a roofing job with some other buddies the morning of May 5; but if the police wanted him to tell a different story, he would do that.

When he finished telling them what they wanted to hear, Jessie assumed they would let him go home, and he still hoped to get some of the reward money for a new truck for Big Jessie. With his simple logic, it did not occur to him that he had just implicated himself in the murders. For the police to claim they did not understand the level of simplicity and susceptibility they were dealing with is as far-fetched as the story they got him to tell. These officers were not stupid or unaware of what they were doing, so we can only conclude that they needed a confession from someone and set out to get it out of this simple soul.

The other tip-off is the total noninvolvement and emotive detachment with which Jessie told the story. It was totally matter-of-fact, almost without affect — not anger, remorse, pity, lust, defensiveness, introspection. There was nothing. The interrogators would have had to be as simple as he was not to realize how strange his demeanor was. But here again, theory led evidence. One thing that forty years of immersion in the criminal justice system has taught me is that if you try

414

hard enough, *you will get the answers you seek.*

Had I been the primary interrogator, I could have gotten Jessie Misskelley Jr. to confess to having witnessed and participated in the alien abduction of the three boys and then depositing their bodies in the drainage creek when the extraterrestrial experiments on them were completed. *But that wouldn't make it true.*

Instead of getting reward money and going home, Jessie Misskelley Jr. was arrested and charged with murder.

No sooner had they booked Jessie than Crittenden County deputy prosecutor John Fogleman appeared before municipal judge William Rainey to claim the police had probable cause to arrest Damien and Jason for murder and to request search warrants for their homes, along with Jessie's and that of Damien's girlfriend, Domini Teer. Part of their probable cause case was the statement William Jones had made to Detective Ridge that Damien had confessed to him. Like others in this strange case, Jones later recanted, but his comments against Damien were effective.

The police didn't wait until morning to move into action. They found Damien and Jason together that night at Damien's trailer, along with his sister, Michelle, and Domini. Damien was wearing a black Portland Trailblazers shirt and Jason was wearing a black Metallica shirt. They arrested the two boys and put them in handcuffs. Jason later said he was shocked. Damien said he was not surprised, because the cops had been virtually camping out on his doorstep for weeks. They took various articles of clothing from the residences, including a number of black T-shirts. In Damien's home, they found two notebooks in which he had put various writings and drawings that seemed to be satanic or occult-like.

Damien never tried to deny his involvement in Wicca, which he interpreted as a positive life force, or his interest in the occult. But when you look at his background, it is easy to conclude that what he was really looking for was an escape from what he considered the banal reality of his life in West Memphis. It was also the likely reason he grew attached to Jason, a mild-mannered and creative kid who shared his interests in ideas beyond the norm.

When they searched the homes, the only evidence the police found in any way linking either boy to the murders were some fibers from Jason's mother's bathrobe and from a child's shirt in Damien's home that were similar to fibers from Michael Moore's shirt. These were common fibers, though, that were used in a lot of inexpensive clothing. No blood or biological evidence was found in either location.

(Recently, new analysis presented by Jason's appeals attorneys John Philipsborn and Blake Hendrix undermines the state's trial testimony that there was any commonality between these fibers. But that would be almost twenty years afterward.)

Both boys were taken to the police station, given polygraph exams, questioned without attorneys and without being able to contact their families; then they were taken to separate cells in the county jail.

Damien was never told whether he had passed or failed the polygraph, but it probably wouldn't have mattered. He has admitted having been too much of a smart-ass at that age for his own good.

"Back then, I prided myself on how much of an ass I was. If they would have come to me and said, 'Oh, we just gave you this lie detector test and you failed it,' I would have said, 'So?'

"If they had said, 'We've got some trouble with your answer,' I would have said, 'Yeah, it sucks for you, don't it?' "

It will come as no surprise that cops don't exactly cherish kids like that.

Meanwhile, once he realized what he had done, Jessie recanted his confession. But it was too late.

■ ■ ■ ■

At nine o'clock the next morning, June 4, 1993, Inspector Gitchell held a press conference. While trumpeting the arrests, he uttered the single most memorable and provocative statement of the entire case. While reassuring the public that the suspects were safely behind bars, he actually revealed very little about the details of the investigation. When he took questions from the media, he refused to comment on a pointed query as to whether those arrested were members of a cult. The reporters were getting restless without a good quote to run with.

Then it dropped on them like the proverbial manna from heaven. A reporter asked, "On a scale of one to ten, how solid do you feel your case is?"

Looking extremely earnest, Gitchell nodded solemnly, as if to show he comprehended the import of the question. Then the corners of this mouth turned up slightly as he replied, "Eleven." He glanced around, saw that his response had been a hit and offered a dignified smile, which bordered on preening. In time, he would come to regret that one-word utterance, that golden nugget of "law enforcement theater." But from that point on, the community was convinced that the case against the three teenagers was open-and-shut.

As I reviewed the case, I hadn't yet thought through a profile or crime analysis, but the link to the three suspects seemed awfully thin, more like a "one" or "two" than an "eleven." Unless there was more to it than I knew about, Jessie Misskelley Jr.'s "confession" seemed as leaky as a sieve. Vicki Hutcheson's story about Jessie and Damien seemed preposterous on its face, especially since it was a well-established fact that Damien couldn't drive. And what else was there: the notion that Jerry Driver thought these kids were capable of doing something bad? Where I come from, we don't call that evidence; we don't call it anything.

There had to be something more that I was missing, or else this was a hysterical and transparent rush to judgment. And as I studied the crime scene photos, I just didn't see anything that said "cult" or "satanic," or presented anything ritualistic in appearance.

On June 7, the *Memphis Commercial Appeal,* which would get many of the scoops and exclusives in the case, published excerpts of Jessie's statement to the police. Satanic panic had taken hold of West Memphis. A rumor circulated that Damien had saved Chris Byers's testicles and had them in his trailer in a jar of alcohol. One neighbor said she had heard that Damien sacrificed babies and

419

covered one of his girlfriends with blood while he made love to her. Domini's mother, Diane Teer, tried to quell rumors that he drank her daughter's and Jason's blood.

Jerry Driver said he'd noticed an increase in teen interest in the occult over the past few years, as witnessed by the charred remains of bonfires, animals and disturbing graffiti. The *Commercial Appeal* described how several teens had been following a mysterious leader known as "Lucifer."

"I've been looking for Lucifer for two and a half years," Driver declared.

Pam Hobbs was interviewed by a local television reporter, who asked, "Do you feel that the people who did this were worshipping —"

Before he could complete the question, she responded, "Satan? Yes, I do. Just look at the freaks. I mean, just look at them. They look like" — and here a dramatic pause — "punks!"

In a prison interview, Damien observed, "West Memphis is pretty much like Second Salem, because everything that happens here, every crime, is blamed on Satanism." Like Bridget Bishop before the Salem Court of Oyer and Terminer almost exactly three hundred years earlier, Damien Echols wore black, acted oddly and had forsaken the commonly accepted church.

He was different, an outsider. And even

though he lived in their community, he was not really one of them. The perfect profile of someone to fear.

"We were the obvious choices because we stood out from everybody else," he commented. He admitted to occasionally spraying graffiti on the concrete sides of underpasses, but he said it was never satanic. He just liked to see his name.

The same day that the *Commercial Appeal* published part of Jessie's confession, a hearing was held in Crittenden County Circuit Court in Marion at which Judge David Goodson appointed attorneys to represent the defendants: Val Price and Scott Davidson for Damien Echols; Paul Ford and George Robin Wadley for Jason Baldwin; and Dan Stidham and Greg Crow for Jessie Misskelley Jr.

There was another piece I found odd and troubling. Recall that the crime scene was an untended wooded area that can be expected to change on a daily basis. On July 4, nearly two months after the murders, Detective Bryn Ridge returned to the area and retrieved two sticks, which the prosecution later used as exhibits. There is an old saying in law enforcement that "the difference between evidence and garbage is chain of custody." How these sticks, these pieces of garbage, were admitted into evidence is beyond me.

This was not the only example of questionable evidence gathering. On the morning of November 17, state police divers working with WMPD detectives set out to search a lake in the Lakeshore Trailer Park, near where Jason had lived at the time of the murders. TV and print reporters suddenly showed up. The divers were only in the water for a little over an hour, from 10:30 to about 11:35 A.M. Yet, they managed to locate the very knife — a large serrated model — that they were somehow convinced was the weapon that had left the vicious wounds on the three victims. Why then? Why there? Was it the only knife in the lake? How would they know? How could they tie it to the child murders without any physical markers? And did they just get lucky to find it so quickly? I've been involved in a number of water searches over the years and I've never seen one go that well. Another piece of law enforcement theater? As soon as I heard about the media being there, I knew this event had been staged for their benefit.

As I say: *If you try hard enough, you will get the answers you seek.*

On August 4, 1993, Damien, Jason and Jessie had all pled not guilty to capital murder charges. They had each told police they were home with their families the night of the murders. Members of both families confirmed this; though, admittedly, that doesn't tend to be the most compelling alibi.

Because his confession implicated the other two, Jessie was given a separate trial. On a motion from his attorneys Dan Stidham and Greg Crow to avoid prejudicial local publicity, the trial was moved north to Corning, Arkansas, near the Missouri state line.

By the time I reviewed the case, it had emerged that Stidham was initially convinced of his client's guilt, not believing anyone would give a detailed confession to a crime in which he did not take part. His strategy going in was to make the best deal he could by getting Jessie to testify against the other two. But the more he investigated, the more convinced he became that Jessie had nothing to do with the murders and had gotten a really raw deal.

Jessie's trial began in snow-covered Corning, with jury selection on January 19, 1994. He was charged with one count of first-degree murder in the death of Michael Moore and two counts of second-degree murder in the deaths of Christopher Byers and Steven Branch. Circuit court judge David Burnett presided and John Fogleman, who had applied for the search warrants, was the lead prosecutor. Despite the change of venue, it seemed as if the entire region was riveted on this satanic-cult murder.

The *Commercial Appeal* reported that a juvenile officer from Missouri was attending the trial *in hopes of learning more about* teenagers who become involved in the occult, because *"The people in rural areas who think this is not going on are sadly mistaken."*

Throughout the trial, Jessie Misskelley Jr. mainly sat with his head down, staring at the floor, as if he really couldn't comprehend the seriousness of what was happening around him. *Arkansas Times* reporter Bob Lancaster described him thusly: *A passivity around him so profound it strains credulity; he sits all day facing away from judge and jury, staring at his feet, slumping farther and farther floorward in his chair as if he might ooze down and become a puddle between his shoes. Hard to see this scrap of person as an agent of evil.* Various people interviewed afterward interpreted Jessie's manner as if he didn't want to be confronted with the enormity of his crime.

Another unusual element raised the level of public and media frenzy. Two experienced documentary filmmakers out of New York, Joe Berlinger and Bruce Sinofsky, had received permission to record both trials and to interview the defendants and many of the key players for a prospective film they were producing for HBO. They made various deals to gain cooperation. For cooperation from Damien, Jason and Jessie, the filmmakers had made a contribution to their defense fund.

The filmmakers, I was told, had gone into the project believing the three defendants had

424

committed satanic murder. That was its juicy appeal. Once they started filming the trial, though, their emphasis shifted as they realized the case was not what it had been cracked up to be.

The focus of the trial, of course, was on Jessie's confession. Under ordinary circumstances, a taped confession would be all the prosecution needed. But Dan Stidham, by now convinced of his client's innocence, wanted to show the jury that in this case, appearances could be deceiving. He brought in Dr. Richard Ofshe, a professor of sociology at the University of California, Berkeley, and a prominent expert on false confessions. Ofshe interviewed Jessie for three hours on December 15; then he attended a hearing in January in which police officers gave their own version of the confession. He was prepared to show all the ways that this was a "classic example" of a coerced confession. In a true confession, there would have been no attempt made by the interrogators to coach, lead, correct or guide what the subject was telling them. He cited eight separate police prompts on getting the time frame right.

In what was only one of a large number of questionable calls in this trial and the one that would follow, Judge Burnett would only let the jury hear a small portion of Ofshe's testimony, reasoning that letting an expert tell the jury what was true and what was false was taking the finding of fact responsibility away from them. I find this rationale to be bizarre, and so did Stidham, since all expert witnesses were going to try to convince a jury that what they said was correct and true.

Another of Stidham's witnesses was a polygraph expert and former Miami PD detective sergeant named Warren Holmes, who was prepared to testify as to the improprieties of Jessie's examination and interrogation, since it was the false information he was given about the lie detector that led him to his confession. Holmes had conducted polygraphs for the FBI, CIA and Royal Canadian Mounted Police, among others. He had worked on such cases as the John Kennedy and Martin Luther King Jr. assassinations and Watergate. But Judge Burnett would not allow him to testify, since polygraph results are not admitted into court. These two rulings effectively tied Dan Stidham's hands on impeaching the only case the prosecution had against Jessie Misskelley Jr.

Even bringing in four witnesses testifying to Jessie's alibi for the date in question wasn't enough to overcome this obstacle. Fred Revelle, a 240-pounder who wrestled under the name "Rowdy Rebel Fred James," said that Jessie was with him that evening at an amateur-wrestling match in Dyess, Arkansas.

"It's not a theory. It's the actual truth," Revelle testified. "I would put my life on it."

And he gave details, as reported the next morning in the *Commercial Appeal:*

Revelle told jurors Misskelley received "a big knot on the side of his head" that night. Outside the courtroom, Revelle said that happened after he tossed Misskelley through the ropes and someone else, trying to toss him back, errantly threw him into the hard side of the ring.

On February 4, 1994, after about nine and a half hours of deliberation over two days, during which they played the confession twice, jurors returned verdicts of first-degree murder in the death of Michael Moore and second-degree murder in the deaths of Christopher Byers and Stevie Branch. It was just what the prosecution had asked for. Judge Burnett sentenced Jessie Misskelley Jr. to life in prison, plus two consecutive twenty-year terms.

The *Arkansas Democrat Gazette* quoted one observer as saying: *"I don't think the prosecution proved its case beyond a reasonable doubt. But I don't think he would have confessed if he hadn't been guilty."*

With the Echols-Baldwin trial scheduled to begin later that month in Jonesboro, Arkansas, the big question was whether Jessie Misskelley Jr. would testify against them. The prosecutors knew they would have to offer him a reduced sentence, and they were willing to do so because they thought it would solidify their case against the other two.

Rumors flew around the community that Jessie would nail his two codefendants. But despite heavy pressure from the prosecution, he told Dan Stidham he would not testify in Damien Echols and Jason Baldwin's trial. His reasoning was typically simple and straightforward: It just wasn't true.

At the same time, prosecutors twice offered Jason a deal if he would implicate Damien. He flatly refused for the same reason Jessie had. He said he hadn't done anything, and neither had Damien.

Now that Jessie had announced his refusal to testify, his confession could not be introduced into the second trial. It would be hearsay, and the defense attorneys would have no witness to cross-examine. In practical terms, however, this was not the advantage to Damien and Jason it should have been. Everyone in the region knew about the confession, and no jury selection question or instruction from the judge could keep it from jurors' minds. No matter what happened at the trial itself, if a juror believed Jessie's confession, it would be difficult to grant Damien and Jason even a reasonable doubt.

CHAPTER 20
STATE V. DAMIEN WAYNE ECHOLS AND CHARLES JASON BALDWIN

On Friday, February 25, 1994, after several days of selection, a jury of eight women and four men was seated in the Craighead County Courthouse in Jonesboro for the Echols-Baldwin murder trial. Outside the 132-year-old redbrick building, the curious lined up for a chance to sit in on what promised to be the biggest spectacle the town had ever seen. Despite the change of venue, Judge Burnett was still presiding, as he did in the Jessie Misskelley Jr. trial.

Like Grundy, Virginia, when Roger Keith Coleman went on trial, someone had put a placard on the courthouse lawn with a picture of a Grim Reaper in a black hood. The sign read: HE WANTS YOU, DAMIEN.

Other than some questionable fibers, the prosecution had no physical evidence and no eyewitnesses to tie the defendants to the murders. Therefore, John Fogleman and his team had to rely on inferential elements and reasoning and statements attributed to either

Damien or Jason. He said as much in his opening statement, while defense attorney Scott Davidson admitted in his opening statement, "You are also going to see that our client, Damien Echols . . . well, I'll be honest with you. He's not the all-American boy. In fact, he's kind of weird. He's not the same as maybe you and I might be."

The public's fascination was further stoked when Domini brought her young son by Damien to court. The baby, Damien Seth Azariah Teer, had been born in September, when Damien was already locked up.

After watching a portion of the trial, an Arkansas State University freshman commented, "Damien Echols — he was just turning around, staring at everybody. He was, like, evil. I mean, I just got the creeps really bad."

The opening portion of the trial primarily established the facts surrounding the murders and the individuals who played a part. Dana Moore, Pam Hobbs and Melissa Byers each testified as to the last time they had seen their sons alive. As someone who has spent much of his career advising on prosecutorial strategy, I think this is a good way to start. It personalizes the victims, their families and the loss, which can often be forgotten in a trial that focuses on the defendants. So if I were Fogleman, I would have done exactly the same.

The only significant evidentiary element that came out of this for those studying the case was that Pam Hobbs's account of the day did not square with what her husband, Terry, had told investigators. But since Terry was not called to testify, there was no impact on the jury.

Officer Regina Meek testified about responding to the call from John Mark Byers about his missing stepson, and became defensive when describing the incomplete Bojangles' investigation. Detective Sergeant Mike Allen described finding the bodies.

The atmosphere in court grew grim as Dr. Frank Peretti described the autopsies he performed on the three boys: the multiple head injuries on Michael Moore and Stevie Branch; Michael's water-filled lungs; the gouging wounds to Chris Byers's thigh, the removal of his scrotum, testicles and the head of his penis, and the missing skin on the organ's shaft. Peretti said it would be difficult to determine time of death, but when pressed, he reluctantly speculated that it could have been between 1:00 and 7:00 A.M. on May 6.

He mentioned scratches and contusions of various sorts on all three bodies, but contrary to the Misskelley confession, he found no evidence of sexual assault.

Perhaps the most significant and grisly part of Peretti's testimony came in response to questions about the damage to Chris's genital area. He stated his opinion that it would take considerable time and considerable surgical skill with a scalpel or a very sharp knife to perform this mutilation under the best of circumstances, such as a well-lit lab. In the dark, in the water, with the locally notorious mosquitoes present, it would be considerably more difficult. Also, since Chris had bled to death, it would be almost impossible to remove all the blood from the creek bank or any other solid ground. The only situation in which there would not be a great residue of blood would be if the body was in water at the time. Yet, he could not see how such a delicate procedure could be performed in water. He didn't think it could be done. That comment left its own tantalizing mystery. If Dr. Peretti himself couldn't have accomplished such a task, how could Damien or Jason have done so?

After testimony from detectives on searching the crime scene and finding the knife in the lake — no evidence was presented tying it to either defendant — the prosecution put Michael Ray Carson on the stand. Michael was a sixteen-year-old ninth grader who spent a week in the county juvenile detention center in August for burglary — breaking into a house to steal guns — during the same time Jason Baldwin had been held there. He testified that on his third day there, he met Jason when they were both involved in a game of spades with two other boys. He said he asked Jason if he was involved with the murders and Jason denied it.

The next day he and Jason were alone cleaning up the cards before returning to their cells for lunch. Michael again asked Jason the same question.

This time, according to Michael, Jason gave it up. "I said, 'Just between you and me, did you do it?' And he said, 'Yes.' "

Michael described Jason talking about how he had dismembered Chris Byers, sucked blood from his penis and scrotum, then put his testicles in his mouth. He added that he was going to kick Jessie's ass for messing everything up, but that he still expected to walk free. The entire conversation, Michael said, did not last more than two or three minutes.

You have to deal with a witness like this the same way you'd deal with a suspect: you need to profile him. You have to evaluate the background of the subject, the situation in which the confession was allegedly made, and whether there are extenuating circumstances, such as whether the witness has anything to gain.

This encounter was supposed to have happened in August; yet Michael didn't come forward until February 1, the final day of Jessie Misskelley Jr.'s trial. Why? prosecutor Brent Davis wanted to know.

"My father told me that I should tell somebody. But I just really didn't want to get involved. I'd just gotten out of jail, and I didn't want to get involved with the court system," the witness answered.

But then he and his father were watching television when a segment came on showing the still-grieving parents. "I saw how broken-hearted they were about their missing children. I got a soft heart," he allowed. "I couldn't take it." He was not offered a reward, he said, and wouldn't have taken it, even if it were offered.

Give me a break! I wish all teens that break into houses to steal guns had this much integrity.

The idea that even a guilty person would confide in this kid he hardly knew, and who was bound to talk, is so absurd that it is difficult to conceive of any jury buying it. At some point after the trial, Michael admitted he had made up the whole thing, but that's getting ahead of our story. I only mention it here because it should have been obvious to the prosecution — whose first job is to see justice done and only secondarily to seek conviction — that there was a pattern to all of this weak and attenuated evidence. The only logic I can come up with is that they needed a witness like this to make the case. But that doesn't make it right. Combined with a supposed participant who had to be

434

led into the basic facts of the case by the police, you have to wonder why they didn't just admit that there wasn't a solid case.

Judge Burnett wouldn't allow into the record evidence that Michael Ray Carson was a habitual substance abuser because that fact wasn't sufficient grounds to challenge a witness's veracity. *Huh?* And he further disallowed a communication to both prosecution and defense from Danny Williams, a counselor who worked at the juvenile detention facility, saying that he had told Michael the details of the murder supposedly obtained from Jason and that he knew Michael was going to lie at the trial. The judge knocked this one out because of patient-counselor confidentiality.

All in all, the deck seemed to be stacked against the defense.

Unfortunately, we've seen this attitude over and over again, going all the way back to William Heirens in Chicago and before. When it becomes more important to close a case than to make sure the state has the right suspects, the system falls apart and no one is served. Perhaps worst of all, a killer remains free and unpunished.

The issue of the knife in the lake got even more complicated when Joe Berlinger and Bruce Sinofsky, the HBO filmmakers, turned in to police a flip-blade knife John Mark Byers had given to Douglas Cooper, one of their camera operators, as a gift. When HBO officials found out about it, they told Sinofsky to turn it over to the police. Gary Gitchell testified that he sent the knife to a genetic analysis lab in North Carolina, which found traces of human blood near the base of the blade that matched both Byers and his stepson, Chris, but not Damien or Jason. This was of interest because prior to the analysis Byers had previously stated under questioning by Gitchell that the knife had never been used. Confronted with the lab report, he remembered cutting his thumb while dressing some venison.

Known by his middle name of Mark, Byers was thirty-six years of age and kind of an outsize character. He was about six-feet-five, with long stringy blondish hair, often sporting a beard, and given to public eruptions of biblically oriented vengeance against the killers of the "three babies," at least when the cameras were rolling. He had been married previously and had a son named Ryan from his prior marriage. He was a jeweler by trade, but he had held a variety of other jobs. In a community in which corporal punishment of children was the norm, he had often been rough with Chris, but he seemed devoted to him. Chris had ongoing problems with hyperactivity, often acting disruptive in class and elsewhere, and Mark and Melissa were trying to manage the condition with doctors and prescription medication. Damien publicly professed belief that John Mark Byers was the real killer; and of the three fathers, Mark Byers was the only one Gary Gitchell had investigated in depth before he became convinced that the three teens had done it.

A number of witnesses claimed to have seen one or more of the defendants in compromising situations. Jerry Driver testified he had seen Damien, Jason and Jessie walking along in long black robes and carrying staffs at least three times, though no one else ever claimed to have seen them attired this way. Narlene Hollingsworth was in her 1982 red Ford Escort wagon on her way back from picking up her mother from her job in a Laundromat, about nine-thirty on the evening of May 5, when she spotted Damien and Domini walking on the South Service Road near the Blue Beacon Truck Wash. She said that Damien's dark clothing seemed dirty and disheveled. Her husband, Ricky, was in the front seat with her; her mother, son Anthony and daughter Tabitha were in the second seat; and daughter Mary, son "Little Rick" and his girlfriend, Sombra, were in the back. "Big Ricky" said it was dark and the spotting was so brief that he couldn't identify anyone. Anthony said the spotting had actually taken place around 10:30 P.M. The prosecution suggested that maybe it wasn't Domini they had seen with Damien, but rather Jason, whose hair was long and blond.

The trial got down to specifics on Damien Echols when Detective Bryn Ridge testified about a conversation he had with Damien on the morning of May 10. Remember, Damien and Jason would not be arrested until almost a month later, but police were already focusing on them based on Jerry Driver's suspicions.

It is clear when you read the trial transcript that Ridge and Damien were operating on two completely different levels. Damien perceived that he was being asked to speculate about the crime based on his personal knowledge and what he had heard about it. Ridge perceived that he was revealing information and motivation that no one but the killer would possess.

Ridge stated that Damien had told him the boys might have drowned and that the bodies would have been cut up, perhaps to scare someone. Eight-year-olds are not big or smart, so they would be easy to control. The one who did this probably knew the kids and was able to convince them to come with him. It may have been intended as a single murder, but the other two had to be killed to keep them from squealing.

The detective also said Damien told him his favorite book of the Bible was Revelations, his favorite writers were Stephen King and Anton LaVey, author of *The Satanic Bible* and other writings on the occult. From this, Damien knew that young children are the most innocent, so they would give more power to the person who did the killing. All people have demonic forces in them over which they have no control, he said, and speculated that the person who did this probably felt good about it. If this were a satanic killing, Damien would expect to find candles, stones, crystals and a knife at the crime scene. Damien also said that whenever a person does something either good or bad, it will come back to that person three times over.

Ridge asked Damien why his fingerprints would be at the scene. This is a common police questioning technique. Damien said he had never been in the woods, so he would have no idea. Ridge did not tell him that no fingerprints from anyone were found.

The prosecution asked Ridge if there was evidence that the murder was a cult activity. He answered in the affirmative, citing the secluded wooded setting, overkill and torture elements; the mutilation and blood ritual involving Chris Byers's penis and other stab wounds; the way the boys were bound and the fact that they were eight, the "witch's number"; and the meticulous cleaning of the site afterward so that no blood or implements remained.

How did he know all this about cult practices? From books and police handouts not available to the public, as well as notes he had taken from his own research, he replied.

Throughout the questioning, Ridge conceded, Damien had steadfastly denied he had anything to do with the murders.

Remember the sticks that Ridge retrieved from the crime scene on July 4? Damien's lawyer Val Price questioned him about why they had waited two months and how valid such evidence could be. "You all did not take that stick into evidence at the time you recovered the bodies?"

"No, sir," Ridge replied. "I didn't take this stick into evidence until the statement of Jessie Misskelley."

Whoa! Jessie was not testifying, so nothing about his statement was supposed to be introduced. Price immediately moved for a mistrial. "The question I asked the officer did not call for him blurting out the fact that Jessie Misskelley gave a confession. The whole purpose for our trial being separated from Mr. Misskelley's trial in the first place was the confession of Jessie Misskelley."

Judge Burnett allowed as how Ridge "shouldn't have volunteered" that information. But in denying Price's motion for mistrial, he commented, "I suggest, gentlemen, that there isn't a soul up on that jury or in this courtroom that doesn't know Mr.

Misskelley gave a statement."

In other words, the defense would have to deal with the worst of both worlds: Jessie's confession hanging in the air and the inability to challenge it! If the jurors believed it, but didn't understand how it was obtained, then Damien and Jason's involvement would be a sure thing. And if Jessie was sent to the slammer for life and he didn't even kill any of the kids, it would have to be worse for the two who he said actually did the killing.

The next witness was intended to explain the motive for this horrible crime and ended up giving perhaps the most controversial testimony of the trial.

Dale W. Griffis, Ph.D., was a self-proclaimed expert on Satanism and cults. A former police officer in Tiffin, Ohio, he said he had served as a consultant to victims, law enforcement, educators and mental-health specialists. Under questioning, he conceded that his master's and Ph.D. degrees were awarded by Columbia Pacific University, which had no national certification and did not require him to take a single class. The school was closed by California court order in 2000. Griffis had been on the campus five times before his graduation. He said the street was his classroom. The title of his dissertation was *Mind Control Cults and Their Effects on the Objectives of Law Enforcement.*

He admitted that he had never talked with either Damien or Jason and couldn't even pick Jason out in the courtroom. He said he had reviewed the crime scene and autopsy photos and had spoken with John Fogleman between ten and twelve times. What he had done, about a year before the murder, was consult with Jerry Driver and receive copies of some of Damien's drawings to determine if West Memphis had a satanic or occult problem in the person of Damien Echols. Griffis said he considered this very good and responsible law enforcement work. This previous exchange would help explain why Damien was on the top of Driver's list as a possible suspect when the three boys were murdered.

"On behalf of my client," Damien's attorney Val Price objected, "it's our position that the mail-order Ph.D. in which a person doesn't have to take classes . . . from a nonaccredited school doesn't qualify as an expert in Arkansas."

"I disagree," Judge Burnett responded. "I'm going to allow him to testify in the area of the occult."

The defense attorneys challenged this ruling, saying there was no scientific basis to Griffis's assertion about the murders being related to satanic ritual. But once again, Burnett seemed to be making inconsistent distinctions between the qualifications of defense experts, like Dr. Ofshe in the Misskelley trial, and prosecution witnesses, like Griffis, who qualified "based upon his knowledge, experience and training in the area of occultism or Satanism."

Once Griffis was allowed to get into the substance of his testimony, Jason's attorney Paul Ford asked him whether these crimes were "motivated by occult beliefs."

"Yes," Griffis replied. He explained that the murders had taken place under a full moon and that there was an absence of blood at the scene because Satanists would save it to drink or bathe in for its "life force." The black hair, fingernails and T-shirts all had occult overtones or suggested occult involvement. So did the staging of the crime near water. The overkill and genital mutilation — check. The pentagram on the front of Damien's seized notebook was certainly indicative of satanic activity. Inside, the pentagram surrounded by upside-down crosses symbolized the merging of white and black witchcraft — Wicca and Satanism.

Does this remind you of the tattoos and heavy metal posters from the Cameron Todd Willingham arson trial?

Griffis said he had never seen victims of a sex crime that wasn't occult tied this way, and that there would be no other reason than occult to tie them in this fashion.

When pressed, Griffis admitted that he had

only investigated two other sex crimes in which victims had been tied, and neither of them was tied in this manner. So basically, he had never seen this type of bondage, but he knew it had to be occult related. He also acknowledged that as far as he knew, there was no evidence of blood having been stored at either of the defendants' residences. Both defense teams pointed out that there were no pentagrams or any other specific evidence of Satanism or the occult present at the crime scene.

It went on from there. Griffis did not know if the murderers knew the ages of the boys, but there is an occult belief that if you do not have sex with a boy before he turns nine, he loses his magical powers.

When both defendants' attorneys protested the use of evidence taken from Damien's house by the juvenile system before the murders even took place, the judge ruled that facts or data do not need to be admissible in court to be used to form an expert opinion. Since it is necessary for the prosecution to prove motive if they can, his reasoning went, proving motive outweighs all other negative effects.

Though Griffis conceded to the defense that many of the indicators in the crime could be interpreted in various ways, they "showed trappings, not just of vague occultism, but of satanic worship in particular."

■ ■ ■ ■

The prosecution closed its case with the testimony of two young girls, one eleven and the other fifteen. They each testified they had seen Damien, dressed all in black, at the J.W. Rich Girls Club softball fields and had overheard him telling a group of friends that he had killed the three boys, and that he planned to kill two more — "I already have one of them picked out" — before he turned himself in. In one of the witness's accounts, Jason was with him when he made this statement.

They said they were about fifteen or twenty feet away, and neither young lady could recall what he had said before or after, nor identify any of the friends to whom he had been talking. There was a police officer on the field, but neither went to tell him. One of the girls said she told her mother afterward, but none of this was reported until after Damien was arrested. And one girl put the date of the game after Damien's arrest. Between Jessie's confession and this account, was it possible West Memphis parents didn't teach their children how to tell time or read a calendar?

Damien Echols's defense team allowed him to take the stand. Jason Baldwin's team kept their client off. Both decisions can be second-

445

guessed and were, though I have always felt that innocent defendants — and it is a credit to the general efficacy of the criminal justice system that they are in the minority — make pretty good witnesses.

Jason, in particular, gave the impression of being so guileless, straightforward and unsophisticated that I think he would have done himself some good. It came out afterward that he very much wanted to testify in his own defense, as well as have his attorneys call character and alibi witnesses. On the other hand, with the atmosphere of satanic ritual so heavily in the air, the mere fact that eleven black T-shirts were found in his home might have negated all other impressions. As Jason later commented, "All that mattered was that Damien was weird and I had black T-shirts." You can never fault a defense attorney for trying to protect his client.

The consensus was that Damien did himself no favors by testifying over the course of two days in his own defense. Reading the transcripts and watching the film of his testimony, I think it had a mixed result. The prosecution certainly made points tying him to an interest in the occult through his seized notebooks, which was damaging.

On the other hand, I thought he came across as candid and unguarded, trying to answer questions as honestly as he could. As a prosecution strategist, I always wanted defendants to take the stand, because I felt a skilled prosecutor, pressing the right buttons, could get the witness to let down his guard and make the jury see him as he actually was.

In the prosecution of Wayne B. Williams for the early 1980s Atlanta Child Murders, that is exactly what we did. I coached Jack Mallard, an extremely skilled prosecutor, to get up close and personal with Williams, who had been smug and controlled on the stand up until then. With his methodical, south Georgia drawl, Mallard bore in on him, violating his personal space, and pressed, "What was it like, Wayne? What was it like when you wrapped your fingers around the victim's throat? Did you panic? Did you panic?"

And in a weak voice, Williams responded, "No," before suddenly catching himself. He flew into a rage, pointed his finger at me and screamed, "You're trying your best to make me fit that FBI profile, and I'm not going to help you do it!"

The defense went ballistic as Williams went nuts on the stand, ranting about "FBI goons" and calling the prosecution team "fools." But the damage was done. For the first time, the jury saw a man capable of murder.

That never happened with Damien Echols. There was no such drama here. Nothing the prosecution did got under his skin. It was as if there was no boiling point. Damien answered the questions with a certain air of weariness, as though he was just waiting to finish up so he could leave.

He said he was into skateboarding, music, movies, watching TV and talking on the phone. He would read any book he got his hands on. He admitted telling Bryn Ridge the things the detective testified to — that everyone had a good side and a bad side. He said, "I have read about all different types of religions, because I've always wondered, like, how do we know we've got the right one, how do we know we are not messing up." After exploring Catholicism, he focused on Wicca.

When Price asked him his opinion on Dale Griffis's testimony, he replied, "Some of it was okay, but he didn't stop to differentiate between different groups. He just lumped them all together into one big group that he called 'cults.' "

He was matter-of-fact rather than defensive on issues the prosecution had considered damning. On the knife found in the lake, he observed, "I had one sort of like that, but mine didn't have a black handle. The handle on mine was camouflaged, and it had the camouflage case and everything. The blade on mine was black. It wasn't silver like that."

When asked if he had ever read books by Aleister Crowley, a pretty hard-core writer on black witchcraft whose name Damien had written in code in his notebook, he replied no, but "I would have read them if I had saw [*sic*] them."

As to whether a killer would feel good about the crimes, he thought that if that person committed the crimes voluntarily, he probably would feel good about it. As far as Damien was concerned, that was just common sense and showed no particular insight into the mind of the killer.

He also said about Detective Ridge, "If he didn't get the answer, he'd try to make me go back and say something else."

"Tell the judge the manner in which they were questioning you during this period of time," Price instructed him.

"During these questions right here [initial standard questions], they were pretty nice. After that, God! After I'd been there awhile, they started cussing me, telling me they knew I did it. They were going to fry my ass. I might as well go ahead and confess now."

A little later, Price asked, "During that time, did you ask for an attorney?"

"Three times," Damien replied, elaborating that Ridge "told me I didn't need to bring him back there, because he was just going to cost us a lot of money, and that in the end he was going to quit, anyway."

Later, Damien said he didn't take the trial all that seriously, because he didn't believe anyone could prove he had committed murder when he knew he hadn't killed anyone. His reasoning was like a more sophisticated yet equally naive version of Jessie's.

After Damien's testimony, the defense tried to call Christopher Morgan to the stand. He was a twenty-year-old from Memphis with a string of drug problems who had told police in California that he might have killed the three boys during a drug blackout. During a hearing away from the jury, he explained that he had been in the area during the murders, but now he denied any part and had recanted his confession to the police. He described a situation similar to what Jessie Misskelley Jr. had gone through, with seventeen hours of questioning and a confession made in desperation. Prosecutors Brent Davis and John Fogleman claimed West Memphis PD had considered him unreliable and had ruled him out as a suspect. Paul Ford replied that Jessie had also recanted right away and was similarly unreliable, and Christopher's testimony would certainly cast reasonable doubt.

Ultimately, Christopher's court-appointed attorney said that his client would not testify; and if he was compelled to do so, he would invoke the Fifth Amendment on each question because of various charges that were pending against him. Judge Burnett bought into this and not only excused him from taking the stand, but placed a gag order on all the attorneys so that they could not even mention Christopher Morgan's existence to the jury and give them another highly questionable confession to consider.

For their final witness, Damien's defense team called Robert Hicks, a police training officer from Virginia who had done his own study of satanic cults as they related to violent crime. Like my FBI colleague Ken Lanning, he had found no empirical evidence that such a phenomenon actually existed or that listening to heavy metal or wearing black had anything to do with the propensity to commit ritual violence. Point by point, he refuted Griffis's ideas and said that even his phrase " 'trappings of the occult' is absolutely meaningless in considering any kind of violent crime."

Jason's team firmly believed there was nothing on the record that implicated their client and therefore rested without calling any witnesses. Jason had gone into the trial believing so strongly in the American system of justice that despite his arrest and incarceration, he didn't believe he could be convicted. When prosecutors came to him before the trial and offered him a lesser charge if he turned against Damien, he refused. He refused again when they cut his sentencing deal in half from forty years to twenty. Jason said that even if they let him walk away scot-free in exchange for testifying against Damien, he wouldn't do it, because they were both innocent.

In his closing statement, prosecutor Brent Davis pointed to photographs of the three dead eight-year-olds and said, "The normal motives for human conduct don't apply. There's something strange going on that causes people to do this."

Then he went on to cite Damien's manner in the courtroom: "You can judge him from the witness stand. This guy's as cool as a cucumber. He's nearly emotionless, and what he's done in terms of the satanic stuff is a whole lot more than just dabbling or looking into it for purposes of an intellectual exercise.

"As bizarre as it may seem, and as unfamiliar as it may seem, this occult set of beliefs and the beliefs that Damien had, and his best friend, Jason, was exposed to all the time — those are the set of beliefs that were the motive or the basis for causing this bizarre murder."

John Fogleman's part of the closing argument was both strange and controversial. He began by admitting that nothing specifically tied the defendants to the crime. However, if jurors evaluated the totality of the evidence, it all pointed in one direction, and pointed there beyond a reasonable doubt.

He held up a grapefruit and, in turn, picked up the two exhibit knives: the one found in the lake and the one that had belonged to Mark Byers. Paul Ford rose to object; this was not a scientific experiment and the subject grapefruit had not been introduced into evidence. As had been his pattern throughout both trials, Judge Burnett sided with the prosecution.

Fogleman gave the grapefruit a whack with each of the knives. While admitting that this was not conclusive as to the specific knife that was used in the murder, he pointed out that the marks on the grapefruit's skin left by the lake knife matched wounds on Christopher Byers's groin. In other words, there were small wounds an approximately even distance from each other, corresponding to the serration on the knife. The Mark Byers knife did not.

But as I watched the tape of Fogleman's argument, I sat up with surprise. No criminal in my experience had ever brought a knife down flat against a victim's skin surface. You use a knife to stab or gouge. So this demonstration didn't — and still doesn't — make any sense to me. It had no relationship to a real-life situation — just more of the strange suggestion and innuendo that had characterized this entire trial.

When it was his turn, Damien's attorney Val Price picked up a picture that had been seized from Damien's bedroom of a goat-headed figure holding two torches. He acknowledged that it was "a weird, strange-looking picture, but so what? It's still all right in America to have weird things in your room, and it doesn't mean you're guilty of murder, and it doesn't give any kind of motivation.

"It's not our job to prove what happened May fifth. It's the state's job, and they haven't done it."

The case went to the jury at five on the afternoon of March 17, 1994. They deliberated until 9:40 P.M., then came back the next morning at nine-thirty. They reached their verdicts at three-thirty that afternoon.

We asked Damien if he expected a guilty or not guilty verdict as he waited.

"You're torn," he replied. "It's like they always say, 'You're supposed to be innocent until *proven* guilty.' Well, in my mind, it is impossible, *physically impossible,* for someone to prove you've done something that you haven't done. In a teenaged mind, that violates the laws of physics. But also, people who've never been in a situation like this can't comprehend the state of shock you're in, the trauma. It's like they set a bomb off at every single level of your being. They've destroyed you — psychologically, emotionally. I mean, in every way you have just been devastated, had your entire world destroyed. *You can't think the way you normally think.*"

As the jurors filed into the courtroom, all Damien specifically remembers is that they "were staring holes in me."

When all were assembled in court, the bailiff handed the jury forms to Judge Burnett, who read them out loud. Damien Echols and Jason Baldwin were both found guilty of capital murder.

As it was later revealed, the jury did take up the Misskelley confession in its deliberations and used it as evidence to convict the two defendants.

The next day, the jurors returned and, after hearing what lawyers for each side had to say, spent a little over two hours deliberating their punishment recommendation. They found that the crimes had been committed, as the legal expression stated, in "an especially cruel and depraved manner," which could mitigate any positive considerations for the defendants. For Damien Echols, the perceived ringleader, it was death by lethal injection. For Charles Jason Baldwin, his follower who had no prior history of bad behavior or run-ins with the law, it was life in prison without parole.

When Judge Burnett posed the formality, "Do either of you have any legal reason to show the court or give the court as to why the sentence should not be imposed?" Damien answered no.

Jason, in his typically soft and timid voice,

responded, "Because I'm innocent."

"Well," the judge declared, "the jury has heard the evidence and concluded otherwise."

The trial and its outcome confirmed the community's worst fears. Indicative of this was a headline in the *Arkansas Democrat Gazette* the same day it reported the sentences that read: MOMS STILL SCARED IN WEST MEMPHIS.

The *Commercial Appeal,* the newspaper that had done much of the lead reporting on the case, ran a lead editorial that began:

> "You better get to know your kids."
> That's the message that West Memphis Police Inspector Gary W. Gitchell said he had taken from his 10-month immersion in one of the most shocking and grisly murder cases this region has known.

The editorial went on to suggest that satanic involvement had warped the three defendants' thinking and robbed each of them of a conscience.

So, through this and other similar accounts, perception became reality.

CHAPTER 21
DAMIEN AND LORRI

"After I got to the prison, I was literally sick for about two weeks," Damien recalled for us. "I couldn't eat. I couldn't sleep. I was vomiting continuously. At that moment, you're so beat down. . . ."

His voice trailed off, until he started another thought. "You know, I used to get letters that said, 'If that were me and I was innocent, I would have been kicking and screaming and yelling and saying, *I'm innocent!*' '

"No, you wouldn't — not after they beat you the first time. After that, you're going to shut up and do what they tell you to do."

This was something Damien said he learned early in his stay at the Varner Unit, the Arkansas Department of Corrections (DOC) maximum-security prison near Pine Bluff, which houses the state's death row. For eighteen days, he states, prison guards beat him regularly. It was not because they thought he was a child killer. "They didn't care what I had or hadn't done. It was just, 'Welcome to the neighborhood.'

"I was so weak, so sick, in so much pain, that I thought I'd die."

He characterized his environment as "living on concrete twenty-four hours a day."

He was hit so many times in the face in those early days that it damaged his teeth. "Then you have two choices — either live in pain or let them pull your teeth."

He went on, "Whenever I was in fear for my life, it was always from a guard, never another prisoner." Remember, he was just eighteen years old.

Eventually, Damien and the other two would have a large and influential support network. At the time, though, no one helped him, including — as it turned out — me.

Years later, while working for Peter Jackson on a film about the case, director Amy Berg showed me a series of letters. They had been found by appeals attorney Stephen Braga as he was reviewing Freedom of Information files from the Bureau. It was postmarked 29 September 1994 and addressed simply: F.B.I. Academy, Behavioral Science Unit, Quantico, V.A. [sic] 22135. The spelling and syntax weren't perfect, but the printing was neat and uniform and the message very clear:

I got your address from a friend who said you may be able to help me. I was convicted on 3 counts of capitol [sic] murder, but had nothing to do with any of them. I was framed by the West Memphis police department. They know who really committed the crime, but they refuse to do anything about it. I am going to be executed for a crime I did not committ [sic], and am desperate for help. Even if you cannot help me, could you tell me of someone who can?

I greatly appreciate you taking the time to read my letter. Thank you.

Sincerely,
Damien Echols SK 931
2501 State Farm Road
Tucker, Ark. 72168

I didn't recall ever seeing this letter, but I must have, because my handwritten initials are on the typewritten reply, next to the initialed signature of Robin Montgomery, the special agent in charge of the Critical Incident Response Group under which my Investigative Support Unit operated. This means I must have written the reply. I even misspelled "capital" as Damien did.

Dear Mr. Echols:

Reference your letter sent to the Investigative Support Unit postmarked September 29, 1994. In your letter you state that you were convicted of three counts of capitol murder, but that you had nothing

459

to do with them. I must advise you that the FBI is not authorized to intervene in criminal matters under the jurisdiction of the State of Arkansas. If you believe that you have information that provides legal grounds for an appeal of your conviction or sentence, you should provide that information to your legal counsel, who could then file your appeal with the appropriate court in the state of Arkansas.

Sincerely yours,
Robin Montgomery

In other words, a bureaucratic kiss-off. *We only help the cops, not the bad guys. If you're so sure you're innocent, go through the regular channels.*

Actually, what I was probably thinking was somewhat more detailed than that. With the incredible workload we had, I was probably grateful that we weren't authorized to take up prisoners' requests. But even more pointedly, I would have had a reaction similar to my first misplaced impression of Lorri. *So you're innocent, just like every other convicted killer? Okay, take a number.*

In practical terms, we just didn't have any mechanism for working that side of the street. Even in a situation like the David Vasquez case in Virginia, it was a law enforcement officer who suspected he was innocent and *he* brought the case to us.

If there was anything that kept Damien going during those first few years of his imprisonment on death row, it was his own introversion, which had often been a problem for him in the past. "What would break other people down would be the solitude in there. I would literally see people go stark raving bats. People can't take being alone twenty-four hours a day. I *need* time alone. If I don't have time by myself, I can't deal with it."

But, by and large, his most effective coping mechanism was simply to turn off.

"Before Lorri, my life was horrific. Before Lorri stepped into it, literally, I used to buy sleeping pills off the black market in the prison just to sleep for days at a time and not have to think."

By the time I entered the case in 2006, we all knew there was only one reason Damien Echols had not yet had his rendezvous with the Arkansas death house. It was not due to the so-called fail-safe built into the criminal justice system. It was not due to the work of dedicated law enforcement officers or learned judges. It was not even an enterprising investigative reporter who strove for years to expose the truth. It was an outraged public and grassroots movement prompted by the 1996 airing of Joe Berlinger and Bruce Sinofsky's two-and-a-half-hour HBO documen-

461

tary, *Paradise Lost: The Child Murders at Robin Hood Hills.* This was the film that brought in Lorri and the Jacksons and everyone else.

"Without that film," says Steven Mark, my attorney who became a critical researcher on the case, "Damien Echols would have been long underground with a stone over his head."

Or, as Damien himself put it, "They thought, 'These kids are white trash. No one's ever going to look into this case. Nobody's ever going to ask any questions. They look crazy, so therefore people are going to swallow it.' They thought they would arrest us, put us on trial, murder me, and no one would ever ask any more questions."

As Lorri explained to me in our first phone call, she had been living in Park Slope in Brooklyn and working as a landscape architect for a firm in Manhattan when a friend brought her to a screening of *Paradise Lost,* even though she professed no particular interest in documentaries. She became obsessed with the topic, convinced of the WM3's innocence, and was compelled to write to Damien on death row. When Damien wrote back, she felt an immediate bond, even though she was twelve years older than he, a worldly professional woman who had traveled internationally, undergone an amicable divorce and lived the urban lifestyle.

"There was a connection that I'll never be

able to explain. It was immediate, from when we first started writing. And then when we started talking to each other, we just couldn't talk enough — the things he was interested in. . . ."

Her visits to Damien in prison solidified the bond she had sensed. "When I first started writing, he was young, but he was such a fascinating person. From the get-go, here's this guy who's in prison in Arkansas, has a more fascinating mind than anyone I'd ever met. And that's all I ever really cared about. I needed someone with a fascinating mind. I think it was probably the first time I came down to see him, I remember coming back and telling my friend, 'I'm done. I can't even look back.' "

In 1998, she left New York and moved to Little Rock, Arkansas, the place closest to the prison where she could get a job in her field. She went to work for the city's parks department.

It took Damien some time to come to terms with having a significant person in his life. "In those early days, I would wake up in the middle of the night, grinding my teeth, and think, 'I hate you for making me feel this way.' Because on top of everything else that I'm going through, this is the last thing I need in my life right now. And it was hurting me, and in a way it was because it was bringing me back to life.

"I really had, in those two years before she found me, I had started to die, to wither up and fade away and die inside. And it was like she was forcing me to come back to life, and it hurt the way physical therapy would hurt."

In December 1999, she and Damien married in prison. As his wife, she would be allowed to have contact visits with him rather than having to talk through a pane of glass.

The relationship, as one may imagine, was fraught with strain. She was consumed by her focus on getting Damien, Jason and Jessie out of prison, but she had lost much of the previous life she had in New York. Having given up her landscape architectural job, she had little money; and as she wrote to Damien, *I haven't been poor in such a long time.* She knew they both needed the large network of supporters that had developed across the country, but at the same time Lorri found it difficult to "share" Damien with them. Some days he would receive hundreds of letters and felt he had to answer each one of them.

I have never said this before about a woman who married a convict on death row, and I don't know if I'll ever say it again, but Lorri Davis is a true hero. Because of her interest, conscience, passion for justice and love — in that chronological order — she sacrificed a promising career and an exciting cultural and social life in one of the world's great cities. Instead, she dedicated fifteen of her most productive and precious years for the cause of justice. It is no wonder that despite more than a decade and a half on death row, Damien never ceased to be amazed that Lorri had come into his life.

"That's what made me quit smoking," he commented. "When Lorri came into my life, I decided I didn't want anything to distract or diminish this experience in any way, whatever it is that's going to happen. I don't want anything going on that's going to disrupt this connection. I put the cigarettes down and never picked them up again. I put the sleeping pills down and never picked them up again."

I've always known that maximum-security penitentiaries can be brutal places. But I have reserved most of my concern and compassion for the victims of crimes and their survivors. In this case, however, the idea of a poor teenager being beaten and facing other institutionalized cruelties — not to mention the always-present specter of death for something he did not do — turns my stomach. I frankly don't see how he made it day to day.

"I think the people who don't make it are the ones who can't find another world to live in," Damien observed. "We had to build a world, Lorri and I, and build something where we didn't think about that prison. Whether it was improving meditation techniques, whether it was doing artwork, whether it was writing, whether it was physical exercise, whatever it was, I had to find ways to push myself, to keep pushing myself further every single day so that I felt like I was making progress. I felt like I was making improvement. And it distracted me from the prison."

"Damien is the most disciplined person I've ever met," said Lorri.

"I built up to where I was doing five to seven hours a day of meditation, over a thousand push-ups a day, running in place for a couple of hours at a time."

Still, the prison lighting, nutrition and medical care, and the lack of sunlight and outdoor exercise, were taking its toll on Damien's eyesight and health. Lorri worried constantly.

She also had to worry about every aspect of the appeals case. "We had a lot of funding. But as soon as you'd get it, it would be gone," she said.

The reason there was money or support at all was because of the same factor that had brought her and Damien together. After seeing the HBO film, a number of people got together in Los Angeles to form the Free the West Memphis Three Support Group. They included Burk Sauls, Kathy Bakken, Grove Pashley and Lisa Fancher. The group raised money, developed a website and spread its message around the United States and the world. Every time there was a hearing, its members would marshal supporters from all over to come to Arkansas.

Their efforts were augmented by the celebrities who had lent their names to the cause. In fact, they did a lot more than lend their names. They maintained an active interest, contributed their own money, held benefit concerts and made sure the case stayed in the public consciousness. Actor Johnny Depp, Dixie Chicks lead singer Natalie Maines, Pearl Jam rock guitarist and songwriter Eddie Vedder, and musician Henry Rollins, among others, remain close friends of Damien and Lorri to this day.

And there were two others who would turn out to be absolutely critical.

In Wellington, New Zealand, director Peter Jackson and his writer-producer wife, Fran Walsh, saw the documentary in 2004 and were moved to get involved. Jackson had attained worldwide fame with his blockbuster movie version of J.R.R. Tolkien's *The Lord of the Rings,* but he had done fine work before that, such as *Heavenly Creatures,* with Kate Winslet, for which he and Fran had also written the screenplay. That film was based on the gripping, horrifying story of the cold-blooded 1954 murder of Honora Parker by her sixteen-year-old daughter, Pauline, and Pauline's fifteen-year-old friend, Juliet Hulme, probably the most notorious murder case in New Zealand history.

Peter and Fran sent in a contribution through PayPal with a note that said if there was anything else they could do to help, to let them know. In her own special, highly intuitive way, Lorri sensed a spiritual kinship. In thanking them for their donation, she wrote a long e-mail expressing her feelings and laying out what she thought they were facing in the struggle to get Damien and the others freed.

In December 2005, Peter and Fran were scheduled to be in New York for the premiere of Peter's remake of *King Kong* and invited Lorri to attend. They met and grew even closer.

"I think they were so shaken by the documentary *Paradise Lost*," said Lorri, "they thought surely everything would have been taken care of. Surely, they would be out of prison. And when they learned that they weren't, Fran told me, they got in a room together and Fran said, 'Let's help them.'

"So they already had it in their mind from seeing Damien in the film, and wanting to help, and I think it was just the fact that I wasn't crazy, Damien was innocent and an intelligent being, and was being tortured. And Fran has this innate sense, there's something about her, that loves this work, and she's good at it. She came on board. I didn't know what I was doing. I'd try to figure out things as I was going along. We hired a few horrible lawyers, had money stolen."

Not being American, Peter and Fran didn't know whether their public influence would help or hurt the WM3 effort, so they kept it private. But as it turned out, with all the other efforts that had been launched, they represented the tipping point in the entire process.

"When Fran and Pete came on board — they're directors, they're producers, they know how to run a big project," Lorri said.

Damien added, "They would ask, 'Why is this not being done now? Why didn't someone get on this the second we said do it?' Peter is scary smart. He can look at a situation and know what people are going to do three or four moves down the road. And he'll tell you, 'We're going to do this because they're going to do that, and then we'll be in a position to do this.' And every single time, what ever he said would happen, happened just as he said it would."

"And Fran's the same way," said Lorri. "Her intelligence is off the charts. So to have the two of them in there . . ."

Soon she and Fran became active correspondents. Lorri discussed all critical strategy with Fran and Peter. Eventually they became long-distance shoulders she could lean on; and when needed, to cry on.

Peter and Fran's strategy and backing

brought me to West Memphis in 2007. Fran had read our books and knew a lot about profiling and criminal investigative analysis.

"Fran was adamant she wanted John Douglas on the defense team," Lorri told Mark Olshaker.

I asked her, "Can I mention you and Pete?" She said I could, once I agreed to take part.

"I called Steve Mark back and mentioned Dennis Riordan, our lead appeals attorney. They'd gone to college at Colgate together, so I think Steve realized this was something concrete."

About a year later, when we were all meeting in New York about the case, Peter and I got into a discussion about *The Lovely Bones,* Alice Sebold's exquisite and heartbreaking novel, which Peter was preparing to film. I went over some ideas with him about how the villain, a remorseless child killer, would behave. Knowing of my involvement with *The Silence of the Lambs,* he asked me to consult on the film. I ended up coaching actor Stanley Tucci on how to play this monster realistically. I was highly gratified when he was nominated for an Academy Award as Best Supporting Actor.

But before that happened, I had this real-life case to pursue.

CHAPTER 22
FITTING THE PROFILE

Joe Berlinger and Bruce Sinofsky released a second film in 2000. *Paradise Lost 2: Revelations* detailed the efforts of the Free the West Memphis Three Support Group and chronicled the thus-far unsuccessful appeals process. Burk Sauls, Kathy Bakken, Lisa Fancher and Grove Pashley all figure prominently in *PL2,* as does Lorri.

The film brings up the curious death of Melissa Byers, in home and in bed, on March 26, 1996. Melissa had had a long-standing substance abuse problem, even before she and her husband, John Mark Byers, met. Her death cast further suspicion on him, and he didn't seem to understand why a group of mainly West Coast agitators were coming in to support the three who had killed his stepson.

"To me, it's like a Jeffrey Dahmer fan club, Charles Manson fan club, Ted Bundy — you could name them all," he told reporters. "Some people want to come to the rescue of a savage to get maybe their fifteen minutes of notoriety on TV."

Byers, who'd had previous run-ins with the law, hadn't exactly kept his nose clean in the years between the two films. He had been accused of taking $20,000 worth of property from a neighbor's home and pawning it; he reportedly held a gun on potential interveners while two teens in his neighborhood beat each other up. He later said in the stolen merchandise charge, he and Melissa were covering for his son Ryan and his friends.

In 1999, while on probation after conviction for that crime, he was arrested for selling twenty tablets of the prescription tranquilizer Xanax to undercover narcotics officers. His court-appointed lawyer plea-bargained, but he ended up doing fifteen months of hard time in maximum-security institutions, even though he had never been a violent offender. The first day he was in prison, three inmates jumped him. That encounter left him with a concussion, broken nose, dislocated shoulder, four broken ribs and bruised kidneys. His description to us of getting to the point where you just tune out the screams of the other prisoners is remarkably similar to Damien's.

PL2 also shows how Dan Stidham, Jessie Misskelley Jr.'s attorney, brought in Brent Turvey, who calls himself a criminal profiler and "forensic generalist." Stidham had wanted a profiler involved from the start, but he couldn't afford it. During the appeals, Kathy Bakken got in touch with Turvey, who agreed to look into the case pro bono. After examining photos of the bodies and other crime scene evidence, Turvey concluded that the murders must have taken place elsewhere and that the creek area was only a dump site. In a long and detailed consultation, he also disagreed with Dr. Peretti about many of the wounds on the bodies, declaring they were not made with a knife, but rather were bite marks.

"This is the single worst case of sexual mutilation I've ever seen," Turvey declared, and suggested they might get closer to the true killer or killers if they could get dental impressions from the various suspects. A forensic odontologist subsequently ruled out all three defendants from the bite marks.

Turvey also believed it would have been difficult for one offender to pull off the triple murder by himself, so there would probably have been two UNSUBs.

When I came into the case, I disagreed with this analysis. First of all, I didn't see any way there were separate abduction, murder and body disposal sites. I was certain it all happened in one location. It would be virtually impossible to abduct three active boys, control and keep them quiet while they were transported to a different location, kill them in a brutal manner, and then carry the bleeding bodies into the woods, all without being seen or noticed. If there were more than one offender, the difficulty would be multiplied. Anyone criminally experienced and sophisticated enough to pull off something like that would not undertake such a high-risk venture.

But the possibility of more than one offender was low in my mind. When I was assuming this was a sexually based crime, it didn't seem like the kind of scenario where two perverts would be partnering and watching each other. Later, when I knew more about the facts and changed my assessment, it seemed even less likely that two UNSUBs would be involved.

His contention that the crime scene and dump site were different made no sense to me. I couldn't visualize the offender carrying three victims' contorted bodies, clothing and bicycles back into Robin Hood Hills, dropping the bikes in the water one place, placing the bodies elsewhere, and then hiding the clothing under the creek bed with sticks. Why wouldn't he have just burned or thrown away the clothing? Turvey's scenario just didn't scan.

None of these exotic theories made any sense to me. The crime had to be simpler and more straightforward.

Between 2000, when *PL2* leaves off, and 2006, when Lorri contacted me, in some ways a lot had happened and in others almost nothing had. The sum total was that life didn't get any easier for some of the key figures in the case.

While raising her and Damien's son, Seth, Domini Teer married and divorced and married again. She ended up living in Arizona.

Pam Hobbs left Terry in 2002 and divorced in 2004. That same year, Vicki Hutcheson recanted her testimony that she had accompanied Damien to an *esbat,* explaining, "He was just like any normal kid his age."

She suggested that it was her only way of getting out of her own legal difficulties, and apparently the ploy worked. She also said the police brought up the possibility that the authorities would take away her son if she did not cooperate. The theft charges were never brought against her and she kept her child. "I testified to it, but I lied on the stand," she said.

Dana and Todd Moore divorced. There had long been local talk about the couple's problems with alcohol. Just a year after the murders, Dana had struck and killed a pedestrian while driving on a rural road in Crittenden County. She was charged with driving under the influence, but her lawyer had pled the charge down. She was fined, put on probation, and ordered to pay restitution.

Michael Carson moved out to California,

continued to get in trouble with the law, and continued to ply his trade as a jailhouse snitch. Eventually he, too, would call into question his testimony that Jason Baldwin had confessed the murders to him. "I was really in a bad state," he reflected. "They [the prosecutors] knew the drugs I was taking." Essentially, he said he couldn't remember whether Jason confessed, merely told Michael what he had been accused of, or that he heard it from somewhere else. Since his assertions were so bizarre, my own conclusion is that he made them up in his drug-induced haze.

Meanwhile, the appeals were going nowhere. Judge Burnett turned down every new motion the defense brought before him, and the Arkansas Supreme Court consistently upheld each of his rulings.

The only ray of hope was a new state statute in 2001 that allowed the new scientific capabilities of DNA analysis to be raised in support of actual innocence.

Studying the victimology, I found nothing in the three victims' behavior that would categorize them as high-risk.

On the other hand, Robin Hood Hills itself was potentially a high-risk area because it was isolated and densely wooded. Cries for help would be difficult to hear. For the same reason, it was relatively low-risk for the offender. Eight-year-olds would be vulnerable targets, though three boys together would decrease their chances for harm. It would be difficult to control three victims at once unless there was more than one offender, as the prosecution put forth, or if a single offender had a gun or knew the victims and therefore could assert verbal authority over them.

A significant behavioral consideration was the location, nature, and severity of injuries and their intended lethality. The offender was very methodical about the killings. He made all three victims remove their clothing. This tactic, as an M.O., had been observed in other cases where the offender not only intended to instill fear into the minds of victims by removing their clothing, but also to cause embarrassment and vulnerability to the point where victims would not want to run out totally naked into a public area. The offender knew this tactic would be an effective means to control young victims.

Another controlling technique that I had never seen before in other violent crimes was using shoelaces from the victims' tennis shoes to hog-tie them. According to the reports, Chris Byers was tied by half hitch and double half hitch knots; Stevie Branch was tied in a similar fashion and the knots were all half hitches. Michael Moore was bound with square knots on his left wrist and ankle and half hitch knots on his right wrist and ankle.

I saw several possibilities for the different

knots used in the Moore bindings:

- Multiple offenders.
- The offender himself used two styles of knots familiar to him.
- The offender had one of the victims help him bind Michael.

Having victims tie one another has been observed in previous cases. But what couldn't be concluded from this one aspect of the case was whether there was more than one offender involved. A forensic expert for the prosecution testified during the trial about the types of knots utilized by the offender, but never gave an opinion as to the significance of the difference.

The offender was criminally clever to utilize the shoelaces as bindings. The question, though, is *why* did he want to hog-tie the victims? If the intent was to kill the boys, why tie them up?

Behavior reflects personality and the behavior exhibited by the offender at the crime scene reveals his personality characteristics. The method and manner in which this offender perpetrated this crime would be indicative of who he is and what he is like as a person. The commission of a violent crime involves the personal attributes of what we recognize as an individual's "normal" behavior. Such normal behavior is unique to that individual.

In addition to the uniqueness revealed by how and with what the victims were hog-tied, other behavioral indicators reflected on the offender as well. Postoffense behavior reflects that he felt the need to hide the victims' clothing at the scene. He did so by sticking small branches he found at the scene into the clothing and pushing it under the muddy water and out of view. The victims were also hidden from view. As a final act, the offender felt the need to toss the two bikes into the bayou drainage ditch and out of sight.

Once I had studied and absorbed all of the case materials, I set out to create a profile and analysis.

Before you can deal with the specific personality of the UNSUB, you have to figure out *what kind of murder it is.* We break down intentional homicides into four broad categories:

1. *Criminal Enterprise* entails murder committed for profit or material gain such as money, goods, territory or favors.
2. *Group Cause,* in which two or more people with a common ideology sanction an act committed by one or more of its members that results in death. Gangs and religious and hate

groups would fall under this heading.

3. *Sexual Homicide* involves a sexual element or activity as the basis for the sequence of acts leading to death. Performance and meaning of this sexual element vary with the offender. The act may range from actual rape involving penetration — either before or after death — to a symbolic sexual assault, such as insertion of foreign objects into the victim's body.

4. *Personal Cause Homicide* is an act of interpersonal aggression that results in the death of a person or persons who may or may not be known to the offender. The homicide is not motivated by material gain or sex and is not sanctioned by a group. It is the result of an underlying emotional conflict that propels the offender to kill.

Of course, these categories can overlap based on the offender's particular psychopathology. Sedley Alley's murder of Suzanne Collins, for example, was a mixed presentation. It was primarily a personal cause homicide because it was motivated by anger and aggression, but it certainly had sexual overtones, displaced onto Suzanne from other problems in his life.

After laying out the topics to be dealt with, I always begin by explaining just what Criminal Investigative Analysis is. As I wrote in my report:

> Criminal Investigative Analysis is a process whereby crimes are reviewed in their totality from both a behavioral and investigative perspective. It involves reviewing and assessing the facts of a criminal act; interpreting offender behavior before, during, and after the criminal act; developing strategies; profile of unknown offender(s); assessment of suspects; interview and interrogation strategies; search warrant information based on research, prosecutive and trial assistance, and expert testimony in the areas of motive, MO, and signature (ritual) analysis.
>
> The purpose of Criminal Investigative Analysis is to generate potential leads, as well as suspects who, based on past case experience and research, would most likely perpetrate the type of crime being investigated (i.e. homicide, rape, arson, kidnapping, etc.). In most cases an analysis is requested in order to provide investigative direction when the perpetrator's motive and intent are unknown. An analysis may "reinforce" the course or direc-

tion of the investigation or may in fact "redirect" an investigation if it appears the investigation has been somehow misdirected or maligned. From prior investigative experience, cases have been misdirected by misinformation relative to eyewitness testimony; lack of investigative experience; false confessions; contamination at the crime scene; and/or the mishandling of evidence during the collection and preservation of the scene.

Regarding the Cameron Todd Willingham supposed arson case in Texas, I have expressed concern that my FBI unit might have gotten it wrong if we had analyzed it, due to inaccurate scientific information that came from local practitioners.

In other words, to explain the murders of the three victims it is important not only to analyze the crime with respect to what is observed behaviorally, but also to integrate that analysis with known facts through investigative interviews and forensic evaluation of evidence.

The situation turned out to be similar here in West Memphis.

When initially reviewing the case materials, my first impression was that the case was a lust murder, a subcategory of sexual homicide, with Chris Byers being the primary target. This was based in large part on the findings of medical examiner Frank Peretti, who opined that Chris was emasculated by use of a sharp instrument. Recall that he testified the emasculation was so surgically precise that even he would have had difficulty performing such precise surgical acts even under the best operative conditions. I later found out that Dr. Peretti had never been board certified, and as I would soon learn, much of his analysis was out-and-out wrong.

We define "lust murder" as any case in which the assailant cuts, stabs, pierces or mutilates the sexual organs of a victim. A distinguishing characteristic of the lust murder involves extreme mutilation and body dismemberment. The attack is frenzied in appearance, but it is primarily focused on the genital areas of the victim. The lust murderer often bites victims in the breasts, buttocks, abdomen, thighs and/or genitals.

The most common method of killing for the lust murderer is strangulation, blunt-force trauma or stabbing with a sharp instrument. The crime may display overkill: excessive trauma or injury beyond what is necessary to cause death. Dr. Peretti described Chris's wounds as having the appearance of gouging, bite marks, cutting and blunt-force trauma. While he stated that the cutting wounds were caused by a knife, he did not address the cause for the gouging and bite marks.

The more I looked at the crime scene

photographs and studied the reports, the more I was convinced something was not right about this. Lust murders tend to be disorganized, and in nearly every case the offender does not know the victim or victims. But the evidence here told me just the opposite. The crime was not only organized, but it showed a strong degree of what we call criminal creativity or flexibility. That is, the killer did not come to the scene with ropes, so he was not planning on binding anyone. Rather, when he decided to do so, he utilized what he found at the scene — the boys' own shoelaces.

Also, he had the presence of mind — the need, in fact — to hide the clothing and bicycles, something he would not have needed to do if he were a stranger who could get out of the area quickly.

Then there was the fact that the genitals were only mutilated on one of the three victims. That also didn't square with a lust murder of three individuals. Clearly, from the binding, he wanted to control all three, but only emasculated one. No, that didn't make sense, either. And even though the bodies were found in water, I would have expected to see some evidence of blood in the surrounding area. No, there had to be another reason or explanation for the castration.

This was not lust. This was personal cause between the UNSUB and at least one of the three boys.

Not trusting the evaluation of Dr. Frank Peretti, the defense team enlisted Dr. Werner Spitz, one of America's foremost forensic and anatomic pathologists, and author of the standard text *Medicolegal Investigation of Death,* then in its fourth edition, and Dr. Jon Nordby, a Ph.D. in forensic sciences.

They examined the evidence just as I did, with only the promise of an objective and dispassionate analysis, regardless of whether it helped or hurt the defense effort. Their conclusions were stunning.

Both experts independently concluded that most of the injuries, other than blunt-force trauma to all three bodies, including the horrific genital wounds on Chris Byers, were the result *not of a meticulous castration and skinning of the penis* as Dr. Peretti had testified, or to lacerations with a serrated knife on the others, but to *postmortem animal predation.*

Frank Peretti had been wrong about knife wounds, and Brent Turvey had been wrong about human bite marks. It was all starting to make more logical sense.

Experiments clearly demonstrated that the bite marks on all three bodies corresponded exactly with test bites inflicted by alligator snapping turtles. Interestingly, it was our personal attorney, Steve Mark, who first discussed this possibility with Fran Walsh, simply by speculating about other alternatives to the court testimony and researching the types of animal predators indigenous to the area. Steve and Fran developed the idea over a series of emails.

This confirmed for me that it was not, in fact, a lust murder or, as I had already concluded, a ritualized, satanic crime. Whoever killed these three boys did so because of a specific reason having to do with the offender and at least one of the victims.

This did not start out to be a murder. It was perpetrated by someone whose initial intent was not to kill the victims, but rather to taunt, punish, and/or "teach them a lesson." The reason for this conclusion is that the offender did not immediately kill the victims. They were alive for a period of time as they were being stripped naked and hog-tied. It is my opinion the offender went too far with his taunting and punishment and knew he would be implicated if he let the children go free *because he knew the victims and lived in the immediate area.*

There was another rational and logical criminal reason why the offender hid the victims, their clothing and bicycles in the creek and drainage ditch. The offender did not want the victims to be found immediately, because he needed time to establish an alibi for himself. This was one of several reasons I discounted the Mr. Bojangles connection and considered the homeless man a coincidental red herring.

I believe the three boys came into the woods of Robin Hood Hills by the most common method from the neighborhood side, crossing the large drainage pipe. It is inconceivable that they carried their bikes across this very narrow-width bridge. Nor is there any evidence they entered the woods at another location or were killed somewhere else and disposed of in Robin Hood Hills. It required much balance crossing the bridge, and the risk of falling off the bridge while carrying their bicycles was high. The boys would have left their bicycles hidden in the tall grass and weeds before they each walked across the pipe bridge. This is an important aspect of the crime to consider, because the offender, in all probability, would have spotted the bikes, crossed the pipe and committed the crime. Then he would have thrown them into the bayou drainage ditch after crossing back over the pipe bridge and heading in the same general direction where both he and the victims lived.

I believe the UNSUB was looking for the boys, or at least one of them, when he spotted the bikes. The most likely explanation is that they were not where they were supposed to be; and when he found them, he was already angry. It is even possible that when he found them, they were involved in some kind of sexual discovery and therefore fully or partially undressed, which would have fueled his anger even further. It is also possible that one or more of them simply mouthed off to him, which increased his need to punish or humiliate them.

At some point, he lost control of the situation, or realized he had gone too far. This might have been where the blunt-force trauma to the boys' heads came in. He could have had a closed knife, the butt of a gun or some other object with which he struck them. If one did mouth off, most likely Chris Byers, based on what his parents and others said about his cockiness and impulsivity, then he might have been struck harder, and that represented the point of no return. He could easily be identified by the victims; so in his mind, he had to destroy the evidence — he had to kill them. Had he been a stranger or a drifter, he could have just gotten the hell out of there, and he would have been relatively safe. Not so with someone known to the boys.

I would classify this individual as an "organized" offender and describe him as being self-centered, egocentric and narcissistic. He resents people, but he does not avoid social situations. He looks at social situations as an opportunity to manipulate and use others for his own personal gain. The organized type is known for his cunning and is methodical in his everyday activities. Because of his criminal intellect, based on his previous criminal activities, he is seen as adaptive and flexible when criminally active; however, he prefers to perpetrate crimes in close proximity to where he either resides or is employed — his "comfort zone."

The organized type is cognizant of not leaving evidence at the scene that could be forensically linked to him. Stripping the victims, hog-tying them, using sticks to submerge and hide the victims' clothing, throwing their bicycles in the water, all reflect the offender's criminal mind.

It is not uncommon for the organized type of offender to be overly cooperative post-offense. Because he lived in the general neighborhood and knew the victims, he realized law enforcement would be asking him questions relative to the case and his whereabouts at the time. The organized offender's cooperation is intended to deflect suspicions away from him as a suspect.

Due to the brutality exhibited by the offender at the scene, it can be said with confidence that he would have the reputation from past behavioral "problems" as having an unpredictable and extremely explosive and violent personality. He probably came from a bad background in which there was family violence and/or he was physically abused.

Although this crime may, in fact, be the first time he has killed anyone, it is not the first time he has violently attacked someone.

Damien and Jason had no indicative violence in their pasts; and while Jessie was known for a hot temper, he channeled his aggression into pursuits such as wrestling. He was also known to be very gentle with children and often babysat in his neighborhood. Though the three were raised in a culture in which corporal punishment was common, none were abused.

Predicting the age of an offender at the time of a crime is difficult. Both chronological age and behavioral age need to be considered. However, based on the method and manner of death of the three victims, coupled with the offender's behavior postoffense, which included secreting the bodies and disposing of the clothing and bicycles in the water, what can be said with a high degree of certainty is that this triple homicide was not a crime perpetrated by a youthful offender or offenders, or one without any history of past violent behavior. It is inconceivable to me that three teenagers could pull off a crime like this and not leave any evidence of themselves behind. I have never seen it done.

While the violence-prone UNSUB responsible for these homicides may not have killed before, he did not simply evolve and emerge on May 5, 1993, as a triple murderer. He had been "working up" to that capacity for years or decades before. He would almost assuredly have some kind of violence, cruelty and anger management issues in his background.

In any case involving the murder of children, investigators always look to the family and immediate adult social circle first, just as in the JonBenét Ramsey case. In all my years of experience, I have never seen a mother or other woman perpetrate this type of crime. So had I been an initial investigator, I first would have looked closely at the father and two stepfathers. If none of them panned out, I would move out in concentric circles of closeness; while at the same time, I would follow up on all forensic evidence, possible witnesses and other leads.

Another potential area of inquiry would be the nearby Mayfair Apartments complex that was known to house transients and sometimes had been a residence for drug users and sellers and paroled sexual offenders. It was unlikely that the three boys would have known any of the residents, but not impossible. Perhaps one of the residents could have spotted one or more of the boys and followed them. An experienced sexual offender would have developed techniques for talking to and controlling potential victims. And since he lived in the area and would be known for his criminal past, he would have to cover up the crime as best he could. I would have tried to find out if anyone had suddenly left the area right after the murders.

With what I knew from the pathologists' reports, I discounted the likelihood of this possibility. There was no evidence of any sexual bodily penetration; and though nude bondage can certainly have a sexual context, the boys' bodies were forced into strange contortions, and nothing appeared to have happened based on the bondage.

So none of the evidence pointed to multiple offenders, teens, ritual or symbolism, Satanism or sexual assault.

In sum, I found not one shred of evidence and nothing in the behavioral backgrounds of Damien Echols, Jason Baldwin or Jessie Misskelley Jr. to suggest that any were guilty of murder.

CHAPTER 23
WEST MEMPHIS HEAT

When I sent my report to Dennis Riordan, the response was dramatic. As Steve Mark recalls, "Fran and Lorri particularly were very pleased, as well as relieved that the foremost FBI profiler had validated three points: It was not a satanic murder; the three teen defendants could not have carried it out; and that this was a personal cause homicide, suggesting the offender knew at least one of the victims. So far, it had been like a one-sided tennis match. Suddenly, with John's report, the tempo of the match shifted and all the spectators looked up and said, 'Whoa!' "

What my profile and analysis showed, the Jackson-Walsh team said to me, was that both they and the police investigators had been looking in the wrong direction and concentrating in the wrong area in trying to figure out who killed the three boys. If it was not a satanic killing, and not likely a stranger murder, where should they be looking?

"What John's report did," says Steve, "was

refocus the team in a specific direction, away from strangers and toward those who had some relationship to the victims. Specifically, it made them devote more attention to Terry Hobbs as a potential person of interest."

I remember it was hot as hell when I went down to West Memphis in 2007 at the request of Lorri, Fran and Peter. Five people had died from the heat. I was grateful for the air-conditioning in the Holiday Inn in Memphis, where I was staying.

The heat was representative of the oppressive daily burdens many of the residents faced. This was a population of tough, hard-working people, most of whom had not had the advantages of higher education, influential social contacts or opportunities to get ahead. Of the people I came in contact with, most of them smoked — and smoked a lot — and few had had access to good medical or dental care. They lived in small houses or trailer park communities, and the American tradition of upward mobility was severely limited in West Memphis. There were so many stressors in their lives that alcohol, domestic violence, divorce and other social problems were rampant.

But I also noticed that no matter what they had to face, these were people of abiding faith. Churches of various denominations were all over the place. The locals were also friendly and hospitable, and those who weren't instinctively wary of an outsider like me poking around into their personal business greeted me warmly and welcomed me into their lives.

One of my first stops in West Memphis was the police station. I went there with Lorri, a Memphis investigator named Ron Lax, who was working with the defense, and his associate Rachel Geiser. As we sat in the file room going over additional evidence, cops passed by in the hall with curious looks on their faces.

The inspection confirmed what the investigators told me after I submitted my written report: Though WMPD had talked to John Mark Byers several times and looked into his background, they had never interviewed Todd Moore or Terry Hobbs. Given the nature of the crime, this was a pretty staggering oversight.

One item we came across that surprised me was that Damien was not the only one who had contacted my unit at Quantico. So had WMPD. I would have been unit chief at the time, but I knew nothing about it.

It was an over-the-phone consultation. We did a lot of those, in which a local chief or detective would call and describe a case rather than send all of the materials. We would try to give them guidance as to what type of individual to look for and what strategy to follow. In this case, the police talked to two other agents in the unit, who gave them advice about what kinds of questions to ask during door-to-door canvassing. There was no record of any follow-up at the time.

When I returned home from this trip, I happened to get a call on another matter from Ken Lanning. Ken had offered advice in the JonBenét Ramsey case while he was still in the FBI that the prosecution team hadn't liked and was subsequently shut out of the investigation. I asked Ken if he'd ever had anything to do with the West Memphis murders before he retired.

"Oh, yeah," he replied. "Someone from the prosecutor's office called me based on the guide I'd written, described the case and told me they were pursuing it as a satanic murder."

"What'd you tell them?" I asked.

"I said I thought they were letting the theory drive the investigation. I said, 'If you bring up that this is a satanic murder, they'll laugh you right out of court.' "

"What happened then?"

"Nothing. They never called me back. Next thing I know, I'm reading about it in the papers — that the motive is satanic ritual."

During my years at Quantico, I had learned never to dismiss anything Ken Lanning had to say — a lesson lost on at least these two prosecution teams. The only thing Ken was wrong about, as it turned out, was that the West Memphis district attorneys were *not* laughed out of court, and that is precisely where the tragedy of murder was compounded with the tragedy of miscarried justice.

Todd Moore had a strong alibi: He was working at his job driving a truck during the time the boys went missing. After he got off work, he and Mark Byers went looking for them together. Other people saw them.

While Terry Hobbs was with other people for most of the day and evening, there was about a two-hour window — from about 6:40 to 8:30 P.M. — when he wasn't with anyone else. This was tantalizing as a potential clue because he had said he was with his friend David Jacoby the entire afternoon and evening. Jacoby had contradicted this, saying they were only together for about an hour and a half. Moreover, Terry claimed he hadn't seen Stevie all day, having left for work before the rest of the family arose. But a neighbor, Jamie Clark Ballard, stated that she had seen Terry calling after Stevie near his house about six-thirty on the evening of the murders. Stevie was on his bike, and Chris and Michael were running behind him. All three boys were laughing.

About two weeks after the murders, Terry

left town. He said staying there was too much to handle. Clearly, we needed to get more information on him.

Dana and Michael Moore each flat-out refused to talk to me, and John Mark Byers and Pamela Hobbs were unresponsive. But Terry Hobbs, now split up from Pam, agreed to see me. I hadn't had the opportunity to prepare or do any real background investigation on him. But I didn't want to lose what might be my only chance to meet with him, so I figured I'd better take the offer while I had it.

Terry and I met on a Monday evening from about eight to ten in a garden restaurant at a mall outside Memphis. He was pleasant and considerate, and he had a reasonable-seeming answer to every question I posed. He came across as a father still grieving after all these years. He had loved Pam and Stevie, and he deeply regretted the factors that led to his divorce. I know how the loss of a child can put an unbearable strain on a relationship, and he implied that everything in the marriage had been going downhill since the murders.

I mentioned that I understood he'd had a tough childhood; his father had been pretty rough on him. Terry shrugged and dismissed the observation, as if to say that it was no worse than most and that he had gotten past it. We ended our conversation amiably and I said I might want to talk to him again at some point. I left the interview thinking that I might have been barking up the wrong tree.

I met again with Ron and Rachel. We went through every record or reference we could find on Terry. With two professional private detectives working the case, that turned out to be quite a lot. Rachel interviewed his ex-wife and learned of a highly disturbing incident involving a former neighbor named Mildred French. She and Ron assembled a complete dossier. A new portrait of Terry Hobbs was beginning to emerge.

But before we tried to approach him again, I wanted to talk to his best friend David Jacoby, the one who the police believed provided his alibi for the night of the murders.

Jacoby lived in a single-level house with white siding with a yard surrounded by chain link fencing. When I approached, I saw him sitting shirtless in the yard under an umbrella, apparently working on his business papers. At the time, he was working as a driver for a trucking company out of Little Rock. I was in "Bureau casual": I had taken off my dark suit jacket and tie. Still, he was far more appropriately attired for the heat than I was. I could already feel the sweat developing in all the old familiar places.

There was a female pit bull chained up that

looked as if it had recently had a litter. I originally wanted to be a veterinarian and I still notice such things. I also noticed that if I took a couple of steps in the wrong direction, the dog would have the opportunity to decide physically if I were welcome or not.

Fortunately, it didn't turn out to be an issue. David Jacoby looks like a civilized version of the traditional mountain man, with a craggy face framed by a full head of grayish-brown hair and a long, untrimmed graying beard. His manner was completely civilized as well. When I told him who I was and what I was there for, he courteously asked me to sit down.

What I wanted him to do, I explained, was take me through the timeline of May 5, 1993. The story that had emerged originally was that after Terry dropped Pam off at the restaurant where she worked, he went over to David's house to play guitar with him. At two points in the evening the two of them had gone out to look for Stevie. But the real question was: *Was he with Terry the entire evening?* He had avoided talking to the media, but answers he had given to investigators, including Rachel, had contradicted some of the earlier assumptions, including that he had been with Terry the whole time in question.

So I needed to get a definitive answer to this if I could.

At the time of the murders, both David and

Terry worked for the Memphis Ice Cream Company and lived close to each other, so they got together frequently. He verified that Terry came over to his house shortly after he dropped off Pam at work, which would have made it about 5:15. He had his daughter Amanda with him, and David's wife Bobby was home with him. Terry came over frequently in those days to play guitars with David, which was what they did that evening.

I asked David to think carefully about what happened after that. He said it had been a long time ago and the evening was clouded in his memory by the trauma of the tragedy, which he said accounted for some of his confusion. But as he thought about it, he recalled Terry saying that he'd better get home and see if Stevie was there, because he hadn't been home when Terry left with Pam. He told David that Stevie knew he wasn't supposed to be out after dark. This would have been some time between 6:00 and 6:15 p.m. He couldn't remember if Terry had left Amanda with him when he went back home, but thought he probably did, which is what he had told Rachel when she interviewed him.

David also recalled that when he had opened the front door to let Terry in, he saw two boys on bicycles and one on a skateboard. He was pretty sure that one of the boys was Stevie. If that were the case, I noted, it contradicted Terry's longstanding statement that he had left the house to go to work while Stevie was still sleeping and had not seen him all day.

It was about an hour later when Terry returned. He asked David and Bobby whether Stevie had come by. When they both said no, Terry and David decided to go out and look for him. He was pretty sure they took Amanda with them.

Their first stop was the Mayfair Apartments, where they asked if anyone had seen Stevie or his two friends, Michael and Chris. They then drove to the area south of Ten Mile Bayou, but didn't see anything. Then they drove back to David's house, where Terry dropped him off. He thought they were out for about fifteen or twenty minutes.

David and Bobby were alone in the house until Pam came over, which would have had to be some time after nine when Terry picked her up from her restaurant shift. She drove over in her own car and Terry came just afterward in his truck. She was hysterical, saying that Stevie was still missing and she wanted to go out looking for him. He didn't think she was in any shape to drive, so he convinced her to let him take her around to some of the locations Stevie frequented, like the cub scout meeting place, which he thought was either a local church or school. They returned without finding the boy.

Sometime after that, he went back out

searching with Terry and Jackie Hicks, Sr., Pam's father. At some point they came across Mark Byers and Dana Moore, also looking for the boys. When they approached the drainpipe crossing, he noticed bicycle tracks, and also muddy footprints small enough to be children's on the pipe itself.

As they got close to what turned out to be the murder scene, Terry reported to David that he heard something that sounded "evil." He had a bad feeling about the place, so he turned around and they went the other direction. David thought this was odd because he was looking for Stevie and wouldn't want to think he was in that "evil" place, but he didn't say anything.

I had the same reaction. If you are afraid for your son and you sense something bad, a parent's natural instinct would be to go toward it to protect him, not recoil from it.

They were out looking until about 3:00 A.M., at which point David went home to get some sleep.

By the time David got back home the next afternoon, about 3:30, the boys' bodies had been found.

I listened to all of this calmly and made sure my outward gestures were matter-of-fact. But the whole time I'm realizing, *My God, Terry doesn't have an alibi for the entire evening!* The apparent time discrepancy was real and there was a window of opportunity when he wasn't with David. David was so forthcoming with me, as he had been with Rachel, I could only conclude that no one from the police had asked him for his version, or he certainly would have told them. This fit right in with no one having formally interviewed Terry just after the crime as they had Mark Byers. I couldn't — and still can't — figure out why.

I explained the dynamics of the crime to David and why I thought the offender had to be someone who knew the children. He had to control three children at once, and even if he were threatening them with a gun, it would have been virtually impossible to keep at least one from running away. So it was most likely someone they would naturally listen to. I told him I believed the offender had seen the bikes, crossed over into Robin Hood Hills, and found the children. His first reaction was anger, so he tried to punish them in some way. When he lost control and the situation got out of hand, he felt he had no recourse but to kill them. Otherwise, his life and reputation would be ruined.

We discussed the area together and I showed him that if it had been a stranger, he most likely would have both come in and gone out the truck wash side of the woods rather than the neighborhood side, and we knew from the position of the bikes in the water that he had either entered or left through the neighborhood — probably both.

David was visibly shaken as I departed. He was specifically upset that he hadn't looked into the crime more closely on his own before this.

The first time I tried to talk to Pam Hobbs, she wouldn't let me in. It took Ron Lax calling and convincing her I was not out to "get anyone" or make her look bad to get her to talk to me. By the time she agreed to see me, the investigative team and I had been able to probe deeper into her ex-husband's background and I felt more prepared.

We met at her mother's place, a small brick house on a corner lot about a half-hour drive from West Memphis. There was a FOR SALE sign on the front lawn. Several members of her family sat in on the conversation around the dining-room table.

I told them I had spent most of my career working for the prosecution, but here they had gotten it wrong. At first, like Mark Byers, they were resistant, and who could blame them? After I went through the steps of the case and my analysis, I asked, "Am I describing anyone to you?"

It seemed as if every person around the table exchanged a glance with every other person before they all agreed: Terry.

"Why is that?" I probed.

They described the physical and emotional

abuse Pam had received from Terry. They said he had also hit his first wife, Angela. They described the times Terry had beaten Stevie, treating him very differently from Amanda, his natural daughter with Pam. Pam said that two weeks before the murder, Stevie asked her to leave Terry. " 'He loves Amanda,' " she quoted him as saying, " 'but he doesn't love me.' "

The family also suggested that Terry's relationship with the girl did not seem normal and may have been inappropriate, or worse. They confirmed my information that Terry's father had been a Fundamentalist minister, who was often brutal with him.

The most significant violence in Terry's past involved family. In November 1994, Pam and Terry got into one of their frequent disputes, which ended with Terry striking Pam across the face with the back of his hand. Pam called her family, and her brother Jackie Hicks Jr., with whom Terry had clashed before, rushed over. When Jackie started fighting with him, Terry pulled out a .357 Magnum he had loaded with hollow-point bullets and shot him in the gut. Terry said he had used the gun in self-defense; he served six months in prison for aggravated assault. Jackie underwent surgery and lived for another ten years, but he died from a clot released during a follow-up surgery.

As I listened, the family recalled other

incidents and tried to put them together. For example, they reminded Pam that when Terry dropped her off that evening at five at the Catfish Island Restaurant, where she worked, they couldn't be sure where he was until he picked her up at 9:00 P.M. There had been a sighting of him with the kids around 6:30 P.M., which he had denied. When he did pick her up, he behaved strangely. Without saying anything, he walked right past her into the restaurant and called the police. What had he been doing the previous four hours? If he was so concerned about Stevie being missing that he went looking for him in the woods, why didn't he call Pam at work to share his concerns? They also told me they all believed that the stress of Stevie's murder and Jackie Jr.'s shooting had caused Jackie Sr.'s death.

Interestingly, one source of the tension between Terry and Pam was his continuing insistence that she "get over" the murder and get on with life. I try to remain as objective and dispassionate as possible in what I do, but when I hear *anyone,* however well meaning, tell a close survivor to get over it, my blood starts to boil.

By the time I left, Pam no longer believed the West Memphis Three were guilty of the murder of her son. And she was ready to say so publicly.

CHAPTER 24
TWO STEPFATHERS

I purposely had not watched either of the *Paradise Lost* films until after I did my analysis so I would not be influenced in my evaluation. But I did watch them before I went down to Arkansas and knew that Mark Byers had come across as the prime alternative suspect in the second film. The first had laid the groundwork, in which he seemed a wild, *Deliverance*-type character, ready to blow off someone's head or pick a fight at the least provocation. But this, I already knew, was an illusion, a caricature.

In fact, by the time I reached the front porch of his trailer in a community in Millington, Tennessee, fourteen miles north of Memphis, I already had some pretty firm ideas about him that didn't fit in with my profile.

Byers was an extrovert, with no history of personal violence beyond punishing his children with a belt. His lawbreaking had been nonviolent and primarily examples of criminal enterprise: jewelry fraud, drugs and petty theft. He also had some experience as a drug informant. But he was known to be friendly with and well liked by neighborhood children. When you hear this, if there is anything improper in any of the relationships, you generally hear at least an innuendo from someone. There was none of this in the reports about Byers. Also, I had studied the timeline of the night of the murder, and he could be accounted for the entire time.

When he answered his door, I introduced myself amidst the barking of dogs. *This guy really is big,* I thought. Mark is an intimidating presence. He seemed extremely wary and had clearly had enough of lawmen, even retired lawmen like me. Having seen the HBO film, I also knew he'd be aware of how I was likely to perceive him.

"What do you want?" he demanded. "Who approached you to come here? You're that former FBI guy. Get off my property!"

As he stood in the door frame, I said, "Mr. Byers, I'm not here to point a finger at you. I don't consider you a suspect, but I would like to talk to you because it's my strong belief that the three people in prison did not kill your son Chris."

"They got the right guys, Goddamn it!" he insisted.

He came out onto the porch, but he didn't invite me in. In my white dress shirt and dark slacks, I was sweating like crazy in the heat. You could feel the oppressiveness every time you breathed in.

He told me that Damien Echols was the lead killer and that the motive was satanic.

"No, it wasn't," I replied. "And I'd like you to give me an opportunity to go through my analysis with you."

I heard his wife, Jackie, who was standing by the screen door. "Mark, we need to hear what he has to say."

Mark and Jackie had met in a bookstore in 2001, five years after the death of Melissa, Chris's mother. Jackie had tripped over her shoelace and fallen. Mark was the only one who came to her aid. They married the next year. Interestingly, she had never heard of him and knew nothing about the case; so before they got engaged, he insisted she watch the two *Paradise Lost* films to "know what you're getting into."

As he stood there looking down skeptically at me, I explained who I was and what kind of work I did in the FBI. Jackie came out on the porch and listened with interest, although she didn't say anything at first. They were both smoking, which made it seem like there was even less air to breathe.

I took them through what the steps of the crime would have been and why I believed that Satanism or ritual violence did not fit into the scenario. I tried to show them that when you stripped away all of the preconceptions and emotional overlays and looked strictly at the physical and behavioral evidence, you were left with a personal cause homicide situation. And it was one that didn't even involve a knife — his, Damien's or anyone else's. I showed them why Jessie Misskelley Jr.'s confession made no sense and how the police must have known it.

I told him that the killer knew his stepson.

I think I'd been there talking for about a half hour when Mark told me to sit down. That was the first time I thought maybe I was getting through. Before long, they invited me inside. There were several photographs of Christopher. Three friendly dogs circled around me on the soft sofa I sank into.

Almost right away, I could tell that this guy was not the out-of-control hillbilly I'd seen in the two *Paradise Lost* films. He was introspective and clearly intelligent and well informed. Jackie proved herself to be widely read on criminal justice and the kind of work I did. Her questions were incisive. I had already met many dysfunctional couples down here, but these two — he on his third marriage and she on her second — seemed like a genuine, emotionally strong and committed team. "She has been a big part of the stability in my life," he commented. "I tell people she is the glue that has kept me stuck together."

One of the first things I raised was how

Mark came across in the films. I asked him why he thought he had come across so negatively.

He didn't shy away from responding at the time, and confirmed it later for Mark Olshaker and me. "I was trying to take care of Melissa. I was trying to take care of Ryan. I really didn't have time for myself to mourn and grieve, and I was extremely angry because someone had murdered my son. But I was trying to keep my family together.

"Then in the second film, Melissa had passed away, Ryan was gone. I'd been all by myself. I'd tried to commit suicide once. I'd committed myself twice into rehab just because I couldn't handle it anymore. I'd had a lot of suicidal thoughts and was deeply depressed."

This is important because it gets to the heart of the mistakes in the case and an overarching theme throughout this book. If we go on first impressions and appearances, if we apply stereotypes and conventional wisdom, we run the terrible risk of misjudging people. The West Memphis Three were misjudged by the entire legal system, and Mark Byers was later misjudged by the wider court of public opinion. Notwithstanding the self-proclaimed practitioners who pop up on every TV talk show and the clichés that are so easy to parody, behavioral profiling gets below these surface judgments to find the real factors that cause people to do what they do. That was how I was able to get past the cartoon image to the real John Mark Byers.

"I was nervous just being around him," Byers later recalled of his first encounter with me, "thinking he was profiling me. He said he'd done that a long time ago."

Once inside, I found it even more difficult to breathe in the close environment, but Mark and Jackie seemed more comfortable now. Describing the crime scene and motivation, I went through my analysis: The murders were not the work of a complete stranger, drifter or sexual pervert; the incident had started out as an attempt to taunt and punish the victims, not as a murder, but the perpetrator had lost control and couldn't risk being identified; no weapons or implements that could be used to commit the crime were brought to the scene, such as binding rope or cord; while the UNSUB may not have committed murder or any other serious crime before, he had a violent past and, if left unchecked, a violent future; hiding the clothing with sticks and throwing the bicycles in the water showed criminal sophistication beyond the level of a teen; this individual lived in the area and had a psychopathic personality; he could look you straight in the eye and tell you he didn't do it.

How could one person tie up three kids? Jackie wanted to know.

Because they knew him and either respected or feared his authority, I explained. It was also possible that he may have ordered one boy to bind another. From what I knew of Chris's personality, he may have stood up to this vicious bully, his defiance causing the situation to get out of hand.

Mark Byers listened thoughtfully. At last, he said, "You're describing someone like Terry Hobbs."

He admitted that he had had unanswered questions ever since the trial and that his suspicions about Terry had been strong enough that he decided to try an experiment. "Gitchell had told us that he recovered a briefcase with some pictures in it, a knife, a gun and some drugs. But he didn't ever produce it. Well, I said to Terry, 'You remember seeing that picture of Damien on your couch?'

"And he goes, 'Yeah, I remember seeing it. Pam must have took it.' And here in our house, he told Jackie and me he'd always suspected Pam was messing around with Damien. So he started adding to this picture story that I totally fabricated."

Mark also described glancing at Terry during the trial when Michael Carson was testifying about Jason's supposed confession to him. "You could just see him, like it was almost too good to be true."

The turning point, I think, was when I told

them what David Jacoby had said about Terry having seen the children that evening, while Terry had claimed consistently that he hadn't seen any of them, including Stevie, the entire day. "That's when I freaked out. That was a lightbulb moment for me above all others," Mark Byers later told us.

I asked him if he thought Christopher might have been the one who rebelled against the offender and caused him to lose control. "I do think it's a strong possibility," Mark replied. "I have spent many hours wondering exactly what did happen. And as things have unfolded, I still don't have the answers."

But he added, "Christopher would be the first to tell him, 'You're not my daddy. I don't have to listen to what you say.' And if something was wrong, it would be, 'I'm gonna go tell my daddy!' He would have been the first to have done that."

When I left, Mark hugged me. And I have to say, when all is said and done, he is among the participants in the case for whom I have the highest regard and respect. For all his admitted flaws and problems, he was the one who wanted the truth right from the beginning. When presented with as much of that truth as we had to offer, he was the one who showed the integrity and strength of character to accept it, make peace with the young men he had thought guilty and then fight vigorously for their freedom and exoneration. If those on the law enforcement side had had the broadmindedness and courage of John Mark Byers, three innocent young men would not have had to suffer for so long; and justice for his son Chris, Michael and Stevie would not have proven so elusive.

"John Douglas came to visit me," Mark said later. "He gave me the answers I needed, and my worst fears were confirmed. I didn't think the state would mess up that badly. I thought they were here to protect and serve. I've always been brought up that way."

Terry agreed to my request to meet with him again, this time in a suite at the Memphis Holiday Inn where I was staying. And this time I was armed with information relative to the *real* Terry Hobbs. I was forthright and told him I felt better prepared this time. I noticed that Terry was carrying an unopened can of soda. I suggested he sit down, but he preferred to stand. I have seen this before when I've interviewed inmates in penitentiaries. Standing can be a technique for asserting a dominant position over the other person.

"You had me good, Terry," I began. "When I talked to you the other day, I really didn't know your background. But since then, I've had a chance to do some investigation, and find you were really bullshitting me. A lot of the things you told me just aren't true. You're a good liar, Terry, but not that good."

He didn't react, except to grasp the soda can a little tighter.

"You have a violent history," I continued. He looked at me as if I were just mentioning an incidental detail, like the color of his hair.

I employed a technique I've often used in the past. I call it, "This Is Your Life," taking him through key events I had learned about.

"You minimized it before, but I know your father beat the hell out of you, and you beat the hell out of Stevie." I had learned that he used to whip Stevie viciously with a belt, making him hold his hands up in the air away from his body. Others in the family had described the welts these punishments left. "You've been manipulative, lying. . . ."

Everything I mentioned led to a "big deal" shrug or a "So what?" When I mentioned the altercation with his brother-in-law, Terry calmly explained that Jackie Jr. was choking him, and the only way to make him let up was to threaten him with the gun.

I pointed out that shortly after the murders, he and Pam had gone to stay at Pam's family's home in Blytheville, Arkansas; and shortly after that, Terry left Pam there and went to stay in Hardy, Arkansas, about 120 miles away. This meant that he was never questioned or examined by the police. Again, "So what?" Remaining in West Memphis was just too much for him, he said.

He didn't flinch when I brought up the accusations that he had molested his daughter, Amanda. Normally, when you confront a man with a serious or outrageous charge that isn't true, he'll go ballistic. Terry didn't admit the charges, but he didn't bother denying them. The only thing I noted was that he was holding the can increasingly rigidly, as if it might be used as a weapon. He kept pacing.

Then I brought up an incident with his neighbor that had taken place twenty-five years ago, long before the murders. And that was when he finally became visibly agitated, as if he were shocked I found out about it.

In 1982, Terry and his first wife, Angela, and their child were living in Hot Springs, Arkansas. He was in his midtwenties at the time. Several times, his next-door neighbor Mildred French said she saw Terry outside staring at her through the window. One time, she heard a baby crying and what sounded like the child or Angela being beaten. She went over and rang the bell. Terry opened the door and asked contemptuously what she wanted. Mildred, who was about thirty years older than he, said that if he ever touched his wife or baby again, she would call the police.

Several months later, on December 8, 1982, she was stepping out of the shower after cleaning up from some yard work when she said Terry grabbed her from behind and then put his hands on her breast. She screamed and repeatedly yelled for him to get out. Finally, when he realized the window was partially open and she could be heard from outside, he ran out. Mildred stated that she was afraid he would beat, rape or kill her. She was certain she had locked the front door.

In 2009, Terry Hobbs filed a civil suit against the Dixie Chicks singer Natalie Maines, who had been a major advocate for the innocence of the West Memphis Three. Terry's action claimed she had defamed him at a concert by suggesting he might have been the killer of the three boys. As part of that suit, Mildred French detailed the events of Terry's intrusion in a sworn deposition:

That night, after I told my landlord about the attack, my landlord set up a meeting in which both Hobbs and I sat down face to face in front of the landlord. Terry's father-in-law was also there. I said to Terry, "Tell them what you did to me." Terry said, "I didn't do nothing." After I articulated what Hobbs had done to me, Terry looked me square in the eye and said calmly, "It never happened." He was cool and collected as he told me it never happened. If you had not known for certain Terry was lying, you would not have been able to tell by his demeanor that he was lying. I was sickened and frightened by Terry's ability to deny his horrific and perverted actions and seem calm in doing so. I looked at Terry and told him, "You are a liar and you are sick." Terry looked back at me with cold, dead eyes and said, "Yeah, I'm sick."

The landlord evicted the Hobbses, and Terry was charged with assault and criminal trespass. The case was dismissed in exchange for his agreement to go to counseling.

We went round a little more; me bringing up incidents and him either denying or shrugging them off. After a little while, he declared, "I've had enough of this shit," and walked out, still carrying the unopened soda can. He had not sat down the entire time.

It was neither my job nor my role to say whether I thought Terry Hobbs was involved with the murder of his own stepson, as well as Chris Byers and Michael Moore. I had been brought in to analyze the case from a behavioral perspective and offer an opinion on *what type of individual or individuals* had committed the crime. Knowing of Todd Moore's background and alibi, and having looked into and interviewed Mark Byers, I knew they could be eliminated from the suspect list and were, in fact, genuinely grieving parents and victims. Having done my analysis and having scrutinized and spoken to Terry Hobbs, what I could now say was that had I been advising WMPD on the case initially, I would have put him on the front burner of the investigation.

When I returned home, I received an extremely gratifying email from Fran and Peter that read in part: "You have single-handedly done more to humanize this case and advance the cause of Damien's innocence than anyone we know."

I just hoped we were moving closer to seeing justice done.

CHAPTER 25
ARKANSAS REVISITED

I went back to Arkansas later that year. On November 1, 2007, I participated in a press conference that Dennis Riordan and his law partner Donald Horgan led at the University of Arkansas at Little Rock, William H. Bowen School of Law. The other participants were Dr. Werner Spitz, Dr. Richard Souviron, who has been the chief forensic dentist for the Medical Examiner's Office of Miami-Dade, Florida, since 1967 and an expert on bite mark identification, and Thomas Fedor, a criminalist, DNA expert and blood and body fluid analyst with the Serological Research Institute of Richmond, California. Like me, each of them had worked on the case using the perspective from his own field of expertise.

The case was now styled *Echols* v. *Norris et al,* in the federal Eastern District of Arkansas. Larry Norris was the director of the Arkansas DOC, a position often used as the respondent in such appeals cases. Riordan explained that the federal habeas corpus appeal he was heading was different from most that are launched after all state remedies have been exhausted, because this one was based not on procedural flaws at the trial or state appeals court level, but on actual innocence. If that threshold could be established, then other procedural blocks to a new trial would be swept away.

"Actual innocence, in a legal sense, in the federal court means the following," Riordan stated. "Is there new evidence that was not available at the time of the offense? When you view it with all of the evidence concerning the case, would a federal judge then be able to say, with confidence, that any reasonable juror would have a reasonable doubt about the defendant's guilt? To state it differently, does the new evidence suggest that no reasonable juror would find the defendant guilty beyond a reasonable doubt? And a third way, can the judge be confident that with this new evidence, if that defendant were tried today, he would be acquitted? We are here today to discuss the evidence that establishes that no reasonable juror would convict Damien Echols, essentially knowing what we know today."

Riordan reviewed the problems with the Misskelley confession and the problems with the knife evidence. He posed the question, "How could three teens brutally murder three kids and not leave any evidence?" Then he turned the podium over to Donald Horgan, who introduced the DNA specimens submitted to Bode Technology in Virginia, a leading forensic analyzer and the prosecution's lab of choice.

Horgan announced that Bode was given samples from the three victims and from the three defendants and asked to analyze any possible links to DNA profiles of genetic materials collected from the victims' bodies and the crime scene. *There were no matches.*

He said that private investigators had obtained samples of DNA in the form of discarded cigarette butts from Stevie Branch's stepfather, Terry Hobbs, and a voluntary oral swab sample from David Jacoby, Terry's friend who was with him the night of the boys' disappearance. Thomas Fedor analyzed the samples and compared the Bode results.

"The result of that analysis, in May 2007, showed that a hair from the ligature used to tie up Michael Moore could be associated with Terry Hobbs," Horgan declared.

Fedor then explained that the hair in the ligature could only be tested for mitochondrial DNA — inherited from the female only and therefore not exclusive — meaning it could come from 1 1/2 percent of the population, including Terry Hobbs but none of the defendants. A hair found on a nearby tree stump could have come from 7 percent of the population, including Terry or David Jacoby, but none of the defendants.

Horgan confirmed that Dr. Spitz, Dr. Souviron and several other highly regarded experts all came to the independent conclusion that the injuries Dr. Peretti identified as knife wounds, and that Brent Turvey identified as human bite marks, were actually the result of postmortem animal predation, just as had been reported to me. This included the emasculation of Chris Byers.

Dr. Spitz, white-haired and still speaking in the accent of his Israeli upbringing, elaborated, "When these pictures came to me, I couldn't understand what this issue was all about because it was so obvious that these are animal products." With his usual authority, he concluded, "There were obvious claw marks. On all the victims, there was no evidence of sexual abuse. There was no evidence anywhere of anal penetration or mutilation. There were no other abnormalities on the bodies that would in any way conform with that which was alleged to have occurred."

Spitz also thought the ME was wrong in another area. He did not believe that Chris Byers bled to death from the genital wound or any other trauma. "I think they all drowned. The injury in the groin area was almost bloodless or was bloodless for all intents and purposes, and showed ripping, chewing by a predator animal, a carnivorous animal, a large animal with evidence that this did not occur during the life of the boy. So there could not have been bleeding from that source."

Dr. Souviron concurred, completely refuting Dr. Peretti's testimony. It was Souviron's bite mark analysis that made the case against Ted Bundy, finally putting away for good one of the most notorious serial killers in history, and his opinion carried a lot of weight. He then took apart prosecutor John Fogleman's closing demonstration with the knife and the grapefruit. "That is the most ridiculous statement that I've ever heard anybody make. And to sell that to a jury is unconscionable, in my opinion."

Riordan's takedown of self-proclaimed cult expert Dale Griffis was equally withering. After reviewing his mail-order Ph.D. and loony satanic theories, Riordan held up a book entitled *Secret Weapons.*

"Here is his new book, 2001, in which he details how he discovered that two thirteen-year-old girls were taken over by the CIA, given electroshock treatment, and at the age of fourteen became military pilots and committed assassinations for the CIA and then were brainwashed to forget it. And it was only with his assistance that he was able to recover the memories of this abuse of these thirteen-year-old girls by the CIA. This is a man who stands on the same level as those who claim that the World Trade Center bombing was a result of explosives in the basement, and that all of the Jews in the building were given notice so they could get out before the bombing was committed. There is probably no greater disgrace in the history of death penalty litigation in this country than that Dale Griffis was placed on the stand in a death penalty case to testify and offer testimony as the basis for executing Damien Echols. And with that, I would like to turn to someone who actually does know something about analyzing crime, John Douglas, twenty-five years with the FBI criminal analysis unit."

I detailed my findings that the West Memphis homicides were not perpetrated by a stranger or a teenager, but rather by a relatively criminally sophisticated individual; that the original intent was not to kill; that there would be no remorse. I declared that although the UNSUB might have known one of the boys better than the other two, there was no preferential victim and that any more severe wounds on one boy over another would have resulted from the way that boy reacted to him.

I repeated what I had told Mark Byers: Someone who could commit this crime would be a psychopathic personality who would show no remorse and easily lie about his involvement.

This was a personal cause homicide, I stated, perpetrated by someone who knew the victims and so was able to control all three at once by verbal command; was familiar with the neighborhood; and had criminal sophistication based on age and aggressive experience. When he found the boys, his initial intention was to degrade and punish, but the scene got out of hand. Perhaps one of the kids mouthed off to him or tried to run away, and he became more violent. At a certain point quickly reached, he had passed the point of no return and therefore had to kill all three to cover up his initial crime. He then had to delay finding and identifying the bodies until he could get back and establish an alibi: hence the immersion of the bodies and the hiding of the clothing and bicycles.

I also pointed out that I had never seen a case involving more than one teen in which they wouldn't turn on each other. "That would be very unusual for guilty teens.

"So, looking at this case," I concluded, "besides being a travesty of justice, this is not a satanic murder."

The reporters present asked a number of questions. Several focused on whether it was the team's intention to shift the murder charge from Damien Echols and the other two to Terry Hobbs.

Riordan was quite clear on this. "The last thing as defense lawyers we would intend to do is indict and convict someone beyond a reasonable doubt of this case. The evidence as to Hobbs, even less so to Jacoby, I don't think should be viewed that way. But is it evidence that would lead any reasonable juror to acquit Damien Echols? Yes, it would."

I had accomplished much of what I'd set out to do after analyzing the case. I had made my point that this was neither a ritualistic nor a multiple offender crime, that it was not perpetrated by teenagers, and that it was almost certainly not a stranger who killed the three boys. Perhaps as important, I had managed to convince the Byers and Pam Hobbs of this.

We all understood that the reason Damien was still alive was the public — at first through viewing *Paradise Lost* and then through the grassroots efforts so many people put together. And if we knew if Damien, Jason and Jessie were ever to get out of prison, that effort had to continue at a high level.

Getting two out of three of the victims' parents to publicly express doubt or disagreement with the original verdict was part of the strategy for keeping up the public pressure. Damien had always worried that his, Jason and Jessie's social status would mean they would be "thrown away and forgotten." That wasn't going to happen now.

As the defense team and the WM3 supporters worked toward getting the state supreme court to mandate an evidentiary hearing or a new trial, I went back to Arkansas.

Amy Berg, who was down there directing the documentary project that would become *West of Memphis,* said that David Jacoby liked me and was impressed with the evenhandedness of the analysis I'd given him, so he agreed to see me and help us work through a strategy.

One thing that had become clear to me is that David had always loved Stevie Branch and had been deeply affected by his death. He had thought justice had been done when the three teens were arrested, tried and convicted. Now he understood that the horrible deaths were still unpunished. He didn't want to believe Terry Hobbs had any involvement, but more than that, he wanted to help get to the truth.

We arranged a series of what we refer to as "pretext calls." I came over to David's house and coached him on what to say to Terry on the phone. We wanted to know how Terry would react if he felt his "lifeline" were being severed; in other words, what would he do if he felt he was losing his only alibi.

David called him sounding extremely nervous. There was this former FBI man named Douglas snooping around and asking a lot of pointed questions. He told Terry I was pointing out discrepancies in the timeline that made it clear the two of them were not together all evening and that their stories did not match up.

I was breaking him down, David told Terry. Terry immediately replied that he didn't have to talk to me and followed it with a string of expletives. "I wouldn't give him the time of day"; "Tell him he can go to hell"; "Tell him to take a hike"; "Tell him, 'Look, don't come 'round here again' "; "I'd tell him to hit the road"; and "John Douglas is a jerk and a half," was some of his advice.

Even though these were pretext calls, as I listened next to him, I could tell David was speaking from his own core of truth. "I felt like I could have done more that night," he told Terry.

While Terry said nothing to incriminate himself, he tried hard to give David confidence, to boost his belief that everything had been okay and proper between the two of them that night and reassure him that everything was all right. "We weren't anywhere close to the crime scene."

David kept saying how he was afraid there would be a new trial and that he would have to testify. Terry counseled him that he didn't have to talk to anyone and if he was asked he should just say that he couldn't recall.

And anyway, Terry emphasized, there wasn't going to be a new trial.

"The police know who done it. They're sitting in prison."

Chapter 26
A Deal with the Devil?

The events that took place — and those that didn't — between 2007 and 2011 were difficult to endure for those involved, but relatively straightforward to summarize.

Not long after the press conference, at a rally supporting the West Memphis Three, the Dixie Chicks lead singer, Natalie Maines, commented on some of the recent findings and suggested that Terry Hobbs should be considered a suspect. She posted a similar comment on the band's website.

In September 2008, Judge David Burnett maintained his near-perfect record of consistency against the West Memphis Three by denying a defense request for a new trial based on DNA testing and what had been learned about the animal predation to the bodies. Burnett ruled the evidence "inconclusive."

On November 25, 2008, Terry Hobbs filed suit against Natalie Maines, under her married name Pasdar, claiming defamation.

Honorably, Natalie insisted on defending the suit. In July 2009, depositions were taken, including one from Mildred French that brought into the open the assault charge that had so thrown Terry during our meeting. He spent two days under oath and did himself no favors. Neither did the testimony of his former wife Pam or his friend David Jacoby, who contradicted his claim that they were together looking for the boys the entire evening. Stevie's aunt Jo Lynn McCaughey swore that Terry had sexually molested Amanda and that shortly after the murders she had observed him uncharacteristically washing his own clothes. Other relatives described his regular and cruel mistreatment of Stevie.

In her own deposition in the lawsuit, Pam Hobbs said:

> After the murders my sister Jo Lynn Mc-Caughey and I found in Terry's nightstand a knife that Stevie carried with him constantly and which I had believed was with him when he died. It was a pocketknife that my father had given to Stevie, and Stevie loved that knife. I had been shocked that the police did not find it with Stevie when they found his body. I had always assumed that my son's murderer had taken the knife during the crime. I could not believe it was in Ter-

ry's things. He had never told me that he had it.

The picture that emerged, while not dispositive of murder, was pretty devastating.

On December 1, 2009, Judge Brian Miller, of the Federal District Court for the Eastern District of Arkansas, issued a summary judgment in favor of Natalie Maines Pasdar and ordered Terry to pay her over $17,000 in legal expenses. According to the *Jonesboro Sun,* Terry's response was *"I don't give a damn what the judge says, I'm not paying the Dixie Chicks a thing."*

In November 2010, in response to an appeal of Judge Burnett's ruling, the Supreme Court of Arkansas ordered the lower court to hold an evidentiary hearing to determine whether the now-available DNA evidence might reasonably have exonerated the defendants and whether a new trial should be held. Judge David Laser, of the Second Judicial Circuit, was appointed to replace Burnett, who had been elected to the state senate. By that point, Stephen Braga had begun representing Damien. He was a prominent and high-profile litigation attorney with the Washington, DC, office of the large international law firm Ropes & Gray.

And all the while, Damien Echols, Charles Jason Baldwin and Jessie Misskelley Jr. remained behind bars.

"It had literally gotten to the point where I'd been in prison half my life," said Damien. "I literally could not remember what it was like to be free anymore. That's when I started getting that desperate, hollow feeling. I could no longer even envision what it would be like to be out. It gets to the point when you can only see one way, and it goes on *forever.*"

"It was hard for me to hear Damien say things like that," Lorri commented, "because I could always see the end. Every day, I *knew* that it was going to end — not to say that in that last year, that was the hardest year for me because we both knew it was so close and they kept pushing it off. You just have to make yourself stronger."

Stephen Braga took over the lead role in Damien's defense in December 2010. By that point, Damien and Lorri had developed the highest regard for him — a regard that I share and certainly continues to this day.

Also during this time, Damien Echols and Mark Byers exchanged written apologies for having accused the other of being a killer. Mark started wearing FREE THE WM3 T-shirts and attending rallies. What he wanted, he said, was what he had always wanted: justice for Chris and his two close friends.

The evidentiary hearing was postponed several times for administrative reasons, sending Damien, Lorri and the others on an emotional roller coaster. Each time the light at the end of the tunnel grew a little brighter, the tunnel stretched longer in front of them. Finally the hearing was set for December 2011, but they worried that the prosecution would somehow stall indefinitely.

There was another worry. Damien's health had been steadily declining. Even if they won the hearing, the prospect of a year or more preparing for a new trial, finding unbiased jurors, the trial itself — all seemed daunting.

Facing the prosecution's intransigence and knowing his clients were correct about Damien facing incarceration well into the future, even if they were successful, Braga agonized over a way to bring the entire legal fiasco to a rapid end. The ultimate decision maker on the prosecution side would be Scott Ellington, the new prosecuting attorney for the Second Judicial District. Braga's narrative of what happened is a fascinating and illuminating inside story:

As the defense prepared for the evidentiary hearing — a point at which considerable resources would have to be expended — Steve Braga's local counsel Patrick Benca said he would soon be having his annual lunch with his law school classmate Dustin McDaniel, who happened to be the attorney general of the state. Was there anything about the case Steve wanted Patrick to bring up with him?

"Now, McDaniel's office wasn't prosecuting the case, but they were helping Scott Ellington. And we thought strategically that we would ask McDaniel if he would agree to dispense with the evidentiary hearing in December and just go right to a new trial. Why should the state of Arkansas have to pay twice? Why should the defendants have to wait twice as long? Clearly, there's enough evidence for a new trial. Why don't we just go right to it?"

McDaniel wouldn't agree to that, but he was interested and perceptive enough to ask Patrick what the real bottom line was: What was he really after?

"And that made Patrick and me think, and what we really wanted was, we really had to get Damien out of prison. I mean, he was really suffering. And the thing that I don't think a lot of people appreciate is that the death sentence makes a difference. If you can reach a certainty that he's not going to be executed, that's a big deal!"

Aside from the obvious stresses of living so long on death row and never knowing if or when he might face the lethal injection, Damien's health was deteriorating significantly. His eyes were failing because of the perpetually dim lighting and poor nutrition, and he was not allowed outside into the sunshine. His mouth and jaw hurt all the time because of untreated injuries from guards having repeatedly smashed him in the face.

And he had developed alarming symptoms of cardiovascular disease.

"So we went through Patrick and told McDaniel that we wanted to get our guy out. He said, 'Well, if they're willing to plead guilty, I'll get them out in two weeks.' "

Braga didn't want Damien and the others to plead guilty, because they weren't guilty; and even if he were willing to go that route, he didn't think he could get them to agree. *But what about a nolo,* he wondered.

Nolo contendere is an alternative to pleading either guilty or not guilty. However, it has the same effect as a guilty plea and is generally construed as an acknowledgment, if not an admission, of guilt.

Both Braga and Ellington were relative newcomers to the case and carried none of the potentially paralyzing emotional burdens of past history. Steve was hoping to open up some room for compromise.

"The message came back to us that they would accept a nolo plea.

"So then I decided after talking to Patrick and thinking about it, a nolo plea still might be a tough sell. But an Alford plea would be a step better — right? — because the way I look at it is a nolo plea, plus an affirmative manifestation of innocence. You get to state it on the record, and the world knows you're proclaiming your innocence."

In 1970, the U.S. Supreme Court heard the

case of *North Carolina* v. *Alford,* in which Henry Alford pled guilty to second-degree murder in the shooting death of another man, even though he steadfastly maintained his innocence. In explaining his unusual plea, Alford stated, "I pleaded guilty on second-degree murder because they said there is too much evidence, but I ain't shot no man, but I take the fault for the other man. We never had an argument in our life and I just pleaded guilty because they said if I didn't they would gas me for it, and that is all. . . . I'm not guilty, but I plead guilty."

The High Court recognized the right of a defendant to plead guilty while not confessing and still asserting his innocence. It is an extremely arcane legal maneuver.

"I actually don't expect them to accept the Alford plea. I've been doing this for thirty years — *no one does an Alford plea.* They say, 'If you're going to plead guilty, plead guilty. If you're not going to plead guilty, go to trial.' "

Surprisingly, the prosecutors responded that they would consider the Alford, but only if all three defendants would agree. Clearly, the state was looking for a way out of the legal morass, but they didn't want to be done with two and still have to try the third.

Damien said yes, and then Jessie agreed. But Jason balked.

For all the years he had suffered in prison,

Jason remained as adamant as he had been when he'd originally rejected a plea deal. He said he would stay in jail the rest of his life if need be rather than admit to something he didn't do.

Ultimately, though, Jason softened his position when presented with the facts of Damien's health and the reality that if he didn't go along, it would ruin the deal for everyone. In an act of great moral character and compassion, Jason agreed to take the Alford plea for the sake of his friend.

"To me," said Stephen Braga, "Jason's withholding of the Alford plea until literally the eleventh hour is one of the clearest indications that these guys are innocent, because anybody guilty would take it in a heartbeat."

On August 19, 2011, Damien, Jason, Jessie and their attorneys appeared in a packed courtroom before Judge Laser. He vacated the previous murder convictions, heard from representatives of the prosecution and defense, and ordered a new trial. Then he asked each of the defendants to stand and made sure they each understood the proceedings and what they meant.

"Mr. Echols," he asked, "how do you wish to plead in this case?"

In a voice that was measured and unemotional, Damien replied, "Your Honor, I am innocent of these charges, but I'm entering an Alford guilty plea today based on the advice of my counsel and my understanding that it's in my best interests to do so, given the entire record of this case."

Judge Laser asked the other two in succession and received similar responses. As had been agreed to by the parties, he sentenced them to time served — eighteen years and seventy-eight days — and released them.

After these moments of high legal drama, Judge Laser spoke from the bench, gracefully summing up the entire case over which there continued to be so much disagreement. One had the feeling that had Laser been the original presiding judge, the outcome might have been completely different, and almost two decades of nearly unimaginable trauma might have been avoided.

"I'm aware of the controversy that's existed," he began. "I'm aware of the involvement of the people in this case. I don't think it will make the pain go away to the victim families. I don't think it will take away a minute of the eighteen years that these three young men served in the Arkansas Department of Corrections. What I just described is tragedy on all sides. And I commend the people in the case that have assisted toward the end of seeing that justice is served to the best that we can do.

"Sometimes outside help is, in fact, a big help, and for those of you who have been participants in that regard here, I commend you personally and publicly for having done that."

Lorri smiled with pride and relief.

For Stephen Braga, Dennis Riordan and the rest of the defense team, the Alford plea represented an act of grace, an inspired and humane solution to an ongoing and intractable miscarriage of justice that still had the potential to send his client to an early grave.

Without the deal, Braga told us, "It would be at least two and a half years or three years before there'd be closure. So you'd have to go through the following hoops: You'd have your December hearing. If we won that, the state had an opportunity to appeal, so they could have appealed up to the Arkansas Supreme Court. That would take a year or so. If we won that, it would come down to Judge Laser and we'd have a new trial. We'd have to win that before a jury of Arkansas citizens, who, to this day, remain pretty polarized in this case. My view of the world is it's pretty clear what happened to these guys, that they were wrongfully convicted and they're innocent. But there are a lot of people who don't think that. And if you have a criminal trial and you don't get everybody unanimously — one holdout — then you've got to do it again. And so the risks were just too severe. Nothing was going to happen in the short run, and I didn't think Damien was going to survive."

For the prosecution, in my view, the plea arrangement represented a deal with the Devil: a face-saving scenario that essentially indemnified them for the nearly two decades of suffering they had inflicted on three young men, and the denial of justice and truth to three dead boys and their loving survivors.

In what we can only hope was a statement of uninformed ingenuousness rather than cynical duplicity, Scott Ellington declared, "I have no reason to believe that there was anyone else involved in the homicide of these three children but the three defendants who pled guilty today."

Come on, folks! Does anyone for one nanosecond believe that a responsible district attorney, *under any circumstances,* would let three men out of prison who, he honestly believed, had brutally slain three 8-year-old boys and denied it?

As Steve Braga told us, "It's part of the calculus of the Alford plea — and this goes to my strategy and my discussions with Patrick and my selling it to Damien and thinking it all through — that if this works, what's it going to look like? What's the public going to say? Is the public going to say, 'They pled guilty to get out, they're guilty,' which I don't want, or is the public going to say, 'They must be innocent because they never would have let them out if they thought they were guilty.' And that's what we concluded would happen, and that happened in ninety-nine-point-nine percent of the reactions. And I do believe that no true-believer prosecutor would have let these men walk out if he thought they were triple child murderers."

Ellington got to the real heart of the matter a little later when he candidly told reporters, "When the [state] supreme court handed down this decision on November the fourth of last year, reopening issues of juror misconduct and all these other matters on the basis of new DNA, then that caused some troubles. And this judge was most likely going to grant a new trial. And if this judge granted a new trial, the defendants, most likely — I mean, we would do the best we could to put on the evidence — but most likely these defendants, to say the least, could very easily have been acquitted."

Despite this rationalization, to his credit, Ellington did not glory in his three technical guilty pleas, but he explained his decision on the basis of: (1) terminating prolonged litigation, (2) avoiding another potentially prolonged appeals process, and (3) preventing a possible "civil lawsuit against the state that could have resulted in many millions of dollars."

John Mark Byers wasn't concerned about what it might cost his state when he told the press outside the courtroom, "This is not right, and the people of Arkansas need to stand up and raise hell because three innocent men are going to have to claim today that they're guilty for a crime they didn't do. They're innocent. They did not kill my son and it's wrong what the state of Arkansas is doing. And I'm sick of it, because the real killer is walking around free!"

After the celebrations and the first tastes of freedom, Damien, Jason and Jessie set about the task of getting on with their lives. Never having lived outside of prison walls as adults, this was bound to be a strange and unpredictable process.

Jessie went back to the comfort and familiarity of his family in West Memphis.

The day after he was released, Jason flew to Seattle — his first time on an airplane, and his first time out of Arkansas — to visit a friend, who was living there. He liked it so much that he decided to stay. After a round of traveling to talk about the case and the various media projects associated with it, he settled down in his first apartment to enroll in community college. He hopes to go to law school, work with the falsely accused and eventually become a law professor. He and his girlfriend, Holly Ballard, an Arkansas native whom he met in 2008 after she'd been writing to him in prison for four years, are serving as executive producers of *Devil's Knot,* a movie about the case based on the book of the same name by reporter Mara Leveritt.

Damien and Lorri are also in the movie business now, among other creative endeavors. While still in prison, they worked with director Amy Berg to coproduce *West of Memphis,* Peter Jackson and Fran Walsh's revealing and insightful, full-length documentary, which has been distributed theatrically around the globe.

For most of eighteen years, Damien sat and stared at four concrete walls to the point where he said he couldn't even exercise his distance vision. Now, with Lorri by his side and the help of loyal and supportive friends, he was free to explore a whole new world.

CHAPTER 27
MEETING MR. ECHOLS

Though I had worked closely with Lorri, Fran and Peter and the rest of the defense team, it wasn't until January 2012, at the Sundance Film Festival in Park City, Utah, for the screening of *West of Memphis* that I met Damien and Jason for the first time. I had not wanted to talk to any of the defendants in prison lest it affect my objectivity so this was the first opportunity. Being now so familiar with the evidence and photographs, the trial footage and all of the news interviews, in my mind Damien and Jason were a strange composite of their 1993 teenage selves all the way up to videos of their release from prison as men in their thirties.

As it happened, it was in the parking lot as my wife Pam and I were going into the theater for the screening that I saw Damien with Lorri. She came over to greet us and introduced Damien. He threw his arms around me and thanked me for my part in his case. At that moment, I felt I had known him as long and as well as I had known Lorri. Seeing him in person for the first time, looking healthy, happy and trim, I immediately projected back to the horror of his nearly two decades on death row.

The film was very well received by the Sundance audience. In the lobby I spotted Mark and Jackie Byers and waved to them. They came over and Mark hugged me and thanked me. Then I saw Pam Hobbs, who did the same. It seemed a long time ago that they hadn't even wanted to hear what I had to say, and that Mark practically threatened to throw me off his property. But that "long time" was only about a quarter of the time the West Memphis Three were wrongfully imprisoned.

After the screening, Fran and Peter held a dinner for the defense team at their hotel. Jason and Holly were there and it was good finally to meet them. Peter placed me at one end of the table and Dennis Riordan at the other. This was more than just a movie after-party. The first thing Peter said after we sat down was, "All right, what are we going to do next?"

Steve Braga, who had had the most recent "close encounter" with the Arkansas legal process, said he thought the logical move was to get back in touch with Scott Ellington. Now that the three were safely out of prison, he was the one who would have to be convinced that justice demanded a large final step of removing the murder conviction.

I said this would not be easy, because elected prosecutors are political animals and an overriding consideration for them is going to be: *What will the constituents think?*

"We think John should be the one to talk to him," Steve suggested. "He'll have the credibility because in his career he's worked with both prosecution and defense."

He told me that Ellington was going to receive a private showing tomorrow — Sunday, January 22. "He probably won't like it," Steve commented.

"You're probably right," I agreed. He said he'd let me know the next step after they heard back from Ellington.

Pam and I flew home on Sunday and that night Steve called to say that Ellington did want to talk and would call me the next morning at 9:00.

My conversation with the district attorney lasted about an hour and a half. I can't relate all of the specifics, because some issues and investigative points remain highly sensitive until the entire case is finally resolved. Knowing how he felt about the film, I figured he was going to jump down my throat, but he was polite, measured and attentive.

I was surprised he did not know more about the facts and record than he did. Steve had predicted this and figured it would make

Ellington more open and objective.

"I don't know if they're guilty or not," I recall him telling me early in the conversation.

I interrupted him to say, "Scott, I can tell you: They're not guilty. They had nothing to do with this crime."

So I took him through the entire case, just as I had with Peter and Fran, Jackie and Mark Byers, and Pam Hobbs and her family. He continued to be highly attentive and seemed to take it all in.

When I finished up, he asked, "So what does the defense want? I gave them an Alford plea."

"They want to be exonerated," I said. "They're out of prison, but they've been convicted of three murders with sexual overtones that they didn't do."

We went back and forth on this for a while, with Ellington remaining noncommittal until finally he said something to the effect, "The timing is not good."

I wasn't sure what he meant by that, but thought it probably had something to do with his being fairly new in the office and him wanting to establish his credibility with the public. Many of his constituents might already be unhappy with him because of the plea deal, I reasoned, so pushing for exoneration could be political suicide.

Three months later, I learned he was planning to run for Congress.

The effort continued. But as of this writing, the case of the West Memphis Three remains in legal limbo. Damien, Jason and Jessie, though free, are still convicted killers in the eyes of the law. New witnesses have come forward whose sworn affidavits appear to shed additional light on Terry Hobbs and what he allegedly said and did. Scott Ellington promised Steve Braga, who has left Ropes and Gray to open his own firm, that he would follow up. But after nearly two decades, the actual murderer of Michael Moore, Chris Byers and Stevie Branch continues to elude justice.

Damien and Lorri continued their close association and friendship with Fran and Peter in other ways. While Damien was in prison, he wrote and published the first volume of his autobiography, *Almost Home,* a book that is now a valuable collectors' item.

His startling literary insight and writing talent are self-taught. When Mark and I met with him and Lorri to talk about the case, he reflected, "My mom had me when she was fifteen years old. My dad was sixteen years old. I dropped out of school in the ninth grade, and that's the most education anyone in my family has. My stepfather could not read or write a single word other than his own name."

By the time he had been out a few months,

amidst the same kind of hectic travel and appearance schedule Jason had undertaken, he had completed his second volume, a heartbreaking, empowering and beautifully written memoir of his life before the case and while in prison, *Life After Death.* He and Lorri are coproducing a feature film version with Fran and Peter, starring their supporter and now-close friend Johnny Depp. Amy Berg is directing. Damien completed the book while living in Fran and Peter's recently purchased American apartment. While Damien wrote, Lorri supervised the finishing work and decorating for Fran. Lorri is anxious to get back to her landscape architecture and design career, and Damien is exploring various forms of art and expression as he continues to adjust to a new world.

As Lorri said, "Damien went from living in complete poverty in a trailer court to death row in a prison, to this amazing city and this amazing place we're staying in. To watch him learn how to move around in this world, my biggest thing was just to stop messing with him and just let him do it."

But it wasn't all easy or charming or an adventure of endless wonder. The most ordinary of tasks that most of us take for granted could completely throw him.

"One day, I decided to go out and just explore the city. So Lorri asked me, 'Will you take these checks and put them in the bank?'

And I said okay. So she gives me this check and I go to the bank and I freak out — I don't know what a deposit slip looks like. And there's this line of people looking at me like I'm a jackass because I'm holding up progress and I just turned around and got out of there.

"And I'm thinking, 'I've been beaten almost to death, I've been starved, been tortured in just about every way a human being can be tortured. *Why am I freaking out because I can't fill out a bank deposit slip?*' "

Lorri said, "While we were on the road so much after the release, Damien's healing process was on hold. Only now is he really healing, mentally and physically."

And he is ready to move on. "This case has eaten up half my life. I don't want to give it any more."

In the six years I spent with this case — far shorter than so many others — I came to realize how much time and effort it took from so many supporters, celebrities and experts to get three clearly innocent young men simply freed. That's not even talking about getting them exonerated or getting the real killer to trial.

Of course, some people still cling to the opinion that the West Memphis Three were child killers and that the effort to get them out has been a sham. They may be among the ones who still feel that Stevie, Chris and

Michael were killed by satanic cultists.

After all was said and done, one of the most scurrilous comments came from Jerry Driver, the man who got Damien into this mess in the first place. It was uttered during an interview included in *West of Memphis*. Sitting complacently in his recliner, he said of Damien, "I think he did. I'll put it this way — I know he could have. Whether he did or not, I know he could have."

Damien, in some ways, is more philosophical than I would be. Several months after he was freed, reflecting on the chain of events and the people who brought him to trial, conviction, prison and a looming lethal injection, he noted, "I don't even really believe in the word 'evil.' Most of the time, what I see that people call evil, I see as stupidity or lack of empathy."

Brandon Garrett, a law professor at the University of Virginia, published a book in 2011 based on his extensive research, *Convicting the Innocent: Where Criminal Prosecutions Go Wrong*. Steve Braga said, "Garrett identifies five common failings leading to wrongful convictions — false confessions, junk science, jailhouse informants, ineffective assistance of counsel and bad judging. They're all in this case! So this case is the poster child for wrongful conviction."

I would like to think that this legal nightmare never would have taken place if there had been better juvenile officers, better investigators, better scientists, better lawyers, a better judge, better jurors and even better media. But there weren't. So I hope this case will serve as an object lesson and cautionary tale, except we know that similar horrors are still happening all over.

Damien himself has said that theirs was not an unusual case. They just got lucky that two guys decided to make a film about them. It makes you realize how tenuous was his deliverance and the magnitude of the challenge we face in making our criminal justice system better and more reliable.

The defendants didn't originally agree to the film because they thought it would get them out. They agreed because the filmmakers paid them for participating and that money was used to help support their severely underfunded defense. And that decision was what ultimately led to their salvation.

Sitting with Lorri, Mark Olshaker and me over lunch in a restaurant near where they were living, Damien said, "If you take out one single link in the chain, I'm still in prison or I'm dead. If you take away HBO, nobody would have heard about the case. If you take away Lorri, nobody would have been driven. Take away the WM3-dot-org people, everybody would have seen the movies and said, 'That's too bad,' but there's nothing they would have done. When I look at the list —

Peter and Fran, Johnny Depp, Eddie Vedder, Natalie Maines, Henry Rollins, Steve Braga, Dennis Riordan, Don Horgan, John Douglas, Steve Mark, Burk Sauls, Kathy Bakken, Lisa Fancher, Grove Pashley . . . I mean, hell, every single person in this case . . . If you take any of them away, it's like a house of cards that collapses."

CHAPTER 28
THE DAY OF THE DEAD

In the fall of 2007, twenty-one-year-old Meredith Susanna Cara Kercher, a Leeds University student from Coulsdon, Surrey, south of London, had just begun a yearlong adventure. She was taking a course in modern history and political theory as an exchange student at the University of Perugia in the beautiful medieval and Renaissance city, about a hundred miles north of Rome. She wanted to follow her father, John, into a career in journalism, and she had worked at Gatwick Airport, near her home, to raise money for the overseas program.

Called "Mez" by her friends, of which there were many, Meredith shared the four-bedroom upper floor of a tiled-roof, white stone and stucco cottage at Via della Pergola 7 with three other young women: twenty-year-old American exchange student Amanda Marie Knox, of Seattle, Washington, and Italians Filomena Romanelli and Laura Mezzetti. Filomena and Laura were just starting out as attorneys in local firms. Amanda, an honors student from the University of Washington, came over around the same time as Meredith. She was studying Italian at the Stranieri, officially the Universita per Stranieri di Perugia — the University for Foreigners of Perugia.

Meredith and Amanda were both pretty, smart and personable. Amanda was the wholesome outdoorsy type, outgoing and bubbly, a guitar-playing free spirit. She was an honors graduate of Seattle Prep, an elite Jesuit high school to which she'd won an academic scholarship. She had been to Japan as an exchange student, had recently visited German relatives and said she wanted to master at least seven languages. She worked part-time at a bar called Le Chic, operated by Diya "Patrick" Lumumba, an immigrant from Congo, well known and popular in Perugia. Patrick had come to Perugia in the 1980s to study political science at the Universita per Stranieri, where Amanda was studying, and stayed on after graduation. In addition to the bar, he produced concerts at the university. When he met Amanda, Patrick thought her looks and personality would attract patrons.

Meredith, the youngest of four children, was equally bright and accomplished. Like Amanda, she was a child of divorce. She had an exotic beauty, the product of an English father and a Pakistani mother, whose ethnic characteristics had mixed perfectly in their daughter. She was more reserved and introspective, but with a zany, goofy side that came out when she was in relaxed social situations. In addition to her flatmates, she had a posse of British girls with whom she hung out when they could tear her away from her studies.

The house they shared had a panoramic view of the city, though some locals considered it situated in a bad neighborhood. Laura and Filomena, in their late twenties, had found the house through a leasing agent and then posted flyers to find the additional tenants they'd need to handle the rent. Their rooms were at the front of the cottage, and Meredith's and Amanda's were in the back, in an addition that overlooked a ravine. Four Italian guys — Giacomo Silenzi, Stefano Bonassi, Marco Marzan and Riccardo Luciani — lived on the lower floor.

Thursday, November 1, 2007, the day after Halloween, was All Saints' Day, a national holiday in Italy. Meredith was alone in the cottage that evening after having watched a movie at a friend's house. Amanda was staying over at the flat of her new Italian boyfriend, Raffaele Sollecito. A twenty-three-year-old computer science and engineering student from Bari, whose father was a prominent urologist, Raffaele had a mop-topped Harry Potter look. She had met him at a classical music concert on October 25, and they had been pretty hot and heavy ever since. Raffaele's parents had also divorced; and in his second year of college, his beloved mother had died suddenly of a heart condition. He couldn't get over not being home when she passed away and was still mourning her.

On the night and day in question, Filomena was staying with her boyfriend, Marco Zaroli, and the other five Italians were visiting their families for the holiday weekend.

Amanda returned to the house around ten-thirty on the morning of November 2, according to her account, and found the front door ajar. There was no spring latch, so the door had to be locked with a key. Meredith's bedroom door was closed; and if she was still sleeping, Amanda didn't want to disturb her. So Amanda went to shower in the small bathroom the two girls shared.

As she stepped out and was about to dry herself, she noticed what looked like dried blood droplets on the sink and the floor mat she was standing on. There were no towels, she suddenly realized. Maybe Meredith had had a bad period, but she was always so meticulously neat and clean that it all seemed strange.

Amanda went to her bedroom to fetch a towel and dry off. She played music on her computer while she got dressed. Then she went into the bigger bathroom off the kitchen, which Laura and Filomena shared, to borrow their hair dryer. As she was drying her hair, she suddenly noticed the toilet was unflushed and the bowl was filled with feces and toilet paper. This was not something any of her roommates would do, and she was sufficiently creeped out to quickly leave the house and rush back over to Raffaele's flat, where she described to him what she had encountered.

She called Meredith's British mobile phone, but she got no answer. Then she called her Italian mobile, which was registered in Filomena's name. Still, she got no answer. A few minutes later, Filomena called to say she was very worried because she had also been trying to reach Meredith.

Taking Raffaele with her, Amanda went back to the cottage and took him first to the larger bathroom. Then they checked out Filomena's room, which was a mess. It looked as if someone had rummaged through everything and left clothing strewn about the floor. Most alarming, there was a rock near her desk, and one of the bedroom windows was broken.

Even though Filomena's computer was sitting on the desk, Amanda was convinced the house had been burglarized and went to look in Laura's room. Nothing had been touched. This wasn't adding up. She knocked on Meredith's door again; still, no answer.

When Filomena called again, Amanda told

her about the broken window. A few minutes later, at 12:47 P.M., the now-panicked Amanda called her mother, Edda Mellas, in Seattle, where it was 4:47 A.M., and told her what had happened. Edda told her to call the police. Since Amanda's Italian was only barely passable, Raffaele called his older sister, Vanessa, who worked in Rome for the Carabinieri, the national quasi-military police. Like Edda had, she told him to call the Carabinieri immediately, which he did on the emergency 112 number.

Meanwhile, the Polizia Postale — the Postal Police — arrived on the scene. They had been contacted by a woman about a half mile up the road who had found Meredith's mobile phones in her garden. Telephone regulation in Italy is under the jurisdiction of the post office, and they had traced ownership of both phones to Via della Pergola. The two plain-clothes officers — Michele Battistelli and Fabio Marzi — found Amanda and Raffaele outside, saying they were waiting for the Carabinieri. They brought the officers into the house and Amanda showed them around. She didn't understand the distinction in police services and thought these were the officers Raffaele had called.

Downstairs flatmate Marco Marzan showed up with a friend, Luca Altieri. He explained that Filomena had asked him to come after Amanda's worried call. Shortly afterward,

Filomena arrived with her best friend Paola Grande, who was also Luca's girlfriend. Filomena examined her room and discovered that nothing was taken, not even cash or jewelry.

All focus was now on Meredith and her locked door, but the Postal Police were reluctant to take any action until the Carabinieri arrived. Finally, around 1:15 P.M., Filomena asked Luca to break down the door. He kept kicking it until it broke from its hinges and flew open.

The room was covered in blood. Meredith's beige duvet was on the floor. Filomena saw a bare foot sticking out from underneath.

Amanda rushed in the direction of Filomena's screams, but Raffaele intercepted her and pulled her away. Inspector Battistelli ordered everyone out of the house, then called police headquarters.

It was All Saints' Day, also known to many Christians as All Souls' Day or the Day of the Dead.

I didn't know much about the Meredith Kercher murder case until Mark Olshaker brought it to me with the comment that it seemed to have remarkable echoes to the West Memphis Three. He had become convinced that like Damien, Jason and Jessie in West Memphis, Seattle college student Amanda Knox and her Italian boyfriend, Raffaele Sollecito, had been railroaded into a conviction for the murder of Amanda's housemate. Several lengthy phone conversations with Amanda's stepfather, Chris Mellas, had further convinced Mark that her family firmly believed in her innocence. I didn't want to draw any conclusions of my own unless I could fully examine the record and evidence.

When I delved into the case, I was struck by both the similarities and the differences between this case and WM3. In some sense, Knox is a photo negative of WM3, with the same ultimate effect.

Both involved horrific, gory murders of low-risk, innocent young people who had the promise of their whole lives to look forward to.

One took place in a scruffy southern city on the edge of the interstate, a place many kids considered "West Nowheresville" and yearned to flee as soon as they were old enough. The other happened in a historic Umbrian hill town that attracted adventurous students from around the world.

One involved defendants who were marginal outsiders from poor and broken families whom the rest of the world considered losers. The other involved a beautiful young woman and a handsome young man, both solidly middle-class with promising futures ahead of them.

Both hinged on a questionable confession

after many hours of police interrogation without a lawyer present — one by a scared and confused seventeen-year-old boy; the other by a girl just out of her teens who barely spoke the language being shouted at her.

Both were rushes to judgment, prosecuted as satanic ritual murders on the basis of fear and superstition rather than solid evidence And analysis.

Both became passionate, controversial, international causes whose balance was finally tipped by the lack of a match between the defendants and DNA found at the crime scenes.

Knox also had the kind of sensational elements that had captured world imagination with the Ramsey case: a beautiful girl and a vicious, senseless murder in the house where she lived. But in this case, the beautiful girl was all grown up, and there were actually two girls: one a victim, the other a suspect.

Through Mark's exchanges with Amanda's family, I was contacted by Steve Moore, a retired FBI agent currently working as deputy director of public safety at Pepperdine University in Malibu, California — not a bad job if you like the beach and warm weather as much as I do. Steve had been in my behavioral science classes during new agent training at Quantico. Though we knew and had worked with a lot of the same people, I didn't remember meeting him. He had never met

Amanda, but he had become so moved by her case that he decided to conduct his own investigation, with the family's cooperation but independent of them.

I have not been universally praising of all my FBI colleagues over the years, but when I looked up Steve Moore, he turned out to be the real deal. He had spent his entire FBI career dealing with violent crime; and as his last assignment, he ran the FBI's Los Angeles-based "Extra-Territorial Squad," which was tasked with responding to any acts of terrorism against the United States in Asia and Pakistan. He agreed to organize and supply me with all of the relevant case materials, including records, photographs, videos and various transcripts. He told me he respected my work and me too much to try to influence me in any way and genuinely wanted to know if I felt he was on the right track in interpreting the evidence.

Before the case was resolved, Steve would admit to me, "When you told me about the grief you took after the Ramsey case, I didn't really understand how petty and mean people can get. In my whole life, I have never been vilified by people like I have since I got involved in the Knox case."

I reviewed all of the material presented to me and read everything I could, both positive and negative. All of the evidence pointed squarely in one direction: Amanda Knox and Raffaele Sollecito were innocent.

Clearly, Italian criminal justice authorities did not want my help. What I could do, Steve, Mark and I concluded, was to speak out as much as possible and try to educate people as to what this case was really about rather than the salacious tale of sexual obsession with which the media had so fallen in love.

As it turned out, Amanda and Raffaele did not suffer quite so long as the West Memphis Three, but they still spent four years in prison — the first without being formally charged. They were convicted in October 2008 and released by an appeals judge in October 2011. Nearly everything about their case demonstrates the same systemic weaknesses and personal failings as the Arkansas case. The only other difference, ironically, is that in Perugia, they had the real killer in custody almost right away. Yet that didn't stop the persecution of the other two defendants.

The overwhelming initial public impression in this highly publicized case was that the beautiful, seductive "Foxy Knoxy" was guilty of brutally murdering her roommate in a frenzy of satanic lust. Books have been published asserting her guilt, and even today, world opinion is wildly mixed on whether she should have been let out of prison. Let's go through this case and see why it quickly became a travesty of justice and why Italian authorities *should have been able* to determine that right from the beginning.

CHAPTER 29
THE FACTS OF THE CASE

Let's start with the crime scene.

Meredith Kercher had been stabbed multiple times, including three deep wounds in her neck.

When Luca Altieri and Filomena Romanelli and then Raffaele Sollecito and the police first saw her blood-soaked body, eyes open and naked but for a T-shirt pulled up over her breasts, she was on the floor with a pillow beneath her hips and the bloody duvet pulled up over her chest. In the trial, prosecutors Giuliano Mignini and Manuela Comodi would claim this was evidence that a woman had committed the crime and that covering the body was a sign of compassion or pity.

I disagree. For sheer depravity, this murder was absolutely horrific. As soon as I looked at the crime scene photographs, there was no question in my mind that the killer had not an ounce of compassion for Meredith. There was no question in my mind that the killer had no compassion for anyone or anything that could pass for a conscience.

When we see actual evidence of a "soft kill," such as manual strangulation with a handkerchief or towel, say, followed by a carefully covered or "comfortably" wrapped body, we think of parental or close-relationship murder. This scene had none of those indicators. A blanket thrown haphazardly over a body indicates nothing about a male or female UNSUB. If anything, it shows contempt for the victim, or, if the head is covered up, depersonalization. Or it may simply represent an offender's discomfort with looking at a mutilated body while he carries out a burglary or whatever else he set out to do.

If the placement of the pillow means anything at all, it could have been put there by an assailant to make sexual assault easier. The pulled-up T-shirt also fits the pattern of a sexually motivated crime. There was a bloody handprint on it, and streaks of blood on the wall, as if the UNSUB had tried to clean his hands.

Two towels were under the body and a third lay on the bed, also soaked with blood. A shape that appeared to be a knife was imprinted in blood on the bed. Several bloody shoeprints on the tile floor led from the bed toward the front door. These were later identified as belonging to a Nike shoe. Finally there was a bloody print from a bare foot on the mat in the bathroom that Meredith and

Amanda shared.

Meredith's handbag was on the bed. It appeared to have been gone through. In addition to her missing mobile phones, cash and credit cards were also gone. Though the scene showed clear signs of either a burglary or a staged burglary, prosecutors used this evidence against Amanda as well, claiming she stole from Meredith to pay her rent. Had they looked seriously into her background, they would have found that she worked part-time for several years to help pay for her studies in Italy. Given this past behavior, I would consider theft completely out of character, and as a motive for such a hideous murder out of the question.

The Postal Police cleared the house and sealed it off. Around three in the afternoon, Public Minister (equivalent to a district attorney, magistrate *and* senior investigator) Giuliano Mignini arrived with Luca Lalli, the coroner and a professor of pathology at the University of Perugia. Mignini was a portly, balding tyrannical type in his midfifties. Lalli noted the three stab wounds on Meredith's neck and determined that the cause of death was blood loss and suffocation.

Already mistakes were starting to pile up. Lalli did not take Meredith's temperature, which meant, as in the West Memphis case, there would be no subsequent method of establishing time of death.

At this very point, the public case against Amanda Knox began. As she and Raffaele and the other flatmates waited outside, she was observed whispering to Raffaele, cuddling and kissing him. She later said she had been crying and he had been trying to comfort her, but the image of that lip-lock soon made news around the world. Her roommate had just been brutally murdered and she seemed intent on public displays of affection with her handsome Italian boyfriend. Monica Napoleoni, head of homicide for the police flying squad, the *squadra mobile,* or quick response team, spoke to the couple and decided they seemed unemotional and indifferent to the murder.

The same phenomenon occurred in the Ramsey case, and I have seen it over and over. Once the media and the public establish a mental image of a suspect or even a potential suspect, that image is almost impossible to shake.

When police and the crime scene team had finished, all of the flatmates and their friends acceded to police requests to go to the *questura,* the police station, for questioning. After the first round of questioning several hours later, some of Meredith's English girlfriends happened to meet Amanda in the waiting room. They later said she had given them details about the killing. In trial, prosecutors charged these were facts only someone who had seen the body could know. *Or perhaps someone who had been around a police station for hours while everyone was focused on the crime?*

Amanda didn't leave the station until around six the next morning. There were conflicting reports that she "seemed calm, as if nothing had happened," and "paced nervously." From my experience, I cannot imagine a twenty-year-old woman who had never been in trouble with the law, and suddenly found herself in a foreign police station being questioned about the murder of her flatmate, *not* being nervous and frightened, *whether she was innocent or guilty.* Anyone in such a situation who appears calm, as John Ramsey appeared before JonBenét's body was found, is merely suppressing outward emotion. I guarantee it.

Later that day, police went with Amanda back to the house. The prosecution would describe her as having sobbed uncontrollably outside. Eventually her tears, or lack of them, became a major point of contention in the case. But there are enough eyewitnesses at various times to suggest that she cried quite a bit in the hours and days after the murder.

Following the visit to the house, they took her back to the station for more questioning. Despite the intensive probing over several days, she was officially considered a witness at this point and was not asked if she wanted an attorney.

Back in London, the Kercher family's agony was nearly beyond description. Meredith's mother, Arline, was chronically ill, and Meredith was in the habit of calling her daily. So when she and John didn't hear from her and couldn't reach her on her mobile phone, they were instantly worried. John, a journalist, had heard the rumors of an English student murdered in Italy; but it was not until about five-thirty in the afternoon, the day after the murder, that one of his press contacts was able to confirm for him that it was his beloved daughter.

He went back home to Coulsdon to be with the other children, Stephanie, John Jr. and Lyle. Arline was in the hospital, but she had already spoken to someone in the British Foreign Office. As soon as she got out of the hospital, and she and John could make arrangements, they flew off with Stephanie to Perugia. Around the same time in Seattle, Amanda's mother, Edda Mellas, made plans to journey to Perugia, soon to be joined by her former husband, Curt Knox.

All of the flatmates were again questioned at the police station on November 4, then brought back with Giuliano Mignini to the house to see if any kitchen knives were missing. None seemed to be; but as they were examining the knives, Amanda again broke down uncontrollably.

On the evening of November 5, police asked both Amanda and Raffaele to come to the station to discuss apparent inconsistencies in their accounts. And here occurred another incident that slammed the public relations lid on Amanda. While Raffaele was being questioned, Amanda sat in a waiting room. As the free-spirited, athletic Pacific Northwest girl she was, Amanda was into yoga. When she felt stiff or stressed, she would often resort to her routine of yoga stretches and poses.

Late in the evening, a male police officer observed her stretching, admired her flexibility and asked if she could do a split. Whether out of fear, openness or pride in her body, she complied, much to the officer's delight. But out of this incident developed the widely reported story that she was doing cartwheels in the police station as she awaited questioning on Meredith's murder.

Napoleoni and other homicide detectives questioned Raffaele for more than six hours, until after 3:00 A.M. During that time, according to the police, he began wavering on his story that Amanda had slept over with him and that they'd been together the entire night of the murder. Maybe she had gone out for a while — around 9:00 P.M. or so — and hadn't come back until 1:30 A.M.; he wasn't sure.

What seems to have happened is that in his fear and fatigue, Raffaele eventually confused and transposed the nights of October 31 and November 1. On Halloween night, Amanda did go out around nine o'clock, dressed as a sexy cat with a nose and whiskers that Raffaele had painted on her face. Halloween celebrations were a much bigger deal to the foreign students than to the Italians, so Raffaele stayed home that night and waited for her. She returned around 1:00 A.M., just as he told police occurred the next night.

This turned out to be the real beginning of the case against the two, and the parallels to Jessie Misskelley Jr. and so many others are almost uncanny. Amanda and Raffaele became suspects despite the fact that bugged rooms in the *questura* and tapped telephones that picked up numerous private conversations between them revealed not a hint of any secrets or conspiracy.

When they got around to interviewing Amanda, it was well after midnight. They brought her into an interrogation room and told her that Raffaele had said that Amanda had left his flat about nine on the critical evening to go to Le Chic and hadn't come back until after 1:00 A.M. They had checked the records of Amanda's mobile phone. The last exchange was a text from Patrick Lumumba saying she didn't have to come to work that night because business was slow and a texted reply from her: **Ci vediamo piu tardi, buona serata,** which translates as "See you later. Have a good evening." After that point, both she and Raffaele had turned off their cell phones for the night, uncharacteristic for both. When asked about it, Amanda said she was afraid Patrick would change his mind.

Now things started getting rough for her. Confronting her with Raffaele's story, the investigators suggested that "See you later" was not a routine, banal sign-off but an actual arrangement to meet later that night.

Who was she protecting? they wanted to know. *Who was it?* According to Amanda, when she didn't have an answer, they kept pressing her. A policewoman called her "stupid" and a "liar" and slapped her on the back of her head. They repeated the blow every time she didn't give them an answer. They gave her nothing to eat or drink and didn't allow her to go to the bathroom. It was as if they were going to keep punishing her until she remembered.

When she asked for a lawyer, they told her it would go worse for her if a lawyer was present.

According to Rita Ficarra and Lorena Zugarini, two members of the *squadra mobile,* no one hit Amanda or insulted her. She was given food, water and hot drinks and allowed to go to the bathroom whenever she wanted. She was asked if she had a lawyer or wanted one and she said no.

The interrogation dragged on. Amanda remained in detention for many hours. She was scared, exhausted and totally strung out. They couldn't get her to admit anything about being with Patrick Lumumba that night, so one of the police officers asked her to relax and explained that sometimes severe emotional trauma causes a mental block. Since she couldn't *remember* anything, she should try to *imagine* what had happened in the house and what her and Patrick's parts had been. That exercise often releases the emotional barrier.

As outrageous as this might sound, the "let's pretend" ploy is not an uncommon interrogation technique. I have used it myself, sometimes with great success, in questioning suspects.

In a particularly heinous 1985 abduction, assault and murder of a high-school girl named Sharon "Shari" Faye Smith in Columbia, South Carolina, I interviewed a suspect who had been traced by a combination of profiling, forensics and first-rate police work.

His name was Larry Gene Bell, and we all knew he was guilty of the crime. We also knew his lawyer would never let him on the stand to testify; so if we were going to get a confession, it had to be soon. I told him about our profiling program and how we knew that these crimes were often committed by men with two warring instincts within their psyches. I told him I understood how this might be one of those situations and to try to imagine how the crime might have taken place.

At the end of his narrative, he looked up at me with tears in his eyes and said, "All I know is that the Larry Gene Bell sitting here couldn't have done this, but the *bad* Larry Gene Bell could have."

That was as close as we ever got to a confession, but it was enough. Larry Gene Bell was executed by electrocution on October 4, 1996, for the murder of Shari Faye Smith. I was glad to see him go.

This investigative technique is like anything else in law enforcement. There are good practitioners and sloppy ones. You have to figure out whether you are "unlocking" the suspect's mind — giving him a face-saving scenario and a means to confess — or if you're leading him into a world of fantasy.

When you're dealing with a subject who is exhausted and at the end of her emotional rope, so empty and disoriented that she *literally can't think straight,* then you've misused the practice. Like the detectives who questioned Jessie Misskelley Jr., there was no question here of getting to the truth by asking the subject to *imagine,* or to "dream" as in the David Vasquez interrogation in Virginia.

As Steve Moore commented, "If any FBI agents who reported to me had conducted this interview, I would have had them prosecuted."

Altogether, Amanda was interrogated over a forty-hour period (an average workweek) by twelve detectives. This is known as "tag teaming." The interrogators remain fresh and at the top of their game while the suspect grows increasingly exhausted and isolated. All he (Jessie) or she (Amanda) wants is for the interrogation to end.

In 1956, CIA director Allen Dulles sent a memo to FBI director J. Edgar Hoover outlining brainwashing techniques used successfully by Communist operatives in North Korea. The document has since been declassified. It lists and explains techniques such as introduction of fatigue, inducing a feeling of helplessness in attempting to deal with the impersonal machinery of control, and developing a feeling of dependence upon the interrogator. Similar techniques have been employed to interrogate terrorist suspects at Guantánamo Bay.

They didn't want Amanda alert and lucid to give an accurate account. *They wanted to break her.* And they did everything they could that wouldn't leave physical marks on her body.

Under this haze of fatigue and fright, Amanda spun a tale of meeting Patrick at the Piazza Grimana basketball court, across the street from her house, around eight-thirty and going back with him to her house. Though she said it was dreamlike and she couldn't tell if it had actually happened, she "recalled" Patrick having sex with Meredith, but she didn't remember whether he had had to force her. But she vaguely remembered him killing her with a knife afterward, which implied that she was in the room at the time.

There may have been another reason for the full-court press on Amanda that night. The police may have perceived that time was running out for them. Since they were tapping Amanda and Raffaele's phones, they knew that Edda Mellas was on her way to Perugia to stand by her daughter. She would never let Amanda continue to speak without an attorney present, no matter what the investigators said.

Giuliano Mignini came in at 5:45 A.M. to take her official statement. Everything she had said previously was as a witness, so it couldn't be used against her. Between the original "confession" and the official statement, several key details changed, such as the time and the added detail that she had heard Meredith scream. Everyone agrees that after she signed the statement, she was given food.

At noon, the police formally arrested Amanda at the police station. They had their killer.

Pathologist Luca Lalli, accompanied by a female officer, conducted a physical exam on Amanda Knox and took DNA swabs and saliva, urine and head and pubic hair samples.

When Amanda recovered her wits enough to realize, like Jessie Misskelley Jr., what had just happened to her, she was shocked. She immediately felt as though the police had led her down the primrose path to a murder charge. Up until now, she had been feeling vulnerable because of how close she thought she had come to being another victim of the killer.

Clearly, for the police to question Amanda and Raffaele intensively over the course of several days, for them to hammer on Raffaele until he changed his story to say that Amanda left him for several hours the night of the murder, for them to interpret a simple text message with its most unusual and outlandish meaning, for them systematically to stress Amanda to the point of stripping her of all logic and emotional resources and essentially get her to make up a story they liked, someone already had to have had a theory of the case that he or she wanted all the facts to fit into. Aside from all the other pressures she was under, Amanda had a poor command of Italian, and the translator was essentially helping the police, not making it easier for her to communicate.

A compulsive diarist, Amanda wrote in her green notebook journal that day that she already doubted *the verity of my statements because they were made under the pressures of stress, shock and extreme exhaustion.* She noted that she had been hit on the back of her head when she didn't give interrogators the responses they wanted and was threatened with a long jail sentence if she didn't co-operate.

She was clearly strung out and confused. A guilty person would either acknowledge to herself that they had caught her or, if she thought the journal might be made public, steadfastly deny the charges to vindicate herself. Amanda does neither. She is *very doubtful* of what she has said and even cuts the police a break in saying she understands their behavior.

If Amanda had taken part in murder, she certainly would not have gone about her business and come back to the house. She had the means and the time to get out of Italy before authorities caught up with her. She did not exercise this option because it never occurred to her she might need it.

At a news conference on November 6, Perugia chief of police Arturo De Felice announced the arrests of Amanda Knox, Raffaele Sollecito and Patrick Lumumba for the murder of Meredith Kercher. The case, he assured reporters, was "substantially closed." An outraged Lumumba, insisting he had no idea what this was all about, had been arrested at home and taken from his family earlier in the day.

That same day, executing a search warrant, the *squadra mobile,* or flying squad, officer Armando Finzi searched Raffaele's flat and took away, among other items, a kitchen knife he found in a drawer among other knives. How did he know the murder weapon came from Raffaele's kitchen rather than from the crime location itself? And how did he know that particular blade, rather than any others in the drawer, was the murder weapon? Investigator's instinct, he proudly proclaimed.

Later, the lab would report having found a tiny amount of Amanda's DNA on the handle — no leap of logic since she had prepared food in Raffaele's kitchen — but also an equally tiny speck of Meredith's DNA near the tip. Since she had not been in Raffaele's flat, this looked as if it might be real evidence.

But there were a couple of problems. To start, it was never definitive that Meredith's blood was ever on the knife blade, as was acknowledged in the final appeals report, and the testing may have been manipulated or amplified to indicate her DNA in ways that were never apparent to other independent testers. Moreover, the blade, which effectively had been selected by the investigators at random, did not match the blood outline on the bed and was too large to have made two cuts in Meredith's neck. Mignini didn't let this stop him, though. All it meant was there must have been two knives.

The chain of custody would have been laughable if it weren't so pathetic. Finzi admitted he had given the knife to another officer, Stefano Gubbiotti, who had been at the murder scene that day, meaning an easy case could be made for cross-contamination. He put the knife in a box and stored it before it was sent to the lab in Rome, so there is no way of telling what happened to it or who touched it in the meantime.

Later, the results of the DNA assay itself would be challenged by numerous experts as being too small a sample to render a reliable match.

On November 8, the three defendants were arraigned before Judge Claudia Matteini. Under Italian law, they easily could have been released pending trial, but the judge ordered all three held for a year, concerned particularly that Amanda and Patrick would flee.

If you read Amanda's "My Prison Diary,"

which was given to me by investigators helping with her case, you see no evidence of guilt or culpability. It is more observational than anything else. Clearly, it was written for herself, no one else. In it, she expresses confusion about the whole situation rather than anger or even sadness. She knows she has to wait out the workings of the system, but she fully expects to be out and going home soon.

Even the diary was used against her in a selective leaking campaign. As Candace Dempsey, a Seattle-based Italian-American journalist, noted in her comprehensive and insightful book *Murder in Italy,* the language problem became a further opportunity for the prosecution and media. This is a section that was translated into Italian, leaked to the press, and then translated *back* into English:

That night I smoked a lot of marijuana and I fell asleep at my boyfriend's house. I don't remember anything. But I think it's possible that Raffaele went to Meredith's house, raped her and then killed her. And then when he got home, while I was sleeping, he put my fingerprints on the knife. But I don't understand why Raffaele would do that.

This all sounds pretty damning and definitely locks Raffaele into the murder scene

— particularly, if you accept, as I do, that the diary was not intended for anyone else's eyes. But like some diabolical version of the children's party game telephone, this is how the passage actually read in context in the *original* English:

Raffaele and I have used this knife to cook, and it's impossible that Meredith's DNA is on the knife because she's never been to Raffaele's apartment before. So unless Raffaele decided to get up after I fell asleep, grabbed said knife, went over to my house, used it to kill Meredith, came home, cleaned the blood off, rubbed my fingerprints all over it, put it away, then tucked himself back into bed, and then pretended really well the next couple of days, well, I just highly doubt all of that.

Giuliano Mignini now had a complete theory of the case, which was outlined in a judge's report issued by lead judge Claudia Matteini on November 9. The logic of arriving at his conclusion, if I follow it correctly, is decidedly *Alice's Adventures in Wonderland*. The inconsistencies between Amanda and Raffaele's stories had to do with timing. The first led them to speculate that the call to the Carabinieri had been placed a few minutes after the Postal Police arrived, rather than before, which would imply that the two young lovers had never called the police at all on their own initiative, only to cover themselves when an investigation was already under way.

But here's where it gets interesting: If Raffaele suddenly changed his story and said there was a gap of time when Amanda wasn't with him — when she said she was going to Le Chic to meet Patrick — then she was lying and she must have gone back to the house. But then if she said he was with her all night, then he must have been with her in the house when she and Patrick killed Meredith, which meant that he was involved, too. As goofy as this sounds, it is the same type of approach WMPD followed; that is, take the "best" part of each account or piece of evidence to come up with a theory that meets the police's needs.

And what was that theory here? Actually, there were two. One was that Meredith and Amanda's friendship had broken up over a number of issues, including Amanda owing Meredith rent money and refusing to do her part in keeping the house clean. In other words, assuming either or both of these charges were accurate — which I do not believe — so as not to have to pay her back and/or resentment over being called out for being something of a slob, Amanda solicited the help of two male friends and plunged a knife three times into Meredith's neck.

This falling-out must have happened

shortly before the murder, because up until then, the two had been close friends, hanging out at bookstores, restaurants and clubs together and going together to Perugia's celebrated EuroChocolate Festival in late October, only days before the murder.

The investigators seemed to be projecting their own distaste for Amanda's perceived habits into a murder scenario. In the judge's report, they took her to task when *she found traces of blood, which she did not worry about cleaning, and noticed that in the other bathroom the toilet water was full of feces that she was astonished to find but did not try to clean.*

So Amanda helped indict herself by not touching a potential crime scene.

But that motive was only a secondary theory. Mignini's main theory of the case started out with Patrick having a crush on Meredith, who allegedly had turned him down, and with Raffaele, as shown from writing on his online blog, seeking "extreme sensations," which he apparently felt Amanda was capable of fulfilling. The murder, then, was either part of a drug-fueled satanic ritual, a sex game that got out of hand, or else Amanda decided she wanted to have an orgy. When Meredith wouldn't play along, Amanda and the others had to kill her.

Sounds convincing, no?

Giuliano Mignini, locally born and bred and

a student of history, must have known he was acting on precedent. Perugia had been the site of a series of witch trials in the fifteenth century, and the public minister understood the bewitching power of certain women.

Upon reflection, the investigators decided it was more likely that one of the men had plunged in the knife while Amanda held Meredith down. As far as I can tell, there was no evidence, forensic or otherwise, to support this. Mignini figured the crime, whatever *it* was — orgy, murder or satanic ritual — and whatever the exact motive, had been planned ahead of time. Since there was a strong satanic component, it was supposed to take place on Halloween. But since that didn't work out, the Day of the Dead would be just as auspicious.

This line of reasoning reminds me of "Dr." Dale Griffis's wacky logic in WM3. There were a bunch of cultic holidays on the calendar; and if you acted on either the day before or the day after, it had the same effect. When you think that people's lives and freedom are being determined by listening to this kind of nonsense, the effect does become scary indeed.

Curiously, though he and other investigators considered Amanda and Raffaele prime suspects, they never even seemed to consider Filomena Romanelli, who had pretty much the same alibi as Amanda, or Giacomo Silenzi downstairs, who had already been identified as Meredith's sometimes boyfriend. This pattern of arbitrariness would characterize the entire investigation.

But the police knew they had the right girl. As Edgardo Giobbi, head of Central Operation Service in Rome, put it, "We were able to establish guilt by closely observing the suspect's psychological and behavioral reactions during interrogations. We don't need to rely on other kinds of investigation as this method has enabled us to get to the guilty parties in a very quick time." I guess this is their idea of profiling.

Here is an exercise I've tried a number of times with people who either assumed or insisted to me that Amanda Knox was guilty:

What would you say if your teenaged daughter, studying abroad, called you one day to say that she had suddenly taken it upon herself to stage a satanic-themed orgy, and when her roommate refused to go along, she stabbed her to death?

If you have, or are close to, a teenaged girl, your response would be, "Absurd!"

If I then asked you *why* it was absurd, your response would be, "Because she would *never* do anything like that!"

When I asked you how you *knew* that about her, you would reply, "Because she's never done anything like that."

You would undoubtedly be right, and you would have just participated in some basic profiling. And the same exercise would be valid for a son like Raffaele.

Past behavior predicts future behavior. It is one of the elemental tenets of what we do. Just as we could tell a lot about what John and Patsy Ramsey were capable of by evaluating their past behavior and treatment of their children, we can tell a lot about what Amanda and Raffaele are capable of by looking into how they've acted in the past. Nothing in Amanda's neo–flower child background or behavior suggested that out of nowhere, she would suddenly become homicidally violent, especially to someone she lived with and was close to.

Don't people without a past history of violence ever commit murder? Yes, they do. But not without a motive.

So what supposedly gave Amanda the idea to kill her friend brutally that night? Giuliano Mignini had an answer for that, too. Raffaele was a fan of Japanese manga comic books, particularly those featuring violent themes and sexual domination of women. They found one in his possession they thought fit the bill, *Blood: The Last Vampire.* They also found a short story online that Amanda had written the year before that involved a rape.

If Mark and I were prosecuted for what we've written about, we'd be in jail for the rest of our lives.

Under questioning, Amanda and Raffaele admitted smoking hashish that night, and it was not the first time for either one of them. While certain substances — alcohol being prime among them — do lower inhibitions, they do not make you a different person or prone to committing violent acts that you wouldn't do while sober or straight.

True, a person who commits vehicular manslaughter while driving under the influence would likely not have done so if he had not been drinking. But that is a question of *diminished capability,* not *altered intent.* This individual simply couldn't drive as well. The crime had nothing to do with transforming his character or choices.

That's one aspect of profiling. Now let's look at another as it applies here. What elements of the crime, the forensic evidence, the statements of the witnesses or anything else led Giuliano Mignini to conclude this murder was satanic or orgiastic in nature, or that Amanda Knox and Raffaele Sollecito had anything to do with it? Where are the clues? Where are the behavioral indicators? I've studied this case quite closely and I just don't see any.

Aside from the fact, as we've noted, that satanically motivated murders by sane people are essentially nonexistent, the kind of group cause homicide Mignini had conceived was almost as unlikely. Gangbang-style rapes are not uncommon, though they seldom involve another woman. This had all the hallmarks of a break-in/robbery/sexual assault/murder scenario, which is also unfortunately not uncommon. But sadistic or power-excitation rapists don't welcome watchers; it spoils the sense of control, and it is just too easy to be ratted out afterward. Unless DNA or other strong forensic evidence turned up to the contrary, there was nothing about this scene to indicate more than one assailant.

By this point, both the Italian and British media had picked up the story. The once-venerable London *Times* ran the headline: MEREDITH KILLED AFTER REFUSING ORGY, and that was one of the tamer ones.

The beautiful, mercurial Amanda was a defendant almost too good to be true. This was a classic archetypal morality play: Virtue against evil; the good girl against the bad girl. What could have possessed this sultry temptress to kill her equally lovely friend, enlisting the help of her sexy Italian boyfriend and black African boss, even though Patrick had a young, beautiful wife at home? Oh, the powers of seduction this American must have!

Reporters had already picked up on her Foxy Knoxy moniker, presumably through her Facebook page or similar source. What they didn't mention was that Amanda had picked up the nickname years before as a preteen for her elusive moves on the soccer field. But it fit in so well with the seduction narrative and balanced so perfectly with the well-scrubbed, all-American "girl next door" image (*Which is she?!*) that it seemed like another gift from the gods of media. As with Ramsey, the tale they wove was simply *a better story* than the one that made sense. And as with Ramsey, the mainstream media shamefully took to parroting the sensationalistic tabloids, giving their lurid accounts validity.

The clue to the real Amanda actually lay in her voluminous diaries. As Nina Burleigh stated in her book *The Fatal Gift of Beauty: For most of her life, Amanda explained herself to herself in her scribbled pages. She didn't spend much time looking for answers in front of the mirror.* By that we mean her introspection was based on her mind and what she was pondering, rather than trading on her looks or appearance.

As far as the press and local observers were concerned, though, she couldn't do anything right. A couple of days after the murder and shortly before she and Raffaele were arrested on November 6, she was observed in a local clothing store called Bubble sorting through a table display of panties with him. Raffaele was reported to have said to her, "We go home and have hot sex." ("Hot" in Italian had the connotation of wild, rough or kinky.) Let us stress *reported* because the salesman who *sold* the anecdote to a British tabloid did not speak English, so in reality had no idea what they actually said to each other.

Whatever their intentions for the afternoon, the fact was, she had not been allowed back into the house and had run out of clean underwear. She paid for the purchase herself; and instead of jumping into bed, they ate lunch and then met with Amanda's two Italian flatmates. But prosecutors were so taken with this lingerie outing that they had the Bubble manager testify at the trial.

They also made a great to-do and feigned prudish shock over the vibrator Amanda supposedly kept in plain view in the bathroom she shared with Meredith. Obviously, this girl was sexually insatiable. What they did not say was that it was two inches long and in the shape of a pink bunny. It had been given to her as a going-away joke by her best friend, Brett Lither, and was kept, unused, in a container with the rest of her toiletries.

Throughout the ordeal, Patrick Lumumba maintained his alibi that he had been at Le Chic the entire evening; and because it wasn't busy, he had been talking to a visiting Swiss professor there for several hours. On November 11, a teacher from Zurich confirmed the story. It looked as if the police case was falling apart.

But then they caught a break. Actually, it was the first *real* break of the case.

On November 16, forensic police in Rome scored a match on fingerprints lifted in Meredith's bedroom. They belonged to Rudy Guede, a twenty-year-old Ivory Coast native who had been living in Perugia since he was five. His father, Roger, a construction worker, abruptly decided to move back to the Ivory Coast when Rudy was sixteen. But Rudy got lucky. A wealthy local businessman named Paolo Caporali, who had met him playing basketball on a court the family had built, took him in and informally adopted him. Paolo had tried to give him every advantage and a stake in life, finding him jobs, introducing him to the right people, and encouraging him to study and better himself. When Rudy dropped out of hotel management school, Paolo found him another job. When he couldn't or wouldn't keep it, Paolo finally threw up his hands. All Rudy wanted to do was hang out at bars, play basketball and video games, and chase girls.

What cracked the case was that all immigrants in Italy were fingerprinted, so Rudy's prints were available.

Rudy, on the other hand, was not. He was a known habitué of Perugia's bars, disco and club scene; so when friends stopped seeing him, they wondered. He lived in a room near Via della Pergola and had met the women who lived in the house through the men downstairs, with whom he was friendly and with whom he dealt in illicit substances. But he had left or, probably more accurately, fled the city soon after the murder. On November 20, he was arrested for riding without a ticket on a train near Mainz, Germany. Once German police figured out who he was, and what he was wanted for, they extradited him back to Italy.

Authorities took DNA samples from the toothbrush in his room, which they were able to match up with samples in Meredith's body and on toilet paper in the larger bathroom.

That made it extremely awkward for Rudy to deny he'd been at the crime scene. His story was that he was in the house on the fateful night. He had run into Meredith at a Halloween party the night before; they'd flirted and arranged to meet the next night. He came to the house as planned and they began engaging in consensual sex play. But before the activity reached climax, Rudy suddenly felt the urgent call of nature as a result of kabobs he had eaten earlier in the evening. While he was sitting on the toilet in the larger bathroom and listening to his iPod, a stranger must have broken into the house and attacked Meredith. When he heard the commotion, he got up and rushed to help her.

This accounted for the unflushed toilet.

He grappled with a white male stranger, but since he hadn't had time to pull his trousers all the way up, he stumbled and the intruder rushed off. When he saw Meredith covered with blood, he tried to help and comfort her, which explained the bloody towels and why his DNA was all over the scene, as well as a shoeprint matching his Nikes. He panicked when he heard a sound downstairs and ran out. He realized that if authorities found him there, they might think he had attacked Meredith. He blamed himself for not having the presence of mind to call an ambulance, but he was in total shock.

Apparently the shock had worn off sufficiently by 2:00 A.M., when he was seen by several witnesses dancing in a local nightclub.

Nowhere in his account did he mention Amanda Knox or Raffaele Sollecito.

One of the most common defenses in rape cases is that it was not forced, that the victim was actually a partner and only changed her story later. If this victim is dead, however, this complicates the defense. What are you going to say — that after consensual sex, he killed her? So you have to add a third individual to actually perform the murder. For Rudy Guede's story to carry any weight, he would have had to call for help as soon as he saw Meredith's condition.

Given the matchup of fingerprints and DNA samples and the absence of any evidence to support a ritualized or group cause homicide, had I been advising the police I would have said, "Looks like you've got your killer. He had the means, motive and opportunity. How can I help you with his prosecution?"

Of course, that's not the way it actually went down. The day before Rudy's arrest, Giuliano Mignini bowed to the inevitable and signed an order for Patrick Lumumba's release. Amanda was thrilled because he was now cleared and she thought it would mean that she and Raffaele would soon be cleared as well. Not only did this not happen, but it signaled the end of her friendship with Patrick. Eventually he filed a defamation suit against her for naming him as a killer.

Mignini didn't let Patrick's release damage his theory of the case. He merely plugged in Rudy to fill Patrick's place. He even played basketball on the same court where Amanda was supposed to have met up with Patrick. The equation still worked: Amanda Knox plus Raffaele Sollecito plus one black African.

But looked at another way — the correct way, in my professional judgment — the like-for-like swap of Rudy for Patrick is one of the most compelling pieces of behavioral evidence for Amanda's innocence.

If the police were right and Rudy was part

of a murderous trio, why wouldn't Amanda have named him to begin with? She had an important and friendly relationship with Patrick, who was also helping her support herself. She had no relationship with Rudy and barely knew who he was. Why would she have defamed Patrick to protect Rudy? Another way of posing the question is: If her confession was true and it finally came out when it did because she was just so worn-out that she no longer had the energy or wits to lie, why did she mention Patrick rather than Rudy?

The answer is: Because the police had already identified Patrick from the text exchange, so he was in her mind and she knew they were interested in him. In her fear and exhaustion, trying to do anything to get the police off her back, he was the only person she could come up with in any context. She didn't know Rudy well enough to even think about using his name.

Any other scenario makes absolutely no sense, and Giuliano Mignini, Judge Claudia Matteini and the Perugia Police Department should have known that.

It got worse. Late in the evening of November 22, Amanda was taken to see a prison doctor she hadn't met before, who told her he had the results of tests that had been taken in the police station and it looked like she was HIV positive. He told her it could be a mistake and they would conduct another test to be sure, but Amanda was terrified. She wrote in her journal that she was afraid of dying and missing out on marriage, children and her whole life.

They made her list everyone with whom she'd ever had sex and include the method of birth control, if any. Given the language gulf and her own relative inexperience, she wasn't even sure what they meant by having sex, so she listed seven individuals with whom she'd had some degree of intimacy. When this information was inevitably leaked to the Italian press, they stated she had had seven lovers in the two months she'd been in Italy.

The next week, they told her the test had not been positive and she was healthy.

Even considering the rampant incompetence of the Italian forensic personnel in this case, it is nearly impossible to believe that this was a simple mistake. It was an obvious trick to get her to admit private and intimate information about herself that could be used to further the image of her as a sexually manipulative vixen. The sham medical report had nothing to do with Amanda's health. It was a cold-blooded ploy to prejudice opinion against her.

It took weeks for Italian authorities to release Meredith Kercher's body, and then more time for Arline and John to bring her back home to England. They buried her on December 14, 2007, after a funeral service at her parish church, St. John the Baptist, in Croydon. More than four hundred mourners attended.

CHAPTER 30
LEGAL LIMBO

Given that they were "flight risks," as well as apparently highly dangerous individuals who might kill "again," the court ruled Amanda and Raffaele had to remain in jail pending trial. Even a subsequent plea from Amanda's mother, Edda, that Amanda be placed under house arrest in Perugia was denied because Amanda hadn't shown any remorse for her crime. Sound familiar? They would have to remain imprisoned, in legal limbo, until the creaky wheels of Italian justice finally rolled around to trying them.

Forty-seven days after the murder, police went back to the crime scene to look again for evidence. How anything collected this long after the fact could even be considered evidence is beyond me. The bra clasp they retrieved was not in the same place on the floor that video of the original crime scene showed it to be. Remember, just as with the kitchen knife: *The difference between evidence and garbage is chain of custody.*

I think the reason for this strangely timed evidence hunt is clear. Once the Nike shoe-print was proven to belong to Rudy Guede, the prosecution had nothing to tie Raffaele Sollecito to the scene, and they needed it in a hurry, just as the WM3 prosecution needed the knife from the lake. Whatever the logic, they found a metal bra clasp, presumably Meredith's, and brought it to the lab for processing. Subsequent analysis, they said, revealed a trace amount of Raffaele's DNA.

It also revealed the DNA of three other unidentified individuals, but now the prosecution had the "scientific" evidence it was looking for.

Between Edda, her husband Chris Mellas, her ex-husband Curt and their daughter Deanna, Amanda's family tried to make sure some member was always there in Perugia for her. Her grandmother Liz Huff, Edda's sister Christina Hagge and Christina's husband Kevin, Edda's brother Mick and his wife Janet also spent time in Italy emotionally supporting Amanda. So did Curt's wife Janet and Amanda's younger half-sisters Ashley and Delaney. And it wasn't just family. Amanda's close friend Madison Paxton spent considerable time in Perugia. The fact that they were allowed visits of only a few hours a week made their lives all the more torturous.

About half a dozen other friends came over to visit her in prison, including David

Johnsrud, Jessica Nichols and Andrew Se-
liber.

Back in Seattle, an important ritual during
Amanda's imprisonment was the weekly
telephone call. Each Saturday morning family and friends would gather at Edda and
Chris's house for the allotted ten-minute
conversation during which they'd all try to
lift each other's spirits and make Amanda
feel as if she still had some connection to
back home. There were usually a bunch of
people present and sometimes the modest
kitchen where the speakerphone was located
was packed to overflowing.

The ordeal was proving not only emotionally harrowing but also financially ruinous.
The Knox and Mellas families were going
through their collective savings and had
mortgaged everything they had, but they were
dedicated to bringing their girl home.

Several people stepped up to help in any
way they could. Thomas Lee Wright is a
former motion picture executive for such
studios as Paramount and Disney who became a prominent film producer and writer.
He and his wife had moved to Mercer Island,
Washington because they didn't want to raise
their daughter and son amidst "all of the
Hollywood craziness." Their daughter Sara
had been close to Amanda at Seattle Prep,
sharing mutual passions for theater, writing
and athletics. When Tom heard about the

607

charges against Amanda in Italy, he was distressed but felt it must have been a misunderstanding that "would be cleared up in a matter of days."

"Ten days in was when I realized it was not going to clear up and [Amanda and her family] were in a heap of trouble. So I called Edda and dove in with both feet."

Judge Michael Heavey, whose daughter Shana was another of Amanda's friends at Seattle Prep, partnered with Tom in establishing Friends of Amanda (FOA). They recruited attorney and media commentator Anne Bremner as an advocate for the cause and were joined by Jim Lovering, a retired businessman who became the organization's archivist and Internet wizard. Together they created two websites: "Friendsofamanda.org" would post up-to-date information regarding the case for her supporters and the media. "Amandadefensefund.org" would be run by the family and accept contributions for her defense. FOA mobilized a wide array of resources and received hundreds of thousands of hits from around the world. Among other tasks, they eventually collected hundreds of thousands of documents and pieces of evidence.

As was true with West Memphis and the effort spearheaded by Lorri Davis, Wright, Heavey and Lovering's work demonstrates the Herculean undertaking that any legal defense represents. And this one was complicated by a trial and imprisonment that took place 6,000 miles and nine time zones away.

Despite his media background, Tom made the decision early on that he would not approach the case as a writer or a filmmaker because he didn't want any of his decisions to be clouded by story considerations or the prospect of personal gain. He only wanted to be a friend and felt he needed complete objectivity to be effective. He was the one who brought my old colleague Steve Moore into the case after Steve sent an email to Friends of Amanda volunteering his services. Tom took it upon himself to vet all volunteers carefully to make sure they had competence and no ulterior motives or hidden agenda. After lunching with Steve near Pepperdine in Malibu, Tom showed him crime scene footage the police had taken. Steve was aghast at the apparent incompetence and cavalier attitude.

Their influence reached not only far, but high as well. On her way to the airport to attend the 2008 Democratic Convention, Washington Senator Maria Cantwell stopped off at the Heavey home in West Seattle and met with Edda for more than an hour, pledging to do everything she could. Her support was both public and behind-the-scenes and didn't let up until Amanda was freed.

Senator Cantwell had searing personal

experience that allowed her to empathize with the Mellas and Knox families. In 1977, when she was nineteen, her twenty-one-year-old brother Daniel was charged with the murder of a twenty-six-year-old woman who had rented an apartment from his and Maria's mother. The case went on for three years with three prosecutors, two sets of defense attorneys, two changes of venue and two trials before a jury took only twenty minutes to acquit Daniel. Maria Cantwell knew the devastation a false charge brings to a family.

Ultimately, along with Cantwell, who remained a vociferous public advocate, personages as diverse as developer Donald Trump and Secretary of State Hillary Clinton would call for justice for Amanda.

Everything about the case against Amanda Knox and Raffaele Sollecito was based on supposition, preconceived ideas and questionable testimony. Near the end of March 2008, as both defendants cooled their heels in Italian prisons awaiting an appeal by the Corte Suprema di Cassazione (Supreme Court of Cassation) in Rome regarding their imprisonment before trial, Rudy Guede asked to speak to Giuliano Mignini. It seemed he had just remembered that the intruder he'd run into the night of the murder was, in fact, Raffaele. He also remembered hearing Amanda's voice.

Rudy gained himself no credibility with his shifting story, but it wasn't enough to get the other two out. The Italian Supreme Court upheld Mignini's satanic ritual/sex orgy theory and even cited the Nike shoeprint as evidence, even though Rudy later admitted the print was probably his. Raffaele also had a pair of Nikes.

Amanda spent her twenty-first birthday, July 9, 2008, in Capanne Prison. Her mother was allowed to visit, but not to bring a cake.

CHAPTER 31
TRIAL

By the time the pretrial motions began on September 19 at the Palace of Justice in Perugia, under Judge Paolo Micheli, the three defendants were among the most famous people in Italy. Amanda's fame and infamy had long since spread to England, and she was being covered seriously by the American media as well.

The key to the fascination, I think, was similar to what I had seen in the Ramsey case and was wrapped up in the presumption that she was guilty. First of all, why would Italian authorities arrest her and put her in jail awaiting charges and trial if she were just an innocent little American schoolgirl? Some of the papers had taken to calling her "Angel Face" and both "Luciferina" and "Bambi." What made her fascinating was the existential human mystery of *why* someone that lovely would kill another girl who was supposed to be her friend, and *how* she had deployed her sexual wiles to get two men to go along with her.

To counter this image, the Knox-Mellas family hired a crisis management consultant at a public relations firm, further impoverishing themselves. And, of course, they were roundly criticized for it by various members of the media for trying to manage the news, which has the same fatuous logic as saying if someone needs a lawyer to defend him, he must actually be guilty.

Still, the prosecution team continued to promote the story that far from being friends, the two girls didn't get along because Amanda was a deadbeat on the rent and didn't do her share of the housework, even though neither assertion was ever verified, and neither is exactly a common motive for murder.

This supposed animosity between Meredith and Amanda could have been disputed effectively were it not for another of the mistakes by officials in the case. While examining the computers belonging to both young women, police managed to destroy both hard drives, which obliterated some key material on Amanda's laptop. Specifically, there were dozens of digital photos of Meredith and Amanda hanging out and having fun together and numerous emails between the two that would have testified to their blossoming friendship. Whether this was an act of deliberation or ineptitude, we cannot say, but either way, it removed a troublesome impediment to Mignini's theory of ongoing tension between the two flatmates.

At the hearing, Rudy's lawyers asked that his case be separated from the other two and that he be given an abbreviated, fast-track trial, which was his right in Italy. They said he didn't want to be tarnished by the evidence against Amanda and Raffaele. Defendants who go this route often receive reduced sentences for saving authorities the trouble of a drawn-out legal affair.

When Amanda finally got a chance to speak, she described the terror of the police station and tried to explain why she had named Patrick. "Meredith was my friend, and I had no reason to kill her," she stated. "I am innocent. I wasn't in the house that night. If I said the opposite before, it was because I was forced to do so because the police pressured me."

Since Italian courts only sit about two days a week and take breaks for all sorts of things, the pretrial procedures lasted nearly two months. On October 27, Judge Micheli announced that Rudy Guede had been found guilty of murder in his fast-track trial and was being sentenced to thirty years in prison and payment of several million euro to Meredith's family. Amanda and Raffaele would be tried for murder, sexual assault and theft, among other charges.

The trial of Amanda Knox and Raffaele Sollecito began on January 16, 2009, at the Perugia Corte d'Assise. Judge Giancarlo Massei presided, assisted by Deputy Judge Beatrice Cristiani and six lay judges, all of whom would decide the defendants' fate. That is the trial system in Italy.

Coverage of the case had gone global and there were media representatives from all over the world. Fashion commentators critiqued Amanda's daily outfit and appearance. The apparent rise or fall of her weight was of keen interest.

Joining Giuliano Mignini in the prosecution was Manuela Comodi. They called the already-convicted Rudy Guede once during the trial, but he exercised his right to remain silent and so was sent back to prison.

Ironically — or maybe not — Giuliano Mignini had to go back to Florence from time to time for his own trial on charges of intimidating witnesses and illegally tapping phones of journalists and police officers in the notorious "Monster of Florence" case. That series of crimes, in which sixteen young lovers were killed with the same gun in the foothills outside of Florence between the late 1960s and mid 1980s, became a national psychodrama in Italy. Though a number of suspects have been identified, charged and convicted over the years, many feel the case remains largely unsolved. Mignini reopened the case in 2002, claiming, according to ABC News, that "the murders were the work of a satanic sect, dating back to the Middle Ages, that needed female body parts for their Black Masses, to serve as the blasphemous wafer."

This would all be comical if it wasn't so deadly serious.

I wondered whether Mignini's relentless prosecution of Amanda and Raffaele was essentially a face-saving scenario to detract attention from the charges against him having to do with the Monster of Florence. If he could bring in convictions in another case to which the whole world was riveted, perhaps the disgrace in the former case wouldn't stick.

As witness after witness appeared over the course of weeks, the questionable facts, character innuendos and specious theories were paraded before the judges. Again, the issue of the timing of the first call to the Carabinieri arose; but the Postal Police could not pinpoint the time of their arrival, so it was their word against the defendants' on when the call was made.

Several witnesses claimed to have seen Amanda Knox and/or Raffaele Sollecito outside the house at critical times, but these witnesses came across as confused and mistaken. One woman who the prosecution hoped would pinpoint the time of death by her report of an earsplitting scream turned out to be hard of hearing and mentally ill to the point of needing hospitalization. Another eyewitness, a homeless man who had conveniently testified for the prosecution in two other serious crimes, turned out to be a heroin addict and couldn't even get the date straight.

Paola Grande, Filomena's friend who had come to the house with her on the day Meredith's body was discovered, testified that, indeed, Amanda was upset and did cry. The next day, Filomena Romanelli herself got on the stand, confirmed Amanda's tears and stated that the American and British girls were friends and had gotten along fine. And Amanda was not a deadbeat; she always paid her rent on time.

The prosecution was able to squeeze out a few complaints that they claimed the three flatmates shared about the American girl. The bill of particulars included: not doing enough of the housework, not always cleaning the toilet, playing the same song frequently and monotonously on Laura's guitar, doing yoga exercises at odd times and in inappropriate situations, and generally being "too outgoing."

These may be the kinds of annoyances an

attentive mother might scold you for, but they are not the sort of issues that lead to murder in otherwise rational people.

Giuliano Mignini put several of Meredith Kercher's English girlfriends in Perugia on the stand, hoping they would reveal a huge rift between the two flatmates. But most of their testimony was bland, and the worst they could come up with were a few petty complaints they thought Meredith might have had. The ones who were with Meredith on Halloween actually helped Amanda's case by saying they had seen no sign of Rudy that night, and he did not flirt with Meredith and make a plan to see her the next evening.

Whatever negative things the British girls had to say about Amanda were in marked contrast to what they had — or, more accurately, *hadn't* — said about her prearrest — namely, that Meredith had grown to dislike her.

The prosecution rested in June, having heaped theory upon theory; but if one studies the transcript and reports, they had proven absolutely nothing. Not a single witness or piece of forensic evidence could put Amanda Knox anywhere near the scene of the crime.

On June 12, Amanda took the stand in her own defense, straining to make herself understood in her imperfect Italian. All of the opposing lawyers got a chance to get their licks in on her, but her story remained consistent. At one point, she explained that during the long night of questioning, interrogators told her they already had the other suspect in custody and all she had to do was mention his name. When she couldn't, they hit her and called her stupid. Then they told her that giving them an account of what had happened was the only way she could avoid spending thirty years in prison.

When a friend from Seattle came to testify as a character witness for Amanda, he was questioned about her sex life in Seattle, about which he knew nothing. Then, to show how wild and uncontrollable she was, the prosecutors produced the record of a citation she'd been given when a party at a house she and some roommates had rented near the University of Washington campus had gotten out of hand and a neighbor had called the police complaining about the noise and some participants allegedly throwing rocks at cars. It was actually a moving-out party the housemates had collectively hosted.

We have examined the actual citation — Amanda's only prior brush with the law. In form it looks like a typical parking ticket, and in the incident description, the officer states that he did not see any damage and that Amanda came outside and presented herself as one of the residents, which is why she was the one listed on the citation. She apologized for the noise and said she knew nothing about any rock throwing. To me, this shows her sense of responsibility. She easily could have ducked the officer and let someone else take the rap. The punishment consisted of a $269 fine that all of the housemates shared and a warning that rock throwing was "dangerous and juvenile," which Amanda accepted on behalf of the actual offenders.

These petty grievances are part of a clear and subversive pattern. Mignini and his team had nothing substantive against Amanda, so they threw in anything they could think of to convince the judges and the public what a bad girl she was, and therefore how evil and capable of violent murder.

Mark and I have spoken with many people around Amanda. It became clear to us that the Amanda Knox the prosecution and the media described did not exist in real life. She was a creation designed to serve their very specific needs and purposes.

Teachers and fellow students at Seattle Prep described Amanda with terms such as "bright," "sweet" and "kind." One teacher noted that in history class debates, she would always take the side of the smallest country.

In both academics and athletics, one teacher said, "she was a brilliant example of determination. She kept working at something until she could do it well." In a Seattle

Prep production of *Annie* Tom Wright's daughter Sara had the lead role and Amanda was one of the orphans. It was directed by John Lange, one of Amanda's favorite teachers and a close friend to this day. As Tom recalled, she decided she was going to do multiple backflips as part of the dance routine, but in every rehearsal kept landing on her bottom. By the first scheduled performance she still hadn't completed the routine successfully but was determined to keep trying.

"On opening night, for the first time she nailed it," Tom reported, "and all of the other orphans just stopped and broke into spontaneous cheering."

Despite the defense's success in portraying Rudy as a habitual crook with several breaking-and-entering and theft charges, as well as his previous use of a knife in some of his crimes, Mignini forged on with his narrative that was supported by nothing other than his own supposition. He created an elaborate fifteen-minute video presentation, reported to have cost more than $200,000, taking the jurors visually through the crime, with identifiable animated avatars representing Rudy, Raffaele and Amanda. Intercut with this "recreation" were graphic crime scene photographs. There was nothing to back up anything the video purported, but this piece of imaginary fiction helped seal the relationship between the defendants and the horrific murder in the jurors' minds.

On October 9, after a long summer recess, Judge Massei announced there was no need to appoint independent experts, as was common for disputed evidence or testimony in Italian trials, declaring, "We have all the evidence we need."

Before that, John Kercher suffered a stroke that sent him to the hospital for several days, with severe dizziness and double vision for weeks afterward. He did not know whether stress from the murder and the trial was the cause, but I have seen many families so afflicted in the aftermath of a murder. Facing up to such a horror requires everything you have to give, and more. While I don't believe that stress causes illness, it certainly capitalizes on the body's weaknesses. My heart goes out to the entire Kercher family and always will.

As had occurred years after the conviction in the West Memphis case, a group of American scientists met in Las Vegas while the trial was ongoing and declared that the DNA evidence from the knife and bra clasp were useless and should have no bearing on the case.

They put their finding succinctly in writing and made them public: *The DNA testing results described above could have been obtained even if no crime had occurred. As such, they do not constitute credible evidence that linked Amanda Knox and Raffaele Sollecito to the murder of Meredith Kercher.*

The trial lasted eleven months and heard 140 witnesses. On November 20, 2009, Giuliano Mignini rose to give his closing argument. It went on for eight hours during which he repeated his story about the orgy, even though neither Luca Lalli nor any other expert could show evidence of a sexual attack. Even Rudy Guede's DNA found in Meredith turned out to be particles of skin cells rather than semen.

Mignini's entire argument was an exercise in speculation, and not even informed speculation. He merely told a story of Amanda meeting Rudy by chance, making a plan to go back to her house and going to get Raffaele. They confronted Meredith; the two women had it out; then they attacked her with knives.

The jury of judges and laymen deliberated for twelve hours, finally announcing its verdict on December 4, 2009. Both defendants were guilty. Amanda Knox, the ringleader, was sentenced to twenty-six years in prison; Raffaele Sollecito to twenty-five. In addition, she had to pay a multi-million euro judgment to the Kercher family and another fifty thousand to Patrick for defamation. Amanda sobbed. Raffaele said nothing. Giuliano Mignini's only regret, he said, was that the defendants weren't given life sentences.

Amanda and Raffaele's families were stunned and appalled. The still–shell-shocked but always-dignified Kercher family merely said they would have to accept the evidence and the verdict. Meredith's brother Lyle said, "We are pleased with the decision, but this is not a time for celebration. It's not a moment of triumph. We got here because our sister was brutally murdered."

According to the 427-page report written by the judges, they and the six jurors did not believe Mignini's assertion that Meredith's murder was planned or the result of animosity between her and Amanda, but they did believe that Amanda and Rudy played a significant role in her death.

The "most plausible hypothesis," they asserted, held that Rudy went to the house, and was let in by Amanda and Raffaele despite the likelihood that they were in Amanda's bedroom having sex at the time. Once admitted (Amanda knew him only vaguely and Raffaele not at all) Rudy came on to Meredith, who refused him. For some reason, Amanda and Raffaele, who were there, came into the bedroom and helped Rudy have his way with Meredith rather than defend her. From there, things got out of control, resulting in Raffaele attacking her with his pocket knife, causing her to scream, which, in turn, caused Amanda to stab her repeatedly with Raffaele's kitchen knife:

The motive is therefore of erotic sexual violent nature, which, originating from Rudy's choice of evil, found its active collaboration from Amanda Knox and Raffaele Sollecito. This is a translation, by way of CNN, but you get the general idea.

Like all of the government's other hypotheses, this one makes no sense. There was no premeditation, according to the judges; yet they did accept that the kitchen knife on exhibit was the principal murder weapon. In other words, Amanda brought a large kitchen knife from Raffaele's kitchen, but with no nefarious purpose in mind. Was she intent on cooking that night and liked her boyfriend's knife better than her flatmates'? Was she slicing chicken or dicing vegetables when she heard Rudy trying to rape her girlfriend and, already holding the knife, just decided to join in the fun? And, after all that, did she wash it off, bring it back to Raffaele's place and put it back in the knife drawer, where the police found it?

I have never seen a judge's ruling so bizarre or nonsensical. It defies reason that it could have been conceived and written by an adult with any logical capacity whatsoever, much less an experienced jurist. To think that these two young people would be sentenced to spend a quarter of a century each in prison based on such a flight of fantasy is nothing less than sickening.

Violent crimes aren't that elaborate or far-fetched. *Never.* A few basic things happen that lead to tragedy. Convoluted, counterintuitive scenarios are what happen in fiction. Given a certain set of evidence, which is a more coherent narrative — one of the explanations the prosecution or judges bought into, or that a local disco guy without a job, with a history of burglary and drugs, broke into a house he already knew, stole money, found one of the women residents home, began to sexually assault her, panicked and killed her, then escaped?

That scenario is clear-cut and logical: Rudy needed money. He went to the house on Via della Pergola, didn't see any signs of habitation, so he broke a window with a rock and climbed up and in Filomena's room. He was a lithe, athletic basketball player so this was hardly the feat of herculean skill the police and prosecutors seemed to think. It was the beginning of the month so it was likely rent money would be lying around. But first, as he had done on other occasions — past behavior predicts future behavior — he helped himself to food in the kitchen. His DNA bears this out. He then had to use the bathroom, and was probably surprised when he heard someone enter the house. This explains the toilet not being flushed; either he rushed out suddenly to see who it was or didn't want to alert the other person that she was not alone.

He then had to neutralize the other person, who turned out to be Meredith. It could have been any of the four women — the scenario and outcome would have been the same.

It is clear from the crime scene that Meredith did not submit meekly. There is blood all over the place, which indicates she bravely fought like hell. Once she was rendered helpless, he could have had his sexual way with her, or even masturbated on or over her body as she was dying. The scene also tells me that he didn't even leave right away then. He probably continued to look around for anything he might want to take, and threw the blanket haphazardly over her body so he wouldn't have to look at her and confront what he had done.

He was sophisticated enough to lock Meredith's bedroom door, delaying discovery of the body.

He went home through a circuitous route so as not to be spotted, and along the way ditched the two mobile phones he had stolen. When he got to his room he cleaned up and changed clothes. Anyone involved with this scene would have been covered with blood. Perhaps he even broke into the downstairs and took clothing belonging to one of the men. Then from home, he went out to the clubs to dance the night away.

This action has two overlapping interpretations. First, he was so morally unconcerned with the murder that it didn't stop him from having a good time. Second, he needed to establish an alibi. He would have figured that the exact time of death would be difficult to establish, so if he were seen by the club habitués, it would seem that he had been there all evening. But even this goes back to the first interpretation — you have to be a pretty cold and conscienceless individual to pull this off.

Why jump through logical hoops with Amanda and Raffaele when this scenario is so coherent? As a profiler, I applied the same questions to this case as I had to the Ramseys'. We have to ask ourselves: What would turn an ordinary, happy day into a murder? What occurred on Christmas Day, after exchanging gifts, having dinner with friends and anticipating a Disney cruise, to make either of JonBenét's parents kill her? *Nothing!*

Likewise, what went on the day after Halloween to cause happy, bubbly, often goofy and recently-in-love Amanda to grab a kitchen knife and stab it repeatedly through her girlfriend's throat? Again: *Nothing!*

CHAPTER 32
APPEAL

Less than a month after the verdict, Rudy Guede's sentence was cut from thirty to twenty-four years on appeal, then to sixteen and then fourteen. It was explained that he was the only one of the three defendants to offer an apology to the Kercher family. It wasn't, however, for killing their daughter, which he never admitted. It was for failing to rescue her.

Or was the reduction of sentence a pro-active technique — an incentive to keep him from saying anything damaging to the prosecution's case against Amanda and Raffaele? This is a law enforcement establishment that handed out numerous commendation awards for excellence in the Kercher murder investigation; another proactive technique.

Of all the amazing things about this case, the most amazing of all is that, like the West Memphis Three, it got to trial at all. The authorities had the real killer as soon as they apprehended Rudy Guede and they should have known it. It was not a difficult case to analyze or figure out. On top of everything else, his DNA was all over the crime scene.

How, in the name of all that is rational, could Amanda and Raffaele have participated in this satanic orgy of sex and murder Mignini so imaginatively described and yet not leave any of their own DNA on the scene?

Mignini said they cleaned it up, and used the recently purchased container of bleach at Raffaele's apartment as proof.

So tell me, Mr. Public Minister Mignini, how do two unsophisticated kids who've never gotten into serious trouble in their lives suddenly figure out how to erase every bit of their own invisible DNA from the crime scene, yet manage to leave gobs of Rudy's? If you would answer this question, Mr. Public Minister, I would be mightily impressed, because I've worked with some of the best crime scene investigators in the world and none of them know how to do it.

Had you gotten to Rudy first, maybe it would have been different. As scary and threatening as Amanda was to you and all you believed in, you still might have left her and her boyfriend out of it if you could have. You had your real killer. His story made no sense at all and was disprovable at practically every turn. But by the time Rudy turned up, it was too late; you'd already proclaimed that an American girl, an Italian boy and a black African had committed the murder. To back down at that point would have been embarrassing and would have destroyed your precious theory of the case.

What you did so successfully during the trial was get the jury to do the same thing you made Amanda do during her long night of interrogation: *imagine* what might have happened at Via della Pergola 7 that horrible night.

You were willing to ruin two lives and mislead a grieving family for the sake of your own honor and ego. But let's be honest. It wasn't just you. There is plenty of responsibility and blame to go around.

On January 22, 2010, Mignini was convicted of abuse of office in relation to his Monster of Florence investigation. He was sentenced to sixteen months in prison, all of it suspended.

By this point, negative reactions to the verdict were popping up all over the world. The case was giving Italian justice a black eye. In a major public relations pushback in July, forty-three officers involved in the investigation of the Kercher murder were given meritorious service awards.

As the appeal drew near, Steve Moore decided to find out what he could about Amanda on a personal level to see if there was any validity to the wild and wanton portrait Mignini had painted.

On September 12, he went to the Knox family residence and conducted an interview with Amanda's sister Deanna, then twenty-one, and Amanda's best friend, Brett Lither, then twenty-three. He was not expecting them to be objective or unbiased, but he wanted to get insight into her background. Steve is a good and experienced investigator, so he knows how to ask the right questions and how to interpret the responses. He shared the results with me with the family's knowledge, but he purposely did not ask for their permission or consent.

From the time she was small, according to Deanna and Brett, Amanda was known to "stick up for forgotten people." Brett gave examples of how Amanda would be nice and supportive to her even when she felt she was being unpleasant or feeling depressed. So many friends seemed completely devoted to her.

Was she a pure, snow-white virgin? Hardly. Was she a high-spirited girl looking for romantic adventure in Italy? Certainly. But as to the suggestion that Amanda was a manipulative, sexually charged vixen, both women just laughed. They said she was "dopey" and "inexperienced," and so naive about boys that she didn't even get it when one of them was hitting on her. When they saw the list of her seven sexual partners, they said of the five they knew, all were "geeky young white virginal boys" and questioned whether she'd gone "all the way" with each of them. The way they knew her, they confirmed that if she was told to list her previous partners, she was so cautious and obedient that she would include anyone with whom she'd had any sort of intimate contact. Her sex life, they said, was "plain vanilla."

At a barbecue at the Knoxes' house, Steve conducted another discussion with eight of Amanda's other friends, both boys and girls. The portrait that emerged was similar.

The important point here is not the specifics of what Deanna or any of Amanda's friends revealed, but the general image. None of these kids was sophisticated enough to fool or mislead Steve, who had interviewed al Qaeda terrorists. He confirmed my impression that the Amanda Knox created by Giuliano Mignini was a myth.

Two weeks after these conversations, on September 28, 2010, Pepperdine University fired Steve after he refused repeated directives to drop the case and stop speaking out in support of Amanda. Previously they had offered him $25,000 if he would resign and sign an agreement never to discuss why he was leaving the institution. He refused this offer as well. So when they fired him, the story at the time was that administrators felt his advocacy was making things awkward for the university's program in Florence. I hate to see men or women lose their jobs for what they believe in, but I certainly respect the integrity behind it.

Would Amanda's plight have attracted so much attention and support had she not been a beautiful American girl? Probably not. On the other hand, were she not a beautiful American girl, it's doubtful she would have been charged at all. As it was, she had to be neutralized and punished for her perceived power to charm men into murder. In an earlier age, one suspects, the high priests of Perugia would have known what to do with her.

The Knox-Sollecito appeal began in November 2010 under Judges Claudio Pratillo Hellmann and Massimo Zanetti. They appointed two forensic experts from Sapienza University in Rome, Stefano Conti and Carla Vecchiotti, to review the collection and analysis of the DNA evidence.

Like just about everything else in Italian justice, the trial dragged on for months through sporadic court sessions. Meanwhile, Amanda and Raffaele remained in prison.

For the January 2011 issue of *Maxim,* the magazine did a profile on me, relating my FBI experience and describing how I now consulted with police departments and legal teams. The article mentioned that I was working to clear both the West Memphis Three and Amanda Knox.

"In both cases — West Memphis and Knox," I was quoted, *"the police allowed theory rather than evidence to direct their investigations, and that is always a fatal error."*

This attracted the attention of *Il Messaggero,* the national newspaper that is the most widely read daily publication in Rome and Central Italy. Editor Paolo Graldi assigned Krista Errickson, an American writer with extensive international journalistic experience, to interview me. She was assisted by Italian journalist Gianmaria Giulini. Krista contacted me and I agreed to talk to her.

Of the more than five thousand cases I've worked on, she asked, how many of these had been international? About 250, I replied — mostly in Canada, England, Australia, Germany and South America.

After probing my background, experience and investigative techniques, she asked for my conclusion on the Knox-Sollecito case, the one the paper's readers would be most interested in. I answered her:

"From the profiles I created, none of the behavioral or forensic evidence leads to Amanda and Raffaele. There is no history or experience related to violence in their backgrounds. Guede has the history; he was an experienced criminal, he had the motive, and all evidence points to him. The crime scene does not indicate the presence of three individuals in the room where Meredith was murdered. Behavior reflects personality. And that behavior fits only Rudy Guede."

The article concluded with me saying: *"I know Meredith's family wants this nightmare to end. But they have the person that killed their daughter: It is Guede. Only Guede."*

Apparently, this was not what the paper wanted. Krista "was ordered to fall in line" by Graldi and come up with a version more to their taste, which would result in undercutting everything I said. There were admonitions added to the effect that I didn't have the real evidence and there is "no legal recognition of [my] profession [in] Italy."

If she didn't agree to do this, the article would run with an editorial response tacked onto the end by *Messaggero*'s legal expert Massimo Martinelli, who, according to Graldi, had been on the Knox case "since the beginning." The Martinelli response was six paragraphs, characterized by commentary such as this (in translation):

We have an interview of such that would be seen as interference, seemingly humble, in respect to the work of the investigators, and the prosecution's theory: in reality, the entire prosecution is swept away with one stroke, and without many issues, in personal opinions of Douglas.

Graldi's note to her included the warning (translated): *So unless you will edit the article to an acceptable form, Martinelli and I cannot bring ourselves to accept the interview in this form, because it would only cause problems.*
Krista was appalled and refused to have it published this way. She called me and said, "John, I want to pull the article. I don't want to do this to you, but I'll leave it up to you." I asked her to send me a translation of the proposed new version; when I read it, I agreed completely.
"Pull it!" I said; and I told her to warn the publisher that if they published it in that form, I would sue them.
She then sent a long e-mail to my attorney, Steve Mark, explaining why it would not run, along with "Before" and "After" versions. She recounted:

This was an assignment, requested by the editor and publisher of *Il Messaggero*. . . . It seems what John had to say is not what they expected to hear. Again, I deeply regret this outcome. I spent three days in a complete daze. I felt as if I had been hit by a bus. Paolo Graldi, the editor, is someone I have worked with, and moreover, has been a very close personal friend for over 17 years. This shook my faith to its very foundations. After a 2 hour phone argument with Graldi, the last thing he said to me was, "This article, as you wrote it — is too dangerous for Italy."

I admired Krista's integrity. Not only did she refuse to recast the article, she resigned from *Il Messaggero* after twenty years as a contributing political writer.

Fortunately, some other people also considered the truth above all else. Appearing in court on July 25, 2011, scientists Stefano Conti and Carla Vecchiotti demolished the prosecution's assertions and singled out its lead forensic examiner, Patrizia Stefanoni, for gross negligence in the handling, processing and interpretation of the evidence.

The month before, Greg Hampikian, a DNA expert, professor at Boise State University and the founder and director of the Idaho Innocence Project, announced, according to the *Idaho Statesman,* that *"the prosecutors drew the wrong conclusions from that evidence, twisting it to fit their preconceived theory of Knox's guilt."*

"I looked at the data," Hampikian said, *"and it was just horrible."*

He even staged an experiment that replicated his theory of DNA transfer in the case. Using techniques identical to how the knife DNA sample was collected, he got DNA from another researcher's soda can to show up on a clean knife the researcher had never touched.

In her closing statement, given in Italian, Amanda told the judges, "People always ask, 'Who is Amanda Knox?' I am the same person I was four years ago. The only thing that now separates me from four years ago is my suffering. In four years, I've lost my friend in the most terrible and unexplainable way. My trust in the authorities and the police has been damaged. I had to face charges that were totally unfair, without any basis. And I am paying with my life for something I haven't done."

On October 3, 2011 — nearly a year after the procedure began and four years since Amanda and Raffaele had been locked up — the appeals court overturned the convictions, stating in their opinion that the original verdict "was not corroborated by any objective element of evidence." They described the interrogation sessions of Amanda as of "obsessive duration" and acknowledged that the account she gave was due not to fact but "great psychological pressure."

The Kercher family released a statement:

We respect the decision of the judges but we do not understand how the decision of the first trial could be so radically overturned. We still trust the Italian judicial system and hope that the truth will eventually emerge.

Amanda and her family left Italy the next day.

At long last, justice was served.

■ ■ ■ ■

CLOSING
ARGUMENTS

■ ■ ■ ■

CHAPTER 33
IN SUMMATION

The United States Attorney is the representative not of an ordinary party to a controversy, but of a sovereign whose obligation to govern impartially is as compelling as its obligation to govern at all; and whose interest, therefore, in a criminal prosecution is not that it shall win a case, but that justice shall be done. As such, he is in a peculiar and very definite sense the servant of the law, the two-fold aim of which is that guilt shall not escape or innocence suffer. He may prosecute with earnestness and vigor — indeed he should do so, but, while he may strike hard blows, he is not at liberty to strike foul ones. It is as much his duty to refrain from improper methods calculated to produce a wrongful conviction as it is to use every legitimate means to bring about a just one.

— Justice George Sutherland in
Berger v. *United States,* 1935

In his 1936 memoir essay, "The Crack-Up,"

F. Scott Fitzgerald observed: *The test of a first-rate intelligence is the ability to hold two opposed ideas in the mind at the same time, and still retain the ability to function.* For those of us in law enforcement who at least strive for a first-rate intelligence, criminal justice provides an ultimate challenge: How do we vigorously hunt down criminals and prosecute and punish crimes, while trying to make sure that no innocent person suffers at the hands of a sincere but imperfect system, administered by practitioners representing every one of our collective human faults and foibles?

How, for instance, can we condemn the long procedural morass and delaying tactics for Sedley Alley, yet condone them for Damien Echols?

When I was a kid, there was a television series that virtually every boy and many girls of my generation will recall. It was the *Adventures of Superman,* and in the intro, over a tableau of the superhero posed, hands resolutely on hips, in front of a waving American flag, the narrator proclaimed how he fought "a never-ending battle for truth, justice and the American way."

When I began my law enforcement career in 1970, along with most of my colleagues, I believed that truth and justice would always prevail. Regardless of the jurisdiction or individual law enforcement agency, we were all playing on a level field. As investigators, I believed, it was our job to help solve crimes and apprehend criminals using all of our skills and every investigative tool available to us.

In retrospect, I was somewhat naive. It is not a level playing field, and all investigators and agencies are not equal. I still believe that the overwhelming majority of us are dedicated to following the letter of the law and our own personal codes of conduct. Unfortunately, as in any other profession, there are some individuals and departments that believe they are performing their jobs properly when, in fact, they are using faulty, outdated and sometimes illegal techniques and practices.

It has taken too many years to realize and accept that while our justice system is still the best in the world, it is far from perfect. And I now wonder about some of the cases my colleagues and I received from law enforcement agencies within the United States and worldwide. Did the investigators effectively contain and control the crime scene? Did they effectively collect and preserve evidence, avoid contamination and maintain chain of custody? Were the medical examiner and/or forensic pathologists adequately certified, and were specimens correctly evaluated? Were interviews and interrogations conducted without leading or coercion? Was the prosecutor influenced by any factors outside the case itself, such as reelection or political ambition?

For some cases, I now have to wonder: *Did I get it right?* And that will always be a troubling question.

That, in a nutshell, is what we're dealing with. And that is why we all must be vigilant and involved and questioning to see that the system works as well as it can.

Which brings us back to Superman and his never-ending battle. None of us is Superman, but by the very nature of the challenge, this pretty much *has to be* a "never-ending battle." Within a system that must be administered fairly and uniformly, we must never lose sight of the *individual* aspects: the individual victim, defendant and facts of the case. In so doing, we reach an understanding of appropriate responses in each situation.

The facts in Sedley Alley's case were unambiguous. The facts in Damien Echols's case were extremely ambiguous. There is a long continuum between the two, in which each position calls for a response appropriate to its own particulars.

I know this is far easier said than done, and we'll never get it perfect. But it is a goal that is easy — and critical — to strive for.

The investigations, research and writing of this book have made me realize how vulnerable any of us can be when the system goes awry. When that happens, the system can take on a life and momentum of its own, just as powerful and potentially devastating as when it functions properly.

Writing this book has also forced me to look back at some of my earlier cases and reflect on some of the assumptions under which I operated.

First and foremost, when a local law enforcement agency came to us for assistance, we had to assume that they were providing us with good data. On cases where I was actually able to get out into the field, I could make my own evaluation. But when all of the information was presented to us, we were limited. In most situations, that didn't matter because we had the key elements we needed, such as crime scene photos, descriptions and victimology.

If I had been asked to get involved in a case like the Cameron Todd Willingham suspected arson, I would have relied on what looked like good science, and I would have come to the wrong conclusion. Had I been brought in to investigate the West Memphis Three, I would have known immediately that it wasn't a satanic ritual murder, but I would have been totally misled by the medical examiner's report into concluding that it was a lust murder.

I would recommend several steps that could

help prevent innocent men and women from facing incarceration and execution.

If we start with Brandon Garrett's key problem areas — false confessions, junk science, jailhouse informants, ineffective assistance of counsel and bad judging — we can start to see what needs to be done.

First, I advocate an independent national forensics lab, separate from the FBI and all other law enforcement agencies. Despite previous documented problems, I strongly believe in the current excellence and integrity of the FBI National Laboratory, now located in a modern facility at the Academy in Quantico. But with potential death penalty or other serious cases, there should be no question of influence or hidden agenda. It is still possible for an investigator to convey subtly to someone in the lab that this particular piece of evidence is critical to the case, or that the jury has to be able to understand a certain fact in unequivocal terms, or any of a number of other requested outcomes.

Also in the realm of evidence, we have seen that too many confessions are coerced or in some other way are not legitimate. I would therefore require that *all police interrogations* be recorded — preferably video, as well as audio — in full. If this is not done, the evidence should be inadmissible in pursuit of a death penalty eligible verdict. Signed written confessions should not be sufficient.

Steve Braga has thought long and hard about these questions. As he has put it, "Every interrogation should be videotaped from beginning to end. If you don't want people to see what you're doing in there, then you're doing something you shouldn't be doing."

One of the recurring arguments against the death penalty is the incredible amount of money expended on seemingly endless appeals. There are various estimates on how much it costs to get a convicted defendant to the point where he can be executed, but most of them are in the seven-figure range. In this age of diminished resources, that is not a sum to be trifled with. A similar argument can be made for any case where a long appeals process is likely.

On the other hand, if we could reform the issues that cause wrongful or questionable convictions and solidify public confidence that we have done so, think of how much will be saved by not having to go through the extensive efforts required to cure wrongs like the West Memphis Three and Cameron Todd Willingham cases.

If we could put some of that money into providing more funding and better resources for defense attorneys, I believe we would save in the long run.

To me, a fundamental defect in the system is the election of prosecutors and judges.

Again, as Steve Braga observed, "When you have elected prosecutors and elected judges, and you have a high-profile criminal case, they don't win any votes by giving somebody a fair trial and having somebody walk away from a murder charge, particularly one as gruesome as [West Memphis]. And so, look at what happened here — the two prosecutors are now judges, the trial judge is now a state senator, the district attorney wants to be a U.S. congressman. There's a real political gain to be made. There's a real political self-interest at play."

I've been on the prosecution's side for the vast majority of my career, and it's almost always the side of the angels, as far as I'm concerned. But that "almost" is a huge modifier and represents a wide chasm. One of the most important means of bridging that chasm is for prosecutors to understand and accept their proper function. This, in fact, might do more than any of the other proposals if it could ever become a reality.

Everyone on that side wants a conviction; I understand that. No one wants to fight that hard and lose. As Steve Braga commented to Mark Olshaker, "When Dennis Riordan brought in Werner Spitz and John Douglas and Michael Baden and Vince DiMaio, among others — the world's leading experts — and they say, 'Your coroner got it wrong. These weren't knife wounds. We all agree.

650

Six of us independently agree these aren't knife wounds but animal predation,' then somebody on the prosecution side has to be stand-up enough to say, 'Okay, let's take this seriously' — not 'Oh, my God, how are we going to defend against this? Let's keep fighting.' At some point, you've got to recognize a mistake.

"The Supreme Court has a landmark decision called *Berger* versus *United States* back in the 1930s. It's not the prosecutor's duty to convict. It's the prosecutor's duty to insure that justice is done."

Along these lines, there is no trustworthy and effective national governing body with objective standards that certifies experts in all of the key forensic areas, such as odontology, fingerprint identification, hair and fiber, ballistics, and so on. If a judge concludes that someone is an expert, the jurors are naturally inclined to put a good deal of weight on that individual's testimony. By the same token, if a judge so decides, he or she can prevent another individual from offering a learned opinion. We saw Judge Burnett mishandle both of these instances in West Memphis.

Then, if the defendant is convicted and later found not guilty based on the reexamination of faulty forensic analysis, investigators, prosecutors and judges will often say that the jurors heard the evidence and *they* determined that the defendant was guilty.

This kind of irresponsible projection is a neat way for them to alleviate their own responsibility and place blame on the operation of the jury system.

In the 2011 Casey Anthony murder case in Florida, the judge allowed an "expert" to testify relative to the smell of decomposition in the defendant's car. Making no judgments about the accuracy of this observation, there are no standards for determining the smell of decomposition, and there should be.

In 2004, the FBI linked a terrorist bombing of a train station in Spain, which resulted in mass casualties, to an American living in Oregon, based on a fingerprint recovered at the scene. This individual was arrested, but was later released when the print was linked to an Algerian responsible for the crime. Three of the Bureau's top fingerprint experts, including the division head, had gotten it wrong.

Ultimately, one of the things that most bothers me in dealing with miscarriages of justice is that these mistakes force us to divert focus from the victim of the crime, which is where I always feel it belongs. By rushing to judgment, taking convenient shortcuts and ignoring evidence, law enforcement officials make innocent defendants into new victims, and thereby deny justice twice.

The name Amanda Knox should be known

only incidentally, as the shocked and grieving friend of the beautiful Meredith Kercher. The names of Damien Echols, Charles Jason Baldwin and Jessie Misskelley Jr. should never have even been associated with innocents Chris Byers, Stevie Branch and Michael Moore. And people like John Mark Byers should be able to have faith that the system has done right by them.

The cases and circumstances we have discussed are representative, but far from unique.

The so-called Norfolk Four spent nearly a decade in prison for a 1997 rape-murder it has now been proven they did not commit. The key evidence against them was four individual confessions, all coerced. Jessie Misskelley Jr. and Amanda Knox can certainly relate to that.

In March 2012, Al-Akhbar's news service reported that at least ninety Iraqi teens had been stoned to death in the previous month by armed religious extremists guided by the nation's Moral Police. Their crime: Devil worshipping. The evidence, according to a Moral Police statement: *They wear strange, tight clothes that have pictures on them such as skulls and use stationery that are shaped as skulls. They also wear rings on their noses and tongues, and do other strange activities.* Damien Echols and Jason Baldwin would understand.

It all comes down to this: Whenever theory supersedes evidence, and prejudice deposes rationalism, there can be no real justice.

ACKNOWLEDGMENTS

Like crime-solving itself, producing a book is very much a collaborative effort, not only between the two of us, but also the solid team that has worked with us and backed us up each step of the way.

First, we want to acknowledge and thank Michaela Hamilton, our talented, sensitive and insightful editor at Kensington. It is largely her enthusiasm that has seen this project through, and we are grateful to the entire publishing staff. We are so grateful to the entire team at Kensington.

Our fine agent, Jake Elwell at Harold Ober Associates, understood from the beginning what we wanted to do this time, then helped us shape and refine our ideas. He has been a continual friend, offering support and acting as a sounding board. Likewise, our attorney, advisor and friend, Steven Mark, who, in addition to everything else, is responsible for a substantial portion of the West Memphis Three research and organization. Sarah Lessa is in charge of our website, *www.mindhunters inc.com*. Dave Lessa helped immensely with its planning and design, and Nikki Cheshire conducted our photo research. All three are welcome additions to the Mindhunters team. And as always, Mark's wife, Carolyn, remains our in-house counsel, Mindhunters, Inc. chief of staff and our first-line reader, among her many other talents and virtues.

Profound gratitude goes out to the many individuals who freely contributed their time, talents and insights. Since they all helped so much, we will simply list them alphabetically: Bob Barnett, Philip Bermingham, Stephen Braga, Jackie and John Mark Byers, Ben Cheshire, Jack, Trudy and Stephen Collins, Lorri Davis, Damien Echols, Krista Errickson, the Honorable Bob Graham, Peter Jackson, Amanda, Curt and Deanna Knox, former special agent Kenneth Lanning, Ken Light, Jim Lovering, Chris and Edda Mellas, former special agent Steve Moore, Madison Paxton, John Ramsey, Mark Smit, Lynne Sparks, Mark Stein, Fran Walsh, *Jonesboro Sun* editor Chris Wessel, and Tom Wright.

And finally, to all of those who continually strive to see justice rendered — and right the wrongs when it is not — you have our sincere and undying admiration.

John Douglas and Mark Olshaker
October 2012

ABOUT THE AUTHORS

JOHN EDWARD DOUGLAS served as a special agent of the FBI for over twenty-five years. He is widely admired as the leading expert on criminal personality profiling and modern criminal investigative analysis. A veteran of the Air Force, he has written numerous books including the #1 international bestseller *Mindhunter.*

MARK OLSHAKER is an Emmy Award–winning filmmaker, *New York Times* bestselling non-fiction author, and critically acclaimed novelist who has worked with Douglas for many years.

Both authors live in the Washington, D.C. area. Please visit them at www.lawanddisorderbook.com.

The employees of Thorndike Press hope you have enjoyed this Large Print book. All our Thorndike, Wheeler, and Kennebec Large Print titles are designed for easy reading, and all our books are made to last. Other Thorndike Press Large Print books are available at your library, through selected bookstores, or directly from us.

For information about titles, please call:

(800) 223-1244

or visit our Web site at:

http://gale.cengage.com/thorndike

To share your comments, please write:

Publisher
Thorndike Press
10 Water St., Suite 310
Waterville, ME 04901